THE ANGRY EARTH

THE ANGRY EARTH

DISASTER IN ANTHROPOLOGICAL PERSPECTIVE

EDITED BY

ANTHONY OLIVER-SMITH
AND
SUSANNA M. HOFFMAN

ROUTLEDGE
NEW YORK LONDON

Published in 1999 by
Routledge
29 West 35th Street
New York, NY 10001

Published in Great Britain by
Routledge
11 New Fetter Lane
London EC4P 4EE

Library of Congress Cataloging-in-Publication Data

   The angry earth: disaster in anthropological perspective / edited by Anthony
     Oliver-Smith and Susanna M. Hoffman.
       p. cm.
   Includes bibliographical references and index.
   ISBN 0-415-91986-X (hb). — ISBN 0-415-91987-8 (pb)
     1. Natural disasters — Social aspects. 2. Hazardous geographic environments.
   3. Human beings — Effect of environment on. I. Oliver-Smith, Anthony II.
   Hoffman, Susanna M.
   HV553.A585 1999
   353.34—dc21   98-49959
                                                                 CIP

To a Pioneer
in the Anthropology of Disaster

Anthony F. C. Wallace

CONTENTS

ACKNOWLEDGMENTS

ANY VOLUME THAT HOPES TO PRESENT THE FACETS OF A SINGULAR topic takes the work and aid of many people. Firstly, the editors would like to thank all of the contributors who worked diligently toward the production of their chapters over the course of several years. In addition, we would like to tender thanks to Walter Peacock of the International Hurricane Center and Florida International University for his constructive critical assessment of our project in its formative stages. Louise Lamphere and Jan Brukman provided invaluable insight and assistance on a number of the papers. Victoria Wise added fine polish. Sara Staron, Rodney Stubina, and Jessica Egol provided us essential assistance in the production of the manuscript, and we are grateful to them all. Finally we wish to express our gratitude to those at Routledge Press whose invaluable efforts brought the book to culmination: our editor William Germano, and his excellent assistants, Nick Syrett and Gayatri Patnaik; John McHale for his "alarming" cover; and Brian Phillips, who guided the book to its binding.

CONTRIBUTORS

Robert Bolin is professor of sociology at Arizona State University. His research focuses on social and cultural factors in vulnerability to natural and technological disasters. His most recent book is entitled *The Northridge Earthquake: Vulnerability and Disaster on the Margins of Los Angeles* (Routledge forthcoming).

Gregory V. Button is a former journalist who has covered many natural and man-made disasters. He earned his Ph.D. in anthropology at Brandeis University in 1993 and is currently an assistant professor of anthropology in the School of Public Health and the Department of Anthropology at the University of Michigan at Ann Arbor.

Paul L. Doughty is Distinguished Service Professor Emeritus of Anthropology and Latin American Studies at the University of Florida. He has worked in earthquake situations in Mexico, El Salvador, Guatemala, and Peru. He has served as chair of Florida's anthropology department and was president of the Latin American Studies Association. He is the author of numerous articles, monographs, research reports, and books, including *Peru: A Cultural History* (with Henry F. Dobyns) and *Huaylas, An Andean District in Search of Progress.*

Christopher L. Dyer is an applied anthropologist in the Department of Marine Affairs, University of Rhode Island. His research interests include human responses to coastal hazards and disasters, disaster theory, and maritime anthropology. Dr. Dyer has done research on the *Exxon-Valdez* oil spill, Hurricane Andrew, and the North Cape oil spill in Rhode Island. He has published numerous articles and reports and is senior author of *Folk Management in the World's Fisheries,* with J. R. McGoodwin (University of Colorado Press 1994).

Susanna M. Hoffman is a former associate professor of anthropology, and is now an independent writer and researcher. She has worked in Thera, Greece, for almost thirty years and conducted research on contemporary America for more than fifteen. Among her anthropological works are the award-winning films *The Nature of Culture* and *Kypseli—Women and Men Apart: A Divided*

Reality, and numerous articles. She has written a number of popular books, and her articles and columns have appeared worldwide in newspapers and magazines. Since losing her home and office in the Oakland firestorm, she has been researching and writing on the subject of disaster from New York City and Telluride, Colorado. She received her doctorate from the University of California, Berkeley.

James R. McGoodwin is a distinguished maritime anthropologist in the Department of Anthropology, University of Colorado, Boulder. His research interests include fisheries management, disaster impacts on coastal communities, and the maritime culture of Newfoundland and Mexico. Dr. McGoodwin is the author of numerous publications, including *Crisis in the World's Fisheries: People, Problems and Policies* (Stanford 1990), and co-editor with C. Dyer of *Folk Management in the World's Fisheries* (University of Colorado Press 1994).

Michael E. Moseley received his Ph.D. from Harvard University, where he was an associate curator before joining Chicago's Field Museum of Natural History as a curator. He became professor of anthropology at the University of Florida in 1985. His field studies of ancient Peruvian settlements, agricultural systems, and natural disasters span more than twenty-five years and include intensive investigations in the Moche and Moquegua Valleys. He is the author of *The Maritime Foundations of Peruvian Civilization, Peru's Golden Treasures,* and *The Inca and their Ancestors.*

Anthony Oliver-Smith is professor of anthropology at the University of Florida. He has carried out research on disaster impacts, mitigation, and reconstruction in Peru, Honduras, the United States, and Jamaica. He is the author of *The Martyred City: Death and Rebirth in the Andes* (1992) and the editor of *Natural Disasters and Cultural Responses* (1986). His other research interests include resettlement, social movements, and culture and the built environment.

S. Ravi Rajan is an assistant professor of environmental studies at the University of California, Santa Cruz. He is the author of *Modernizing Nature: British Colonial Foresters, Ecodevelopment Agendas and Post-Colonial Legacies, 1840–1960,* forthcoming from Oxford University Press. Rajan has also been an activist with a number of environmental NGOs and currently serves on the board of directors of Pesticides Action Network, North America.

Payson D. Sheets, professor of anthropology at the University of Colorado, is a fifth-generation native of that state. During his graduate studies at the University of Pennsylvania (Ph.D. 1974), he climbed Mt. Pacaya in Guatemala while it was erupting. The experience fundamentally altered his research interests to the complex reciprocal effects of active volcanism and the human condition. He has conducted archaeology-volcanism research in El Salvador, Guatemala, Costa Rica, and Panama since 1969.

Lois Stanford completed a Ph.D. in anthropology at the University of Florida in 1989. She currently serves as an associate professor of anthropology at New Mexico State University. She has researched and published on the impact of globalization, economic organizations, and rural communities in Mexico. In an interdisciplinary collaboration with Robert Bolin, she has researched and published on local organizational responses to natural disasters, including both the Loma Prieta and Northridge earthquakes in California. A co-authored book with Robert Bolin, *The Northridge Earthquake: Vulnerability and Disaster on the Margins of Los Angeles,* is forthcoming from Routledge Press.

Mohammad Q. Zaman earned his Ph.D. in anthropology at the University of Manitoba and has taught for many years in universities in Bangladesh, Canada, and the United States. He now works as an international consultant for the Asian Development Bank and the World Bank. His other research interests concern resettlement, development, and social change.

ANTHROPOLOGY AND THE ANGRY EARTH:
AN OVERVIEW

SUSANNA M. HOFFMAN
AND ANTHONY OLIVER-SMITH

DISASTERS SOMETIMES STRIKE WITH THE SUDDEN IMPACT OF AN EARTHQUAKE or nuclear meltdown. At other times they accumulate over long periods of time with the slowness of a drought or toxic exposure. In whatever manner they arrive, abrupt or subtle, disasters are all-encompassing occurrences. In their wake they sweep across every aspect of human life: environmental, biological, and sociocultural. By their very constitution, disasters spring from the nexus where environment, society, and technology come together—the point where place, people, and human construction of both the material and nonmaterial meet. It is from the interplay of these three planes that disasters emanate, and in their unfolding, they reimplicate every vector of their causal interface.

Social scientists began to look into disaster early in the twentieth century when Samuel Prince studied the implications for social change in the munitions explosion in Halifax harbor (1920).[1] However, the potentials for social structural research in Prince's work were not pursued for another half century. Instead, most early research concentrated on the physical agents of natural and technological events, contriving ways to counteract them, and, since the plight of disaster victims placed unscheduled demands on society, on the management of affected populations. Social scientists approached disasters as unpredictable and extreme happenings that dismayingly fell upon human communities. They considered disasters departures from the norm and contended that recovery from them was to return as quickly as possible to a predisaster status quo, at least in terms of visible damage or calculable duress. From the 1950s to the 1970s interests centered on the behavior of individuals and organizations in the warning, impact, and immediate aftermath stages of disasters. Little historical perspective and scant sociocultural pattern were taken into account.

Around 1980, however, a new position emerged. Disasters, and the hazards leading to them, were reevaluated and redefined as basic, often chronic elements of environments and, more significantly, as happenings humans themselves to some degree construct (Hewitt 1983). The formation and formulations of social realms were added into the disaster nexus. Societies established settings within dangerous zones and, due to political and/or economic forces, often placed certain segments of their populations in more perilous situations than others. Community members were neither unaware nor inactive. They fashioned appraisals of their physical milieu, their subsistence and commercial pursuits, and the sorts of risks they undertook. They generated ideologies and strategies to enable their lifestyles and explain their circumstance. Researchers also began to take into account that human technology was a double-edged sword. While enhancing security in some domains, such as hurricane prediction or antiseismic engineering, it also promoted human vulnerability to calamity. From the dawn of human life to the age of atomic fission, human craft imperiled both environment and habitat. Social scientific disaster researchers realized that catastrophes could be neither understood nor mitigated merely by exploring the physical platform of human existence. Social factors were equally relevant. Subsistence methods, use of resources, construction of shelter, invention of tools, dictates of social structure, distribution of power, attachment to place, mores, and many other sociocultural elements were entangled within the vortex of catastrophe.

The introduction of social factors in causation made it clear that disasters further involved diachronicity. Calamities emanated from processes that developed over long periods of time as much as from sudden crises. Conditions that spawned or eventually terminated in what people then viewed as dire, harmful, and often horrific emergency had in fact accrued manifestly or latently under their noses. The processes involved ranged from people's adaptations to their physical underpinnings, to the human manipulation and elaboration of physical surroundings, to the construction of sociocultural institutions, beliefs, and ethos.

As researchers have developed their understanding of the cloth from which both natural and technological calamities are woven, the theoretical and methodological pertinence of anthropology for the study of disaster has become evident. In its substantive platform, anthropology as a social science takes into its reckoning the three planes that interface in calamity: the environmental, the biological, and the sociocultural. Thus, anthropology's fundamental investigative format well matches the analytical requirements posed by disaster studies (Torry 1979). In addition, the developmental and comparative perspectives of anthropological research ally with the particular requirements of disaster research. Anthropology looks at human existence from its advent. The study incorporates archaeology, long historical record, and the slowly unfolding contexts of human life. Anthropology places the small against the large and contrasts the circumstances of one society against another. It assays individuals and groups and their intricate sociocultural worlds along with their integration within greater social, cultural, economic, and political orbits, exactly the confluence that defines the usual disaster circumstance. The field further attempts to draw general conclusions from the consistency of numerous singular summations. Anthropology addresses social and cultural continuity and change, a pivotal issue in research on disaster impacts. Disasters bring into intense focus matters of human adaptation, a topic that lies at the very heart of anthropological examination. Disasters reveal basic aspects of how a society conforms to the features of its physical environment and the crux of its survivability. Lastly, from its onset anthropology has encompassed all peoples and places, with most of its research taking place in non-Western contexts. So far, the majority of disaster research, largely emanating from the fields of sociology and geography, has taken place in Europe and America, although most disasters currently take place and fall upon people elsewhere.

In recent years, anthropology has added significant breadth to the study of disasters. In the first place, anthropology has contributed to disaster research its keystone methodology—ethnographic fieldwork. The advent of ethnographic methods, including narrative, has greatly elucidated the articulations of disaster recovery and the microcosmic social organizational shifts and adjustments that occur. In concert with archaeology, anthropology has revealed how cultural systems often incorporate long-developed harmonies or contradictions with their environments. People, at least in their original circumstance, establish routines contrived to overcome the challenges of their environments and allow for their continued existence. Indeed, local communities generally show great understandings of their environments, and all too often disaster intervention based on less-than-holistic research disrupts native adaptations and diminishes rather than augments disaster recovery. Earlier disaster research that concentrated almost entirely on immediate responses to calamity and first-tier agency intervention left unexplored the fluctuations in recovery that transpire over time. Yet, disasters are enduring events with many punctuations in reaching their inevitable outcomes. Anthropology's long-term perspective and in-depth fieldwork have added significantly to comprehending the protracted repercussions calamities provoke. The anthropological eye has further enhanced comprehension of factors that lead to people's vulnerability, bringing to light such matters as age, gender, social class, language, religion, ethnicity, and other distinctions. From ground level, anthropology has asked who are the likely victims of calamity, and what are the practices that lead to unequal shares of safety?

TRENDS IN THE ANTHROPOLOGY OF DISASTER

The anthropological study of disaster has to date been conducted by a small group of researchers. Despite various approaches to the study of disaster, all are more or less united in their outlook on the problem. Disaster is seen as a process leading to an event that involves a combination of a potentially destructive agent from the natural or technological sphere and a population in a socially produced condition of vulnerability. The development of the process and subsequent event produce damage or loss to physical facilities and to major social-organizational components of a community, to the extent that the essential functions of the group are interrupted or destroyed. Individual and group distress and social disorganization of varying severity follow.

Each of the trends in the anthropological inquiry into disaster bears great utility for the study of disaster in general and elucidates method and data from across a wide variety of contexts concerning human catastrophe. No volume has as yet offered a compilation of anthropological inquiry into disaster, although the 1990s—the United Nations' International Decade for Disaster Reduction—leads us into the twenty-first century in an era of increased frequency and severity of both natural and technological calamity. Catastrophes with more lasting and debilitating consequences have proliferated worldwide. Neither modern knowledge nor technology has precluded threats from nature raining upon human populations nor debarred menace emanating from within its own workings. Threat from technological disaster has particularly shadowed modern times. Along with the greater occurrence and severity of catastrophe, the economic impacts of disaster have exponentially broadened. Accordingly, great interest in disasters has grown among academics, policy makers, and the general public. Environmental researchers are now realizing that the subject lies close to the core of their concern. As for anthropology, disasters far more commonly impact areas where anthropologists work, including remote and rural regions that were the principal terrain of past investigation and urban industrial centers where both the population and practice now expand. Along with the anthropological themes, such as adaptation, political economy, and social change, which disasters highlight, catastrophes have been shown to provide researchers a unique opportunity for examining the organization of society and to test the theories of the field.

Four major trends, with various subtopics, have emerged within the anthropological study of disaster. All four interrelate. They also contribute to and draw upon research in other disciplines.

Archaeological/Historical

In the last few years, the fields of archaeology and culture history have both seen the development of particularistic studies of disaster, and research

(1) ord - time
depth &
background
comprehension

from these fields has greatly enhanced the understanding of the time depth to disaster. Studies have focused, for example, on cycles of catastrophe millennia old and the responses to such chronic conditions. The two discourses have greatly enlightened knowledge of the physical and social processes that lead to disaster events and of the subsequent adjustments and adaptive factors involved in cultural survival or demise. They reveal political economic vulnerabilities centuries in development. The diachronic perspective both studies have provided is, in fact, so significant that it overarches into all other areas of the anthropological study of disaster. Archaeological evidence perforce concentrates on material aspects of cultures: habitat, art, uses of terrain, extent of political realms, and mortuary remains. Nonetheless, this sort of evidence sheds light on such factors as what sustains a society's resilience to disaster. Archaeology also indicates which segments of society reemerge after a disaster, which, how, and why some disappear, and what mixture of strategies a culture might have compiled to face or inadvertently provoke repetitive catastrophe. The historical background of disaster comes to light through chronicles, archives, and annals. The relevatory documents may not particularly concern disaster; often they focus on political and economic matters, especially demographic shifts and food production. Even so, they disclose the creation of vulnerable social segments, the policies, prejudices, and actions that comprise the disaster conundrum, and the minute and sometimes surprising ways in which societies recover. Long-term fieldwork further adds to the time-depth perspective and background comprehension. Understanding pre-disaster conditions goes far to clarify the specific nature of risk, duress, and limitations.

Political Ecology

(2) PE
approach -
investigate
environ.
use &
misuse
by looking
at political
& economic

The second trend in the anthropological study of disaster is the political ecology approach. It stems from the conjuncture of cultural ecological and political economic viewpoints that have expanded within anthropology in recent years. Also broad and multifaceted, the purview spans the many and critical issues of human relationships to the environment as they relate to and are revealed by disaster. The approach could be deemed to fall within the sociocultural realm, since in the strictest anthropological sense, all societies are viewed as perceiving and approaching their environment through cultural means. However, as this branch of disaster study investigates the political and economic structures, policies, and forces that influence and shape the human use of the environment, and stresses environmental use and misuse in a way that other sociocultural investigation does not, it merits separation as a distinct focus.

The political ecology point of view defines disasters as less the result of geophysical extremes, such as earthquakes, hurricanes, and floods, and more the function of ongoing social orders as they overlie physical environments. The hazards that lead to disaster, natural or technological, emerge directly from human activity upon environments and the intensity of human environmental intervention. Human societies and their environments are considered fundamentally inseparable, engaged in a continuous process of mutual constitution and expression. Groups create physical niches for themselves and within them produce ecological settings that enable continuity and reinforce social and ideological constructs. Within this investigation falls a culture's use of its physical base to produce the food and other necessities that lead to subsistence. The distribution of goods prompts scrutiny as well, especially in that the various ways social assets are apportioned contribute to the safeguarding and welfare of some, jeopardy and disadvantage for others. The adaptation of a society to its physical realm and the resiliency of populations to imperilment come into play, as do a people's internal partitions and their dependencies upon other populations. These factors all advance or reduce a society's coping capacity when facing hazard. As aspects of adaptation and resilience, political ecology documents linkages among many features such as agricultural intensification, population increase, environmental degradation, and increase in vulnerability. If environment is a test to which constructed social and physical worlds are the answer and continued survival the aim, from the purview of political ecology, disasters serve as one template through which societies show their score.

Within the political ecology scheme, the conceptual scope of adaptation has recently taken a U-turn. It has circled to include not only the issues of success or failure of people within environments, but also the viability of the environments themselves as they are impacted by people. The question of how well a society is adapted to its environment must now be linked to the question of how well an environment fares when fused with a society. The matter of mutuality has risen to the forefront. Disasters that stem from ecological impairment and the mismanagement of physical features and forms clearly express imbalance in mutuality.

In this and other matters, the concerns of the political ecology approach extend beyond the local to the worldwide. In an era of increasing disaster, the question arises as to whether not just particular groups but the entire human community has in its practices diminished its survivability. Warnings of decreased ozone and increased warming, alterations in one place that result in calamities in another, the all-encompassing and all-consuming nature of contemporary industry and industrial society, unmoderated global transit, traffic, and commerce intensify hazards for all (some carrying the potential for complete cataclysm) and elevate the issues examined by political ecology to the global plane.

Sociocultural/Behavioral

Human social realms and cultures are profoundly affected by disaster. Anthropology's third approach to the study of disaster encompasses all the social and cultural issues beyond those that deal directly with environmental matters. It deals with the populace, its organization, and the invisible constructs communities share. In the face of disruption people construct assessment, shape perceptions, and invent explanation. After a disaster they recover and reconstruct. How they respond to the calamity or potential for a calamity both recounts and reinvents their cultural system. The scope of the sociocultural/behavioral investigation of disaster is again complex and vast. Within it have arisen a number of subthemes, some large enough almost to be considered trends on their own. They include, among others: disaster behavior and response; cultural interpretation of risk and disaster; and post-disaster social and cultural change.

Disaster Behavior and Response

Anthropologists from their first encounters with people in situations of calamity began to explore the conduct and reactions of individuals and groups toward the disaster events and disaster aftermath that engulfed them. Disasters are emphatic and all-absorbing occurrences, and their effect upon the thoughts and actions of those disrupted is manifold. No social scientist in proximity could ignore the turbulence disasters ignite. Thus, the examination of behavior and response continues as an important research focus that anthropology shares with other social sciences.

To begin with, people experiencing calamity unquestionably undergo a drastic and traumatic immediate crisis, even when that crisis arrives with the slow onset of a drought. The crisis demands and encompasses response. The behaviors implicated range from the biological to the philosophical. Subjects of the disaster then proceed to traverse an extended recovery period. The recovery process, while it varies considerably from disaster to disaster and people to people, passes through a number of stages, each of which involves complex acts. However, no matter where calamities take place and from what sort of occurrence, disaster reaction and recovery among all people experiencing them bear certain striking similarities and have consequently drawn intense exploration. Disaster victims must answer needs for shelter and sustenance. They tend to merge into an immediate unity that later fragments. They undergo interplay with the surrounding community, aid givers, and governing forces that harkens to core anthropological precepts. Individuals and societies face numerous cosmological dilemmas and concrete problems that provoke distress and require solution. People search for meaning and explanation, bringing to the fore matters of religion and mortality. They launch observances and rituals. They devise ways to express grief and mourning. Frequently people lose essential places—not merely homes, but gathering sites, formal public hubs, and environmental features that convey a sense of community and identity, foregrounding issues of place attachment, self, and social definition. Relocation and resettlement after disaster profoundly affect populations. Both frequently spur dissension among survivors and between survivors and various other factions in the disaster juncture—neighbors, aid givers, governments. People may become disrupted in time perception, habits, and patterns, which not only reveals what the contexts of their lives were once, but propels them to build their milieu anew. Issues of morality, ethics, law, and legality arise. Access to resources and property becomes impacted, and economic shifts result. Questions of resource sharing and inequality spring up, along with particulars of self-interest versus community welfare. Disasters are, in fact, often seen as material events in which the core concerns are goods, property, status, and situation. Outside monies and products often enter a disaster scene and generate dependencies previously nonexistent. Relationships and allegiances change. New groups and affiliations emerge. Participants frequently seize disasters as opportunities to alter leadership and to disassemble or reassemble power arrangements. Hegemony enters. Not uncommonly, disasters become contexts for the creation of political solidarity, activism, and new agendas. Disasters may propel old social factions to inhibit new agendas, or they may incite old institutions to readjust. Included in the examination of behavioral responses are also the many sociopsychological issues that accompany crisis, trauma, and victimization. Amid all the other factors, neither reaction nor recovery, nor, for that matter, initial vulnerability, turn out to be unidimensional. All can differ drastically by factors of age, race, ethnicity, class, and gender.

Cultural Interpretation of Risk and Disaster

People view hazards, calculate risks, and assess what, in fact, constitutes a disaster in various cultural and individual ways. Among factions within a society, perceptions are sometimes uniform, sometimes critically diverse. Among victims, or potential victims, and various sorts of non-victim outsiders, verities sometimes concur and sometimes they do not. Accordingly, hazard perception and construction, risk calculation and even the definition of calamity, and the way these concepts are contested, also figure in the social cultural study of disasters.

All people, before and after a calamity, assay the nature and value of their environment and counterpose that assessment with what they deem perilous or safe. Encompassed, as well, is the way in which people construct or "frame" their vulnerability, including at times the denial of it. People employ various means to control flow of danger from entering their sense of risk.

Those means span from the perception of dangers that cannot outwardly be verified to the negation of threats that are objectively extant. The perception of risk is linked to the values and prioritizing of values that guide a group's behavior and affect their judgments. Food, money, social position, and preferred lifestyles may outweigh jeopardy. Calculating their entire circumstance, people, in essence, gamble. Assessment also differs between natural and technological hazards, between those endangerments "known" or recognized about an environment and presumed to be controlled by unpredictable innate forces and those that are invisible or emanate from the actions of supposedly trustworthy people. Subjects common in the anthropological work on perception and assessment include the contrasts in risk measurement that emerge between local and expert knowledge or between developers and environmentalists. Also covered is the role of culture and values in the formation of risk perception. Matters of risk perception are methodologically difficult to study because they address theoretical questions about the cultural construction of reality. They further incorporate ideologies of social, physical, and cosmological settings.

As an adjunct to issues of risk, danger, and vulnerability perception within societies, the anthropological investigation of disaster has evolved to incorporate questions of the definition and ownership of disaster, or the "framing" of calamity. Who gets to declare disaster? on what terms? for whom? to what ends?—these are matters that provoke social discourse and often dissension. It follows that both the topic of framing and the struggle over it have come under anthropological scrutiny. Particularly pertinent in this modern age is not only how a disaster frame arises, but who dominates the construction of the frame and, consequently, takes command of persuasion. Studies have focused, as well, on who defines "need," what agency is bona fide, who declares when a disaster is over, and what happens to victims and the environment when a disaster is not perceived as a disaster.

Post-Disaster Social and Cultural Change

A long-standing tradition within disaster research has considered hazards and catastrophes as instruments of change in the structure and organization of societies. Although relatively unaddressed since Prince's sociological study in 1920, anthropological research has revived this tradition. In fact, the topic holds interest for both anthropology's sociocultural investigation and its political ecology inquiry. Deliberation on the topic centers on the behavior of individuals and groups in the various stages of disaster impact and aftermath and on the eventualities that take place in the course of time. Attention has surrounded the emergence of groups and new leadership; the adjustments and interactions of individuals, organizations, and differing social segments; the intervention of external institutions and organizations along with the time of their arrivals and lengths of their stay; and the permanence and transience of all the above.

Ethnographic fieldwork clearly reveals that disasters affect religion and ritual, economics and politics, kinship and associations. Disasters affect technology, the attitude toward and management of environment, and the construction of physical and cultural ecologies. They stir conflict. If not actual change, disasters certainly bring about the potential for change. Disasters often expose to both insiders and outsiders conditions that need alteration. Whether such changes are realized or not enters the inquiry. Undeniably, the introduction of change versus the retention of the former state of affairs sparks contention among the many disaster parties and factions.

The strength of sociocultural persistence, that is, the constancy of people's habits and ways, comprises the contrasting side of the discussion. Disasters impel societies and cultures to reassert prior patterns as much as spur them to undergo transformation. Anthropology has been central in expanding research into predisaster conditions and how they influence post-disaster recovery even among differing groups impacted by the same disaster. The historical background of a society profoundly influences revival and reformulation, or as has sometimes been said, "the past of a community lives on in disaster response." At the same time, in the anthropological point of view, calamities clearly figure as a pivot point motivating change.

Applied/Practicing

The field of anthropology has long held a branch of applied and practicing anthropologists, those utilizing the understandings of the discipline toward direct use and specific goals in consultantship with business, industry, government, and nongovernment organizations. Since people experiencing disaster face numerous difficulties that require expedient and operable answers, the field of disaster studies has also attracted anthropologists with practical and applied aims. The applied approach constitutes the fourth trend in the anthropological investigation of disaster.

Similar to disaster research in other fields, almost all aspects of the anthropological investigation of disaster implicitly carry an applied consideration. Virtually every focus of the investigation in some measure expounds the problems of individuals, communities, and societies engrossed in disaster. However, a growing corpus of work in anthropological research explicitly addresses applied concerns and methods. Work has varied depending on the type and scope of disaster, but applied anthropologists have directed attention and action to issues of prediction, prevention, and mitigation. They have been concerned with warning systems, the construction of habitat and workplace, and relief efforts. Traditional adaptations to environments and indigenous technical knowledge have been suggested as approaches to reducing disaster

deaths and damage and decreasing vulnerability. The work of applied or practicing anthropologists has shown that immediate local persons and institutions often better understand how to channel and distribute relief than do
outside agencies, although it is also evident that local managers bear faults
and prejudices of their own. Anthropological analysis of victim and agency
discourse has demonstrated how each party constructs relief and the reconstruction process differently. Fieldwork has revealed that relief aid is often
distributed unevenly in societies and helps or hinders people according to criteria such as sex, generation, social rank, and ethnic background. It has further demonstrated how ignorance and disregard of local customs in aiding
disaster victims can compound the obstacles and plights survivors suffer. By
ignoring traditional alliances and support groups, external aid organizations
often additionally disrupt communities. Post-disaster resettlement schemes as
well often neglect kinship and other salient local arrangements. Relief agencies sometimes objectify victims and produce dependency among recipients.
Not infrequently, disaster aid is entirely culturally inappropriate and insulting. In addition, anthropology, along with sociology, has looked into the
organizational makeup of aid agencies themselves, examining their agendas,
competitions, time scales, and value orientations.

All four trends in the anthropological examination of disaster nourish a
broad anthropological concern, the development and verification of theory.
No anthropologist or other social scientist can observe a people generate a
culture or society from *tabula rasa* to complete formation. All human social
and cultural situations come to the observer's eye well established and deeply
rooted in time and custom. Disaster, however, draws a researcher as close to
basic elements of culture and society as ever found. Disasters take a people
back to fundamentals. In their turmoil, disassembly, and reorganization, they
expose essential rules of action, bare bones of behavior, the roots of institutions, and the basic framework of organizations. They dissolve superfluous
embellishment and dismantle unfounded or casual alliance. They erase the
polish of recent development. As a result, disasters offer the investigator
amazing situations in which to analyze hypotheses pertaining to the constitution of society and culture, to reap data sustaining or confounding such max-
ims, and, potentially, to create new suppositions.

Studies emanating from disaster research have already provided anthropologists opportunity to take to task our discipline's adherence to models
derived from a Western point of view and to critique the concept that societies
and cultures always operate with fixed or "normal" patterns of behavior.
Catastrophes have demonstrated that some societies constantly adjust to
chronically shifting contingencies, and in some contexts the nonroutine is
routine. Disaster research not only hones theories of sociocultural change,

methodologically it underscores the uses and values of qualitative data and quantitative.

Although anthropologists have made little use of disaster situations to advance the field, great possibilities lie there. The assessments derived from disaster circumstances all lead to anthropological acumen.

diff. anth
approaches
diverge
but also
interweave

While the various anthropological approaches to the study of disaster to a degree diverge, clearly they also interweave. The archaeological/historical perspective not only unearths material and food production strategies, but through artistic artifacts uncovers the constitution and development of socio-cultural ideologies that maintained people in perilous locales. Political ecological explorations overlap with cultural interpretation of risk and disaster. Together they bring to heed such considerations as who controls cultural reinvention and how such control is achieved. The sociocultural purview, in its concentrations on disaster response, psychosocial trauma, perceptions of risk, and change, flows into the applied practicing approach. Applied concerns frequently parallel those of the political ecology. Other research directions exist, flowing into the major trends: for instance, the constitutions of natural resource communities and the effects of disaster on them; the linkages between development and disaster; and the interplay of disaster and health. Together all add to the diorama of anthropological disaster research.

THE ANGRY EARTH

The hope of this volume is twofold: to serve as an exemplar for the anthropology of disaster's developing concerns and to outline and establish a baseline for further anthropological research in disaster.

In the sections of the book that follow, we examine in more detail many pertinent anthropological motifs in the study of disaster. The various chapters cover both technological and natural disasters and include cultures and societies from almost every continent.[2] The articles investigate the interrelation of disasters, environment, and culture, including the definition of disaster; the archaeological record of the long-term environmental patterns of catastrophe; the cultural construction of disaster and how individuals and groups affirm, manipulate, or negate events; the configuration of disaster response; the patterns of interaction and articulation between agencies and victims, including when agendas differ; and, finally, the continuity of cultural realms in the face of chronic calamity or after disasters occur. The organization of this volume does not directly follow the outline of perspectives in the anthropological study of disaster. Nor is every aspect of every concern covered. Rather, these chapters represent a selection of topics from the various concerns, each section containing chapters from differing perspectives. Every section is introduced with a heading that explains its relevance to the holistic platform of anthropological disaster research.

We begin with a section, "Disasters, Environment, and Culture," that is, in essence, a preamble to the rest of the volume. To examine disaster we need a launching pad; we need to know what a disaster is. Defining disaster has not been a simple or agreed-upon matter. The term and concept have, indeed, attracted much argument and discussion. Anthony Oliver-Smith's chapter "'What Is a Disaster?': Anthropological Perspectives on a Persistent Question" addresses the definition and multidimensional nature of disasters from the anthropological point of view.

Section II, "Environmental Pattern, Hazards, and Culture: The Archaeological Perspective," illuminates the time-depth perspective that the anthropological examination of disaster finds indispensable. The two chapters demonstrate what the record of no longer extant people can show about the relationship of disaster to human communities and the long-term continuum of social and cultural life in zones having chronic disasters. The chapter by Sheets, "The Effects of Explosive Volcanism on Ancient Egalitarian, Ranked, and Stratified Societies in Middle America," remarks upon the survivability or friability of certain social structures and political economic systems. Archaeological evidence in Central America demonstrates that simplicity of social stratification is directly related to flexibility, and that flexibility is related to a society's ability to regather and survive calamity. More complex organizations bear less elasticity. The implications for the present-day global structure of our world are disquieting. Moseley's chapter, "Convergent Catastrophe: Past Patterns and Future Implications of Collateral Natural Disasters in the Andes," ominously exposes the boundaries of cultural resilience. Given one major disaster, communities and cultures of the Andes could muster and continue. When two or more disasters compounded, one perhaps slow, another abrupt, the culture's resilience is diminished and collapse can result. As well as attesting to the value of anthropology's diachronic perspective, both chapters are texts in cultural ecology and political economy.

Bridging the archaeological perspective into history and leading into Section III, "The Cultural and Social Construction of Catastrophe," Oliver-Smith's chapter, "Peru's Five-Hundred-Year Earthquake: Vulnerability in Historical Context," chronicles the duration involved in manufacturing the sociocultural conditions culminating in calamity. The vulnerability that resulted in the 1970 Peruvian earthquake is seen to be the consequence of both inappropriate environmental and political economic changes imposed on the Andean region since the conquest. Bolin's and Stanford's "Constructing Vulnerability in the First World: The Northridge Earthquake in Southern California, 1994" also examines the social production of vulnerability. They argue that vulnerability exists not only within third-world, non-Western contexts, but within the developed world as well. They compare and contrast four separate communities in the aftermath of the same disaster. Economic stability, home ownership, and incorporation into larger realms by education and employment drastically affected the differing responses and the ultimate viability of the communities. Their portraiture illuminates a political economic discourse. The question of who defines a disaster in a multilayered global world, along with the overlapping sociocultural matter of ideological "framing," comes to the foreground of Gregory Button's chapter, "The Negation of Disaster: The Media Response to Oil Spills in Great Britain." Button shows how one of the world's major technological disasters, one that profoundly affected thousands of people, as well as a second ensuing one, had become essentially ignored due to the power of hegemonic framing strategies by the media. Buttons shows how politics and power penetrate the perceptual. His treatise combines both behavioral response and political ecological points of view.

No volume could cover all the varieties and layers of cultural response to disaster, but certain of the inquiries are addressed in the chapters of Section IV, "Varieties of Cultural Response." Various studies of communities in the aftermath of disaster reveal that there are characteristic phases in the disaster recovery process victims pass through. Hoffman's article, "The Worst of Times, the Best of Times: Toward a Model of Cultural Response to Disaster," canvasses that seemingly universal narrative. Survivors traverse from almost euphoric mutuality to disharmony, from seeing new horizons to watching the old reclaim them. Oliver-Smith in "The Brotherhood of Pain: Theoretical and Applied Perspectives on Post-Disaster Solidarity" puts under the microscope one stage of that recovery process as experienced by people of Yungay, Peru, after the catastrophic avalanche of 1970. He dissects and analyzes why the behavior occurs. Both Hoffman's and Oliver-Smith's accounts represent sociocultural recapitulations. Hoffman's delineation of the different recovery experienced by women and men in the Oakland firestorm of 1991, "The Regenesis of Traditional Gender Pattern in the Wake of Disaster," sketches how recovery and response to disaster are not uniform. The study underscores the importance of narrative methods in achieving the more fine-grained and ethnographic analysis required to expose the multidimensional nature of disaster circumstance. Zaman, in "Vulnerability, Disaster, and Survival in Bangladesh: Three Case Studies," explores the interplay of natural hazards with sociopolitical and economic dynamics that link systemic vulnerability and impaired disaster response. In Bangladesh government programs compound marginality, poverty, and survival. Dyer's and McGoodwin's chapter, "'Tell Them We're Hurting': Hurricane Andrew, the Culture of Response, and the Fishing Peoples of South Florida and Louisiana," unites political ecological analysis to the disaster recovery process. The chapter reviews two natural resource communities responding to the same disaster and shows how wider cultural values and integration affect recovery and determine how effectual or ineffectual a community's rebound will be.

Paul L. Doughty's chapter, "Plan and Pattern in Reaction to Earthquake: Peru, 1970–1998," develops a discussion of cultural response and the crucial interplay of outside agents in the disaster complex. His piece introduces Section V, "Agencies, Survivors, and Reconstruction." Doughty chronicles a twenty-seven-year recovery process from the 1970 Peruvian earthquake until the present. Agencies and policies come and go. Traditions shift, changes and persistence occur. His and the following chapters also illuminate the implicit and explicit aspects of applied and practicing concerns within the political and sociocultural factors in catastrophe. In "Bhopal: Vulnerability, Routinization, and the Chronic Disaster," Rajan documents the making of a tragedy, plus the augmentation of that tragedy, that characterized the disaster surrounding the gas "accident" in Bhopal, India. There industrial, bureaucratic, and medical personnel so miscalculate and mismanage a disastrous event that charged and polarized political consequences emerge. Dyer takes into the spotlight a single disaster agency in "The Phoenix Effect in Post-Disaster Recovery: An Analysis of the Economic Development Administration's Culture of Response After Hurricane Andrew." He examines the Economic Development Administration of the United States in its dealings in Florida after Hurricane Andrew. The story is one of considerable success, as the agency incorporates a great deal of sociocultural understanding with a political economic agenda.

We conclude with Section VI, "Disaster and Cultural Continuity." Hoffman's summation, "After Atlas Shrugs: Cultural Change or Persistence After a Disaster," looks at the critical question that hovers over all fields of the anthropological study of disaster: Do society and culture change in response to disaster or not? Capsulizing several case studies, she finds the answer is yes and no.

All the articles in *The Angry Earth* explicitly demonstrate the importance of anthropological perspectives to the study of disaster. Disasters are conjunctural events. They document linkages between past and present, tradition and politics, response and change, behavior, adaptation, and survivability at a time when the issue of survivability confronts us all.

NOTES

1. In this introduction we sketch a broad overview of the field, citing only certain benchmark contributions. More specific references are available in the articles which follow.

2. While this volume lacks a chapter on drought in Africa, the literature on drought and famine in Africa is extensive. For the researcher interested, see Parker Shipton, 1990, "African Famines and Food Security: Anthropological Perspectives," *Annual Reviews in Anthropology* 19: 353–94.

BIBLIOGRAPHY

Hewitt, K. 1983. *Interpretations of Calamity*. Boston: Allen & Unwin.

Prince, S. H. 1920. *Catastrophe and Social Change, Based on a Sociological Study of the Halifax Disaster*. Unpublished Ph.D. thesis. New York: Columbia University.

Torry, W. 1979. "Anthropological Studies in Hazardous Environments: Past Trends and New Horizons." *Current Anthropology* 20: 517–541.

I

DISASTERS, ENVIRONMENT, AND CULTURE

IN THE DEVELOPMENT OF DISASTER RESEARCH, ESTABLISHING AN APPROPRI-
ate definition of the concept has proved to be a challenging
task. The problem is complex because disasters are complex,
generated by a variety of forces, producing a variety of impacts,
varying radically along chronological and spacial scales. Over
the years, some approaches to the definition have focused on
environmental and destructive agents. Others have emphasized
criteria of physical or social disruption. Still others have pointed
to cultural perceptions rather than actual physical impacts. In
fact, disasters, because of their material impacts, their emergence from human-environment relations, and their cultural
construction, possess multiple identities and range over multiple spaces from purely object (nature) to purely subject (social
discourse). In all aspects, however, disasters test the adaptive
resilience of a community within its total environment. Definitions of disaster must take into account trends in increased hazards and vulnerability. Moreover, the definition involves issues
of policy as well as science, since deeming an event a disaster or
not may set in motion programs and practices which impact
affected communities.

1

"WHAT IS A DISASTER?": ANTHROPOLOGICAL PERSPECTIVES ON A PERSISTENT QUESTION

ANTHONY OLIVER-SMITH
University of Florida

INTRODUCTION

DISASTERS HAVE BEEN STUDIED FROM A SOCIAL SCIENTIFIC PERSPECTIVE FOR roughly seven decades. During this span multiple conceptual and thematic foci emerged from a variety of origins, each contributing in different ways to the overall development of the field. Ranging from Prince's (1920) early study of a munitions explosion in Halifax harbor to studies of populations experiencing wartime bombardment to the social impacts of natural hazards and a myriad of operational definitions used in emergency assistance and reconstruction, there has been little consensus on the definition of disaster. In some circles, the lack of consensus has caused concern regarding the intellectual health of the field (Quarantelli 1985, 1995).

However, the intellectual vitality of a field of research does not necessarily depend on a conceptual or definitional consensus. In anthropology, for example, Kroeber and Kluckhohn, after surveying the literature, found 164 different definitions of culture, the discipline's core concept (1952). Since Kroeber and Kluckhohn's time, debate on the concept of culture has raged over such central elements as the material or ideological bases of culture, appropriate methodologies for cultural research, and the nomothetic versus the ideographic nature of the study of culture. Those debates generated markedly different approaches to research topics and methodologies. Although anthropologists probably ascribe to fewer definitions of culture today, total consensus on the concept has hardly been reached. Still, lack of complete conceptual uniformity or consensus has not resulted in intellectual stagnation. Indeed, such debate is the substance of both scientific and humanistic endeavor in general. The continuing discourse surrounding the discipline's core concept has hardly, in my view, been damaging to the integrity of the field, nor has it undermined the discipline's research enterprise. While there are those who would disagree with me, I see the current foment in anthropology as a sign of health and vitality. The intense self-examination that anthropology frequently becomes involved in revitalizes and stimulates new theoretical, methodological, and research questions.

Despite the fact that the lack of consensus about either culture or disaster is not a particular source of concern to me, I do not wish to dismiss the question "What is a disaster?" as insignificant. The definitional debate regarding disaster is significant because it prompts an exploration of past and emerging dimensions of disaster in an increasingly hazardous present, as evidenced in the appearance of new forms of hazard and rapidly changing human-environment relations and conditions. Definitional consensus may be less important than stirring discussions in which conflicts may not be totally resolved, but important issues will be clarified, new perspectives and problem areas developed, and, most importantly, new potentials for practice explored. In effect, multiple definitions are not necessarily injurious to a field if they can be operationalized through appropriate intellectual and methodological procedures to advance orderly and systematic research (Rocha 1995: 5). In this chapter, I intend to review some of the inherent difficulties in defining disaster, as well as the issues central to definitional debates. Further, I outline the contribution of anthropology to the conceptualization of disaster and argue for the development of a political ecology of disaster.

DISASTERS: VARIABILITY AND COMPLEXITY

Why has it been so difficult to reach a consensus on the concept of disaster? On the one hand, disaster is a term that is used fairly liberally in popular parlance. Many events or processes are colloquially referred to as disasters—everything from a failed social event to a regionwide hurricane. The varied popular and literary uses of the term embrace such a wide array of phenomena, concepts, metaphors, and allusions that attempts at precision, clarity, and, perhaps most importantly, simplicity by scientific interests are challenged. By the same token, popular usages and interpretations of the term also on occasion reveal significant dimensions of disasters that escape the perspective of the purely objective stance (Kroll-Smith 1998).

Since disasters are characterized by external variability and internal complexity, the conceptual challenge presented by disasters is doubly problematic. External variability refers to the wide range of "objective" phenomena in natural and technological domains that generate or trigger disasters and produce very different kinds of physical impacts. Covering them all, the word *disaster* is used to characterize events/processes that range from slow-onset processes such as droughts and toxic exposures to rapid-onset phenomena such as earthquakes and nuclear accidents. External variability also encompasses the range of effects of such disasters, extending from immediate destruction and death from, for example, tornados, to impacts not perceived or experienced physically for perhaps many years, as in the case of toxic exposures. External variability alone thus almost defies analysts' abilities to establish a set of common definitional characteristics that can encompass the vast array of phenomena that generate and occur in disasters.

Wittgenstein counsels us regarding the linguistic difficulty of absolute precision, particularly when dealing with categories that encompass widely ranging phenomena. For such categories or concepts, he suggests using the term "family resemblances." Following his discussion of the concept of games, I suggest that disasters form a family, in that what emerges from a consideration of their wide array of phenomena is "a complicated network of similarities, overlapping and criss-crossing: sometimes overall similarities, sometimes similarities of detail" (Wittgenstein 1973: 32e). Wittgenstein employs the metaphor of spinning a thread in which there is a continuous overlapping of fiber upon fiber, but no one fiber that runs through the entire thread. The common feature of the thread, as well as—to extend the metaphor—its strength, lies in the continuous overlapping of the filaments through the whole strand. Furthermore, there is no need to establish definitional criteria limits to make such a set of family resemblances usable as a concept. This is not to say that boundaries cannot be drawn, as they frequently are for special purposes, but boundaries are not necessary to make the concept usable, except for that special purpose (Wittgenstein 1973: 33e).

Multiple, yet similar, definitions of disasters arise exactly according to the specific purposes or goals of various disaster endeavors. Researchers focusing on behavior will define disaster differently from those exploring societal-environment interactions. Organizations involved in disaster management or reconstruction set operational definitions that allow their participation in events and processes that meet the criteria. Thus, the term *disaster* constitutes a set of family resemblances rather than conforming to a minimum list of definitional criteria. The concept has "blurred edges," as Wittgenstein says, but the inexactness of a definition hardly makes it unusable.

Also central to the definitional debate is the internal complexity of disaster. In a disaster a collectivity of intersecting processes and events—social, environmental, cultural, political, economic, physical, technological—transpiring over varying lengths of time are focused. Disasters are totalizing events. As they unfold, all dimensions of a social structural formation and the totality of its relations with its environment may become involved, affected, and focused. These dimensions express consistency and inconsistency, coherence and contradiction, cooperation and conflict, hegemony and resistance. They reveal the operation of physical, biological, and social systems and their interaction among populations, groups, institutions and practices, and their concommitant sociocultural constructions. Like few other phenomena the internal complexity of disasters forces us to confront the many and shifting faces of socially constructed reality(ies). The complexity is embodied in the multiplicity of perspectives as varied as the individuals and groups impacted or participating in the event and process. The multiple forms, enactments, and constructions that a disaster may take also elicit multiple interpretations from many disciplinary approaches, each with widely varying methodological tools and theoretical and practical goals.

The external or objective variability and internal or subjective complexity of disasters are largely responsible for the contested nature of the concept. As Gallie, writing some ten years after Wittgenstein, asserted, ". . . there are concepts which are essentially contested, concepts the proper use of which inevitably involves endless disputes about their proper uses on the part of their users" (1955: 169). Similarly concepts such as "art" or "democracy" are disagreed on by differing parties as to their use and also to their application to particular situations or contexts, with each faction maintaining the correctness of its interpretation with equally compelling arguments and evidence.

I submit, then, that disaster is a contested concept, with "blurred edges," more a set of family resemblances among a wide array of physical and social events and processes rather than a set of bounded phenomena to be strictly defined.

ELEMENTS OF A DEFINITIONAL DEBATE

The discussion regarding the definition of disaster was most intently engaged in by sociologists and geographers, beginning with efforts by Fritz (1961), Baker and Chapman (1962), and Barton (1969). In surveying the literature of the previous three decades, Quarantelli expressed concern over the lack of definitional consensus in the field (1985), noting that disasters had been variously defined in terms of 1) physical agents, 2) the physical impact of physical agents, 3) an assessment of physical impacts, 4) the social disruption resulting from an event with physical impacts, 5) the social construction of reality in perceived crisis situations which may or may not involve physical impacts, 6) the political definition of certain crisis situations, and 7) an imbalance in the demand-capability ratio in a crisis situation (Quarantelli 1985: 43–44). More recently, Quarantelli noted that the overall situation has not changed substantially since his earlier assessment (1995: 222).

To a certain degree, this relative stasis in the debate engaged in largely by sociologists and, to some extent, by geographers and political scientists is true.

However, current debate has been sharpened by the emergence of both the political economic and cultural ecological perspectives that have spread across the social sciences since the 1960s. In the 1970s many anthropologists and cultural geographers started both to broaden the focus of disaster research and embed it in deeper time frames. In so doing, they opened up new theoretical and practical (political) questions and began to reconsider disasters as less the result of geophysical extremes (earthquakes, hurricanes, droughts, etc.) and more as functions of ongoing social orders, human-environment relations, and historical structural processes. The issues they introduced appear in greater current emphasis upon the roles intrinsic qualities of society play in disaster than on the facts of disruption and devastation. The definitional debate now revolves around how key social factors are to be weighted or applied in definitions and from that, how research questions are to be formulated. Thus, in substance, out of Quarantelli's earlier list of understandings of disaster, a set of common concerns relating to defining what a disaster is did arise. Rather than a wildly disparate set of defining characteristics producing contradictory understandings of a disaster, the discussion now centers around the varying emphases (and in some cases labels) the specific issues have (see Quarantelli 1995).

Objectivity versus Subjectivity

Still of concern in the definitional debate is the issue of disaster as an objectively identifiable phenomenon or a subjective, socially constructed process. That is, is a disaster a set of physical impacts or a set of socially constructed perceptions? Rather than a fixed entity, identifiable by certain concrete material characteristics and time dimensions, some researchers see disaster as a relative matter, that is, varying according to the multiple perspectives of the different affected groups (Quarantelli 1985: 45; Kroll-Smith 1998). Such a formulation permits the application of the term "disaster" to a social construction of conditions and/or events in which no destruction, but considerable social disruption, has occurred, leading to the question of what kinds of phenomena should, therefore, be included within the rubric of disaster and what kinds should be excluded.

Definitions that frame a disaster as a socially constructed crisis, in which modes of interpretation and significance rather than physical structures are endangered, are implicitly broad. Such approaches focus far more on the psychocultural impacts as the crucial characteristics of disasters, and assert that emphasis on issues of material or infrastructural damage fails to address the essential elements of disasters. The kinds of material destruction that other definitions emphasize figure in these approaches as perhaps only triggers of the fundamentally sociopsychological or psychocultural essence of disaster. These definitions emphasize the dislocating and disrupting effects on human cognition and culture of a wide variety of phenomena that would include the effects of everything from a level five hurricane, a chemical oil spill, a terrorist attack, an epidemic, or a plant closing. Broad and cognitively based, they can include such phenomena as a structural adjustment program, the AIDS epidemic, the Oklahoma City bombing, Three Mile Island, the Watts riots, and the savings and loan crisis along with the 1985 Mexico City earthquake, Hurricane Andrew, and Bhopal. These definitions enhance the possibilities of comparison among many classes of events and processes. By the same token, including a wide variety of phenomena under the rubric of disaster may also tend to obscure significant distinctions across classes of phenomena (Kroll-Smith and Couch 1991).

Other approaches that attempt to balance social disruption, physical harm, and psychological dislocation as characteristics defining disaster are less inclusive. They emphasize physical impacts but still incorporate a wide array of events/processes. Kreps (1995) explicitly wants to include a wide array of phenomena that "involve social disruption and physical harm . . . keeping the boundaries broad to include environmental, technological and sociopolitical events." Therefore, civil strife of various sorts would be included under the rubric of disasters in addition to natural and technological events/processes. Kreps, however, would hold to definitions that would exclude such social phenomena as economic crises, plant closings, or perhaps computer/high technology failures unless they occasioned specific forms of destruction or mortality.

Nonroutine versus Socially Embedded Events

A further issue in discussions of definitions of disaster involves the nonroutine nature of disasters. Disasters in general are portrayed as nonroutine, destabilizing, causing uncertainty, disorder, and sociocultural collapse. In such descriptions there is clearly an emphasis on distinguishing disasters from ordinary, everyday realities that are characterized explicitly and implicitly as possessing a higher degree of predictability. Disasters disrupt routine life, destabilize social structures and adaptations, and endanger worldviews and systems of meaning (Horlick-Jones 1995).

While the stress on the nonroutine dimension of disasters seems close to common logic, these descriptions seem to incorporate an almost functionalist assumption of general societal equilibrium prior to disaster onset. Such an assumption dangerously ignores that most disasters are ultimately explainable in terms of the normal order. That is, the risks that people run in their natural environments are by and large manageable, but the forms and structures of ordinary life, particularly those associated with the disadvantages suffered by third-world societies, accentuate the risk and the resulting disaster impact. There is, as Hewitt points out, a "tacit assumption of an unexamined normality" (1995: 322).

The Environmental versus the Social Location of Disasters

The next, and arguably the most important, of these debated issues is the "location" problem; that is, are disasters located in society or in the environment? Among social scientists, there is now a fairly clear consensus that definitions focusing on agents (e.g., hurricanes or oil spills) from the natural or technological environment, described by Hewitt as the "hazards paradigm," divert attention from the fundamentally social nature of disaster and impede generalization and theory building (1995: 319). However, the hazards paradigm is still seen as particularly tenacious, persistently influencing sociological approaches even while being rejected.

The debate over the social versus the environmental nature of disasters brings up a side matter that might be called the "what–why" question, although some might prefer the terms "effect" and "cause." That is, is the task of the definition to clarify what disaster is or what a disaster does rather than to explain why a disaster takes place? Some researchers would reject the concept of vulnerability as relevant to defining disasters. For them, the concept of vulnerability, which centers on understanding disaster in the total social and environmental context, is more appropriate for explaining the origin and causes of disaster rather than defining it (Porfiriev 1995). Quarantelli advises that "we should stop confusing antecedent conditions and subsequent consequences with the characteristics of a disaster" (as cited in Porfiriev 1995: 292). Rather, they require that definitions be framed in terms of the behavior of people and groups at a temporally and spatially specific moment. Community perception and response, including organizational involvement, therefore become the crucial issues for defining a disaster (Dynes 1993). Disaster is thus seen largely as a behavioral phenomenon, and the focus of the definitional problem is primarily the behavior of human beings and groups in a specific context of disruption and/or damage as expressed in individual, group, or institutional terms. In this approach, a disaster becomes an array of socially derived effects.

DISASTERS AND DEBATES
IN ANTHROPOLOGICAL PERSPECTIVE

Although anthropologists have been involved in disaster studies since the field gained recognition as a substantive research area in the 1950s (Drabek 1986), they were, for the most part, fairly atheoretical and uninvolved in definitional issues. They preferred to focus on the responses of traditional peoples to specific events (Belshaw 1951; Keesing 1952; Schneider 1957). Firth (1959) and Spillius (1957) were somewhat more concerned with disasters for revealing issues of theoretical importance for social organization. Wallace, however, in his study of the Worcestor tornado, constructed a time-space model of disaster as a type of behavioral event (1956). In his analysis, Wallace posits that a disaster is an event characterized by a series of time stages and spatial dimensions, each associated with different activities and roles embedded both in the predisaster system and the conditions imposed by the event itself (1956: 1–3). Defining what a disaster was appears not to have been particularly problematic to these early researchers. However, anthropology, while rarely specifically addressing the definitional issue, has shared many of the same foci and problematics in researching disasters as have other social sciences, to the effect that many features of the debate are not foreign to the field.

From my perspective as an anthropologist, defining disaster in behavioral or social psychological terms and applying it to a broad array of phenomena, provided the definitional criteria being used are made explicit and the event/process specificities detailed, is not particularly problematic. Indeed, basically behavioral definitions generate interesting and significant research on aspects of behavior of individuals, groups, and organizations as well as social theory, a theme I explore in chapter 8. Such research also has important implications for disaster practice. However, recently I have found that essentially behavioral definitions provide less a starting point than, perhaps, a midpoint to most of the issues about disaster that I, as an anthropologist, find most compelling. These issues concern what disasters reveal about society in: 1) its internal social and economic structure and dynamics in relation to 2) its external social and environmental relations, 3) the nature of its overall adaptation, and, finally, 4) how this knowledge can be employed to reduce disaster vulnerability and damage. Implicit in my approach is the assumption that disasters are as deeply embedded in the social structure and culture of a society as they are in an environment. In a sense, a disaster is symptomatic of the condition of a society's total adaptational strategy within its social, economic, modified, and built environments.

Adaptation has been and continues to be a central concept in understanding the human use of the physical environment. Basic anthropology texts frequently present the concept in terms of strategies of a sociocultural nature adopted by individuals and groups (communities, societies) to cope with the conditions presented by the physical and cultural environments in a way that enables them to survive and/or prosper (Bennett 1996: 253; Peoples and Bailey 1997). The sociocultural system is seen as the primary means by which a human population adjusts to its environment. It enables a community to extract from its surroundings food, shelter, water, energy, and other necessities and to confront and reduce to some relative degree the uncertainty and vulnerability experienced in interaction with environmental conditions and forces that threaten the population (Bates and Pelanda 1994: 149). There are two fundamental features that human beings must address in their relationship to their environments: the natural resources that enable people to meet their needs, and the set of challenges that people must adjust to in order to survive. In other words, if people are to survive and reproduce they must exploit resources efficiently and deal with environmental problems effectively. Environmental problems include abiotic forces (temperature, precipitation, terrain, water, etc.), biotic forces (basically flora and fauna), and the challenge of other human beings who may compete or cooperate with any given population present (Peoples and Bailey 1997: 117).

There are two dimensions or axes that are crucial to how the process of adaptation is played out. The first involves the interplay between individual and group, or between differently constituted groups. What may be adaptive for the individual may be maladaptive for the group, and vice versa. That is, choices made by an individual in the use of resources—water, for example— may prejudice the welfare of the group. The converse is also true. How choices are made is not purely an issue of biological adaptation among human beings, but of a cultural or, specifically, a political nature, reflecting the power relations of the society and how power is expressed in the domains of wealth and prestige. The second involves the issue of choices and actions in a proximate time frame that may bear unanticipated longer-term adaptive implications (Bates and Plog 1991: 18). In essence, a society, as an interconnected network of individuals and groups seeking to satisfy both material and nonmaterial needs and wants, adapts to its physical and cultural environment. The society interacts and modifies its environment, engaging a series of processes over which it has incomplete control and incomplete knowledge, particularly over longer periods of time.

Despite flourishing in numbers and complexity, human societies have not been able to absorb or deflect all forms of hazards presented by the total environment over extended periods of time without impact. The forces and conditions in the built, modified, and/or natural environments that characterize disasters are forms of adaptational challenges to which the society must, but does not always, respond. Insofar as it is impossible to guard against every threat completely, all systems experience degrees of inherent vulnerability. For example, communities are often founded on the basis of proximity to resources, thus enhancing chances of survival, only to find over time that the same proximity to resources also involves proximity to hazards. The hazards must then be responded to in a way that enables the community to withstand their effects. Furthermore, the sheer complexity of our own social and technological systems generates dangers often simply out of slippage among the multiplicity of elements composing the system (Perrow 1984). Disasters, and how well or poorly systems fare in them, are a gauge of the success or failure of the total adaptation of the community. In the way we structure consciously and unconsciously, intentionally and unintentionally, our interactions with the environment, we can frequently be the cause of our own hazardous situation.

The problem presented by hazards and disasters must therefore be framed within the overall pattern of societal adaptation to the total environment.

Traditionally, in cultural anthropology such practices as hunter-gatherer migration patterns, postpartum taboos on intercourse, and band fragmentation (Steward 1955; Sahlins 1972; Lee 1979) were seen to be effective adaptive strategies for hazards in specific environments. Indeed, anthropology has a long tradition of studying among populations living in stressful and hazardous environments and framing research from an adaptational perspective (Torry 1979). However, the source of hazards is no longer necessarily found in the environment. Increasingly, the levels of environmental stress and vulnerability to hazards are being exacerbated by political, economic, and social forces, obliging people to adapt to an institutional environment as well as a natural one (Vayda and McKay 1975).

Viewing disasters from the perspective of adaptation both permits and obliges us to reconsider questions of the adaptive fitness of all societies, particularly those which have traditionally been perceived as having controlled or dominated their natural environments. The question of adaptation to hazards and disasters is paralleled currently by a similar concern about the long-term sustainability of resource use along with present levels of environmental degradation and pollution. The emerging relationship between increasing hazards and disasters and environmental degradation calls into question from the adaptive perspective the long-term sustainability, or, to put it another way, the adaptive fitness of industrial societies.

To return to an issue mentioned earlier, if we separate questions of cause from questions of effect (the "why–what" issue), basically we disengage hazards from disasters and environment from society. To separate the two matters is also to remove from the discussion the question of vulnerability or, that is, those features of society that do not favor survival of all or some of its members. The inadequacy or collapse of cultural adaptations, or "protections," as Dombrowsky refers to them, is certainly one of the core issues of disaster research and practice (1995). By separating hazard from disaster we disengage society from the physical world in which both are constituted. The "why" is implicit in every disaster because disasters either do not occur or are not severe if a community is successfully adapted to its environment. Occurrence and severity of disaster are one measure by which we can judge the success of adaptation to the environment.

If cause is, in fact, an appropriate issue in the definition of disasters, then we need to develop an alternative to understanding why disasters happen and why they take the forms they do. In calling for a perspective that includes both cause and effect, I am not advocating a return to a simplistic environmental "hazards" approach and situating the origin of disasters in environmental forces, so appropriately criticized by Hewitt (1983, 1995). I am instead calling for a more nuanced approach to the relationship between society and environment, underscoring their mutual constitution, interaction, and adaptation (Ingold 1992). In essence, the debate over situating disasters in nature or in society is a pointless dualism. In understanding and defining disaster, the focus should be on the intersection between society and environment in terms of societal adaptation to the total environment, including the natural, modified, and constructed contexts and processes of which the community is a part.

The reason for adopting an adaptational dimension in our understanding of disasters is grounded in the fact that human communities and their behaviors are not simply situated in environments. As Ingold notes, the interface between society and environment is not one "of external contact between separate domains" (1992: 51). Societies are founded and formed in nature themselves, just as nature is culturally constructed and physically altered by society. Nor is this mutual constitution static. Rather, it is an active, complex, and evolving interaction. Society and environment are not separate, but two interrelated and reciprocally formative entities. Environmental features and processes become socially defined and structured just as social elements acquire environmental identities and expressions. Societal development entails development of an environment, and the resulting interplay emerges from the many continual processes of exchange through the porous and shifting borders between them. Society and environment thus are interpenetrating, mutually constitutive of the same world, comprised basically of the possibilities for exchange and action provided by natural, modified, and built environments and of the abilities and capabilities of people and their cultural constructions (Ingold 1992: 52).

Accordingly, disasters occur in societies. They do not occur in nature. However, disasters do not originate exclusively in societies, but rather emerge from societal environmental relations and the institutionalized forms those relations take. The frame or context in which disasters occur is a set of interacting and mutually constituting processes of human society and material culture, each with its own internal autodynamics, and of nature, also with its own autodynamic and self-organizing processes. Disasters thus become defined as failures of human systems to understand and address the interactions of this set of interrelated systems, producing a collapse of cultural protections and a resulting set of effects called a disaster. Disasters can result from the interaction of social, material, and natural systems, producing a failure of human culture to protect. Since our understanding of the effects of our actions and about these autodynamic systems is far from complete, the risk of failure becomes very high (Dombrowsky 1995).

In terms of anthropology, then, disasters are best conceptualized in terms of the web of relations that link society (the organization and relations among individuals and groups), environment (the network of linkages with the physical world in which people and groups are both constituted and constituting), and culture (the values, norms, beliefs, attitudes, and knowledge that pertain to that organization and those relations).

A POLITICAL ECOLOGICAL APPROACH TO DISASTERS

The conjunction of a human population and a potentially destructive agent does not, however, inevitably produce a disaster. The society's pattern of vulnerability—or in other words, its adaptive failure—is an essential element of a disaster. A disaster is made inevitable by the historically produced pattern of vulnerability, evidenced in the location, infrastructure, sociopolitical structure, production patterns, and ideology, that characterizes a society. The pattern of vulnerability will condition the behavior of individuals and organizations throughout the life history of a disaster far more profoundly than will the physical force of the destructive agent.

The complex internal differentiation that characterizes all but the earliest levels of sociocultural integration may distribute the benefits of adaptational effectiveness in widely disparate ways in both the short and long term. From this perspective, the patterns of adaptation developed out of the social systems of the society may be effective generally, or effective only for those favored by the societal power relations or patterns of production and allocation and not effective for those not so favored. The same patterns of adaptation, while reasonably effective for some or many in the short run, may equally sow the seeds of future vulnerability and disasters in the long run.

To understand disasters in the context of the complex internal differentiation that is particularly characteristic of contemporary human societies thus requires the combination of an ecological framework with an analytical strategy that can encompass the interaction of environmental features, processes, and resources with the nature, forms, and effects of the patterns of production, allocation, and internal social differentiation of society. The fact that complex societies, as adaptive systems, are controlled by contesting interests within a society, privileging some sectors with enhanced security while subjecting others to systemic risks and hazards, must also be apprehended by any effective research strategy.

In substance, a political ecology of disasters must be developed. Political ecology situates an ecologically grounded social scientific perspective within a political economy framework by focusing on the relationships between people, the environment, and the sociopolitical structures that characterize the society of which the people are members (Campbell 1996: 6). A political ecology perspective on disasters focuses on the dynamic relationships between a human population, its socially generated and politically enforced productive and allocative patterns, and its physical environment, all in the formation of patterns of vulnerability and response to disaster.

Human-environmental relations are largely structured and expressed through social relations and the value orientations that derive from the arrangements through which a population extracts a living from its surroundings. A political ecology approach recognizes that the social institutional arrangements through which human beings access and alter the physical environment in their quest for sustenance and shelter are key elements in the evolution of disasters. Political ecological analysis focuses on those conditions surrounding the disaster, either threatened or occurred, which shape its evolution. It most particularly emphasizes those structures that shape the developmental features that make the society vulnerable to both socioeconomically and environmentally generated hazards.

This perspective is consistent with recent formulations on development and environmental degradation (Peet and Watts 1993; Schmink and Wood 1987; Painter and Durham 1995) and similarly founded approaches to disaster (Blaikie et al. 1994; Bates and Pelanda 1994; Kroll-Smith and Couch 1991; Peacock et al. 1997). The basic view is that a necessary but not sufficient condition for a disaster to occur is the conjuncture of at least two factors: a human population and a potentially destructive agent. The society and the destructive agent are mutually constitutive and embedded in natural and social systems as unfolding processes over time. Both societies and destructive agents are clearly processual phenomena, together defining disaster as a processual phenomenon rather than an event that is isolated and temporally demarcated in exact time frames.

If vulnerability is to be considered essential to the understanding of disaster, the question of time becomes fundamental. I suggest that the life history of a disaster begins prior to the appearance of a specific event-focused agent. Indeed, in certain circumstances disasters become part of the profile of any human system at its first organizational moment in a relatively fixed location or area. As a society develops through time, it may reduce or increase its vulnerability to selected hazards through sociocultural adaptations. A political ecological approach appears the most capable of encompassing the causation and production of disasters, their development as social and environmental processes and events, their sociocultural construction, and their implications for the overall sociocultural adaptation and evolution of the community (Bates and Pelanda 1994: 147).

CONCLUSION: DEFINING DISASTER
IN THE CONTEXT OF GLOBAL CHANGE

The issue of success or failure of species within environments has traditionally been the focus of adaptation research, but the viability of the environment itself as a self-sustaining system must now also be included. Given the current changes in the nature and number of hazards and disasters, there is a certain urgency for appropriate reconceptualizations and approaches to hazards and disasters. From the anthropological perspective, the question of how well a society is adapted to its environment should now be linked to the question of how well an environment fares around a society. The issue of mutuality is at the forefront. Disasters now more than ever express most clearly imbalances in that mutuality.

Clearly, the continued expansion of certain activities in the world are straining the limits of both human adaptive capabilities and the resilience of nature. The violation of these limits is generating a wide variety of problems in our most basic natural resources, air, water, and land. While not immediately evident in the short run, these problems often slowly gather momentum until they evoke rapid changes in local contexts in ways that negatively impact the health of populations, the renewability of resources, and the well-being of communities. Thus, they lead to disasters of varying degrees of severity. The increasing globalization of biophysical phenomena intertwines socially with a similar globalization of trade and migration. Together both impel a process of intensification of linkages that is creating problems across greater scales in space and reduced spans of time. The root causes and triggering agents, and possibly the solutions of local problems today, may be located on the other side of the world. As Holling so cogently noted, these globalization processes have produced problems that are basically nonlinear in causation and discontinuous in both space and time, and, therefore, inherently unpredictable (1994: 80). Such nonlinearity and discontinuity preclude traditional human adaptive responses. Unable to observe a signal of change, people cannot develop strategies to deal with it. Contemporary societies and natural systems are moving into such basically new and unknown terrain that their novel forms of interaction are taking on evolutionary implications. Basically, people, society, and nature are opening a new chapter in co-evolution, due largely to human inputs on a far more global scale than ever before. Human beings, societies, and local and global environments are influencing each other in unfamiliar ways and in measures that challenge adaptive capacities as well as traditional understandings of structure and organization (Holling 1994: 79–81).

The implications of these conclusions for the study of disasters are profound. They emphasize that the nature of disaster is rooted in the co-evolutionary relationship between human societies and natural systems, and oblige us to intensify our efforts to specify the linkages, now on regional and global scales, that generate these destructive forces within our societies and environments. As we see environmental problems developing, how do we predict and mitigate the disasters they prefigure? Disasters are becoming sentinel events of processes that are intensifying on a planetary scale. Our definitions and our approaches to studying them must now reflect these realities.

BIBLIOGRAPHY

Baker, G., and G. Chapman. 1962. *Man and Society in Disaster*. New York: Basic Books.

Barton, A. 1969. *Commmunities in Disaster*. Garden City: Doubleday.

Bates, D., and F. Plog. 1991. *Human Adaptive Strategies*. New York: McGraw Hill.

Bates, F. L., and C. Pelanda. 1994. "An Ecological Approach to Disasters," in R. Dynes and K. J. Tierney (eds.), *Disasters, Collective Behavior and Social Organization*, pp. 145–159. Newark: University of Delaware Press.

Belshaw, C. 1951. "Social Consequences of the Mount Lamington Eruption." *Oceania* 21, 4: 241–252.

Bennett, J. 1996. *Human Ecology as Human Behavior*. New Brunswick: Transaction Publishers.

Blaikie, P., T. Cannon, I. Davis, and B. Wisner. 1994. *At Risk: Natural Hazards, People's Vulnerability and Disasters*. London: Routledge.

Campbell, C. 1996. *Forest, Field and Factory: Changing Livelihood Strategies in Two Extractive Reserves in the Brazilian Amazon*. Unpublished Ph.D. dissertation. Gainesville, Florida: University of Florida.

Dombrowsky, W. 1995. "Again and Again: Is Disaster What We Call 'Disaster'? Some Conceptual Notes on Conceptualizing the Object of Disaster Sociology." *International Journal of Mass Emergencies and Disasters* 13, 3: 241–254.

Drabek, T. E. 1986. *Human System Responses to Disaster*. New York: Springer-Verlag.

Dynes, R. 1993. "Conceptualizing Disaster in Ways Productive for Social Science Research." Unpublished paper. Newark, Delaware: Disaster Research Center, University of Delaware.

Firth, R. 1959. *Social Change in Tikopia: Restudy of a Polynesian Community After a Generation*. London: Allen & Unwin.

Fritz, C. 1961. "Disasters," in R. K. Merton and R. Nisbet (eds.), *Social Problems*, pp. 167–198. New York: Harcourt Brace & World.

Gallie, W. 1955. "Essentially Contested Concepts." *Proceedings of the Aristotelian Society* 56: 167–198.

Gilbert, C. 1995. "Studying Disaster: A Review of the Main Conceptual Tools." *International Journal of Mass Emergencies and Disasters* 13, 3: 231–240.

Hewitt, K. 1983. *Interpretations of Calamity*. Boston: Allen & Unwin.

———. 1995. "Excluded Perspectives in the Social Construction of Disaster." *International Journal of Mass Emergencies and Disasters* 13, 3: 317–340.

Holling, C. S. 1994. "An Ecologist's View of the Malthusian Conflict," in K. Lindahl-Kiessling and H. Landberg (eds), *Population, Economic Development and the*

Environment, pp. 79–103. New York: Oxford University Press.

Horlick-Jones, T. 1995. "Modern Disasters as Outrage and Betrayal." *International Journal of Mass Emergencies and Disasters* 13, 3: 305–316.

Ingold, T. 1992. "Culture and the Perception of the Environment," in E. Croll and D. Parkin (eds.), *Bush Base: Forest Farm,* pp. 39–55. London: Routledge.

Keesing, F. 1952. "The Papuan Orokaiva vs. Mt. Lamington: Cultural Shock and its Aftermath." *Human Organization* 11, 1: 16–22.

Kreps, G. 1995. "Disaster as Systemic Event and Social Catalyst: A Clarification of Subject Matter." *International Journal of Mass Emergencies and Disasters* 13, 3: 255–284.

Kroeber, A., and C. Kluckhohn. 1952. *Culture: A Critical Review of Concepts and Definitions.* New York: Vintage Books.

Kroll-Smith, J. 1998. "Legislators, Interpreters and Disasters: The Importance of How as well as What Is Disaster?" in E. Quarantelli (ed.), *What Is a Disaster: A Dozen Perspectives on the Issue,* pp. 160–176. New York: Routledge.

Kroll-Smith, J., and S. Couch. 1991. "What Is Disaster? An Ecological Symbolic Approach to Resolving the Definitional Debate." *International Journal of Mass Emergencies and Disasters* 9, 3: 355–366.

Lee, R. 1979. *The !Kung San.* Cambridge: Cambridge University Press.

Painter, M., and W. Durham (eds.). 1995. *The Social Causes of Environmental Destruction in Latin America.* Ann Arbor: University of Michigan Press.

Peacock, W., B. Morrow, and H. Gladwin. 1997. *Ethnicity, Gender, and the Political Ecology of Disasters: Hurricane Andrew and the Reshaping of a City.* New York: Routledge.

Peet, R., and M. Watts. 1993. "Development Theory and Environment in an Age of Market Triumphalism." *Economic Geography* 69, 3: 227–253.

Peoples, J., and G. Bailey. 1997. *Humanity: An Introduction to Cultural Anthropology.* Belmont, CA: Wadsworth.

Perrow, C. 1984. *Normal Accidents: Living with High Risk Technologies.* New York: Basic Books.

Porfiriev, B. 1995. "Disaster and Disaster Areas: Methodological Issues of Definition and Delineation." *International Journal of Mass Emergencies and Disasters* 13, 3: 285–304.

Quarantelli, E. 1985. "What Is a Disaster? The Need for Clarification in Definition and Conceptualization in Research," in S. Solomon (ed.), *Disasters and Mental Health: Selected Contemporary Perspectives,* pp. 41–73. Washington, DC: U.S. Government Printing Office.

———. 1995. "What Is a Disaster? (Editor's Introduction)." *International Journal of Mass Emergencies and Disasters* 13, 3: 221–230.

Rocha, J. 1995. *Adaptation and Cultural Ecological Anthropology.* Unpublished manuscript.

Sahlins, M. 1972. *Stone Age Economics.* Chicago: Aldine.

Schmink, M., and C. Wood. 1987. "The Political Ecology, of Amazonia," in P. Little and M. Horowitz (eds.), *Lands at Risk in the Third World*, pp. 38–57. Boulder: Westview Press.

Schneider, D. 1957. "Typhoons on Yap." *Human Organization* 16, 2: 10–15.

Spillius, J. 1957. "Natural Disaster and Political Crisis in a Polynesian Society." *Human Relations* 10, 1: 3–27.

Steward, J. 1955. *Theory of Culture Change*. Urbana: University of Illinois Press.

Torry, W. I. 1979. "Anthropological Studies in Hazardous Environments: Past Trends and New Horizons." *Current Anthropology* 20, 3: 517–540.

Vayda, A., and B. McKay. 1975. "New Directions in Ecology and Ecological Anthropology." *Annual Review of Anthropology* 4: 293–306.

Wallace, A. 1956. *Tornado in Worcester*. (Disaster Study #3.) Washington, DC: Committee on Disaster Studies, National Academy of Sciences–National Research Council.

Wittgenstein, L. 1973. *Philosophical Investigations*. New York: MacMillan Publishing Co., Inc.

ENVIRONMENTAL PATTERN, HAZARDS, AND CULTURE: THE ARCHAEOLOGICAL PERSPECTIVE

THE SUDDENNESS OF IMPACT IN MANY DISASTERS AND THE URGENCY OF need that they cause have led to a particularly ahistorical approach within disaster research. In most disaster examinations, time is reduced to a relatively shallow duration in which only conditions immediately prior to the calamity are probed and only individual, group, and societal behavior in moments of threat or short-term aftermath is explored.

Such a limited time perspective leaves much unanswered. One relatively unexplored issue concerns the role disasters have played in the evolution of society. Not only the actual occurrence, but also the threat of disaster, influences the ways societies adapt or fail to adapt physically, socially, and culturally to their environments. Archaeological research shows that the success or failure of societies in coping with disaster helps account for large-scale shifts in their cultural patterns.

Specific disasters have specific histories as well. If we are to heed the contention that disasters are socially embedded in the relationship between society and environment rather than "bolts from the blue," then discovering which long-term and cultural trajectories lead to disaster is essential. The diachronic perspective of disasters provides the means through which researchers can analyze the social forces producing vulnerability to hazards.

THE EFFECTS OF EXPLOSIVE VOLCANISM ON ANCIENT EGALITARIAN, RANKED, AND STRATIFIED SOCIETIES IN MIDDLE AMERICA

PAYSON D. SHEETS
University of Colorado

Just as the progress of a disease shows a doctor the secret life of a body, so to the historian the progress of a great calamity yields valuable information about the nature of the society so stricken.
—Marc Bloch

INTRODUCTION

GIVEN THE THOUSANDS OF YEARS OF HUMAN OCCUPATION IN MIDDLE AMERICA and Mexico, the number of times that pre-Columbian societies were affected by volcanism must have been relatively great. The objective of this chapter is to compare the effects that explosive volcanic eruptions had on the ancient societies of Mexico and Central America, to see if any patterns can be detected. The particular focus is to try to answer the question: Did societal complexity play a role in the vulnerability or the resilience of societies affected by those sudden massive stresses? Some societies were resilient to an explosive eruption, reestablishing their social organization, adaptation, and material culture in the devastated area after natural processes of recovery allowed human resettlement. In other cases, societies were more vulnerable to massive environmental change from an explosive eruption, as they were unable to cope with the changed circumstances.

In broad terms, volcanic activity can be both beneficial and detrimental to human adaptation to an environment. The cliché that volcanic soils can be quite rich is accurate, but only after the volcanic detritus has weathered to form that soil. A volcanic ashfall that forms a fertile soil in a few decades can have a lava flow associated with it that requires centuries to form an equally fertile soil. Volcanically active areas often provide obsidian that can be fashioned into sharp cutting and scraping tools, basalt and andesite for grinding implements, and hematite and other pigments for painting pottery and other items that are of value to human occupation. On the other hand, volcanically active areas are seismically active as well, and indigenous societies often developed well-reinforced vernacular architecture for protection. Of the various sorts of phenomena, ranging from benign to devastating, this chapter focuses on the extreme of sudden explosive eruptions and how ancient societies coped or failed to cope with them. There are other highly destructive volcanic events that are beyond the scope of this chapter, including mudflows and hot debris flows. They are not included here largely because they have rarely been researched from both natural and social science perspectives.

It is important in this study to determine the approximate place each ancient society under consideration occupies along the continuum from the least complex egalitarian society to the highly complex state and empire. The evidence of societal complexity that archaeologists seek in the record of ancient societies is centralization of wealth or authority in the hands of a few. Differential wealth generally manifests itself in burials, with richly stocked tombs of the elite contrasting with the more plain commoners' burials. It is also recorded in architecture and artifacts. Differential resource abundance within a society can be seen in the archaeological record in storehouses attached to palaces, and in the palaces themselves as contrasted to the housing of the majority of the population. Centralization of authority can be detected in control of labor, power in military or police functions, or even in religious authority and control—all of which are revealed in quality and use of architecture, distribution of space, and kinds of artifacts. In some cases the record is clear, but in other cases the nature or degree of centralization is ambiguous, and statements must be carefully qualified.

The number of cases of pre-Columbian societies that endured volcanic eruptions that have been researched and adequately documented is small, but it is at least sufficient to begin establishing a comparative framework. Ideally, one would wish to have a sample size sufficient to explore a single variable such as societal complexity, to see the degree to which the internal organization of societies was a factor in their reaction to sudden explosive volcanic stress. But the range of significant variables in volcanological-human societal interactions is very great, and it is often difficult to determine the relative importance of factors such as the nature and magnitude of the eruption, vulnerability of flora and fauna to tephra (volcanic ash) stress, duration and dating of eruptions, chemical and grain size variation of the eruption, climatic variation, weathering rates and recovery processes, in addition to political, economic, demographic, and social factors of affected societies. Thus, anything approaching a statistical analysis is not possible with the present state of knowledge. Although not many cases where explosive eruptions affected pre-Columbian societies have been extensively researched, there are sufficient cases to at least begin to compare and contrast them in this study.

The ideal cases for this archaeological-volcanological study are those in which investigators have dated the eruption well, have done regional analysis of the extent of the tephra blanket, and have conducted regional survey and excavations to document pre-eruption population density and distribution and the timing and nature of the recovery, including soils, flora, fauna, and humans. Societies living beyond the extent of the ashfall are also known in the ideal case and can be examined for possible indirect effects, including housing refugees or taking advantage of the suddenly changed circumstances in the region such as rerouting trading systems. Regional studies determine the pattern of diminishing ash thickness with distance from the source, distinguishing the zone of devastation from the zone of less deleterious effects and from the zone where a slight dusting of ash was beneficial shortly after deposition. An example of the latter are the crops improved by a thin dusting of Mount St. Helens ash from the 1980 eruption, as the ash acted as a mulch and also killed many insects. Soil recovery and plant succession are more rapid on the peripheries of the ash blanket, allowing for earlier human reoccupation. The chemical and physical characteristics of the tephra have been studied in the ideal case, noting how finer-grained and more mafic (basic) tephras weather more rapidly and thus allow for more rapid recovery. The ideal case has documented the pre-eruption subsistence system, whether it was reliant upon wild or domesticated species, swidden or intensive agriculture, a primary staple or a wide variety of foods. Beyond subsistence, the regional economy is understood, whether it was regionally integrated and hierarchically organized or characterized by settlement self-sufficiency. Similarly, the political and religious systems in the ideal cases are well understood, so the impact of the sudden stress as well as the coping and recovery can be studied.

CENTRAL AMERICAN CASES OF VOLCANISM AND ANCIENT SOCIETIES

An important variable in the consideration of cases of volcanic impact (Figure 1) is the depth of burial of sites and their subsistence sustaining areas. With explosive volcanism, burial is essentially instantaneous, and the depth of burial is proportional to the deleterious impact. In conducting regional volcanological-ecological-archaeological research in El Salvador, Panama, and

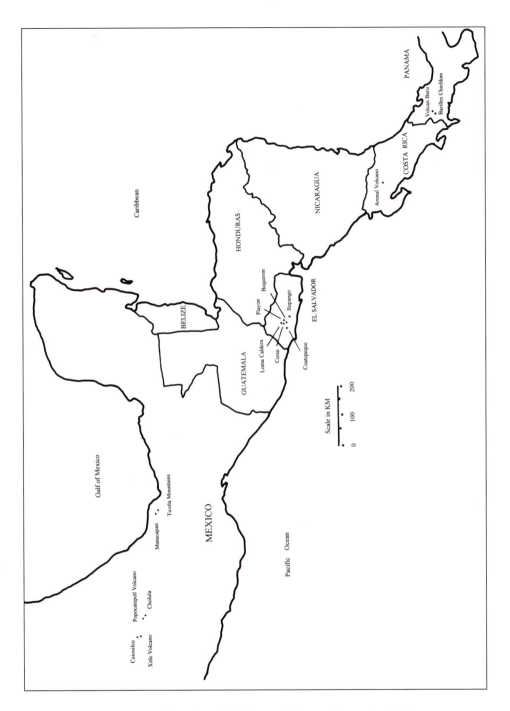

FIGURE 1. *Map of Southern Mexico and Central America. Volcanoes and the pre-Columbian societies affected by them that are the cases explored in this chapter are indicated.*

Costa Rica, I and my project members have found it more practical to search for, find, and investigate sites that are buried by about one half to two meters of tephra. Sites buried by less than that are generally not well preserved by the tephra, and sites buried more deeply are difficult to find and to excavate. Thus, an aspect of practicality ends up assisting this study for purposes of comparability, as many of the sites under consideration in this paper had approximately similar depths of burial with approximately similar tephra impacts on the environment and roughly comparable effects on societies. More deeply buried sites, such as Cuicuilco and Ceren, are also considered here, but in less detail.

The significant variables to be considered in comparing and contrasting cases where explosive eruptions affected pre-Columbian Middle American societies include the nature of the tephra (chemical and physical properties, area and nature of emplacement), the climate, the adaptation and the economy of the society affected, the political system, residential mobility, the density and distribution of population, reliance on fixed facilities, the particular edaphic (soil composition) requirements of cultigens, the regional cultural system including possible competition for resources and warfare, and the internal complexity of the society affected.

Arenal, Costa Rica

People have occupied the Arenal area of northwestern Costa Rica for at least ten thousand years (Sheets 1994). Since its birth almost four millennia ago, Arenal volcano has erupted nine times in a major way, not counting numerous small eruptions (Melson 1994), thus providing the opportunity to study the impacts of sudden stresses on egalitarian social groups with diversified subsistence economies and relatively low population densities. The eruptions that are relatively well dated and understood are here presented within the context of the culture history of the region, as discovered by the Arenal Research Project (Sheets 1994). All of Arenal's eruptions apparently affected egalitarian societies throughout prehistory, as there is no convincing evidence that more complex societies emerged in the area. Thus, the Arenal area provides a contrast with other areas of Middle America where explosive volcanism affected more complex societies with quite different adaptations and political and economic systems and greater population densities.

The hilly research area spans the Continental Divide, with elevations on both Atlantic and Pacific drainages ranging from four hundred to one thousand meters. Mean precipitation varies considerably, with averages as low as thirteen hundred millimeters at low elevation western stations to averages over six thousand millimeters at stations in the east close to Arenal volcano. The wetter areas give new meaning to the term "mean" precipitation. That moisture gradient correlates with a vegetational spectrum from a tropical dry-seasonal forest to a nonseasonal dense rainforest.

Paleo-Indian and Archaic peoples lived in the area in apparently very low population densities. The utilization of domesticated food sources certainly began by 2000 B.C., and probably before 3000 B.C., but the dating of that beginning is not very precise. Maize was cultivated by that 2000–3000 B.C. time horizon, but beans and squash are not confirmed until considerably later. Sedentary villages, with heavy metates and manos, presumably to grind maize, accompanied that subsistence addition. In contrast to many areas of Middle America, domesticated plants supplied only a small fraction of the diet, evidently no more than 12 percent, as reliance was placed on wild flora and fauna even up to the Spanish Conquest. Other aspects of Arenal area culture that showed no change from the Archaic time up until the Conquest are the basic core-flake lithic technology and the use of heated stones in cooking. Project members were unable to detect any changes in the circular houses with activity areas and (presumably) thatch roofs from early Formative times to the Conquest. However, other aspects of culture did change, and the key question considered here is which of the changes can be attributed to the major societal stresses caused by the large explosive eruptions of Arenal volcano.

Eruption	Date (est.)	Cultural Phase	Immediate Effects	Long-Term Effects Detected
Unit 10	A.D. 1968	Historic	Initial Abandonment	Too early to know
Unit 20	A.D. 1450	Tilaran	Abandonment	None
Units 41 & 40	A.D. 800	Silencio	Abandonment	Population concentration in Rio Piedra
Units 53 & 52	A.D. 1	Arenal	Abandonment	None
Unit 55	800 B.C.	Tronadora	Abandonment	None
Unit 61	1800 B.C.	Tronadora	Abandonment	None

TABLE 1. *Principal explosive eruptions of Arenal volcano, Costa Rica. Moderate to small eruptions are not included. "Units" are volcanic ash layers that are numbered sequentially, with the earliest eruption unit having the largest number.*

The Tronadora phase, conservatively dated from 2000 to 500 B.C., is characterized by numerous small villages scattered across the landscape. People lived in circular houses, presumably with thatch roofs, and buried their dead near the houses in small rectangular pits with occasional ceramic vessel offerings. The small pit sizes probably indicate that the burials were secondary (disarticulated). Maize was cultivated and processed with manos and metates, but was probably a minor part of the diet, as numerous wild species were utilized. The ceramics were surprisingly sophisticated in technology and decoration (Hoopes 1987). The phase had been underway for at least two centuries, and perhaps as much as seventeen hundred years, when Arenal volcano was born. That explosive eruption, which deposited the thick tephra layer referred to as Unit 61 (Melson 1994) at about 1800 B.C., resulted in the devastation of many square kilometers of rainforest and gardens, and certainly eliminated human habitation for a large area surrounding the volcano, particularly on the western, downwind side. However, survivors on the periphery of the devastated zone reoccupied the area a few generations later after soil and vegetation recovery had occurred. Toward the end of the phase, at about 800 B.C., Arenal's second huge explosive eruption occurred. It deposited Unit 55 throughout the area, resulting in a similar devastation of flora, fauna, and human populations. As the project team compared pre- and post-eruption conditions of both of these eruptions, we are unable to detect any long-range culture change that can be attributed to the disaster. People certainly had to abandon the area for a few generations, but the reoccupants are culturally indistinguishable from the pre-eruption occupants. That resilience to volcanic disaster continued to characterize Arenal-area society for thirty-five hundred years.

It was during the Arenal phase (500 B.C.–A.D. 600) that population density reached its peak in the area. Although never approaching the high densities of northern Central America during these same centuries, there were more and larger sites than at any other time in the pre-Columbian period. Domestic housing remained unchanged. Human burial was in discrete cemeteries on ridges adjacent to and above the villages. Interment shifted from secondary burials of the Tronadora phase to elaborate primary burials with plots demarcated with outlines of upright stones. A layer of round cobbles was laid between the upright stones, and dozens of whole vessels and decorated metates were smashed on the rocks and left in place. Two volcanic ash layers (Units 53 and 52) fell about midway during the phase, at about the time of Christ, with very little time separating them. Although individually thinner than the other major tephra blankets considered here, these deposits together probably had ecologic and demographic impacts approximately as significant as the earlier great eruptions. They do correlate with a subphase cultural boundary, the shift from the early to the late facet, defined by subtle changes in ceramic decoration. These changes were apparently a local manifestation of regional culture change in Greater Nicoya, rather than an effect of the volcanic disaster. In fact, I believe the important point is that the changes occurred in spite of the eruption, as local displaced populations maintained sufficient contact with regional societies to reflect overall culture change occurring in what is now northwestern Costa Rica and western Nicaragua.

A significant but not drastic population decline occurred at the beginning of and during the Silencio phase (A.D. 600–1300), as both large and small sites declined in number, a change noted in most of lower Central America with unknown causes. That process clearly was not occasioned by volcanism, although it could have been accelerated somewhat by volcanic activity during the ninth century. Chipped stone and ground stone industries show little change, and ceramics indicate considerable continuity, but with the addition of polychrome painting. Cemeteries are located at still greater distances from villages, as exemplified by the Silencio cemetery, located on the continental divide many kilometers from the villages that utilized it. Burial practices remain elaborate and have adopted the stone box technique: using flat-fracturing andesite slabs to create a stone coffin along the two long sides and on top. Remote sensing, with excavations for field verification, divulged the footpaths leading from the cemetery to a nearby spring, to stone sources, and to the villages that used them. During the phase at about A.D. 800 or 900, two large eruptions (Units 41 and 40) occurred in rapid succession and must have had ecologic and demographic effects as drastic as the earlier large eruptions,[1] but as with them, the culture that reestablished itself is indistinguishable from that prior to emplacement. It is possible that the increase in occupation of the Rio Piedra valley during the latter part of the Silencio phase was a result of the eruptions (Mueller 1994: 63). That western end of the Arenal drainage received considerably less volcanic ash from the two eruptions and could have served as a refuge area. If this is correct, it is one of the very few examples of our being able to detect a culture change at Arenal attributable to volcanic pressures. The demographic shift is detectable for perhaps three centuries.

With the disappearance of the last larger sites as well as a decline in the number of smaller sites, the population decline of the Silencio phase continued through the Tilaran phase (A.D. 1300–1500). The quality of ceramic manufacture and firing as well as elaborateness of painted decoration also decline dramatically in this period. The primary cultural affiliation of Arenal-area peoples during all previous phases had been to the west with Greater Nicoya, but that reversed as the primary affiliation shifted eastward toward the Atlantic watershed and the Meseta Central. The reasons for the change are not clear, but it apparently had nothing to do with volcanism. Toward the end of the phase, at about A.D. 1450, Arenal emitted one of its largest eruptions, depositing the thick Unit 20 across the landscape. It appears that the combination of this eruption and the Spanish Conquest with the attendant diseases was too much stress for local native societies, and they disappeared from the area. It is unknown if the societies could have recovered from the effects of the eruption had the Spanish not appeared shortly following it, but given their record of previous recoveries, I suspect they could have. This is an example of convergent disasters, as discussed by Moseley in chapter 3 of this volume.

In summary, the resilience of Arenal-area society to the sudden environmental stresses of explosive volcanism is notable. Only once can we find a significant change in human occupation, beyond the immediacy of the disaster, that persisted and is attributable with a reasonable degree of certainty to volcanism. That one occurrence was the sustained population relocation in the Rio Piedra region that lasted some three centuries. Thus, what is striking about Arenal-area societies is their resilience to explosive volcanism occurring on the average of every four hundred years. The resilience is probably based on a number of factors, each of which is in contrast to the other, more complex societies considered in the rest of this chapter. One is the high degree of village self-sufficiency, as most food, building materials, clay, and stone for chipped and ground stone implements were available locally. Only the material for celts (chisels or ax heads) was obtained from a distance, and that was from not a great distance, only a day's walk away. It probably also greatly aided households and villages in coping with thick ashfalls that domesticated foods were a small portion of the diet. People could increase their exploitation of wild flora and fauna to make up for lost cultivated foods in areas beyond the devastated zones. I suspect another major reason Arenal societies were so resilient to volcanic eruption is that even during the millennia of sedentism following 2000 B.C., they still maintained a reasonably high degree of residential mobility and the technology to support it. The archaeological record for the Silencio phase, for instance, demonstrates that households would "camp out" at cemeteries at considerable distances from their residences, use stone boiling instead of heavy ceramic cooking vessels, and presumably rely heavily on wild flora and fauna as food sources. Finding some maize pollen at cemeteries indicates that people cultivated crops at those distant localities to provide a source of food for inhabitants involved in the elaborate feastings and ancestor worship.

Panama

Archaeological research in western Panama (Linares, Sheets, and Rosenthal 1975; Linares 1977; Linares and Ranere 1980) encountered a case of volcanism affecting a more complex society than in Costa Rica but less complex than in Mesoamerica. The case involves the Barriles chiefdom that developed in the upper reaches of the Rio Chiriqui Viejo from about 200 B.C. until the seventh century A.D. Actually, the Barriles site consists of a series of chiefdoms along watercourses in western Panama and eastern Costa Rica sharing the same culture and, presumably, language but each fiercely defending its own individual polities. Among them there developed an iconography representing aggression, capture, and human sacrifice by decapitation as the society became more complex and competitive. The eruption of Volcan Baru during the seventh century A.D. deposited a layer of tephra comparable in thickness to those deposited by

Arenal on sites mentioned in the previous section. That explosive eruption evidently caused an abandonment of the area by Barriles peoples, and they or their descendants never reoccupied the area. Linares (Linares and Ranere 1980: 244–45) believes some of the Barriles residents who were forced to migrate headed northward over the Continental Divide and founded sites on the Atlantic drainage such as those in the Bocas del Toro area. In contrast to the facility of recovery of Arenal peoples, the Baru tephra had a much greater effect on local populations, and centuries later when people finally did reoccupy the valley, they were not the descendants of the societies that lived there before the eruption. I suspect Baru's impact on its surrounding populations was greater than Arenal's because the Barriles chiefdoms were relying on maize as a staple, with a more intense adaptation, more fixed facilities, and a more complex or rigid political, economic, and social system. That the inhabitants were in a more demographically filled-in landscape with competitive aggressiveness marking intersocietal relationships indicates a lack of land into which migrants could settle. Beyond that ecologic scarcity there was probably a lack of desire and incentive for a relatively intact polity (beyond the zone of negative volcanic impact) to assist the survivors of a stressed polity. In fact, the degree of competitive aggressiveness between polities is greater than in any other of the cases presented in this paper and is apparently a part of the reason why a relatively small eruption had such a dramatic societal impact. Survivors in the two uppermost Barriles chiefdoms could expect hostility if they tried to move farther downriver into other chiefdoms' territories, and thus had to migrate over the Continental Divide into the very moist nonseasonal tropical rainforest to the north, near the Atlantic shoreline. It is possible the surviving chiefdoms were appreciative of the disaster that wiped out their upstream competitors.

El Salvador

El Salvador provides a few cases of eruptions and their effects on pre-Columbian societies, ranging from the immense eruptions of Coatepeque and Ilopango to the highly localized Loma Caldera eruption. The huge Coatepeque eruption, dated to between ten thousand and forty thousand years ago, may predate human occupation in Central America, but if people were in Central America at that time and there are Paleo-Indian sites buried by the Coatepeque tephra, those sites could yield considerable insight into lifeways and adaptations. The societies affected by the post-Coatepeque eruptions were more complex than those affected by eruptions in Costa Rica and Panama. The magnitude of the various eruptions correlates with the magnitude of ecological and societal disruption, but it is a major point of this chapter that the size of the eruption is not the primary variable. It appears rather that the more complex Salvadoran societies were more vulnerable to explosive volcanic disasters than were Costa Rican societies.

Eruption (source)	Date	Km² Covered	Regional Effects
El Playon	A.D. 1658–1659	30	Slight
El Boqueron (San Salvador Volcano)	est. A.D. 900–1100	300 (deeper than 7 cm.)	Moderate
Loma Caldera (Ceren tephra)	A.D. 590 + 90	less than 5	Insignificant
Ilopango (Tierra Blanca Joven)	A.D. 260 + 114 or summer A.D. 175 (by ice cores)	10,000 (deeper than 50 cm)	Massive and long-lasting

TABLE 2. *Four explosive eruptions affecting societies in central El Salvador during the past two millennia.*

The white volcanic ash layer that buried ancient artifacts in central and western El Salvador has been the subject of intermittent interest by archaeologists and geologists during much of this century, beginning with Jorge Larde in 1917 (Larde 1926; Lothrop 1927; Vaillant 1934; Porter 1955; Boggs 1966; Schmidt-Thome 1975; Sharer 1978; Sheets 1979; Hart and Steen-McIntyre 1984.) Called the "tierra blanca joven" or TBJ, it was erupted from a volcanic vent under the west end of Lake Ilopango. It is radiocarbon dated to A.D. 260 ± 114 (calibrated; one sigma range: A.D. 146 to 374), but a more precise dating may be provided by analyses of Greenland ice cores. A volcanic ash began falling in the summer of A.D. 175 in Greenland which might have been caused by Ilopango; both share the same high silica content of 69 percent. Where it is well preserved at Chalchuapa, seventy-seven kilometers from the source, it is over one half meter thick, indicating a regional disaster of major proportions.

The Ilopango eruption occurred in three phases. First, a great explosion deposited a relatively coarse pumice across the countryside, to a radius of about thirty kilometers. That was followed by two colossal ash flows that headed north to the Rio Lempa and west into the Zapotitan valley. These were unusually massive and long, stretching for more than forty-five kilometers. The one that headed west had sufficient impetus to flow up and over the Santa Tecla (Nueva San Salvador) pass at one thousand meters elevation and then down into the Zapotitan valley, even though the vent elevation is only five hundred meters. Both of these first stages were devastating to flora, fauna, and people in their paths, but the third phase was even more damaging regionally. It was an immense blast of very fine-grained volcanic ash that fell over all of central and western El Salvador and must have been significant in adjoining southern Guatemala and southwestern Honduras. The eruption must have blasted ash into the troposphere, so finding Ilopango ash in Greenland ice cores should not be surprising.

Some eight thousand square kilometers might have been rendered uninhabitable. Segerstrom (1950) found that ten to twenty-five centimeters of volcanic ash is too much for traditional agriculturalists to cope with, and natural processes of tephra erosion, weathering, soil formation, and plant succession are necessary before the affected area can be reoccupied by cultivators. Depending on the tephra and the environment, those processes can take decades or centuries. Given an estimated regional population density in central El Salvador of forty people to every square kilometer, one can very roughly estimate that some 320,000 people could have been killed or displaced by the eruption (Sheets 1979). The fact that the TBJ tephra was highly acidic (sialic) rendered the impact more drastic and the recovery delayed. The dozens of sites in the Zapotitan valley buried by some one to two meters of Ilopango tephra are comparable in tephra depth to many of the sites in the Arenal area. The contrast is how different the pre- and post-eruption societies were in El Salvador and how similar the pre- and post-eruption societies were in Costa Rica. To some degree that contrast is due to more rapid culture change in Mesoamerica compared to the Intermediate area (between Mesoamerica and the Andes), and to some degree it is due to greater resilience to perturbation by Arenal societies.

Many areas of central and western El Salvador were abandoned for a century or two (Sheets 1979, 1980). Many archaeologists have noted the striking population decline along Guatemala's Pacific coastal plain at about this time (e.g., Shook 1965; Bove 1989), which was probably a result of the ecologic suppression caused by the Ilopango ashfall.

Flooding is a common aftermath following a volcanic ash deposit in a river's headwaters, as protective vegetation is killed or suppressed. The flooding reported at so many sites in western Honduras at the Formative-Classic boundary (see Table 3) was likely caused by the Ilopango tephra and resultant heavy runoff and redepositions (Sheets 1987). Included are sites such as Copan, Playa de los Muertos, Pimienta, and Los Naranjos. Even some sites as far away as Barton Ramie in Belize witnessed flooding at about this time, but Barton Ramie is a considerable distance from Ilopango, and the flooding might have occurred for quite different reasons. In Middle American areas, where only a few centimeters or millimeters of Ilopango tephra were deposited, the deleterious affects of the eruption were probably minimal and the light dusting could have been beneficial immediately.

Central El Salvador was affected at least three more times by explosive volcanism after the Ilopango eruption (Sheets 1983, 1992a). The Loma Caldera volcanic vent opened up underneath the Rio Sucio and initiated a series of fourteen alternating lateral blasts and airfall volcanic ash and lava bomb units that buried a few square kilometers of the Zapotitan valley, including the Ceren site. From the evidence of artifact placement and plant maturation, the eruption occurred in the evening, during the month of August, circa A.D. 590, with sufficient warning that the inhabitants could lit-

Period	Tephra	Date (approx.)	Thickness (est. from sections)	Effect on Habitation
Middle Classic	Laguna Cocodrilos	A.D. 600	40–45 cm.	Moderate impact on complex society, gradual but consistent decline
Early Classic	Laguna Nixtamalapan & Cerro Puntiagudo	A.D. 400	20–30 cm	None detected, occupation continues
Late Formative	Cerro Nixtamalapan	A.D. 150	40 cm	Significant impact, abandonment, rapid recovery
Early Formative	Cerro Mono Blanco	1250 b.c.	60 cm	900-yr.-long abandonment, major impact on simple society
Late Archaic	n.a.	3000–2000 B.C.	n.a.	Unknown

TABLE 3. *Volcanism and human settlement in the Matacapan area, Tuxtla Mountains, Mexico. ("n.a." means not available.)*

erally "head south," but without enough warning time to remove their possessions. Although it had devastating consequences for the inhabitants of the Ceren village and its environs, this eruption was so small as to have had no detectable effects on the course of societal change in southern Mesoamerica. It was followed a few centuries later by a moderately large eruption of San Salvador volcano (Boqueron eruption) at about A.D. 900 or 1000 that did negatively affect some two to three hundred square kilometers. The Boqueron eruption interfered with cultivation for a few decades and must have had a negative impact on San Andres and surrounding settlements for quite some time, but unfortunately the research at that site remains unpublished. This eruption is an important research topic that, it is hoped, will be explored in the near future. Playon was the most recent eruption to affect the area, beginning late in 1658 and burying thirty square kilometers under lava and a larger area under tephra. Although soils on the Playon lava have barely begun to recover to their pre-eruption state, soil recovery on the tephra is now sufficient to support intensive agriculture. All three of these post-Ilopango eruptions caused severe problems for villages and households near the sources, but they cannot be seen as having had long-lasting societal repercussions and certainly were not massive regional natural disasters. Of the post-Ilopango eruptions, only Boqueron probably had significant negative societal effects lasting perhaps for a few decades.

MEXICAN CASES OF VOLCANISM AND ANCIENT SOCIETIES

Matacapan and the Tuxtla Volcanic Field

Volcanism in the Tuxtla Volcanic Field (TVF), located some one hundred fifty kilometers southeast of Veracruz, Mexico, has been studied recently by Reinhardt (1991), and the following descriptions are taken from his master's thesis. The younger (last fifty thousand years) volcanic sequence covers some four hundred square kilometers, with an average frequency of eruptions of at least four per one thousand years, an activity rate approximately twice that of Arenal during the past four thousand years and comparable to central El Salvador in the past two thousand years. Matacapan, in the Tuxtla Mountains in the Mexican Gulf, has been investigated by Robert Santley (1994). The site zone was occupied twice during the Formative period, but grew to maximum size during the middle of the Classic period.

The most recent eruptions of the Tuxtla volcanos are preserved in the stratigraphy at the Matacapan archaeological site and date to the Late Archaic to the Middle Classic Periods. The earliest of these eruptions occurred about 3000 to 2000 B.C., and its effects on surrounding populations are unknown. Societies at that time would have been egalitarian and probably at least semisedentary, with a mixed domesticated and wild subsistence base. It is likely that village life was emerging in the area at that time, but regional population density would have been quite low compared to Formative and Classic times. The eruption left a relatively thin deposit, some fifteen centimeters, at Matacapan.

The second TVF eruption dates to the Early Formative, about 1250 B.C., and deposited the Cerro Mono Blanco (CMB) tephra. Matacapan was occupied at the time by agriculturalists, and tephra buried the maize ridges of an agricultural field and a dog. The society affected was relatively simple, as egalitarian villages dotted the landscape. The deposit, as I measured it from Reinhardt's drawn sections, is moderately thick, over sixty centimeters. The area was abandoned for some nine centuries, but was reoccupied during the Late Formative. Thus, the second eruption appears to have been much bigger than the first, at least from the Matacapan perspective, and it had exceptionally long-lasting deleterious effects on settlement.

The third TVF eruption, at about A.D. 150, buried Late Formative remains in the Matacapan area under the Cerro Nixtamalapan (CN) tephra. It is about forty centimeters thick on Reinhart's section (1991: 86). Given that the decline of Olmec civilization was largely complete by this time, and the local Classic period societal resurgence had yet to occur, I would presume the volcanism affected relatively simple societies, probably egalitarian villages. As with the second eruption, the area was abandoned, clearly indicating significant initial impact of a substantial eruption. However, the abandonment lasted for only a short while.

At about A.D. 400, during the Early Classic, two closely spaced eruptions (no soil between them) deposited the Cerro Puntiagudo (CP) and then the Laguna Nixtamalapan (LN) tephras. These evidently had less of an impact than the above tephra emplacements, as the site apparently was not abandoned. I measure their thickness from Reinhart's sections at only about twenty to thirty centimeters. The society affected would have been moderately complex, perhaps a chiefdom, but this is uncertain. It appears the stress caused by this relatively thin deposit was within the resiliency of the agroeconomic adaptation, and it is possible that for the cultingens that have roots sufficiently deep to tap into the pre-eruption soil, the tephra could have been beneficial as a mulch layer.

The final Classic period eruption occurred in the middle of that time span, about A.D. 600, and the tephra measures some forty to forty-five centimeters in thickness according to the sections. It sealed an agricultural field with maize ridges under it. Compared to the above examples, this is a moderately large eruption as viewed from Matacapan, and societal complexity as well as population density were at a peak at this time. Coincident with the ashfall is the reversal in Matacapan's fortune. Matacapan's population began to decline during the 600s, a part of which I suspect might have been caused by the ecologic stress of volcanic ash deposition. It should be noted that Santley and Arnold (n.d.) came to quite an opposite conclusion, as they note that volcanism in the Formative caused abandonments and major population resettlements, while volcanism in the Classic did not have the same results. Their suggested explanation is the ability of the state to harness energy and labor on a larger scale and thus cope better with these sudden massive natural stresses.

The relative ecological-agrarian-societal stresses caused by various volcanic eruptions can be researched only if their magnitudes and distributions are understood and can be compared. Because such information is not yet available for the TVF, and lacking other indications, the relative magnitudes can be approximated only very roughly by comparing tephra depths from measured sections. I believe it is significant that the thickness of tephra correlates directly with the societal impacts of the eruptions at Matacapan, as the thinnest of ash layers (CP and LN at about twenty centimeters) did not cause abandonment, but the thicker layers did cause abandonment proportional to their thickness (CMB at about sixty centimeters and CN at forty to forty-five centimeters). The LC tephra, about forty centimeters thick, correlates with a reversal of the demographic and societal trajectories, and the site never recovered. The societal impacts do not correlate, negatively or positively, with societal complexity when viewed from Matacapan. However, viewing societal impacts from only a single site can be very misleading, and regional work is needed for the Tuxtlas to shed light on impacts and recoveries. What is needed to research seriously the interaction of natural and human processes in the TVF (as well as in other Middle American cases) is isopach (depth and distribution) mapping of each unit, with estimates of the magnitude, volume, and distribution of each, and documentation of soil recovery as well as human reoccupation, within a well-dated natural and cultural framework.

Chase (1981) argued that an eruption of San Martin volcano at some time around 600 B.C. in the Tuxtlas caused sufficient damage to the utilized landscape in the Tres Zapotes area to have rendered it uninhabitable, and migrations of tens of thousands of people resulted. He relied on stratigraphic information from Drucker's research at Tres Zapotes from the time of World War II. Unfortunately, the dating of the eruption is rather speculative, as it is not based on extensive data, and sourcing of the tephra is weak. It is conceivable that this tephra might be from the same eruption as the CMB or CN tephra at Matacapan.

Popocatepetl Volcano and Cholula, Puebla, Mexico

For the past few decades a number of separate discoveries of volcanic ash burying cultural features have been made in Puebla, generally to the northeast, east, or southeast of Popocatepetl volcano. For instance, Seele (1973) reported well-preserved maize ridges under white airfall tephra at San Buenaventura Nealtican, and others have reported other maize ridges or artifacts buried by primary or secondary volcanic deposits in the general area. Fortunately, Siebe et al. (1996) are working to synthesize these isolated discoveries into a regional interpretive framework. They have found evidence of three major eruptions of Popocatepetl at about 3000 B.C., between 800 and 200 B.C. (Lower Ceramic Plinian), and probably at A.D. 822 (Upper Ceramic Plinian). The earliest eruption was characterized by a series of phreatomagmatic (magma in contact with water resulting in steam explosions) eruptions resulting in multiple surge deposits followed by a thick pumice deposit and ending with a number of ash flows that carried over fifty kilometers from their sources. The effects on late Archaic populations are unknown but must have been devastating. The recovery of soils, vegetation, and human societies resulted in reasonably dense habitation by the first millennium B.C., which was then buried by the second, or "Lower Ceramic Plinian," eruption. This eruption consists primarily of a thick widespread andesitic pumice deposit followed by ash flows and lahars (mud flows) radiating from the volcano. These primary and secondary deposits buried agricultural fields (e.g., Seele 1973), artifacts, and other cultural features. Even household groups with talud-tablero (sloping panel with overhanging vertical panel) architecture, dating to a few centuries prior to that architectural style's appearance in Teotihuacan, are buried. The eruption's effects on habitation on or near the slopes of Popocatepetl were obviously devastating, but its effects upon Cholula and the Puebla Valley, or upon the Basin of Mexico, are not clear.

The third eruption, called the Upper Ceramic Plinian, is primarily composed of surge deposits from phreatomagmatic explosions followed by pumice falls and extensive lahars. The likely dating to A.D. 822 is from a Greenland ice core, but the detailed geochemistry to confirm that association has yet to occur. Massive lahars filled the Puebla basin and Atlixco valley after the eruption, having apparently devastating effects on settlement. Lahar deposits a few meters thick buried architecture at Cholula.

The cultural, economic, political, and demographic effects of these large eruptions, as well as smaller ones reported by Siebe et al. (1996), remain unknown. Archaeologists have reported cultural and architectural declines and florescences (e.g., Weaver 1993), and two of the declines Weaver reports do approximately correlate with the later two large eruptions. Correlations are intriguing, but establishing probable causalities will require regional interdisciplinary research. Here is a regional integrated archaeological-volcanological project crying out to happen, with the high probability of significant results. Such a project could go far toward understanding the beneficial and detrimental aspects of living in volcanically active areas and explaining demographic and societal declines and surges in this area. The Puebla area is one of the most culturally important areas of ancient Mesoamerica, yet it remains one of the most poorly studied on an integrated regional basis.

The Basin of Mexico: Cuicuilco and Xitle Volcano

In the Basin of Mexico, Niederberger (1979) has documented the emergence of sedentary human communities in the resource-rich lacustrine (lake) environments of the Chalco and Xochimilco basins by the sixth millennium B.C. In the southern part of the Basin of Mexico these communities were devastated by a series of volcanic deposits at about 3000 B.C. Because the time is the same as the earliest Popocatepetl eruption documented by Siebe et al. (1996), I suggest this may be the northwestern component of the same eruption. She refers to the deposits as a series of *nubes ardientes* ("glowing clouds" of hot volcanic ejecta and gasses that flow rapidly downhill) leaving thick white pumice layers. They are thick enough to have caused ecological and human societal devastation, and because of their chemistry and the high elevation, I would expect slow weathering rates and thus slow environmental recovery, on the scale of a few centuries. Adams (1991: 38) finds Niederberger's interpretation convincing and notes that it took some five centuries for human reoccupation of the area.

The case of the Xitle eruption in the southern Basin of Mexico some fifteen hundred to two thousand years ago remains controversial and will probably remain so until a regional multidisciplinary project is conducted to resolve a number of issues. To date, many individual archaeologists and geologists have conducted small and localized investigations, and the interpretations vary widely (one could say "wildly"). Many scholars have noted that the demise of Cuicuilco—apparently the dominant polity of the Late Formative in the Basin of Mexico—the rise of Teotihuacan, and the eruption of Xitle might have been causally interrelated. Parsons (1974, 1976) suggests Xitle devastated Cuicuilco in the first century A.D. and thus facilitated the rise of Teotihuacan. Similarly, Diehl (1976) notes the political ascendancy of Teotihuacan and suggests it was in part because of Xitle's elimination of Cuicuilco as a competitor. Adams (1991: 109) dates the volcanic destruction of Cuicuilco to about 150 B.C.

A major problem in exploring human-volcanic interaction in the Cuicuilco area is dating of the eruption of Xitle. Cordova, Martin del Pozzo, and Camacho (1994), surveying the attempts to date the eruption, note that the early research efforts date it at around 400 B.C., while more recent efforts date it at the third century A.D. and to as late as A.D. 400. They conclude that the most accurate radiocarbon date is 1536 ± 65 B.P., or about A.D. 400. They also feel that Cuicuilco had been abandoned well before the eruption. If these conclusions are correct, the demise of Cuicuilco was certainly not caused by Xitle, and its abandonment might have been caused by the expansion of, and competition from, Teotihuacan, which neatly reverses the causality, plucks it from the volcanological domain, and places it in the cultural domain. Heizer and Bennyhoff (1958) noted the deterioration of Cuicuilco architecture prior to burial by the Xitle lava, indicating abandonment prior to the eruption. If this later dating of the eruption is substantiated, a study still needs to be done to explore the demographic-ecologic-societal implications of burying some seventy-five square kilometers of the most fertile land in the Basin of Mexico under basaltic lava during the early part of the Classic period. Recent research indicates the most accurate dating of the Xitle eruption is about the time of Christ (Claus Siebe, personal communication, 1997), thus putting it at about the same period as the large eruption of Popocatepetl that devastated such a large area of Puebla. Urrutia-Fucugauchi (1996) also dates it to the same time, two thousand years ago.

CONCLUSIONS

Although the sample size is very small, there does seem to be a pattern that more complex pre-Columbian societies were more vulnerable to the sudden massive stresses of explosive volcanism than were the simpler societies in Middle America. Ilopango overwhelmed Late Formative societies in southeastern Mesoamerica, Matacapan was inundated by a Tuxtla eruption, and Popocatepetl inundated Cholula (and perhaps Xitle devastated Cuicuilco). These are cases where those complex cultures did not recover, competitors often took control and prospered, and later cultures were significantly different.

At the other extreme, the simple egalitarian societies living in the Arenal area of Costa Rica showed remarkable resilience to the repeated explosive eruptions of Arenal volcano over almost four millenia. This might seem counterintuitive, as most people living in Western state-level societies today would presume that complex societies with their centralized decision-making, police and military forces, warehouses, and advanced means of transportation and communication would be more prepared for massive emergencies than simple societies. That may be true where rescue and recovery efforts can involve people and institutions hundreds or even thousands of miles away, but it does not seem to pertain to pre-Columbian Middle America.

What might be the characteristics of simple egalitarian societies that would confer resilience against sudden massive stress by explosive volcanism? Based on the Costa Rican examples, I believe that low population densities within and beyond the zone of devastation are important, providing refuge areas without conflict. The Arenal-area societies avoided a single staple food, in contrast to most areas of Middle America, and when their agricultural fields were devastated they could readily replace the domesticated fraction of their diet by intensifying the collection of wild food sources. The Arenal villages were much more self-sufficient than settlements in Mesoamerica, as the latter relied on long-distance trade routes for essential commodities such as salt, obsidian, pigments, jade for axes, and other items. Housing in the Arenal villages was less substantial than in most areas of Middle America, and could be rebuilt in refuge areas more readily. Thus, the built environment was simpler and easier to replace. There is no evidence of warfare in the Arenal area at any time, and thus refugees presumably could have moved into refuge areas without hostility. The low population densities in a highly productive tropical rainforest environment with its abundance of wild food sources must have meant less competition for land and resources than in Mesoamerica.

An unanticipated consequence of this study comparing eruptions, environments and adaptations, and complexities of societies in Middle America is the realization of the importance of the political landscape into which a tephra falls. By ecological, volcanic, and societal expectations the eruption of Panama's Volcan Baru should have had only short-term negative effects on the Barriles chiefdoms. However, the chiefdoms were hotly competitive, as they were in a perpetual state of skirmishing and sacrificing captives from adjoining territories. Thus, when the tephra struck, a relatively minor stress caused abandonment and migration over the Continental Divide. That forced an adaptive change from maize-based agriculture in a highland valley to a much wetter tropical lowland environment where seed crop agriculture was selected against.

The factors which make the more complex Mesoamerican societies more vulnerable to sudden stress include demography, adaptation, ecology, politics, society, and economics. As all settlement units are integrated into a regional economy, with long-distance trade routes supplying essential commodities, the lack of self-sufficiency increases vulnerability to changes beyond their sphere of influence or knowledge. Complex societies with redistributive economies rely on central warehouses, markets, attached specialists, and, thus, are vulnerable when those are suddenly stressed or eliminated. A political landscape of hostility with adjoining or nearby societies can transform a moderate stress into an overwhelming stress, particularly where there is competition for arable land and resources. A packed demographic landscape in areas outside the zone of devastation makes relocation to a nearby refuge area difficult or impossible. Reliance on a staple crop, particularly where the agricultural infrastructure is intensive, may be difficult to cope with when massive agricultural failure occurs on a regional basis.

Thus, the larger explosive eruptions that deleteriously affected complex societies in pre-Columbian Mesoamerica may be similar to some eruptions and their effects in the Old World. Probably the most notable is the eruption of Thera and its devastating effects on Minoan civilization (see Hoffman, this volume, chapter 15), allowing for its competitor Mycenean civilization to prosper and expand.

NOTE

1. Archaeologists and volcanologists investigating the fall of volcanic ash blankets in tropical environments rarely observe the direct effects on the flora, fauna, and human populations in the same way that a modern observer can observe the trees dying and the animals asphyxiating. However, the effects can be inferred with a high degree of probability based on the observed effects of similar ashfalls on comparable contemporary environments. Therefore, phrases like "must have occurred" are used here to indicate a highly probable interpretation that is not a documented fact.

BIBLIOGRAPHY

Adams, R. 1991. *Prehistoric Mesoamerica* (Revised Edition). Norman: University of Oklahoma.

Boggs, S. 1966. "Pottery Jars from the Loma del Tacuazin, El Salvador." *Middle American Research Records* 3: 5. New Orleans: Tulane University.

Bove, F. 1989. "Settlement Classification Procedures in Formative Escuintla, Guatemala," in F. Bove and F. Heller (eds.), *New Frontiers in the Archaeology of the Pacific Coast of Southern Mesoamerica*. Anthropological Research Papers, Arizona State University 39: 65–102.

Chase, J. 1981. "The Sky is Falling: The San Martin Tuxtla Volcanic Eruption and its Effects on the Olmec at Tres Zapotes, Veracruz." *Vinculos* 7, 2: 53–69.

Cordova, C., A. Martin del Pozzo, and J. Lopez Camacho. 1994. "Palaeolandforms and Volcanic Impact on the Environment of Prehistoric Cuicuilco, Southern Mexico City." *Journal of Archaeological Science* 21: 585–596.

Diehl, R. 1976. "Pre-Hispanic Relationships between the Basin of Mexico and North and West Mexico," in E. Wolf (ed.), *The Valley of Mexico Studies in Pre-Hispanic Ecology and Society*, pp. 249–286. Albuquerque: University of New Mexico Press.

Ferrero Acosta, L. 1981. "Ethnohistory and Ethnography," in E. Benson (ed.), *Between Continents/Between Seas: Pre-Columbian Art of Costa Rica*, pp. 93–103. New York: Abrams.

Harris, D. 1973. "The Prehistory of Tropical Agriculture: An Ethnoecological Model," in C. Renfrew (ed.), *The Explanation of Culture Change*, pp. 391–417. London: Duckworth.

Hart, W., and V. Steen-McIntyre. 1984. "Tierra Blanca Joven Tephra from the A.D. 260 Eruption of Ilopango Volcano," in P. Sheets (ed.), *Archaeology and Volcanism in Central America: The Zapotitan Valley of El Salvador*, pp. 14–34. Austin: University of Texas Press.

Heizer, R., and J. Bennyhoff. 1958. "Archaeological Investigations of Cuicuilco, Valley of Mexico, 1956." *Science* 127: 232–233.

Hoopes, J. 1987. *Early Ceramics and the Origins of Village Life in Lower Central America*. Unpublished Ph.D. dissertation. Cambridge: Harvard University.

Larde, J. 1926. "Arqueologia Cuzcatleca: Vestigos de una Poblacion Pre-Mayica en el Valle de San Salvador, C. A., Sepultados Bajo una Potente Capa de Productos Volcanicos." *Revista de Etnologia Arqueologia y Linguistica* 1: 3 and 4.

Linares, O. 1977. *Ecology and the Arts in Ancient Panama*. Dumbarton Oaks Studies in Pre-Columbian Art and Archaeology, No. 17. Washington, DC.

Linares, O., and A. Ranere (eds.). 1980. *Adaptive Radiations in Prehistoric Panama*. Cambridge: Peabody Museum, Harvard University.

Linares, O., P. D. Sheets, and E. J. Rosenthal. 1975. "Prehistoric Agriculture in Tropical Highlands." *Science* 187: 137–145.

Lothrop, S. 1927. "Pottery Types and Their Sequence in El Salvador." *Indian Notes and Monographs* 1, 4: 165–220. New York: Museum of the American Indian, Heye Foundation.

Melson, W. 1994. "The Eruption of 1968 and Tephra Stratigraphy of Arenal Volcano," in P. Sheets and B. McKee (eds.), *Archaeology, Volcanism, and Remote Sensing in the Arenal Area, Costa Rica*, pp. 24–47. Austin: University of Texas Press.

Mueller, M. 1994. "Archaeological Survey in the Arenal Basin," in P. Sheets and B. McKee (eds.), *Archaeology, Volcanism and Remote Sensing in the Arenal Area*

Costa Rica, pp. 48–72. Austin: University of Texas Press.

Niederberger, C. 1979. "Early Sedentary Economy in the Basin of Mexico." *Science* 203, 4376: 131–142.

Parsons, J. 1974. "The Development of A Prehistoric Complex Society: A Regional Perspective From the Valley of Mexico." *Journal of Field Archaeology* 1: 81–108.

———. 1976. "Settlement and Population History of the Basin of Mexico," in E. Wolf (ed.), *The Valley of Mexico: Studies in Pre-Hispanic Ecology and Society*, pp. 69–100. Albuquerque: University of New Mexico Press.

Porter, M. 1955. "Material Preclasico de San Salvador." *Communicaciones del Instituto Tropical de Investigaciones Cientificas*, 105–112. San Salvador.

Reinhardt, B. 1991. *Volcanology of the Younger Volcanic Sequence and Volcanic Hazards Study of the Tuxtla Volcanic Field, Veracruz, Mexico*. Unpublished M.A. thesis. New Orleans: Tulane University.

Santley, R., 1994. "The Economy of Ancient Matacapan." *Ancient Mesoamerica* 5: 243–266.

Santley, R. and P. Arnold III. n.d. *Prehispanic Settlement Patterns in the Tuxtla Mountains, Southern Veracruz, Mexico*. MS in possession of the authors.

Schmidt-Thome, M. 1975. "The Geology in the San Salvador Area: A Basis for City Development and Planning." *Geologische Jahresbuch* 813, S: 207–228.

Seele, E. 1973. "Restos de Milpas y Poblaciones Prehispanicas cerca de San Buenaventura Nealtican, Puebla." Puebla, Fundacion Alemana para la Ciencia, *Comunicaciones* 7: 7–86.

Segerstrom, K. 1950. *Erosion Studies at Paricutin*. US Geological Survey Bulletin 965A. Washington, DC.

Sharer, R. (ed.). 1978. *The Prehistory of Chalchuapa, El Salvador*. 3 volumes. Philadelphia: University of Pennsylvania Press.

Sheets, P. 1979. "Environmental and Cultural Effects of the Ilopango Eruption in Central America," in P. Sheets and D. Grayson (eds.), *Volcanic Activity and Human Ecology*, pp. 525–564. New York: Academic Press.

———. 1980. "Archaeological Studies of Disaster: Their Range and Value." *Natural Hazards Research Working Papers* #38. Boulder: University of Colorado.

———. ed. 1983. *Archaeology and Volcanism in Central America: The Zapotitan Valley of El Salvador*. Austin: University of Texas Press.

———. 1987. "Possible Repercussions in Western Honduras of the Third-Century Eruption of Ilopango Volcano," in G. Pahl (ed.), *The Periphery of the Southeastern Classic Maya Realm*, pp. 41–52. Los Angeles, CA: University of California at Los Angeles Latin American Center.

———. 1992a. *The Ceren Site: A Prehistoric Village Buried by Volcanic Ash in Central America*. Fort Worth: Harcourt Brace.

———. 1992b. "The Pervasive Pejorative in Intermediate Area Studies," in F. Lange (ed.), *Wealth and Hierarchy in the Intermediate Area*. Dunbarton Oaks, Washington, DC.

———. 1994. "Summary and Conclusions," in P. Sheets and B. McKee (eds.), *Archael-*

ogy, Volcanism, and Remote Sensing in the Arenal Region, Costa Rica, pp. 312–326. Austin: University of Texas Press.

Shook, E. 1965. "Archaeological Survey of the Pacific Coast of Guatemala." *Handbook of Middle American Indians* 2, 1: 180–194. Austin: University of Texas Press.

Siebe, C., M. Abrama, J. Macias, and J. Obenholzner. 1996. "Repeated Volcanic Disasters in Prehispanic Time at Popocatepetl, Central Mexico: Past Key to the Future?" *Geology* 24, 5: 399–402.

Urrutia-Fucugauchi, J. 1996. "Palaeomagnetic Study of the Xitle-Pedregal de San Angel Lava Flow, Southern Basin of Mexico." *Physics of the Earth and Planetary Interiors* 97: 177–196.

Vaillant, G. 1934. "The Archaeological Setting of the Playa de los Muertos Culture." *Maya Research* 1, 2: 87–100.

Weaver, M. 1993. *The Aztecs, Maya, and their Predecessors*. San Diego: Academic Press.

Workman, W. 1979. "The Significance of Volcanism in the Prehistory of Subarctic Northwest North America," in P. Sheets and D. Grayson (eds.), *Volcanic Activity and Human Ecology*, pp. 339–372. New York: Academic Press.

3

CONVERGENT CATASTROPHE: PAST PATTERNS AND FUTURE IMPLICATIONS OF COLLATERAL NATURAL DISASTERS IN THE ANDES

MICHAEL E. MOSELEY
University of Florida

WHEN TWO OR MORE NATURAL DISASTERS TRANSPIRE IN CLOSE SUCCESSION IN the same region, as they have in certain Andean cases, the collateral crises produce what can be termed a "convergent catastrophe." Convergent catastrophe is best characterized by means of an analogy with disease. Suffered individually, a natural illness or a natural disaster is generally survived by a healthy population. However, when people are first struck by one malady and then are afflicted by still other disorders, recovery becomes tenuous and the likelihood of demise increases. The potency of collateral natural disasters lies in the compound stress they exert upon biotic communities. Convergent catastrophes are implicated contributors to past cases of economic collapse, fall of government, as well as change in ideology, demography, and health. The nature, intensity, and duration of composite stress varies because convergent catastrophes are generated by variable agencies of hazardous change.

The identification of convergent catastrophes is new to geoarchaeology. Therefore, this essay first reviews the forces that generate collateral hazards in the Andean Cordillera as well as potential symptoms of disastrous processes. It then summarizes several modern and ancient cases of collateral crises. It concludes with a consideration of how present policies can lead to future crises, as my intent is to convey recent research results which identify forms of hazardous stress that contemporary populations and their national planners are neither aware of nor immune to.

FORCING AGENCIES

Incidents of convergent catastrophe increase with elevated frequencies and varieties of natural hazards. The paradigms of plate tectonics (the movement of the earth's crustal plates) and ocean/atmosphere interaction (the climatic interrelations of marine and meteorological currents) characterize the Andean Cordillera as an exceptionally dynamic region subject to many forms of physical change that can be stressful to biological life. Energy is required to change the physical environment, and Andean disasters are driven by two independent, unrelated sources of power. One emanates from the core of the earth, pertains to mountain building, and is modeled by the paradigm of plate tectonics. This energy produces hazards such as earthquakes. Because the central Cordillera is a rapidly growing mountain range, it is subject to ongoing tectonic creep and recurrent seismic shocks (Keefer 1994). The other source of power that drives change emanates from the sun, pertains to climate, and is modeled by the paradigm of ocean-atmosphere interaction. This energy generates hazards such as droughts and El Niño–Southern Oscillation (ENSO) events. Because the central Cordillera is arid to hyper-arid, it is highly sensitive to climatic perturbations of regional and global scope.

The two sources of physical transformation contribute to both high frequencies and many varieties of natural crises. Due to their separate origins, most disasters of tectonic and ocean-atmosphere origins generally transpire independently of one another in time, if not space. The temporal intermittence of crises allows afflicted populations to respond and to recover during eras of relative quiescence. Yet, Andean disasters can also transpire concurrently or in close succession. This generates convergent catastrophe and synergistic stress capable of forcing radical response or cultural breakdown in extreme cases.

DIAGNOSING CONVERGENT STRESS

Diagnosing past cases of convergent catastrophe is new, and some common types of disasters, such as earthquakes, are not yet readily identifiable in antiquity. These limitations create a situation similar to performing an autopsy without being able to recognize the symptoms of certain diseases. The Andean archaeological record is littered with cultural corpses of ancient societies that either died out or metamorphosed into new and different forms. Traditionally, the demise or transformation of bygone societies was explained entirely in terms of cultural causality. However, in the 1970s paleo-flood deposits were correlated with past ENSO events, and flood deposits found in ancient cities and settlements indicated that some extinct societies had suffered severe El Niño trauma. This promoted scrutiny of ENSO disasters as potential contributors to change in the archaeological record (e.g., Craig and Shimada 1986). The roster of ancient natural disasters grew in the 1980s when ice cores from an Andean glacier provided the first detailed records of Holocene climatic conditions in the central Cordillera. Because the ice cores documented atmospheric chemistry, dust, and precipitation at the glacier, they yielded a so-called "proxy," or indirect, but detailed record of the regional climate (Thompson et al. 1985, 1994b). In addition to documenting ancient ENSO events, the glacial cores indicated that severe droughts bracketed several cases of presumed El Niño–induced social collapse. Additional proxy records of past climatic conditions have come from sediment cores extracted from Lake Titicaca. They documented four prolonged droughts, each lasting from one to four hundred years, during the last three millennia (Abbott et al. 1997). Therefore, climatic stress from protracted drought and El Niño events has emerged as a likely contributor to human crises. More recently, earthquakes and large-scale sediment movement have been factored into several cases of collateral disaster also involving El Niño perturbations (Moseley et al. 1992b). Thus, in overview, increasing capabilities for identifying different types of disaster have enhanced the long-term perspectives on natural hazards, disasters, and convergent catastrophes. Once reliable records of past tectonic activity and earthquakes are developed, many consequential catastrophes will certainly prove to be complex ones entailing synergistic stress from multiple agencies of environmental change.

SYMPTOMS OF STRESS AND CHANGE

Deleterious environmental change transpires in many ways and on many spatial and temporal scales. It may be temporary or enduring, continuous or episodic, rapid or gradual. Slow or attenuated transformation can be elusive. Humans see only limited bands of the short- to long-wave spectrum of light, and human perception of time and environmental alteration is similarly narrow. People readily detect stressful processes that impact upon them rapidly and dramatically, yet equally catastrophic processes that impact slowly but cumulatively over generations are poorly perceived or not recognized (Moseley and Feldman 1982). Nonetheless, attenuated hazards are detectable in certain long-term proxy records of past conditions.

The time depth of many proxy records places natural disaster in an evolutionary perspective that has strengths and weaknesses. One limitation of this perspective is that accurate numerical estimates of ancient human fatalities are generally elusive. This mitigates comparisons with contemporary disasters that are often ranked by their deadliness. Disaster-induced deaths are tragic, yet mortalities may lack evolutionary consequences if reproduction among surviving populations leads to demographic recovery. Demographic and social recovery from natural disasters seems to be the long-term norm. Hundreds of deadly earthquakes and ENSO events have struck the Andes during the last five millennia. Yet, the archaeological record is characterized more by cultural continuity than by disruption. This is suggestive of substantial resiliency on the part of human populations.

Long-term proxy records of past conditions indicate that far-reaching evolutionary repercussions arise from natural processes and events that permanently destroy economic infrastructure and impair modes of making a living. Similar to habitat destruction, this type of devastation curtails production, reproduction, and survival. Farmland is the primary resource that has traditionally supported Andean populations. If farmers do not willingly give up fruitful terrain, then deserted farmland is an obvious symptom of fundamental change in human and natural conditions. Recognizing this negative symptom is hindered by its exceptional magnitude. Reaching from Colombia and Venezuela down the Cordillera for thousands of kilometers into Chile and Argentina there are millions of hectares of abandoned farmland. In some areas 30 to 100 percent more terrain was in past production than is presently cultivated. Peru, for example, has some 2.6 million hectares under cultivation, as well as an estimated 750,000 hectares of agricultural terraces that are out of use (Masson 1986). In addition, there are probably 300,000 or more hectares of unterraced ground that was once farmed. Thus, for one nation alone the total amount of abandoned land may exceed 40 percent of that in present production. Loss of agrarian habitat is a pan-Andean phenomenon that is evident both on the ground and in aerial photography. Yet, land loss has never been quantified on national scales. This is because afflicted nations ignore the condition, or at best regard ruined agrarian landscapes as sweeping attractions to titillate tourists. Tourists, though, are not informed of the simplest of potential explanations: Farming is not sustainable when the natural environment is changing.

The physical remains of abandoned agricultural works have been investigated in studies that are relatively few in number, scattered in location, variable in method, but important in their implications. They negate common notions that agrarian collapse was a singular event, such as the consequence of demographic and social upheaval accompanying European pandemics and conquest. Taken as a whole, the studies demonstrate that farmland was reclaimed, cultivated, and deserted at different times and rates in widely separated areas. Therefore, land loss did not transpire all at once as a unique mishap of the past that is unrelated to the present. On the contrary, it is a persistent process that has recurred many times over many millennia.

Along the arid Pacific watershed, where 90 percent of all plant cultivation is sustained by irrigation, abandoned farmland is not randomly distributed. It appears that terrain near watercourses that could be opened by canal systems of modest size and complexity was brought into production more than two millennia ago. Here farming has generally endured. Alternatively, later, more ambitious reclamation that transpired lateral to these core areas and at higher elevations has been less enduring and frequently subject to abandonment (Clement and Moseley 1991). This distribution pattern suggests a potential correlation between the marginality of land, the difficulty of reclamation, and the precariousness of endurance.

Suggested causes of abandonment embrace a wide range of cultural and natural variables (Denevan 1987). In cultural terms, it appears that agriculture has expanded when conditions favorable to the reclamation of new lands are anticipated. When these expectations are not met, or if environmental conditions alter, then agrarian regression ensues either temporarily or permanently (Cardich 1985; Binford et al. 1997; Ortloff and Kolata 1993; Seddon 1994). Known or suspected natural contributors to agrarian contraction and collapse include temperature fluctuations, pervasive drought, severe ENSO events, tectonic events, declining water tables and declining river-flow levels, as well as sand dune incursions generated by terrestrial outwash or declining sea levels. These are all ongoing or recurrent agencies of environmental alteration. Therefore, natural stress upon agriculture is a product of environmental dynamics that are subject to the principles of uniformitarian analysis and explanation.

TWENTIETH-CENTURY ANALOGS

Uniformitarian analysis holds that if loss of agrarian habitat is driven principally by environmental dynamics and natural hazards, then desertion of farmland and its contributory physical agencies will be detectable and empirically demonstrable in twentieth-century time frames. Geoarchaeological evaluation of this hypothesis has employed time-lapse, high-altitude imagery produced by the advent of Andean aerial photography, beginning in the 1940s, and the subsequent availability of satellite data. For many areas imagery taken in different years and decades spans half a century. In conjunction with ground "truth" survey, the imagery provides accurate, unequivocal, time-depth records of recent landscape transformations.

Gradual Land Loss

One study has employed 1951 archival aerial photography and 1985 laser-transit survey to calibrate long-term land loss at Carrizal (17° 28' S, 71° 22' W), a spring-fed irrigation system on the southern desert coast of Peru. At A.D. 1000, fields below the spring covered 13.2 hectares. By the early Colonial Period 48 percent of the land could no longer be farmed when the remaining area was planted in olive trees around A.D. 1575. Ensuing land losses were 13 percent by A.D. 1600; 25 percent during the Republican Period; 6 percent between the 1930s and 1951; and loss of seven olive trees between 1951 and 1985. Successive abandonment of 93 percent of the farmland was the hydrological consequence of a gradual 29.2-meter drop in spring elevation and a concomitant decline in spring flow (Moseley and Clement 1990).

The laws of fluid dynamics dictate that irrigated land will be lost to production whenever and wherever natural levels of water flow decline below the stationary levels of canal intakes. Almost all Andean streams and rivers are down-cutting and deepening their channels. Therefore, surface and subsurface rainfall runoff levels are slowly lowering. This gradual change in hydrological conditions is postulated to be a chronic source of background stress on agriculture wherever irrigation is drawn from eroding water sources (Clement and Moseley 1991). As well as inducing slow forfeiture of land, this background stress also exacerbates loss from other natural causes.

At Carrizal an exceptionally severe ENSO flood event, around A.D. 1360, is associated with widespread abandonment that endured until A.D. 1500 due to drought. Early in the Colonial Period 13 percent of the irrigation system dropped from use as a consequence of several closely spaced disasters. The first, in A.D. 1600, entailed the violent eruption of Huayna Putina (16° 35' S, 70° 52' W), a volcano to the northeast. The eruption was accompanied by very strong earthquakes that produced numerous landslides and large quantities of debris. A very powerful earthquake, estimated at 8.0 or more magnitude on the Richter scale, in A.D. 1604 added to the loose material that reposed on the desert landscape. Massive quantities of earthquake debris were then moved by rainfall and flooding that accompanied the strong El Niño of 1607. Because the ENSO disaster struck a landscape previously destabilized by tectonic disaster, torrential precipitation produced exceptionally severe erosion and deposition (Moseley et al. 1992b; Satterlee et al. n.d.). At Carrizal this convergent catastrophe washed away some olive trees and buried others beneath unusually thick flood deposits, leading to partial agricultural regression.

Episodic Sediment Movement

The A.D. 1600 eruption of Huayna Putina, the ensuing earthquake of 1804, and the strong El Niño of 1607 suggest that paleo-flood events involving disproportional erosion and deposition reflect convergent catastrophes involving tectonic and ENSO disasters. A twentieth-century analog for the synergistic consequences of tectonic events and ENSO events has been developed by a NASA-based study. This investigation digitized and computer overlaid aerial photographic, satellite, and space shuttle imagery to produce a four-decade record of Peru's Rio Santa coastline (9° 02' S, 78° 33' W). The time-lapse record revealed a prolonged cycle of massive sediment movement and landscape alteration involving three different types of natural disaster. The cycle began with a magnitude 7.9 Santa earthquake in 1970. The quake produced hundreds of landslides that released millions of cubic meters of debris with an estimated volume of 0.1×10^9 to 0.2×10^9 cubic meters (Keefer and Moseley 1994). The loose debris reposed on the arid watershed until it was picked up, entrained, and carried to the sea by rainfall, runoff, and flooding produced by the strong ENSO event of 1972–73 and the very strong ENSO event of 1982–83. Debris disgorged into the sea was then reworked by marine currents and deposited along the shore, building new beach up to one kilometer wide. In turn, this initiated a third disastrous process. Strong daily winds off the ocean began transporting the new supply of beach sediment inland in the form of immense sand dunes. As the slow-moving dunes march inland they will bury farmland and large sections of the landscape for long periods before the sand eventually moves to final repose and stabilization against the steep escarpment of the Cordillera (Moseley et al. 1992a).

Cycles of massive sediment movement are not uncommon in long-term perspective because earthquakes and El Niño events are frequent types of natural hazards in the central Andes. Such sediment cycles are potentially reflected in paleo-flood records as episodes of exceptionally severe erosion and deposition. They are also reflected in episodic incursions of massive sand dunes. Dune formation is inhibited where shorelines are formed by rocky cliffs but enhanced where sandy beaches prevail, as in northern Peru. Here sandy shorelines preserve remnant sources of old dune fields that inundated inland areas and disastrously altered where people farmed and lived. Dune disasters result from increased supplies of beach sand that can arise by several means. First, shoreline sediment can increase as a synergistic consequence of earthquakes and ENSO events, as at the Rio Santa. This produces regional dune incursion. Second, supplies of beach sand would also increase when sea levels lowered during Holocene fluctuations. This would produce sand inundations along the entire coast. It is likely that regional incursions will prove more frequent than transcoastal ones driven by sea-level low stands. Still, sand dune disasters do not occur alone but, rather, are indicative of convergent stress involving other agencies of environmental change.

The NASA-based study of the disaster cycle initiated by the 1970 Santa earthquake did not seek to quantify permanent loss of modern agrarian habitat. Yet, large-scale loss transpired because much of the 0.1×10^9 to 0.2×10^9 cubic meters of landslide debris was stripped from farming surfaces or deposited atop them. Between magnitude 6.0 and magnitude 7.0 seismic shocks cross a threshold to produce exponentially increasing volumes of landslide debris. In the Andes more than thirty earthquakes at greater than 7.0 on the Richter scale may occur each century, and recent modeling indicates that each may produce from 40×10^6 to 4×10^9 cubic meters of landslide debris.

Indeed, for Peru the mean erosion rate calculated for earthquake-induced landslides is some 40 percent of the erosion rate attributed to annual river discharge (Keefer 1994). Thus, seismic shocks and earthquake-induced landslides have long been the major contributors to physical alteration of agrarian landscapes.

PAST CASES OF CONVERGENT CATASTROPHE

Populations living in the central Cordillera have always been subject to frequent crises of tectonic and ocean-atmosphere origins. Indeed, a recent synthesis of Andean archaeology implicates natural disaster impact at many major evolutionary turning points in human development (Richardson 1994). Convergent catastrophes are likely contributors to these evolutionary disjunctures. However, composite catastrophes are still difficult to identify. This, in part, is because one disaster often obscures the impact of another, such as an El Niño flood event that follows a seismic shock and washes away earthquake-induced landslides. Therefore, currently identified cases of convergent catastrophes entail overlaying geoarchaeological evidence of disaster on proxy records of climatological stress.

For the central Andes a detailed proxy record of annual wet and dry season climatic conditions during the last fifteen hundred years is provided by two ice cores extracted from the Quelccaya glacier in 1983. The cores reflect ENSO events and other perturbations of rainfall, temperature, and atmospheric chemistry and particulate matter (Thompson et al. 1985, 1994a).

Decadal Drought

One ice core disturbance that stands out as having far-reaching social and political consequences entailed an unusually severe and prolonged drought. The drought began abruptly in A.D. 563 and endured through A.D. 594; precipitation averaged 30 percent below normal during these three decades (Schaff 1988). By this time farming had reached its maximum expansion in many areas, and diminished rainfall presumably depressed harvests by 30 percent or more. Since streams and rivers descending the arid Pacific watershed lose more than 50 percent of their runoff to seepage and evaporation, the decadal drought resulted in little or no water reaching downstream rivermouth areas. Consequently, coastal farming and settlement shifted inland to valley-neck areas around canal intakes where scarce runoff was more available (Shimada et al. 1991).

By subjecting large populations to widespread famine for a generation, the decadal drought exacerbated the negative impact of other disasters. In northern Peru the coastal regions of many desert valleys experienced massive sand dune incursions during the latter half of the sixth century and the beginning of the seventh century. Late in the sixth century an enormous sand incursion inundated the south side of the Moche Valley, swamped agricultural lands, and buried the capital of the Moche polity which held dominion over much of the north coast at the time. The center of government was abandoned, as were many satellite centers. In the aftermath Moche political control was lost over valleys to the south, and a new capital for a smaller nation was established some 165 kilometers to the north and 55 kilometers inland in the Lambayeque Valley neck. At this new city and others there is evidence of tightly controlled facilities for warehousing agricultural foods and other commodities (Shimada 1994; Shimada et al. 1991). Economic and political changes were accompanied by profound alterations in corporate art, iconography, and ideology, reflecting new views of the universe (McClelland 1990).

The environmental conditions contributing to these geopolitical and social transformations are open to several different causal scenarios. One proposes that change was largely or entirely induced by decadal drought. According to this view drought diminished plant cover, which increased erosion, sediment reaching the sea, and coastal sand dune activity (Shimada et al. 1991). This is questionable because the lower regions of the desert watershed are largely unvegetated, and a 30-percent decrease in rainfall and runoff would result in an equal decrease in the competency of rivers to transport sediment from the mountains to the sea where it would supply sand for dune incursions. Alternatively, sand dune burial of the Moche capital and much of its coastal hinterland may reflect either sea level lowering or severe ENSO erosion following a disastrous earthquake, as implicated by the twentieth-century Rio Santa analog for dune formation.

There is evidence of El Niño flood events at the Moche capital (Uceda and Canziani 1993). One late case entailed exceptionally severe erosion that might well reflect prior seismic activity (Moseley and Deeds 1982). Therefore, it is likely that earthquakes and ENSO disasters transpired during the drought, and a complex of natural catastrophe contributed to geopolitical transformation. The decadal drought was the critical component of this complex. Akin to a chronic disease, diminished rainfall and runoff depressed cultural response capabilities to stress from seismic, ENSO, and sand dune disasters and allowed these afflictions to trigger political collapse and social reconfiguration (Moseley and Richardson 1992).

THE DARKEST SIDE OF DISASTER

Hazardous environmental change is as disastrous as humans make it. Some populations build calamity into their future, and Andean countries are doing this on a grand scale. In recent decades all have raised their national debt significantly in order to build very large agrarian reclamation works. Most projects intrude upon abandoned farmland or lie within the ruins of larger-than-modern agricultural systems. In all cases there is no knowledge of why the older, often bigger, farming systems collapsed in the first place. This is because feasibility studies for Andean projects have not acknowledged the presence of ancient agricultural remains or associated monuments. There is both an excuse and a deeper reason for this policy. Ostensibly, it allows developing nations to avoid archaeological mitigation costs. However, this excuse is belied by cases in which mitigation was later sponsored once project financing was secured. The deeper reason that feasibility studies ignore vast agricultural ruins is to preserve the basic premise that large projects reclaim pristine wilderness. The notion that the landscape of the Americas was unfarmed wilderness prior to 1492 is a myth (Denevan 1987). However, the "pristine premise" is essential to modern reclamation. It allows planning for the agrarian future to proceed entirely upon theoretical grounds rather than empirical realities. Theoretical optimism is essential for securing large-scale, long-term financing in the modern global economy. Reclamation projects that raise national debt by more than half a billion dollars must elevate agricultural yields significantly for more than a century if agrarian returns are to repay construction costs. Because there is no scientific basis for predicting conditions a century or more in the future, feasibility studies are political instruments used to fund reclamation on the basis of hypothetical pollyannaism. Unfortunately, theoretical optimism can be made up and marketed only in an empirical void unfettered by the physical evidence of past agricultural performance or by the consideration of future conditions accompanying global warming.

Optimistic forecasts about the centennial viability of current reclamation works are open to serious question. By way of example, this essay has summarized a NASA study of recent regional landscape alteration in the Rio Santa region of Peru. Here a major reclamation project is entering completion that channels abundant Santa waters northward by a "Canal Madre" to four drier desert valleys. In this region known geoarchaeological contributors to past agrarian abandonment include water table subsidence, river down-cutting, strong El Niño flooding, massive sand dune incursions, and severe or prolonged drought. Inferred or suspected contributors include seismic shocks, earthquake-induced landslides and sea level lowering.

Given this background, the long-term prognosis of the Santa project is not one of "sustainable agriculture." During the coming hundred years the region could well experience an earthquake of greater than 7.0 Richter scale magnitude. The new Santa dam is designed to withstand such seismic shock. However, it is not designed for large sediment loads. These loads will come from material still in repose after the 1970 earthquake, debris produced by future quakes, and sediment generated by normal weathering and El Niño rainfall and runoff. Incised ENSO activity and intensity are predicted corollaries of higher ocean temperatures accompanying global warming. The tropical Pacific has warmed measurably (Graham 1995). The frequency of El Niño activity has dramatically increased in the 1990s, and the intensity of the 1997–98 ENSO event has shattered all twentieth-century records. Therefore, massive loads of sediments, exceeding design expectations, are being washed into the newly created Rio Santa reservoir. As this process continues the dam is being transformed into a giant sediment trap that will eventually retain more mud than moisture. As water storage volume decreases, the facility will lose its capacity to mitigate drought, and in dry times newly irrigated farmland will drop out of production. Newly reclaimed land north of the Rio Santa will be further impacted by the sediment that heightened ENSO activity flushes into the sea. Reworked by long shore currents and deposited as beach sand, this material will be picked up by daily winds off the ocean and march inland as dunes that swamp farmland. The NASA study leaves no question about what is happening. The only question is how fast it is happening.

Andean nations raise their national debt to expand agrarian infrastructure under the artifice of "sustainable agriculture." Yet, it is self-evident that stability cannot characterize plants or people when the physical environment is changing. If all Andean landscapes are dynamic, then the nature and course of environmental change must be factored into planning if agrarian reclamation works are to endure. The data and the analytical tools are on hand to make changing agricultural and environmental conditions empirically retrodictive if not predictive. When these resources are not employed propositions of "sustainable agriculture" are as mythical as the "pristine premise." These myths are untenable in a cordillera blanketed by ruins of vast agrarian landscapes. However, they are propagated and embraced by governmental regimes where the construction of reclamation works is synonymous with political profit and patronage. This mythology is further perpetuated by the global political economy because it provides developed nations the rationale for investing in large projects that mortgage the agrarian futures of developing countries for centuries to come. To engage great debt requires firm multinational commitment to systematically ignoring the physical relationships of environmental change, natural disasters, and long-term agrarian performance. Therefore, agricultural land loss induced by modern natural disasters is never quantified. Instead, disaster studies that are conducted focus upon human mortalities and social recovery. Such treatment disengages the present from the past. Therefore, natural disasters cannot be seen or modeled in an evolutionary perspective. Yet, this is essential to divorcing agrarian planning from the constraints of uniformitarianism and empirical data on long-term agricultural performance. The situation is unlikely to change because it is built into the global economy. It will, however, secure a future for the study of catastrophes generated by predictable hazards.

BIBLIOGRAPHY

Abbott, M., M. Binford, M. Brenner, and K. Kelts. 1997. "A 3500 14 C yr High-Resolution Record of Water-Level Changes in Lake Titicaca, Bolivia/Peru." *Quaternary Research* 47: 169–80.

Binford, M., A. Kolata, M. Brenner, J. Janusek, M. Seddon, M. Abbott, and J. Curtis. 1997. "Climate Variation and the Rise and Fall of an Andean Civilization." *Quaternary Research* 47: 235–248.

Cardich, A. 1985. "Cultivation in the Andes." *National Geographic Society Research Reports* (1979 projects) 20: 85–100.

Clement, C., and M. Moseley. 1991. "The Spring-Fed Irrigation System of Carrizal, Peru: A Case Study of the Hypothesis of Agrarian Collapse." *Journal of Field Archaeology* 18: 425–442.

Craig, A., and I. Shimada. 1986. "El Niño Flood Deposits at Batan Grande, Northern Peru." *Geoarchaeology* 1: 29–38.

Denevan, W. 1987. "Terrace Abandonment in the Colca Valley, Peru," in W. Denevan, J. Mathewson, and G. Knapp (eds.), *Pre-Hispanic Agricultural Fields in the Andean Region*, pp. 1–43. London: British Archaeological Reports.

Graham, N. 1995. "Simulation of Recent Global Temperature Trends." *Science* 267: 666–671.

Keefer, D. 1994. "The Importance of Earthquake-Induced Landslides to Long-Term Slope Erosion and Slope-Failure Hazards in Seismically Active Regions." *Geomorphology* 10: 265–284.

Keefer, D., and M. Moseley. 1994. "Catastrophic Effects of Combined Seismic Landslide Generation and El Niño Flooding on Prehispanic and Modern Populations in Peru." *Geological Society of America Annual Meeting Abstracts with Programs* 26, 7: A342.

Masson Meiss, Luis. 1986. "Rehabilitation de andenes en la comunidad de San Pedro de Casta, Lima," in C. de la Torre and M. Burga (eds.), *Andenes y camellones en el Peru andino: Historria presente y futuro*, pp. 207–216. Lima: Consejo Nacional de Cienca y Tecnologia.

McClelland, D. 1990. "A Maritime Passage from Moche to Chimu," in M. Moseley and A. Cordy-Collins (eds.), *The Northern Dynasties: Kingship and Statecraft in Chimor*, pp. 75–106. Washington, DC: Dumbarton Oaks.

Moseley, M., and C. O. Clement. 1990. "Patron de Colapso Agrario en Carrizal, Ilo, Peru," in L. K. Watanabe, M. E. Moseley, and Cabieses (eds.), *Trabajos Arqueologicos en Moquegua, Peru*, pp. 161–176. Lima: Programa Contisuyo del Museo Peruano de Ciencas de la Salud and Southern Peru Copper Corporation.

Moseley, M., and E. Deeds. 1982. "The Land in Front of Chan Chan: Agrarian Expansion, Reform, and Collapse in the Moche Valley," in M. Moseley and K. Day (eds.), *Chan Chan: Andean Desert City*, pp. 25–53. Albuquerque, NM: University of New Mexico Press.

Moseley, M., and R. Feldman. 1982. "Vivir con Crisis: Percepcion Humana de Proceso y Tiempo." *Revista del Museo Nacional* 46: 267–287.

Moseley, M., and J. Richardson III. 1992. "Doomed by Disaster." *Archaeology* 45, 6: 44–45.

Moseley, M., J. Tapia, D. Satterlee, and J. Richardson III. 1992. "Flood Events, El Nino Events, and Tectonic Events," in L. Ortlieb and J. Machare (eds), *Paleo-ENSO Records, International Symposium, Extended Abstracts,* pp. 207–212. Lima, Peru: OSTRUM.

Moseley, M., D. Wagner, and J. Richardson III. 1992. "Space Shuttle Imagery of Recent Catastrophic Change Along the Arid Andean Coast," in L. Johnson and M. Stright (eds.), *Paleoshorelines and Prehistory: An Investigation of Method,* pp. 215–235. Boca Raton, FL: CRC Press.

Ortloff, C., and A. Kolata. 1993. "Climate and Collapse: Agro-Ecological Perspectives on the Decline of the Tiwanaku State." *Journal of Archaeological Science* 20: 195–221.

Richardson III, J. 1994. *People of the Andes.* Washington, DC: St. Remy Press and Smithsonian Institution.

Satterlee, D., M. Moseley, and D. Keefer. n.d. "The Miraflores Catastrophe: A Severe Prehistoric El Niño Flood Event in Southern Peru." Latin American Antiquity, submitted.

Schaff, C. 1988. *Establishment and Demise of Moche V: Assessment of the Climatic Impact.* Unpublished M.A. thesis. Cambridge, MA: Harvard University Extension School.

Seddon, M. T. 1994. *Excavations in the Raised Fields of the Rio Catari Sub-basin, Bolivia.* Unpublished M.S. thesis. Chicago: University of Chicago.

Shimada, I. 1994. *Pampa Grande and the Mochica Culture.* Austin, TX: University of Texas Press.

Shimada, I., C. Schaff, L. Thompson, and E. Mosley-Thompson. 1991. "Cultural Impacts of Severe Droughts in the Prehistoric Andes: Application of a 1,500-year Ice Core Precipitation Record." *World Archaeology* 22: 247–70.

Thompson, L., E. Mosley-Thompson, J. Bolzan, and B. Koci. 1985. "A 1500-year Record of Tropical Precipitation in Ice Cores from the Quelccaya Ice Cap, Peru." *Science* 299: 971–973.

Thompson, L., D. Peel, E. Mosley-Thompson, R. Mulvaney, J. Dai, P. Lin, M. Davis, and C. Raymond. 1994. "Climate Since A.D. 1510 on Dyer Plateau, Antarctic Peninsula: Evidence for Recent Climate Change." *Annals of Glaciology* 20: 420–426.

Thompson, L., M. Davis, and E. Mosley-Thompson. 1994. "Glacial Records of Global Climate: A 1500-Year Tropical Ice Core Record of Climate." *Human Ecology* 22, 1: 83–95.

Uceda, C., and J. Canziani Amico. 1993. "Evidencias de grandes precipitaciones en diversas etapas constructivas de la Huaca de la Luna, Costa Norte del Peru." *Boletin de Instituto Frances de Estudios Andinos* 22, 1: 313–343.

THE CULTURAL AND SOCIAL CONSTRUCTION
OF CATASTROPHE

ALTHOUGH DISASTERS WOULD SEEM TO BE EMINENTLY PHYSICAL EVENTS with great impacts in material circumstances, they are also socially and culturally constructed events and processes. Features of society and culture affect the way disasters unfold, how they are perceived and experienced, and how their effects are distributed. The meeting of a destructive force, natural or technological, and a human community does not inevitably produce a disaster. A disaster takes place when a destructive force intersects with a community in a socially configured pattern of vulnerability. Vulnerability arises from location, sociopolitical structure, production patterns, and ideology. A vulnerability profile is a historical and evolutionary product that influences the way a disaster develops far more than the physical force of the destructive agent.

Interpretations of disaster vary widely according to social and cultural identity and circumstance as well. The construction of meaning and explanation, the perception of risk and vulnerability, and even impact are mediated through linguistic social and cultural grids of individuals and groups, producing significant variability of interpretation to the effect that disasters are as much social texts as material events.

However, to say that disasters are social constructs does not dis-embed them from the materiality of the world. We may "read" the disaster as a social text as it unfolds in its particular context, but the natural forces that created it, or even the hazard processes set in motion by technology, exist as independent agents operating according to physical laws that are ultimately "outside" the text.

4

PERU'S FIVE-HUNDRED-YEAR EARTHQUAKE: VULNERABILITY IN HISTORICAL CONTEXT[1]

ANTHONY OLIVER-SMITH
University of Florida

ABOUT FIFTEEN YEARS AGO, A PERSPECTIVE EMERGED IN THE SOCIAL SCIENTIFIC study of disasters in which an overall reconsideration of disasters as "extreme events" was undertaken. That is, disasters began to be interpreted less as the result of geophysical extremes such as storms, earthquakes, avalanches, droughts, etc., and much more as functions of an ongoing social order, the structure of human environment relations, and the larger framework of historical processes that shaped these phenomena (Hewitt 1983: 25). While attention had traditionally been paid to the social context of disaster threat and impact, the new perspective recasts the relationship between natural hazards and their socioeconomic context, seriously questioning the entire set of human-environment relations in which disasters are seen as unhappy accidents that occur in otherwise "normal" everyday existence. Hewitt, for example, posits that most natural disasters are more explainable in terms of the "normal" order of things than in terms of the accidental geophysical features of a place. Disasters are seen to be far more characteristic of societies than they are of simple physical environments.

In effect, the new perspective asserts that disasters do not simply happen; they are caused. The high correlation between disaster proneness, chronic malnutrition, low income, and famine potential has led many researchers to the conclusion that the root cause of disasters can be attributed to the structural imbalances between rich and poor countries. Indeed, Hewitt explicitly posits that many natural phenomena would not even be disasters or, if they were, would cause far fewer damages, were it not for the characteristic "normal" conditions of underdevelopment in which people have been forced to live in their attempts to adapt to social and economic conditions and contexts far beyond their control. Moreover, the new perspective maintains that such conditions and the forces that created them have also undermined or subverted traditionally effective adaptive strategies developed through long experience with a region's hazards. Seen in this context, the Guatemalans' reference to the 1975 earthquake as a "classquake" or the Peruvians' reference to a "five-hundred-year earthquake" after the 1970 disaster are bitterly accurate assessments of "natural" disaster. The American first lady's remark on viewing the devastation after the 1970 Peruvian earthquake that the United States was going to help the victims until everything was "just rosy again" exemplifies the belief that the disaster was an "extreme event" and returning to normalcy would solve all the problems. There was little recognition that the destruction and misery in Peru in 1970 and after were as much a product of that nation's historic underdevelopment as they were of the earthquake. In effect, then, the perspective of disaster research and analysis shifts from an exclusive focus on "extreme events" to include and give equal weight to the societal and human-environment relations that "prefigure" disaster (Hewitt 1983: 27).

This chapter focuses on these societal and human-environment relations in attempting to understand why the May 31, 1970, earthquake, which at 7.7 magnitude on the Richter scale would have been severe in any human context, in Peru became the worst historic "natural" disaster of the Western hemisphere. The earthquake, which devastated the north central coastal and Andean regions of Peru, can be seen as an event which in certain respects began almost five hundred years ago with the conquest and colonization of Peru and its consequent insertion as a colony into the developing world economic system, which has resulted in the severe underdevelopment of the entire region.

NATURAL HAZARDS IN THE ANDES

In order to assess the relationships between disasters, human vulnerability, and the conditions of underdevelopment in the Andes, it is necessary to survey very briefly the array of natural hazards which characterize the region. The Andes are and have always been a very hazard-prone region of the world. In general the natural bases for this precarious condition lie in two dimensions: climatology and geology.

Strictly speaking, two factors—one climatological and the other oceanographic—interact to produce many of the disastrous atmospheric conditions which afflict the Andean region. Under normal conditions the coastal desert of Peru is one of the driest regions of the world. There is virtually no annual rainfall, and annual temperatures vary only slightly. This context is extremely sensitive to any anomalies in the ocean-to-atmosphere energy transfer system with implications for global weather patterns (Moseley et al. 1981: 234).

Occasionally, major current perturbations in the form of warm air and water masses, known collectively as "El Niño," have pushed down the coast of Ecuador, radically altering the ecosystem of the normally cold Peruvian current, and producing torrential rains in the western highlands. Major impacts include disruption of the marine food chain, with consequent reduction in coastal fishing economies (Caviedes 1981: 288), and torrential rains producing flash floods in the forty-six river systems which descend from the Andean cordilleras, killing people and inundating villages and fields as well as washing out roads and irrigation canals.

prone to floods

The central Andes rise abruptly from the narrow strip of coastal desert and descend somewhat more gradually to the Amazon in the east. The position of the Andean cordilleras is key in the distribution and seasonality of rainfall. The Amazon basin experiences year-round orographic rainfall, and the coastal desert receives almost no rain at all except when the pattern is disrupted by temperature changes occasioned by El Niño. The mountains between the jungle and the desert experience wide variation in rainfall and temperature (Winterhalder and Thomas 1978: 9).

The Andean highland region is noted for its wide variation of microenvironments with complex gradients of climate and vegetation. Such microenvironments, even those in close proximity, often experience extreme variation in temperature and rainfall. Localized frosts are hazards to crops, as are hailstorms, which can be even more devastating to agriculture in specific contexts. The Andean region has experienced both severe regional and local droughts, with little predictable regularity, which may persist for as long as three years, again with devastating agricultural losses and hunger. The uneven topography of the region also figures importantly as a variable in the distribution of precipitation, producing local high concentrations of rainfall, hail, and snow. Heavy rainfall may combine with unstable soils on steep mountain slopes to produce mudslides of varying proportions, with frequent tragic results for human settlements, agriculture, and infrastructure.

droughts

mudslides

In effect, the Andes parallel the plate boundaries, where crustal deformation often produces orogenic uplift, tectonic activity, and volcanism. Indeed, the Andes are the product of the subduction of the oceanic Nazca plate moving eastward from the East Pacific ridge underneath the continental rim of the South American plate which began in the Jurassic period. The surface conformation of Andean environments is the product of the more recent and contemporary geological processes of glacial and tectonic activity, faulting, volcanoes, and erosion and deposition (Winterhalder and Thomas 1978: 6). These processes have produced deep V- and U-shaped valleys, frequently capped by deep glacial lakes dammed by terminal morainic loops. Such formations are characteristic of strong alluvial and glacial erosion exacerbated by both persistent faulting and uplift of the mountains. The two earlier processes of plate collision and volcanism so crucial in Andean geological time, as well as the more recent phenomena, continue to be significant forces in Andean cultural time.

Thus, the Andes, the second highest chain of mountains in the world, are characterized by extreme instability in the form of significant seismic activity, active volcanoes, unstable soils, and avalanches of both minor and major dimensions. The Peruvian Andes have experienced approximately fifty major earthquakes (greater than 7.0 magnitude on the Richter scale) and countless smaller ones since historic records began to be kept (Giesecke and Silgado 1981: 65–67). There are no fewer than ten active volcanoes in the same region. Many of the peaks in the Andes are extremely sharply angled, ranging from forty-five to nearly ninety degrees at their highest reaches, which are often over eighteen thousand feet. The combination of their extreme altitude and their location in subequatorial latitudes with sustained high insolation makes for a pattern of rapid alternation of snowfall and melt and results in extremely unstable glacial icefields susceptible to even slight tremors, producing ice and rock avalanches of varying proportions (Caviedes 1981: 284). When the descent of these avalanches ends in a glacial lake, a major flood is frequently created when the morainic loop dam gives way or is washed over.

Thus, as regions linked by climatological and geological processes, the Peruvian coast and highlands are characterized by a series of natural forces and phenomena with enormous potential for destructive power when combined with human populations in vulnerable configurations. As the location of human habitation for over ten thousand years and the site of major cultural complexity for the last four thousand years, the nature of human cultural adaptation to these complex and unstable environments becomes a compelling issue.

ADAPTATIONS TO HAZARDS IN THE PRE-COLUMBIAN ANDES

The adaptations of pre-Columbian Andean peoples to the existence of these natural phenomena can be grouped into five basic patterns: 1) control of multiple ecological tiers, 2) dispersed settlement patterns, 3) environmentally appropriate building materials and techniques, 4) preparedness, and 5) ideology and modes of explanation. Although environmental forces have played important roles in large-scale culture change in the Andes (Moseley et al. 1981, Kolata 1989), as a whole, these adaptations seem to have been relatively effective in enabling Andean peoples not only to survive, but to flourish, if population growth and cultural complexity are any measures of success. The archaeological record, while revealing the environmental traces of various disaster impacts, is less likely to display evidence of massive mortality and destruction due to sudden-onset disasters. However, the success of these adaptations is supported by the contention that the Inca empire was reaching the limits of its agricultural base. The evidence supporting this contention consists of plentiful examples of extension of cultivation into marginal areas such as ridged fields in flood plains and sunken fields on the coast and terraces on steep highland hillsides (Cook 1981: 108).

In both the coastal and highland contexts the exploitation of a variety of microenvironments has been a basic element of Andean adaptation. The development of Andean civilization has since the earliest days of habitation involved complex interactions between coastal and highland environments, each highly varied and complex environments in their own right. This control of multiple ecological tiers, usually referred to as the "principle of verticality," enabled coastal peoples and, particularly, Andean highlanders, to spread both risk and resources over a wide area, diminishing impacts of localized flood, hail, mudslide, and frosts and at the same time producing a varied diet (Murra 1972).

However, vertical control of the ecology was much more than a strategy of ecological adaptation. Verticality was a broad cultural principle not only shaping the social relations of production and exchange, but also forming an integral part of Andean ideology and worldview (Larson 1988: 20). Following this principle and pattern of dispersed production zone exploitation, pre-Columbian Andean rural settlement patterns tended to be equally dispersed, located on ridges and hillsides as well as in valley lowlands (Rowe 1963: 228; Hyslop 1990: 271–272). The location of Inca towns was dictated by a variety of factors, including access to resources, regional topography, proximity to sacred places, and specific settlement formal function such as garrison or administrative center (Hyslop 1990: 271–272). Most towns, even those planned and constructed by the Inca, were quite small, usually less than one hundred families, and did not resemble urban concentrations in the European fashion (Rowe 1963: 229). Many cities, although by no means all of them, were located in valleys, and, as population grew, particularly on the coast, exploitation of vulnerable flood plain areas was undertaken. However, in some cases, like the region around present-day Arequipa, which possessed both notable fertility and stable water resources but also high seismicity and volcanism, there was virtually no urban development and even relatively sparse rural populations (Cook 1981: 171).

Although major research on Inca architecture and settlement planning (e.g., Gasparini and Margolies 1980; Hyslop 1990) pays scant attention to adaptations to high seismicity, it is clear that the building techniques and materials employed by pre-Columbian Andean peoples provided a measure of safety, particularly from earthquake damage. The corners of walls of Inca buildings were always carefully bonded, and long vertical joints were scrupulously avoided. In houses constructed of adobe, which along with stone was considered an important building material, alternate rows of headers and stretchers, a technique known as "English bond," were used. Rowe considers Inca construction to be far superior technically to the best Mayan or Mexican work (1963: 228).

The Inca empire is justly famous for its fine stonework and feats of engineering skill in the construction of roads, bridges, and buildings. While the monumental stonework of the Incas has withstood many severe earthquakes, perhaps the most significant feature of pre-Columbian Andean buildings was the thatched roofs. All buildings in pre-Columbian Peru had thatched roofs, thus eliminating the threat of collapsing heavy roofs in earthquakes. Other possible anti-seismic design features employed by pre-Columbian Andean peoples include double-structure walls with earthen infill in the middle and trapezoidal-shaped doors and windows. In addition, domestic houses were constructed largely of fieldstone and mud or adobe with thin walls about the height of an average man (Rowe 1963: 222). While such construction and materials were not particularly anti-seismic, the modest height and thinness of walls and thatched roofs of ordinary houses reduced the potential for serious injury from falling debris in earthquakes.

The consciousness of potential threat from the various aspects of the environment led the complex political structure that eventually came to dominate the entire Andean region to establish a system of economic redistribution based on a large number of storehouses for surpluses and emergency use (Murra 1980). These storehouses, known as *qollqas*, were built by the hundreds in regions of dense habitation (Gasparini and Margolies 1980: 118). Indeed, the redistributive system of the state based on the infrastructure of efficient production and the storage capacity of the *qollqas* virtually precluded local long-term hardship as a result of natural disasters (Cook 1981: 108). While care must be taken not to wax too lyrical on the virtues of the Inca empire, from a material standpoint obedient subjects of the Inca were probably better off than the average European of the same era. There is certainly solid evidence of a compendium of empirical knowledge on hazards and hazard mitigation and its effective application in the pre-Incaic and Incaic periods in the Andes. *evidence they*

Further evidence of high levels of consciousness about disasters in the *were v.*
conscious
pre-Columbian Andes is seen in the ideology of the people. As demonstrated by contemporary sociological research, nothing heightens awareness of threat like recent experience of a disaster. While archaeological research reveals evidence of impacts in pre-Incaic and Incaic settlements (Dupuy 1971), evidence of large-scale damage and mortality is very scant. However, several post-conquest chroniclers do comment on recurring natural disasters, such as floods, volcanic eruptions, droughts, and earthquakes, and their resultant destruction and mortality in pre-Columbian Peru, calling into question the complete effectiveness of ancient adaptations.

What is certain, however, is that the region prehistorically experienced recurring impacts of natural phenomena and Andean culture responded both materially and ideologically to this condition. Andean time, like that of the Aztecs and Mayas, was measured in four "ages," expressed by the term *pachacuti*. According to tradition, the world had experienced four creations and destructions prior to the Inca empire.

The term *pachacuti* is composed of two parts, "pacha" meaning space, earth, or world and "cuti" meaning temporal end, moment, or alternative. In Quechua syntax the second term describes or modifies the first (Cuneo-Vidal 1978: 388). Thus, *pachacuti* becomes "world moment" or, as some have interpreted it, "world reversal" in the sense of cataclysm (Bouysse-Cassagne and Bouysse 1984: 57). Something that arrives at its *pachacuti* is over, has reached its end point. Various chroniclers translated the term as a "world or time reversal."

PERUVIAN HISTORY AND THE SUBVERSION
OF INDIGENOUS ADAPTATIONS

Certainly, the coming of the Spaniards in the third decade of the sixteenth century eminently qualified as a *pachacuti*. The destructive and "epoch-ending" character of the conquest is well documented. For the Andean peoples the conquest not only meant the end of the Inca empire, but it prefigured a cataclysmic demographic collapse and distortion or destruction of their adaptive systems to their environment. Although population estimates for the Inca empire on the eve of the conquest range from 37.5 million (Dobyns 1966) to six million (Rowe 1963), a recent effort offers a figure of nine million people for the entire region (Cook 1981: 109). In his study of demographic collapse in Peru between 1520 and 1620, Cook calculates that in the first fifty years of the conquest, the population of nine million fell to one million and in the next fifty years to a mere six hundred thousand or a 98 percent decline for the entire century (Cook 1981: 114).

Although much of this demographic collapse was brought about through indigenous vulnerability to European diseases, the ruthless exploitation of the population by the Spaniards in their quest for wealth doomed millions as well (Spalding 1984). Spanish attempts to control and exploit the massive population that fell under their power began a process the forms and effects of which are still being reproduced today. Many of these attempts to control the population subverted specific indigenous adaptive strategies to their hazardous environments. There are two levels at which this subversion of adaptive strategies took place: the specific and the systemic. By specific adaptations I am referring to actual measures or procedures followed by Andean peoples to reduce vulnerability to or mitigate impact of natural hazards in the environment. By systemic adaptations I am referring to the larger adaptive capacities of the sociocultural and economic system of the Inca empire that enabled a large population to sustain itself in this extremely hazardous environment at levels of prosperity that exceeded or compared very favorably with those of Europe at the same time.

The Spaniards were both ignorant and largely uncaring about Andean notions of territoriality and settlement patterns (Larson 1988: 35). Spanish approaches to settlement location, placing towns often at the confluences of rivers where they were vulnerable to flood and landslide, flew in the face of pre-Columbian experience with the hazards of the Andean environment (Oliver-Smith 1992). The most startling case of putting people in harm's way was the settling of the city of Arequipa in 1540. As mentioned before, Arequipa is blessed with fertile soils and adequate water from seasonal rains and the Chili River. Evidently, it did not occur to the founders of the city to question why such a propitious area for settlement was so sparsely inhabited. Little did the settlers know that the nearby snow-capped peaks were not only located in one of the most seismically active regions of the Andes, but many were active volcanoes as well. In the seventeenth century alone the city of Arequipa suffered total or partial destruction by four enormous earthquakes and a volcanic eruption (Cook 1981: 171–173).

Although the Spaniards initially did not intend to transform the socioeconomic structures of the Andean community that had produced such impressive surpluses for the Inca, they did attempt to make the control over that population and the extraction of those surpluses more bureaucratically efficient through a massive program of involuntary migration and resettlement. In the 1570s it was ordered that Andean communities be concentrated or "reduced" from their dispersed settlements into new planned communities where the people could be more easily controlled.

Spanish building techniques and settlement design were employed in the *reducciones* for Indians and the new towns and cities founded by the Spaniards. Unlike the dispersed pattern of Inca towns in which houses were spaced out along long paths, Spanish settlement design favored the traditional grid pattern of perpendicular streets organized around a central plaza. The streets tended to be narrow and the houses adjoining or close together. Many houses in these Spanish towns had a second-story storage area as well, something which few domestic dwellings had in the pre-Columbian times.

While the building materials used in the pre-Columbian era—adobe, stone, and thatch—continued to be used, some dangerous changes in materials appeared. Clearly, the most dangerous of the changes was the gradual adoption of the ceramic barrel roof tile. Building techniques such as tying walls together at the corners also began to be abandoned, creating conditions for the construction of an exceptionally seismically vulnerable dwelling. Houses with untied walls constructed of adobe bricks built often two stories high and topped with an extraordinarily heavy ceramic tile roof are death traps in an earthquake.

Changes in settlement patterns compounded the danger presented by such dwellings for their inhabitants. The more densely organized Spanish settlements, with their narrow, perpendicularly arranged streets lined with one- and two-story houses of adobe and ceramic tile roofs, created a situation of extreme danger and vulnerability in a seismically active region. Narrow streets, untied walls, heavy roofs, and seismic tremors are a dangerous combination.

The disruption and decimation of the population caused by the conquest and early colonial institutions led to the abandonment of many crucial dimensions of Andean adaptation to their hazardous environment. Survival on the desert coast, for example, was intimately linked to careful management of water infrastructure and resources. The irrigation systems of the pre-Columbian coastal civilizations had developed the science of hydrological engineering to high levels, managing water resources that brought extensive areas of the desert into cultivation. In the aftermath of the conquest, after the founding of the city of Trujillo on the north coast, there was a serious decline in the maintenance of water management systems. In 1578 El Niño appeared, causing heavy rains that destroyed the deteriorated water management system, flooded fields, and destroyed homes (Cook 1981: 139).

Another important adaptation lost not long after the conquest was the institution of the *qollqas*—the storage houses. The assiduous extraction of surpluses by the Spaniards quickly precluded any amassing of stores for contingency purposes. The *qollqas*, so vital in precluding long-term privation after natural hazard impact during the Inca empire, eventually fell into disuse and general abandonment in the first century of the Spanish colony, leaving the decimated and demoralized population even more vulnerable to further catastrophe.

It is beyond the scope of this paper to describe in detail the destruction that occurred throughout the entire structure of Andean systemic adaptations, since this would require a general summation of the vastly complex history of the entire colonial and much of the republican history of the nation. However, we can point to some general patterns of erosion that contributed to the accentuation of the overall vulnerability of Andean peoples to natural hazard.

In areas favorable to mining, large-scale agriculture, or textile manufacturing, the Spanish disrupted traditional forms and relations of production, replacing them with European relations of production. However, even in those areas left relatively undisturbed by European enterprizes, the changes—though slow and imperceptible—over time fragmented and eroded basic relationships of reciprocity and cooperation that bound households and villages into larger units that sustained pre-Columbian levels of prosperity (Spalding 1984: 169). While considerable cooperative institutions still exist in some areas of the Andes today, neither their frequency nor level of activities approach those of pre-Columbian times.

The arrival of the Spaniards further signified major changes in patterns of social organization and structure in the Andes. The separation of society into social and ethnic groups was certainly an important aspect of Inca society, but such a system was elaborated with the purpose of integrating the disparate cultural groups which made up pre-Columbian Peru into all but the very highest stratum of the Inca empire. Inca social organization, however, did not result in the alienation of major groups of populations from the means of production or the mechanisms of distribution. After the conquest, however, the Spanish instituted a series of political and socioeconomic measures which ultimately deprived much of the Indian population of access to adequate land or control over most production. The final result of such policies and later measures taken under the republic was the marginalization of the Indian population, whether as serfs or marginal smallholders or sharecroppers, to the poorer lands on valley slopes and on the high plateaus. Large landholders meanwhile took up both residence and production in the better lands of valley floors.

The economic system which evolved in the colony focused on native production of value for European masters through the institution of market exchange. The shift in the balance between an economy of largely use values to one oriented toward the production of market exchange values constituted a change of profound consequences for the well-being of the Andean social whole (Larson 1988: 47). The extraction of tribute through the shift to production of commercial crops for Spaniards and later Peruvian landlords to sell in the market diverted resources out of communities and created systemic hardship and poverty in most sectors of indigenous society.

Indeed, the extractive nature of the entire system cast a mold which over the centuries since has produced an infrastructure for disunity, not integration, and, ultimately, an agricultural nation which is dependent for food on outside sources. The infrastructure of roads and communications that was imposed over the more integrative Inca system connected highland regions with the primate center of Lima but rarely or poorly with each other. After independence the coastal products of cotton and sugar, and for a brief time, guano, became the primary exports and sources of foreign exchange, and the infrastructure of the coast was developed to aid in their production and exchange. The fishing boom in the 1960s continued this coastal dominance. The highland regions, with the exception of certain mining sectors, provided few resources for foreign exchange and received little investment in either production activities or infrastructure. The political system which evolved to support those extractive institutions and devise that infrastructure in many ways mirrors them both in the flow of political power and wealth. The social system which articulated the various segments of Andean society reflected as well this concentration of power and wealth on the coast and, in particular, in Lima and was echoed in an ideology of racial and cultural bias, that historically denigrated the indigenous population and justified their poverty and rural underdevelopment.

THE GREAT PERUVIAN EARTHQUAKE OF MAY 31, 1970

Consequently, the society that confronted the major seismic event on the afternoon of May 31, 1970, was in many ways already a catastrophe. With an economy characterized by acute boom-and-bust cycles and chronic maldistribution, a rigidified productive system skewed toward foreign exchange generating commercial cash crops as opposed to much-needed foods, an infrastructure which served to articulate only a portion of the nation, a pattern of land distribution only slowly emerging from the nineteenth century, a small and vulnerable industrial sector, rates of illiteracy approaching 60 percent, chronic poverty with all the attendant features of malnutrition, infant mortality, and high morbidity rates, and a historically unstable political system alternating between "elected" coastal elites and military coups, Peru was and continues today to be in a vulnerable condition.

Thus, the worst "natural" disaster in the history of the Western hemisphere, as the earthquake of May 31, 1970, has become known, could only have happened in Peru or a nation suffering under similar conditions. The earthquake affected an area of about 83,000 square kilometers, or an area larger than Belgium and Holland combined. It claimed approximately 70,000 lives, injured 140,000 people, and destroyed or damaged more than 160,000 buildings, roughly 80 percent of the structures in the area. Over 500,000 people were left homeless, and the lives of approximately three million others were affected. Economic losses surpassed half a billion dollars. One hundred and fifty-two provincial cities and towns and over fifteen hundred peasant villages were seriously damaged or destroyed. In addition to homes, industries, public buildings, roads, railroads, bridges, and schools, electrical, water, sanitary, and communications facilities were also destroyed or seriously damaged. The forty-five seconds of the earthquake obliterated much of the fragile material infrastructure of this enormous region. While the above figures apply to the entire affected region, I will direct my attention for the most part to the intermontane valley known as the Callejón de Huaylas in the north central Andes, where I carried out extended fieldwork over a fourteen-year period between 1966 and 1980 (Oliver-Smith 1992).

The high mortality rates in the callejon and to some extent elsewhere in the impact zone were due largely to three major factors: settlement location,

settlement plan, and building techniques and materials. Avalanches loosened by
the earthquake tremors from Andean peaks careened down the canyons of
rivers to obliterate several villages and cities located in these natural channels.
The worst of these avalanches descended from Mount Huascarán, Peru's
tallest mountain at almost twenty-three thousand feet, upon the provincial
capital of Yungay, burying the city and roughly forty-five hundred of its five
thousand inhabitants (Oliver-Smith 1992). The second factor, settlement
planning, combined with the third factor, building techniques and materials,
to produce lethal destruction in town and city streets. When the earthquake
with its severe lateral movement hit, the untied exterior walls of buildings
under the excessive weight of tile roofs fell outward into the narrow streets,
burying people who attempted to escape, while the heavy roofs fell into the
house upon those who remained within. Highland cities and towns entombed
their inhabitants. In the departmental capital of Huaraz, almost a third of the
population, some ten thousand people, lost their lives in this fashion.

The lifeline systems of water, electricity, and medical care were all devastated by the disaster. The valley's urban areas were only partially electrified
before the disaster, powered by the hydroelectric plant located at its northern
extreme in the Cañon del Pato. The rural majority had no electrical power
and no immediate prospect of receiving any. Interestingly, electricity from the
Cañon del Pato had been lighting and powering most highland provincial
capitals as well as the coastal city of Trujillo for some time. Towns and villages that possessed antiquated gasoline generators had to activate them, or
backup systems had to be brought in. Most people who had received electric
power in the callejon, however, remained without it for months, even years in
some cases.

Urban water systems in the callejon were haphazard affairs at best, and
most of them were unable to supply uncontaminated potable water in part
because the ceramic pipes in their shallow trenches or occasionally even
aboveground were vulnerable to impacts. The earthquake totally destroyed
these marginally functional systems, and it took weeks and in some cases
months before water service, such as it was, could be restored.

The pre-disaster health care system in the callejon was largely accessible
only to the urban middle classes and elites, and even then was not adequate
for anything beyond routine maladies. Although hospitals existed in all of the
major towns, they were all seriously underequipped and undermaintained. All
of the hospitals were rendered inoperative by the quake, and ultimately most
emergency medical care as well as longer-term health concerns, such as epi-
demics, had to be met from outside resources.

The fragile infrastructure of roads, railroads, airports, and communication was completely incapacitated by the quake. The rails of the one railroad
system leading into the Callejón de Huaylas were twisted beyond repair by

fissioning and swelling of the earth's surface. They have not been replaced yet, almost thirty years later. All the roads into the callejon were unpaved, and the tremors of the quakes literally dissolved their foundations. Many of them, including the two main routes into the valley, slid off their steep mountain perches, leaving much of the disaster area without access or escape routes for varying periods of time. One of the small airstrips was buried under debris from the avalanche that buried Yungay. The other had to be lengthened before it could accommodate cargo planes bringing in assistance. Indeed, the only airport in the nation capable of receiving the aircraft carrying the enormous outpouring of international aid was Lima's, which created bottlenecks so serious that huge amounts of materials stagnated there in some cases for years after the tragedy.

The bottlenecks in Lima were the symptom of a problem characterizing societies dominated by a primate city through which all goods traditionally flowed. Not only did all earthquake assistance flowing inward have to pass through Lima, but all decisions made regarding the stricken region were vested in a ministry-level organization created for that purpose and at first located in Lima (see Doughty, this volume, chapter 12). The fact that the principal agency in charge of relief and reconstruction was located entirely outside of the disaster zone resulted in a byzantine bureaucratic design and a bewildering division of responsibilities according to type of aid and scope of responsibility, seriously hampering delivery (Doughty 1988: 50). Such was the result of this elaborate bureaucratic structuring that even the president on visiting the disaster zone a year after had to admit that "virtually nothing had been done" for the survivors.

CONCLUSION

The early years of the decade of the 1970s were hard years for the survivors of the earthquake as they struggled to overcome their enormous losses and to rebuild their towns and villages. Despite the fact that aid and assistance have eventually led to some reconstruction, it is mostly cities that have been rebuilt, although roads and electrical and water services are better than they were before the earthquake. Little aid actually reached or has impacted the rural majority. They had to rebuild themselves. Indeed, the maldistribution of aid and the inefficiency of aid agencies over several years following the tragedy gave rise to the saying, "First the earthquake, then the disaster." There is as much truth as there is irony in this statement. Although the statement was clearly directed at the delivery of aid, it implicitly constitutes a mordant criticism of the structure of their society. The survivors saw their society as "disastrous" and the earthquake was just that, an earthquake, indeed a terrifying dimension of their known environment, but one that to a greater or lesser degree they had experienced before and would experience again.

In the last analysis, much of the devastation and misery caused by the May 31, 1970, earthquake in Peru was a product of the historical processes set in motion at the time of the conquest. These processes ultimately subverted the generally effective adaptations to the many environmental hazards worked out by the peoples and cultures of the Andes over the ten thousand years of human residence in the region. Thus, the accentuated vulnerability that the region exhibited and still exhibits is a socially created phenomena, a historical product brought into being by identifiable forces. Furthermore, although the viable adaptations developed by Andean peoples have been subverted, they should not be discounted as fruitful sources for vulnerability reduction and hazard mitigation measures for the future. Peru and other nations in the developing world are not empty vessels to be simply filled with Western technical information on hazard mitigation. As this brief exploration of hazards in the Andes reveals, third-world cultures developed valuable knowledge on hazards which, although largely subverted by the forces of colonialism, may yet, through careful research and combination with global technical expertise, contribute to the reduction of vulnerability and destruction in developing nations.

NOTE

1. A version of this chapter appeared in *Disasters, Development and Environment*, edited by Ann Varley and published in 1994 by John Wiley & Sons Ltd., and is published here with their permission.

BIBLIOGRAPHY

Bouysse-Cassagne, T., and P. Bouysse. 1984. "Volcan indien, volcan chretien a propos de l'eruption du Huaynaputina en l'an 1600 (Perou Meridional)." *Journal de la Societe des Americanistes* N.S. 70–71: 43–68.

Caviedes, C. 1981. "Natural Hazards in Latin America: A Survey and Discussion," in Tom L. Martinson and Gary S. Elbow (eds.), *Geographic Research on Latin America: Benchmark 1980.* Conference of Latin Americanist Geographers, 8: 280–294, Muncie, IN: Ball State University.

Cook, N. 1981. *Demographic Collapse: Indian Peru, 1520–1620.* Cambridge: Cambridge University Press.

Cuneo-Vidal, R. 1978. *Enciclopedia incaica.* Lima: Grafica Morson S.A.

Dobyns, H. 1966. "Estimating Aboriginal American Population: An Appraisal of Techniques with a New Hemispheric Estimate." *Current Anthropology* 7: 395–449.

Doughty, P. L. 1988. "Decades of Disaster: Promise and Performance in the Callejon de Huaylas, Peru," in Anthony Oliver-Smith (ed.), *Natural Disasters and Cultural Responses*. Studies in Third World Societies, No. 36: pp. 35–80. Williamsburg, VA: College of William and Mary.

Dupuy, D. 1971. *Bajo el signo del terremoto*. Lima: Ediciones Paisa.

Gasparini, G., and L. Margolies. 1980. *Inca Architecture*. Bloomington: Indiana University Press.

Giesecke, A., and E. Silgado. 1981. *Terremotos en el Peru*. Lima: Ediciones Richkay Peru.

Hewitt, K. (ed.). 1983. *Interpretations of Calamity*. Boston: Allen & Unwin.

Hyslop, J. 1990. *Inca Settlement Planning*. Austin: University of Texas Press.

Kolata, A. 1989. *La Tecnologia y organizacion de la produccion, agricola en el estado Tiwanaco*. La Paz: Proyecto Wilajawira, Universidad de Chicago, Instituto Nacional de Arqueologia de Bolivia.

Larson, B. 1988. *Colonialism and Agrarian Transformation in Bolivia*. Princeton: Princeton University Press.

Moseley, M., R. Feldman, and C. Ortloff. 1981. "Living with Crises: Human Perception of Process and Time," in M. H. Nitecki (ed.), *Biotic Crises in Ecological and Evolutionary Time*, pp. 231–267. Princeton: Princeton University Press.

Murra, J. 1972. "El Control vertical de un maximo de pisos ecologicos en la economia de las sociedades andinas," in I. Ortiz de Zuniga (visitador), *Visita de la provincia de Leon de Huanuco*. Tomo II, Huanuco: Universidad Hermilio Valdizan.

———. 1980. *La Organizacion economica del estado inca*. Mexico: Siglo Veintiuno.

Oliver-Smith, A. 1992. *The Martyred City: Death and Rebirth in the Andes*. Prospect Heights, IL: Waveland Press.

Rowe, J. 1963. "Inca Culture at the Time of the Conquest," in J. H. Steward (ed.), *Handbook of South American Indians*, pp. 183–410. New York: Cooper Square Publishers, Inc.

Spalding, K. 1984. *Huarochiri: An Andean Society under Inca and Spanish Rule*. Stanford: Stanford University Press.

Winterhalder, B., and R. Thomas. 1978. *Geoecology of Southern Highland Peru*. Occasional Paper #27. Boulder: Institute of Artic and Alpine Research, University of Colorado.

5

CONSTRUCTING VULNERABILITY IN THE FIRST WORLD: THE NORTHRIDGE EARTHQUAKE IN SOUTHERN CALIFORNIA, 1994[1]

ROBERT BOLIN

Arizona State University

and

LOIS STANFORD

New Mexico State University

INTRODUCTION: EXAMINING VULNERABILITY

THIS CHAPTER EXAMINES THE POLITICAL AND ECONOMIC CONSTRUCTION OF vulnerability, applying insights gained from third-world research to a first-world setting. Drawing on Wisner (1993) and Cannon (1994), a framework is developed that identifies factors involved in the production of hazard vulnerability in the United States. The general framework is used to highlight vulnerability issues in two Southern Californian communities following an earthquake of magnitude 6.7 on the Richter scale in Northridge in 1994. The chapter traces the historical, economic, and political construction of vulnerability in the towns of Fillmore and Piru in Ventura County and how these have been revealed in recovery issues following the temblor. As anthropological research in the third world has documented (Oliver-Smith 1996: 314–317), political and economic practices create "at risk" populations through systematic processes of marginalization and exclusion (Blaikie et al. 1994). Thus, disasters are seen as compounding the struggles that are part of many people's daily lives (Watts 1991). In examining the sources of hazard vulnerability, issues regarding the distribution of social power and its particular expression in control over property, politics, and ideologies are central

(Wisner 1993). Instead of studying disasters as resulting from the physical extremes of nature, vulnerability analysis considers social and economic factors that make people and their living conditions secure or unsafe in the face of environmental hazards. Disasters are seen to occur at the interface of vulnerable people and physical hazards—in this sense there are no "natural" disasters (Blaikie et al. 1994; Hewitt 1983; Maskrey 1993).

Defining vulnerability in terms of people's capacity to avoid, cope with, and recover from disasters draws attention to their living conditions, social and economic resources, livelihood patterns, and social power. While physical exposure to risk is a necessary element in vulnerability, it is people's lack of capacities that transform an environmental hazard into a disaster. People's capacities are socially produced and reflect the kinds of resources they can mobilize in disasters. Critical resources include such factors as community preparedness and the abilities of political structures to organize and provide resources during calamities. Vulnerability is complicated by the multiple and intersecting factors that produce risks in specific social formations under varying political and economic conditions. Given that much vulnerability analysis has focused on third-world countries, the concept is linked to poverty and developmental processes that produce deepening social inequalities in a given country (Hewitt 1997). Structured by class, race, ethnicity, and gender, poverty is seen as the specific expression of general political and economic processes that unequally allocate resources and risks.

Recent discussions in the disaster literature have presented schematic frameworks of the major elements and internal relations of vulnerability (Blaikie et al. 1994; Cannon 1994; Hewitt 1997; Wisner 1993). Focusing on the specific sources and forms of vulnerability requires examining people's coping capacities in relation to resource availability. Resources comprise a variety of material and social assets, including finances, information, social support networks, income opportunities, legal rights, and political power. Large and destructive disasters can alter resource availability and governments' allocative schemes in the wake of disasters. Access to resources lies at the heart of Wisner's analysis, which identifies three major components of vulnerability (1993: 21). Livelihood vulnerability reflects people's ability to gain resources through employment or subsistence activities. Those households with higher incomes and secure employment may be said to have resilient—as opposed to vulnerable—livelihoods. People's ability to resume their livelihoods following a disaster varies considerably and reflects the productive regime and social relations of production at a given site. Self-protection and social protection comprise the two other components of vulnerability in Wisner's analysis. These address issues of preparedness and hazard mitigation at both the household and larger spatial levels, including neighborhood, city, region, and/or society (Wisner 1993: 19–21). Self-protection includes aspects of people's hazard exposure in their housing and work sites as well as socioeconomic factors, cultural traditions, and local technical knowledge about how and where to build. Social protection involves the organizational and regulatory realm, including technical knowledge of hazards, warning systems, building code regulations, and land use regulations. State- and local-level organizations designed to manage emergencies and assist in disaster response can be instrumental in social protection (Bolin and Stanford 1998).

By examining political factors, vulnerability analysis also addresses the state's role in both social protection and recovery following disasters. Third-world studies often implicate state practices in increasing vulnerability of populations by embracing development schemes that force rural poor onto marginal lands, deepening their poverty while benefiting the already wealthy ruling class (Blaikie and Brookfield 1987; Escobar 1996). Other studies document cases of politically created famines, exposure of populations to pervasive hazards, discriminatory practices in targeting disaster recovery assistance, and state promotion of dominant-class interests in disaster relief (Hendrie 1997; Maskrey 1993; Oliver-Smith 1986; Waterstone 1992). Researchers differ in their analyses of the state: Some have emphasized the role state planning plays in reducing risks (Burton et al. 1993), while others have documented how state policies can create or exacerbate conditions of social vulnerability (Bolin with Stanford 1998; Hewitt 1983).

ANALYZING VULNERABILITY IN THE UNITED STATES

U.S. researchers have long recognized the presence of particular groups "at risk" to disasters. These include low-income households, ethnic minorities, elders, and female-headed households, among others (Bolin 1994a; Peacock et al. 1997). Vulnerability analysis goes beyond categorizing at-risk groups by investigating the sociohistorical forces that create and shape the risks different groups face. In the United States, well-organized and well-funded disaster response systems allow avoiding or coping with disasters in ways not available to many poor countries of the third world. Yet, despite high levels of aggregate wealth in the United States, sharp social inequalities persist, exacerbated by neoliberal economic policies and economic restructuring that are intensifying income polarization (Harvey 1996). Working in combination with state policies, economic forces produce inequalities that marginalize groups in both wealthy and poor countries. It is well documented that environmental risks and disaster effects in the United States are distributed unequally by class, race, ethnicity, gender, and age (Bolin and Bolton 1986; Morrow and Enarson 1996; Wisner 1993; Davis 1998).

In both the first and third world, marginalization processes create vulnerability by placing specific groups in perilous positions between the inequitable conditions of political and economic systems on the one hand and environmental risks on the other (Cannon 1994: 15). The poor often live in less safe structures that are more likely to be damaged or destroyed by physical hazards. However, spatial and physical aspects of vulnerability tend to be much more pronounced in the third world, where the poor are often forced to live and work in persistently hazardous areas (Hewitt 1997). In contrast, socially and economically marginalized U. S. populations do not necessarily live in areas at greatest risk from natural hazards. Indeed, the wealthy may choose to live in physically hazardous settings, such as in palatial homes perched precariously on the firestorm- and earthquake-ravaged California hillsides (Davis 1998).

In the first world, vulnerability is revealed in people's inabilities to cope with losses and their lack of access to recovery assistance. This dimension of vulnerability is again usually associated with class, ethnicity, and/or gender (Bolin and Stanford 1998; Fothergill 1996). While wealthy households may suffer losses in a hazard event, their property insurance, assets, financial credit, and stable employment generally secure them against the destitution that befalls a poor family exposed to the same event. Although the middle class and the wealthy generally experience greater absolute disaster losses in dollar terms than do the poor in U.S. disasters, in relative terms, the poor generally lose a larger percentage of their material assets and suffer more lasting negative effects (Bolin 1994a).

In the United States, the state assumes an active role in assisting disaster victims, although the nature and degree of financial assistance varies (Bolin 1994b). Even in the United States, disaster relief is not uniform, nor does it benefit all who need it. Research on recent U.S. disaster documents racial and ethnic discrimination in relief aid (Bolin and Stanford 1991; Peacock et al. 1997; Schulte 1991). Federal relief programs traditionally privilege middle-class home owners over renters and the marginally housed, revealing a persistent (if unintended) class preference (Comerio et al. 1996; Wallrich 1996). Despite these biases, the federal and state governments currently provide extensive social protection services and disaster response capabilities. Under the aegis of the Federal Emergency Management Agency (FEMA), a number of short-term assistance programs are available (see Bolin and Stanford 1998). Such programs are designed to buffer the financial shocks a household may experience in a disaster, although the programs are *not* intended to provide 100-percent coverage of all losses. A given household's vulnerability (or resilience) in the face of environmental hazards will be a result of a cluster of factors (class, race, gender, age, etc.) that affect their coping capacities in the context of varying levels of social protection against hazards (Cannon 1994; Hewitt 1997).

RESEARCHING VULNERABILITY

The research reported here focused on households which existing research (e.g., Bolin and Bolton 1986) suggested would have difficulty in coping with disaster; these included elders, Latinos, immigrants, and low-income victims generally. We selected the case study approach as the most appropriate for examining social action patterns and practices over time within a community context (Hamel 1993). In so doing, we followed an established tradition in both anthropology and sociology, reflecting concerns about capturing the complexity and dynamics of social relations (Oliver-Smith 1996).

We conducted documentary research by reviewing newspapers' collections and California Office of Emergency Services (OES) action reports to construct community narratives. Organized chronologically, these materials provided a descriptive record of each community's experiences in the two years following the main shock. Additional data were gathered through a series of interviews with FEMA and OES representatives, county and city agencies, as well as leaders in a variety of non government organizations (NGOs) and community-based organizations (CBOs). Additional interviews with disaster victims focused on households that informants identified as having difficulties obtaining adequate resources for rebuilding. All interviews were taped and later transcribed for content analysis. Through the triangulation of the documentary record, agency interviews, and personal narratives, we identified critical issues in the first two years of the recovery process. Understanding the historical sources of vulnerability within a local context required examination of the factors that created insecure livelihoods and unsafe structures. Additional research was conducted using published historical material and government publications. Further historical insights were gained through interviews with key informants familiar with the history of housing problems and social inequality in Ventura County. The resulting historical narrative assisted in grounding the disaster in the broader historical context in the study communities.

A FRAMEWORK FOR VULNERABILITY ANALYSIS

Based on both existing "models" of vulnerability and factors that appear important in the U.S. disasters, an outline of a theory of vulnerability was developed that identified factors implicated in the production of first-world disasters (Figure 1). Drawn from the authors' book-length treatment of Northridge (Bolin with Stanford 1998), the framework posits a progression of factors that create households vulnerable to environmental hazards. It is the intersection of vulnerable people and physical hazards that produces disaster, as Figure 1 attempts to capture schematically. Identifying general cate-

FIGURE 1. *Progression of factors contributing to vulnerability.*

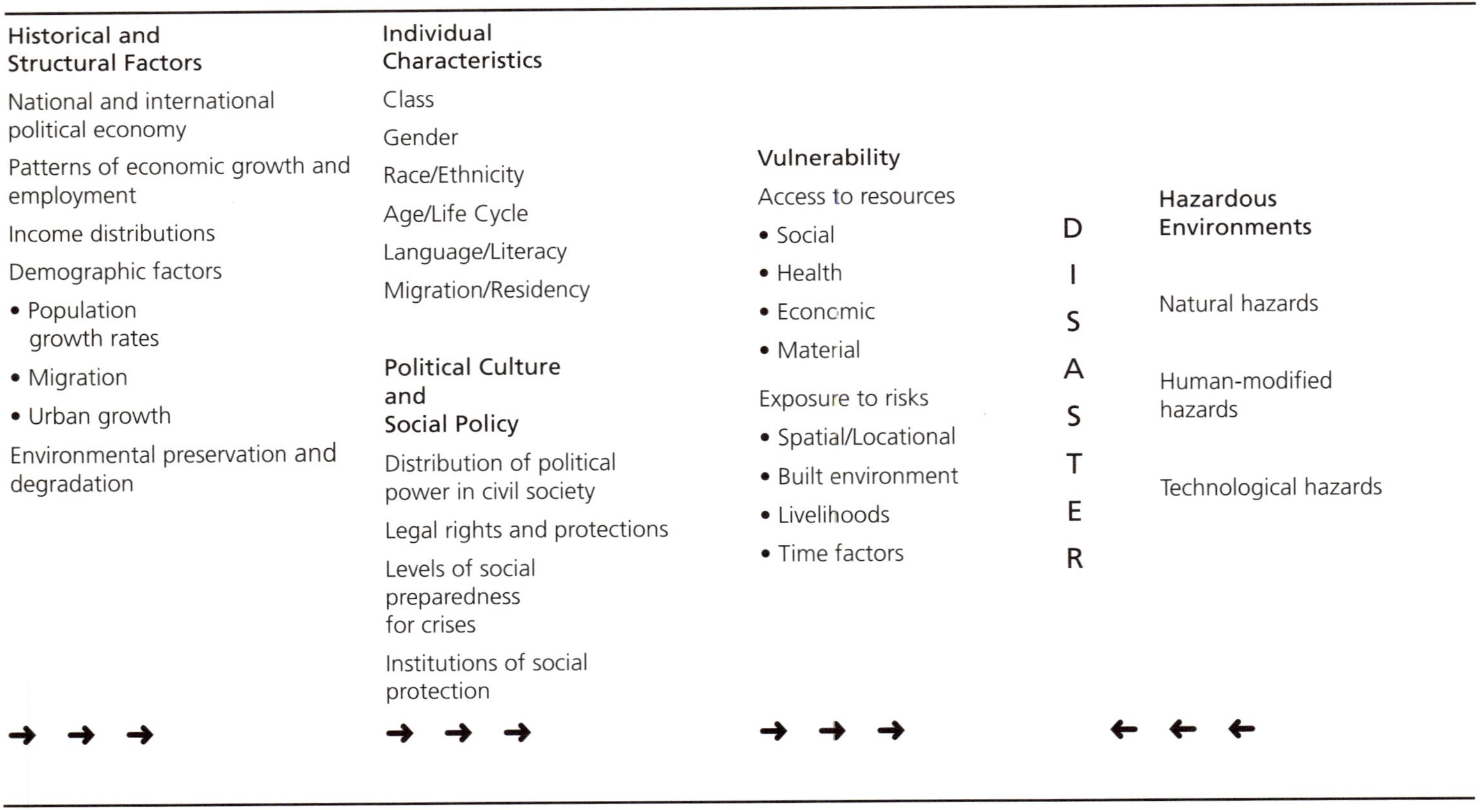

Historical and Structural Factors

National and international political economy

Patterns of economic growth and employment

Income distributions

Demographic factors
- Population growth rates
- Migration
- Urban growth

Environmental preservation and degradation

↑ ↑ ↑

Individual Characteristics

Class

Gender

Race/Ethnicity

Age/Life Cycle

Language/Literacy

Migration/Residency

Political Culture and Social Policy

Distribution of political power in civil society

Legal rights and protections

Levels of social preparedness for crises

Institutions of social protection

↑ ↑ ↑

Vulnerability

Access to resources
- Social
- Health
- Economic
- Material

Exposure to risks
- Spatial/Locational
- Built environment
- Livelihoods
- Time factors

↑ ↑ ↑

D I S A S T E R

Hazardous Environments

Natural hazards

Human-modified hazards

Technological hazards

↓ ↓ ↓

gories associated with vulnerability provides the basis for investigating the specific ways that vulnerability was manifested in Fillmore and Piru (see below).

As demonstrated in numerous studies, social class position comprises a central component of vulnerability, especially when combined with other marginalization factors (Blaikie et al. 1994). Class is generally a marker of access to resources and can include type and stability of employment, income, savings, and education levels. Low-income households may lack the means to prepare for hazardous environments and likewise lack necessary financial resources to recover after disaster. Residential tenure represents an important class-related factor. Renters are dependent on landlords' decisions about rents, security, and building safety standards. Following a U.S. disaster, renters are eligible for different sorts of government assistance from home owners. Home owners generally receive more generous assistance, but in turn shoulder higher liabilities. Home owners may be required to obtain a loan to repair a damaged home, thus incurring long-term indebtedness (Bolin 1994b). Low-income home owners may be in a precarious position after earthquakes if they can neither qualify for reconstruction loans nor afford to pay the difference between minimal FEMA assistance and the actual costs of rebuilding.

Second, while gender has received relatively little attention in the first-world disaster literature (Fothergill 1996; Morrow and Enarson 1996), gender (and gender-based inequality) must be understood as a central feature of social life and a salient factor in understanding vulnerability (Bolin et al. 1998). Only recently have researchers begun to investigate the effects of poverty among woman-headed households on their vulnerability to hazards and the types of obstacles confronted in recovery. Gender analysis must also be contextualized within class, ethnicity, and age, thus combining factors that may significantly disadvantage some households in disaster (Enarson and Morrow 1998).

Third, in multiethnic societies of the first world, race/ethnicity may be linked to the material losses experienced and to differential abilities to acquire resources for recovery. The effects of race/ethnicity in disaster have been documented in numerous U.S. disasters (Bolin and Bolton 1986; Bolin and Stanford 1991; Schulte 1991) and have received extensive discussion in recent work on Hurricane Andrew in Florida (Peacock et al. 1997). Vulnerability analysis calls attention to the social construction of ethnicity, how it is imbricated in class factors, and how it articulates with various environmental risks.

Fourth, a person's age or the age composition of a household has implications for vulnerability. Research indicates that households of the elderly may be physically vulnerable since members may lack the physical ability to avoid rapid-onset disasters or the mobility to acquire recovery resources (Bolin and

Klenow 1988; Eldar 1992). In some instances elders are overrepresented among the casualties of disaster due to frailty and being housebound (Hewitt 1997). Social class is implicated here, as many older householders are retired wage-earners who have reduced incomes, live on pensions, and have limited access to other resources (Phillips 1993), thus complicating potentially costly disaster recovery. In the United States, cuts in entitlement programs for older persons, including health care benefits and cost-of-living adjustments in social security pensions, further marginalize lower-income elder households.

Fifth, language and literacy comprise a potential element in household vulnerability. While this category intersects with ethnicity, as a discrete dimension it has particular relevance, specifically when language and literacy capabilities present barriers to information and resources in disaster (Subervi-Velez et al. 1992). In response to earlier criticisms about failure to serve non-English speakers, FEMA has begun to provide translation services and assistance application forms in a variety of languages. While translation services are important, they do not overcome the problem of literacy of victims. Those familiar with the language of the "bureaucratic culture" in the United States may be very differently culturally "equipped" for dealing with government agencies from recent immigrants, and that familiarity can affect acquisition of needed resources (Bolin and Stanford 1991; Schulte 1991).

Sixth, the issue of migration and/or residency is especially important in U.S. disasters. The Los Angeles area has been the destination of choice for millions of Asian and Latino immigrants over the last two decades (Davis 1998). Within immigrant groups, of course, there is much diversity and social division based on ethnicity, class, language skills, and gender. Factors such as the ongoing economic restructuring in the United States, changes in immigration policy, and continued flow of immigrant workers have created significant stratification within the immigrant populations. Recent immigrants have experienced a significant rupture with a former way of life and must learn anew how to negotiate their way through everyday life in their new community. Changing federal eligibility rules regarding disaster assistance for noncitizens has dramatically increased the significance of immigration status in disaster recovery.

Finally, political ideologies and state practices (see Figure 1) can produce varying levels of social protection (Cannon 1994). Social protection from hazards can be derived from a variety of factors, including hazard warning systems, land use planning, building codes, emergency preparedness, and trained disaster response and recovery organizations. (It is well recognized that Los Angeles is perhaps better prepared than any other U.S. city to manage "normal disasters" [Bolin with Stanford 1998].) Social protection against hazards is manifested in a complex of local, state, and national organizations involved in emergency preparedness and disaster response. Expenditures through FEMA alone are typically measured in the billions of dollars per year and reflect both the property losses of major disasters and the scope of programs offered to victims (FEMA 1995).

Most factors contributing to vulnerability in the first world outlined here are quite similar to those in third-world contexts: class, gender, race/ethnicity, and age/life cycle. In addition, immigrant status and literacy can figure prominently in some U.S. disasters. State-sponsored social protection programs generally play a much larger role in mitigating the effects of disaster in wealthy countries in contrast to poorer countries. No one characteristic is intrinsically a factor in the production of vulnerability to environmental risks. The factors acquire salience only within the different histories of particular places in combination with ongoing features of current political culture and social policies.

The framework calls attention to political and economic factors that shape the particular forms vulnerability may take in the face of geophysical hazards. It highlights both political culture and social policies that affect vulnerability through social protection measures. Political culture can intensify marginalization through the scapegoating of specific groups or by denying public resources to certain groups (e.g., "illegal" immigrants). Hewitt (1997: 154) uses the term "positive disadvantaging" to refer to government actions and social practices that take away people's options and increase the risks they face. But the state can also promote social policies and practices that assist people in meeting their needs or in preparing for environmental disasters. The next section begins a discussion of the research communities using categories identified in Figure 1.

VULNERABILITY IN FILLMORE AND PIRU

Despite its proximity to the vast conurbation of Los Angeles, much of Ventura County remains devoted to open space and agriculture—although it is also host to growing commuter bedroom communities. As a ranching and agricultural area, its roots can be traced to Spanish colonization in 1782, when the Mission San Buenaventura (now the city of Ventura) was established. Cattle ranching and farming were the dominant productive regimes into the early nineteenth century. By the late 1800s, consonant with growth in Los Angeles, Ventura County witnessed an influx of European merchants, Chinese workers, oil speculators, railroad investors, and North American and European farmers, who overwhelmed the small, rural populations of Spanish and Mexican merchants and ranchers. Ethnic differences, land disputes, transformation of the agricultural environment, and the establishment of new communities resulted and set the stage for the growth and development of the two communities examined here by early in the twentieth century. Fillmore was founded as a railroad freight stop in 1887 and Piru was founded the following year on the site of a former Spanish rancho. Development in Ventura

County during the late nineteenth century and most of the twentieth century has pitted land speculators and developers against farmers and ranchers. Most urban growth in the county has been concentrated along the coast and in communities on the county boundary with Los Angeles County. The Santa Clara river valley remained a redoubt of small farms and slowly growing communities, including Fillmore and Piru.

Early-twentieth-century developments shaped the trajectory of these two small communities. In the Santa Clara river valley, agriculture continued to be the main industry, largely concentrated in labor-intensive perennial crops. A force of migrant and resident laborers was used to produce and process these crops, fostering the growth of an ethnically diverse population of Chinese, Japanese, and Mexicans. By 1911, the Limoneira Company operated one of the world's largest citrus ranches (one thousand hectares) in the Santa Clara valley and used mostly Japanese labor. After the 1924 Immigration Act, which restricted Japanese immigration, Limoneira began to meet its labor needs through the recruitment of Mexican immigrant families. By the 1920s, Ventura County was one of the national leaders in citrus production and provided permanent housing and continuous work to Mexican immigrant families (McBane 1995: 76–80).

The 1930s saw agricultural operations expanding in the region, with growers generally supplying housing for a growing Mexican farmworker population. The largest agricultural enterprises, such as La Limoneira and Rancho Sespe, maintained entire communities, with company stores, schools, and recreational centers. In 1954, new highways linked Los Angeles to Camarillo, west of Simi valley (Figure 2). The construction of the Ventura freeway (US 101) provided Los Angeles workers with ready access to communities in Ventura County. With this highway link, rural communities traditionally based in agriculture began to be transformed into bedroom communities on the edge of an expanding Los Angeles. Population increases were concentrated in communities along the Ventura freeway, including Thousand Oaks and Camarillo. Situated further afield from Los Angeles's grasp in the Santa Clara river valley, Fillmore and Piru continued to grow slowly. To control growth in Ventura County, authorities introduced regulations and zoning to protect disappearing farmland and mitigate growing water shortages. Under the California Land Conservation Act of 1965 farmers in Ventura County were given property tax breaks if their land remained in agricultural production. Ventura County zoning ordinances provided exemptions for farmworker housing on agricultural land, thus providing one of the few sources of housing for low-income workers.

In the Santa Clara valley, farmers encouraged the permanent settlement of former migrant workers under Public Law 414 (Immigration and Nation-

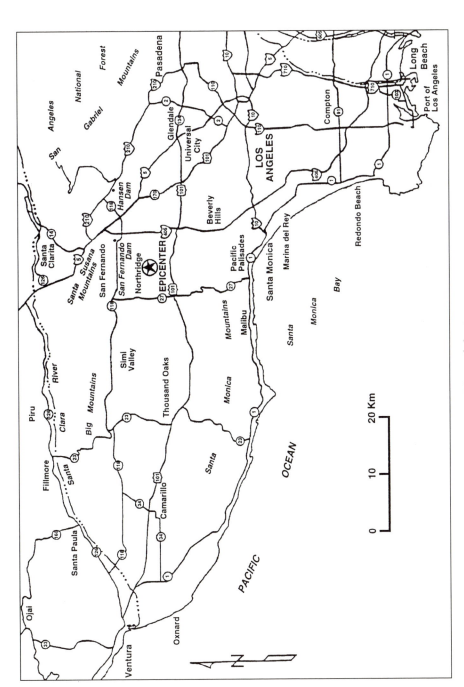

FIGURE 2. Map of the impact zone.

ality Act). Former seasonal migrants were able to obtain legal residence and to establish homes in the region. Within this agricultural context, the rural Santa Clara valley developed a range of different types of agricultural produces, including corporate agribusiness, full-time family farmers, and absentee farmers with full-time farm managers. The complexity of ownership patterns and farm sizes hindered the development of a system rigidly monopolized by large agricultural companies, as is more characteristic of the San Joaquin valley in central California (Palerm 1991).

A corresponding diversity emerged within the farm labor force, now comprised of U.S. workers, primarily Mexican Americans, on the one hand, and documented and undocumented Mexican laborers, on the other. Growers in the region undermined unionizing efforts in the 1970s and 1980s by hiring Mexicans at lower wages than domestic workers. During the 1970s, agriculture continued to shift toward high-value, labor-intensive crops. Reflecting the increased labor demand, county farmworker numbers grew to an estimated fifteen thousand workers employed in agriculture in 1981 (Bee 1984: 3). As a result, affordable housing became a growing problem for farmworkers. Addressing affordable housing problems remains a sensitive political issue throughout Ventura County, especially in Fillmore (Bolin and Stanford 1998).

CONTRIBUTING FACTORS IN HAZARD VULNERABILITY

Given the continuing centrality of agriculture, both Fillmore and Piru have grown slowly, experiencing none of the dramatic growth of northern Los Angeles County, a few kilometers to their east. In 1950, Fillmore had a popu-

TABLE 1. *Selected 1990 census information for Fillmore and Piru, Ventura County, California.*

1990	Ventura County	LA County	Fillmore	Piru
Population	669,016	8,863,164	12,001	1,148
Median Household Income	$45,612	$34,965	$33,482	$27,000
Percent in Poverty	7.3	15.1	13.2	12.0
Percent Latino	26	37	59	76
Percent Housing Owner Occupied	53	39	48	36
Percent Housing Built since 1960	79	49	65	28
# of Occupied Housing Units	228,478	3,163,343	3,521	399

lation of 3,884, growing to 9,000 in 1980 and 12,098 by 1991. Of these inhabitants, in the 1990 census 58 percent identified themselves as Hispanic. By 1980 farmworkers comprised 19.3 percent of all workers residing in Fillmore; of these, most lived permanently in Fillmore (City of Fillmore 1992: 3–18). In contrast to a county median income of $45,000, the Fillmore median household income is low, at $33,500 per year, and 13 percent of the population lives below the official poverty line.

Neighboring Piru is an unincorporated community and remains under the political wing of the Ventura County administration. It is a small rural village on the far eastern edge of the county. Population has grown slowly from 850 in 1950, to 890 in 1960, to approximately 1,148 residents by 1990. Of these inhabitants, more than 75 percent self-identified as Hispanic in the 1990 census. The median household income is even lower than in Fillmore, at $27,000 per year, and approximately 12 percent live below the official poverty line. In Piru, 64 percent of the residences are rented and most are small, old, wood-frame structures. In both Fillmore and Piru, population figures are official census estimates and do not include the numerous undocumented residents and temporary farmworkers who are typically in the area. Both communities are under pressure from developers to expand their housing stock and convert agricultural land into housing subdivisions, as is being done at a rapid clip in Santa Clarita, across the Los Angeles County line.

As outlined in Figure 1, a number of factors must be considered to understand the particular contours of vulnerability in the two communities. Social class and its determining effects on material living conditions are the primary factor. In general terms, much of the Los Angeles metropolitan region, including Ventura County, suffers from a growing shortage of affordable housing for low-income households (Bolin with Stanford 1998). The situation is pronounced in Ventura County and, as noted above, predates the earthquake by decades. The affordable housing situation for farmworkers and other low-income residents was further exacerbated by the temblor's destruction of 375 moderate- to low-income housing units. The majority of lower-income households has been forced to rely on rental housing in areas where little rental housing is available. As a result, two or more households frequently shared single-family residences to share rents, a fact that subsequently complicated FEMA assistance, as FEMA traditionally provides aid to only one family per residential unit. While the city of Fillmore, well before the earthquake, recognized the need for constructing more affordable housing, more than 90 percent of new home construction in Fillmore in the early 1990s was for above-median-income households. The city embraced a contradictory position of acknowledging the need for low-income housing while expanding housing opportunities for higher-income households (Bolin and Stanford 1998).

This policy incoherence has exasperated some community groups who described Fillmore as a city in "denial," dependent on farmworkers as an agricultural labor force yet unwilling to include housing for them in the community. The persistence of these small, rural communities is tied to the economic viability of labor-intensive agriculture. Community survival is necessarily linked to housing for agricultural workers. In response to questions about farmworker housing, one authority commented:

> I think we have to recognize that if we hold agriculture to be dear and valuable, then we have to extend to the worker a more decent, sanitary place to live and a higher value for his service which translates to a higher income. That's the answer. If we really believe in agriculture, then we have to recognize that the people who work it are going to live here and they can't disappear between 6:00 P.M. and 5:00 A.M. God didn't set it up that way. We have to deal with humans, and the day that we make that decision, we're on the right path. As long as we have cheap labor, and people here are satisfied that the problem is the labor force, not the user of the labor force. . . . Well, if they can continue to tag the problem on the worker, why does the farmer have to concern himself?

Prior to the earthquake, housing prices were lower in Fillmore and Piru than across most of Ventura County with its near $250,000 median. While a median price of $189,000 is hardly cheap, the comparatively less expensive housing in the two communities has resulted in a sizable group of low-income home owners. However, these owners often possess houses that are in relatively poor condition and sometimes do not meet housing code standards. These houses may be especially susceptible to earthquake damage if exposed to even moderate ground shaking. Furthermore, few of these households have earthquake insurance, thus placing them at further risk of unrecoverable losses, a condition that eventuated with the Northridge main shock.

Income and housing problems also relate to gender as a marker of vulnerability. In general terms, female-headed households are overrepresented among those households living in poverty. This is a general feature of poverty in the United States, where more than one-third of all such households live below the official poverty line (U.S. Bureau of the Census 1992). Thus, issues pertaining to gender are cross-cut by social class and age. The poverty rate of female headed households in these communities is high; in Piru, 19 percent of female-headed households were below the poverty line, compared to 16 percent in Fillmore. According to 1990 census data for the communities, these rates double to triple for female-headed households with children under the age of five. In addition, in agricultural communities female farmworkers are consistently paid lower wages and are more likely than male farmworkers to have part-time or seasonal employment (Vaupel 1992). Thus, female farmworkers are specifically disadvantaged within a class that is generally low-income and marginally housed. In Ventura County, with its tight housing market, gender in itself is a less significant factor in vulnerability than are the social class and income factors attached to gender.

The salience of race/ethnicity to vulnerability relates to the extent of discrimination and exclusion of ethnic minorities in economic and social life. In Ventura County, the economic and social differentiation within the Mexican-descent population, in conjunction with persistent patterns of Anglo discrimination in politics, housing, and employment, has contributed to a situation characterized by both ethnic cohesion and intragroup conflict (Menchaca 1995). Local Latino/a activists refer to the social isolation of Fillmore's Mexican-descent population and its lack of receptivity toward new Mexican immigrants. Although Mexican-American participation in local politics and civic affairs during the last two decades has increased, there has been no resolution of farmworker issues related to housing, health care, and legal rights. In discussing the persistence of these problems into the 1990s, one Latino activist explained:

> You have a . . . situation where the farmworkers are told to stay out of town, in essence. . . . The local Latinos are hiding. They're not out there because they get intimidated, and they'll get pulled over by the sheriff's department. It's blatant, and it's not nice. Until the Latino community of Fillmore decides that there's blood, ancestry, and cultural ties there. If it wasn't them, the farmworkers, it would be you. . . . Until they decide that's the connection with the farmworkers, they're not going anywhere.

Language and literacy questions connect with the ethnic diversity of the region and contribute to understanding patterns of vulnerability. More than 30 percent of the residents in both Fillmore and Piru indicate that they have a limited ability to communicate in English. (Such figures do not include those in the country illegally.) The lack of Anglophonic capabilities is a potential barrier in pursuing any sort of disaster assistance. Language barriers are complicated further by cross-cultural communication barriers, especially in situations of varying degrees of literacy. In addition, Fillmore has passed an "English only" ordinance for all city government meetings, thereby disenfranchising monolingual Spanish speakers at the local level (Bolin and Stanford 1998).

Immigration and residency issues, when combined with language and literacy difficulties, contribute to households' vulnerability. A key issue here is political vulnerability. Those in the country illegally live, for the most part, covertly, lacking legal rights and having marginal housing and employment circumstances. Additional "illegal immigrants" have restricted housing options

and often live in makeshift shelters or in garages or other nonapproved housing. Recent changes in California law, most notably Proposition 187, deny all
social and educational programs to undocumented Californians. A tightening
of federal disaster assistance has essentially denied "illegal immigrants" all federal assistance. Changes in U.S. welfare laws have likewise curtailed eligibility
and reduced subsidies and assistance programs to *legal* immigrants. Taken
together with an abrasive anti-immigrant discourse in state politics, these factors have produced a climate of fear among immigrants and resident minority
populations alike. While the anti-immigrant discourse is a prominent feature
of California politics, there is little evidence to suggest that undocumented
immigrants used any disaster services, due to fear of deportation.

VULNERABILITY AND RECOVERY ISSUES

The epicenter of the Northridge main shock was under the suburban sprawl of
the San Fernando valley in the city of Los Angeles. As the earthquake was a
"direct hit" on an urban area with a population in excess of ten million, it produced the most costly disaster in U.S. history, with direct losses of at least
U.S.$25 billion and estimated losses now approaching $44 billion (OES 1997).
More than 20,000 residents were displaced from their homes, and FEMA
processed more than 681,000 applications for assistance following the temblor,
disbursing more than $11 billion in individual and public assistance. While Los
Angeles County experienced the majority of losses to housing stock and businesses, Ventura County did sustain an estimated $1 billion in losses concentrated
in Fillmore, Piru, and Simi valley (OES 1997). FEMA and OES provided an estimated $60 million in individual assistance to approximately 30,000 Ventura
County applicants (OES 1997). The Department of Housing and Urban Development (HUD) provided a series of Community Development Block Grants
(CDBG) to Ventura County, totaling nearly $5 million, which in turn were used
to fund housing and business reconstruction programs in Fillmore and Piru. A
portion of these CDBG funds was channeled from the county to local NGOs and
CBOs, which in turn developed small grant programs to assist very low-income
home owners in financing the repair of their homes (Bolin and Stanford 1998).

FEMA individual-assistance programs are intended as supplements, and they
assume victims will use resources from insurance, commercial or federal home
loans, or personal savings to cover disaster losses. FEMA programs are generally
designed to assist householders with initial expenses for temporary housing or
home rehabilitation, so they may begin a return to their social *status quo ante*.
On this count, FEMA programs are specifically *not* intended to improve the situation of an individual beyond what it was prior to the disaster (Wallrich 1996).
FEMA individual-assistance programs are most generous for short-term needs

such as temporary housing assistance and are weaker in the support of longer-term recovery and reconstruction. One consequence of these program limitations is that marginal households may not receive adequate or any assistance after the disaster. It is necessary to distinguish between the *availability* of assistance as provided by FEMA in an elaborate framework of Disaster Application Centers (DACs), and the *accessibility* of that assistance. From the individual's standpoint, relief accessibility is complex and takes up issues of personal knowledge of federal programs, cultural and language skills, legal status, and physical location, with the mediating effects of social class, ethnicity, and gender. It is here that language, cultural, and residency barriers may hinder households in access to resources for recovery. In Fillmore, with its history of an Anglo-dominated power structure and exclusionary practices aimed at farm-workers (and lower-income Latinos in general), local political culture compounded resource access problems for Latino disaster victims.

For recent immigrants from Mexico, and those with strong Mexican cultural ties, there was a pronounced reluctance to pursue any sort of disaster assistance after Northridge, in spite of victims being legally entitled to such assistance. In Fillmore and Piru, social service representatives reported cases of Mexican immigrant households returning to DACs with their FEMA relief checks, in an effort to repay the Red Cross for blankets and food items provided during the early days following the earthquake. For nonresidents, lack of knowledge and experience with the U.S. relief system reflected expectations conditioned by experiences in the Mexico City earthquake of 1985, where government social assistance programs were minimal at best (e.g., Ponia-towska 1995).

Factors that differentiated vulnerable households from others lay in differences in access to both self-protection and social protection, especially in terms of acquiring resources to restore private homes and businesses. In California, rigorous building code and land use regulations are in place to ensure structural safety in the face of moderate earthquakes. Yet low- and lower-middle-income households, typically living in older homes that do not meet current building codes, generally cannot afford the cost of retrofitting homes for seismic safety. For low-income home owners, any additional expenses for hazard mitigation, particularly for uncertain future events, are readily deferred to the existential demands of daily life. Renters, on the other hand, are subject to landlord decisions as to whether seismically to upgrade apartment structures, a decision seldom made in low-rent apartments with minimal profit potential. Thus, in Fillmore, an unreinforced masonry (URM) residential hotel collapsed in the main shock, displacing more than one hundred Mexican farmworkers. The owner of the hotel had previously refused to retrofit the structure to current codes (Bolin with Stanford 1998).

While FEMA offered a number of assistance programs for costs incurred in the early phases of the disaster, applying for such programs necessarily required a willingness to conform to a sometimes complex set of program requirements, including careful documentation of losses and expenses incurred. As noted above, Mexican immigrants expected nothing from the U.S. government and were reluctant to use any federal assistance programs, in spite of an active outreach program conducted by FEMA to encourage applications. Of the twelve taped interviews conducted with Mexican nationals in Fillmore, only one household applied for FEMA recovery assistance. As one victim explained:

> Well, maybe if it had been harder on me, I would have investigated it more. I heard that there were many people applying who really didn't need it, but I didn't go myself because I didn't need much. Thanks to God, the house didn't fall, and here we were. At least we had a roof over our heads. We had water, we always had canned food in the house, so we were fine. I just didn't go because I said to myself, "There are many people who really need it, the ones who have lost their homes, lost their possessions." I said, "God will punish me if I am taking from those people because, thanks to God, I still have my house. It will be a sin if I take blankets from those who need them because I still have blankets in my home."

The politics of immigration also contributed to this avoidance of federal agencies. As one social service agency representative reported:

> Even legal residents were afraid to go file for assistance or ask for services, scared that they would be deported. It didn't matter whether they were illegal or legal. They still had to be convinced that this was their right. They had paid their taxes, and they were entitled to relief services.

Interviews conducted with Mexican immigrants in Fillmore suggested that many Mexicans took advantage of the emergency services, such as food, water, and clothing from local churches and the Red Cross, but they did not apply for assistance at the DACs. (Unlike FEMA, the American Red Cross provides services for all, irrespective of immigrant status.) Respondents referred generally to the fears of undocumented workers but, for security reasons, never identified themselves nor associates as personally affected. Speaking to a question about whether he knew anyone who had been turned down by FEMA for assistance, one respondent told us:

> Oh, man, someone I know? No, not personally. But mainly the

undocumented who don't have papers, they didn't even apply. They were the ones who were really affected. If you don't have papers and you go to the [Disaster Application] Center, they ask you for identification. You don't have a driver's license, no identification, no papers. Those people are still living in houses that were really affected by the earthquake, but because they're scared of the authorities, they are not going to go and apply for benefits. I know maybe four or five who didn't go out of fear. Many people, even those who are working on their papers, applying for residency, they didn't go because someone told them that applying for assistance would hurt their residency application.

Although there are no statistics available, informants in Fillmore and Piru recognized the almost hidden nature of this population and inherent problems in assisting undocumented Mexicans following the earthquake.

Among the vulnerable households in the two research sites were low-income home owners, both Latino and Anglo. Most of these households did not carry earthquake insurance for financial reasons and were dependent on FEMA "minimal home repair grants" (averaging around $2,000 per grant) for repairing earthquake-damaged homes. Most lacked savings to augment FEMA assistance and because of minimal incomes could not qualify for Small Business Administration home loans or commercial home loans for repairs. To assist vulnerable households with unmet recovery needs, a number of NGOS and CBOs developed programs to provide additional resources to assist those who could not qualify for or had received inadequate assistance from FEMA. In Fillmore and Piru, NGOs recognized that many in the community faced income and housing problems prior to the earthquake and that the disaster had created further difficulties in people's daily struggles. In Fillmore, a coalition of churches, local businesses, and civic and service organizations established a nonprofit CBO, called Mano a Mano, in an effort to meet the housing repair needs of a largely Hispanic, relatively poor population. The director of Mano a Mano, a longtime Fillmore activist, explained:

The people have lots of financial problems in addition to problems repairing their homes or businesses. Most are low-income with little savings. With the people I've seen, it's very rare that anyone has earthquake insurance. They weren't financially prepared for recovery costs. They don't qualify for regular loans and are dependent on volunteer services and outside sources. Many still haven't received any money and are concerned about how long the process takes.

For these households, the grants and work crews provided by CBOs, such as Mano a Mano, and NGOs, such as Habitat for Humanity, provided the material and labor resources needed to rebuild homes. The CBOs and NGOs, working cooperatively with HUD and FEMA, provided a locally responsive method of channeling resources to poor and Latino disaster victims with persistent unmet recovery needs (Bolin and Stanford 1998), although they did little to alter the sources of vulnerability rooted in pronounced socioeconomic inequalities deriving from the social relations of production.

CONCLUSIONS

The problems faced by low-income households, diversified by ethnicity, gender, immigration status, and language skills, in Fillmore and Piru bear striking resemblance to other California earthquakes, specifically Loma Prieta in 1989 (e.g., Schulte 1991). The social forces that marginalize and disadvantage certain fractions of the population continue to operate unabated by general economic growth in the state (Davis 1998). The historical sources and current manifestations of vulnerability in California and elsewhere share consistencies regarding groups systematically disadvantaged and lacking response capacities. Studies of earthquakes suggest that the groups characterized as persistently vulnerable are far from unusual. Low-income elders, poor Latino (and African-American) households, homeless persons, farmworkers, undocumented immigrants, and monolingual ethnic groups have been variously identified as encountering problems in acquiring resources and recovering (e.g., Bolin 1994a; Laird 1991; Morrow and Enarson 1996; Phillips 1993). Research on Hurricane Andrew identified numerous marginalized groups in Florida who suffered disproportionate losses and experienced exceptional difficulties in recovering. To varying degrees these involved disadvantaged persons akin to those identified here—people whose already existing social and economic deficits produced barriers in recovery. In the Hurricane Andrew research, these included lower-income African Americans, female-headed households, lower- income elders, farmworkers, marginalized Latino ethnic groups, and Haitian immigrants—all of whom were made vulnerable by low wages, fragile homes and livelihoods, and limited access to post-disaster resources (Peacock et al. 1997). The existence of such persistently vulnerable households raises issues of environmental justice and the unequal risks some bear as a result of poverty and discrimination (e.g., Bullard 1994) in the face of environmental hazards. Without state or NGO interventions to augment their coping capacities and provide social protection, people's lives may become increasingly precarious as resources are exhausted, homes are lost, and disadvantage mounts. The changing nature of federal assistance promises to restrict future assistance to disaster victims, which will deepen the disadvantages faced by some of the most vulnerable households in the United States.

NOTE

1. Funding for research described in this chapter was provided by the National Science Foundation under grant #CMS-9415721, Robert Bolin and Lois Stanford, Principal Investigators. The findings and conclusions presented here are those of the authors and are not intended to represent the views of the National Science Foundation.

BIBLIOGRAPHY

Bee, P. 1984. *CUP 4145: Will 100 Units of Farmworker Housing Be Built in Ventura County?* Unpublished M.A. thesis. Northridge: California State University.

Blaikie, P., and H. Brookfield. 1987. *Land Degradation and Society.* London: Methuen.

Blaikie, P., T. Cannon, I. Davis, and B. Wisner. 1994. *At Risk: Natural Hazards, People's Vulnerability and Disasters.* London: Routledge.

Bolin, R. 1994a. "Postdisaster Shelter and Housing: Social Processes in Response and Recovery," in R. Dynes and K. Tierney (eds.) *Disaster, Collective Behavior, and Social Organization*, pp. 115–127. Newark: University of Delaware Press.

———. 1994b. *Household and Community Recovery after Earthquakes.* Monograph #56. Boulder: Institute of Behavioral Science, University of Colorado.

Bolin, R., and P. Bolton. 1986. *Race, Religion, and Ethnicity in Disaster Recovery.* Monograph #42. Boulder: Institute of Behavioral Science, University of Colorado.

Bolin, R., and D. Klenow. 1988. "Older People in Disaster: A Study of Black and White Victims." *International Journal of Aging and Human Development* 26 (1): 29–43.

Bolin, R., and L. Stanford. 1998. "The Northridge, California Earthquake: Community-Based Approaches to Unmet Recovery Needs." *Disasters* 22 (1): 21–38.

———. 1991. "Shelter, Housing, and Recovery: A Comparison of U.S. Disasters." *Disasters* 45 (1): 25–34.

Bolin, R., with L. Stanford. 1998. *The Northridge Earthquake: Vulnerability and Disaster.* London: Routledge.

Bolin, R., M. Jackson, and A. Crist. 1998. "Gender, Inequality, Vulnerability, and Disaster: Issues in Theory and Research," in E. Enarson and B. Morrow (eds.), *The Gendered Terrain of Disaster: Through Women's Eyes*, pp. 27–44. Westport, CT: Greenwood.

Bullard, R. (ed.). 1994. *Unequal Protection: Environmental Justice and Communities of Color.* San Francisco: Sierra Club Books.

Burton, I., R. Kates, and G. White. 1993. *The Environment as Hazard.* 2nd ed. New York: Guilford.

Cabrillo Economic Development Corporation (CEDC). 1992. *Special Annual Report: 1981–1992.* Ventura: Cabrillo Economic Development Corporation.

Cannon, T. 1994. "Vulnerability Analysis and the Explanation of 'Natural' Disasters," in A. Varley (ed.), *Disasters, Development and Environment*, pp. 13–40. London: Wiley.

City of Fillmore. 1992. *City of Fillmore Downtown Specific Plan*. Fillmore, California.

Collins, F. 1997. "Social and Economic Changes that Will Affect Disaster Recovery: What Voluntary Agencies Should Consider." Unpublished report. Richmond, CA: NorCal VOAD.

Comerio, M., J. Landis, C. Firpo, and J. Monzon. 1996. *Residential Earthquake Recovery: Improving California's Post-Disaster Rebuilding Policies and Pro-grams*. Berkeley: California Policy Seminar Brief Series.

Community of Piru. 1995. *Redevelopment Agency Project Area Sub-Committee Meet-ing*. Unpublished meeting notes, February 22, 1995, Piru, California.

Davis, M. 1998. *The Ecology of Fear*. New York: Metropolitan.

Eldar, R. 1992. "The Needs of Elderly Persons in Natural Disasters: Observations and Recommendation." *Disasters* 16 (4): 355–358.

Enarson, E., and B. Morrow. 1998. "A Gendered Perspective: The Voices of Women," in W. Peacock, B. Morrow, and H. Gladwin (eds.), *Hurricane Andrew: Ethnicity, Gender, and the Sociology of Disasters*, pp. 116–140. London: Routledge.

Escobar, A. 1996. "Constructing Nature," in R. Peet and M. Watts (eds.), *Liberation Ecologies: Environment, Development, Social Movements*. London: Routledge.

FEMA—Federal Emergency Management Agency. 1995. *The Northridge Earthquake One Year Later*. Washington, DC: Federal Emergency Management Agency.

Fothergill, A. 1996. "Gender, Risk, and Disaster." *International Journal of Mass Emergencies and Disasters* 14, 1: 33–56.

Hamel, J. 1993. *Case Study Methods*. Qualitative Research Methods Series, 32. New-bury Park, CA: Sage Publications.

Harvey, D. 1996. *Justice, Nature, and the Geography of Difference*. Oxford: Black-well.

Hendrie, B. 1997. "Knowledge and Power: A Critique of an International Relief Oper-ation." *Disasters* 21, 1: 57–76.

Hewitt, K. (ed.). 1983. *Interpretations of Calamity from the Perspective of Human Ecology*. London: Allen and Unwin.

———. 1995. "Excluded Perspectives in the Social Construction of Disaster." *Interna-tional Journal of Mass Emergencies and Disasters* 13, 3: 317–340.

———. 1997. *Regions of Risk; A Geographical Introduction to Disasters*. London: Longman.

Johnston, B. 1994. *Who Pays the Price? The Sociocultural Context of the Environ-mental Crisis*. Washington, DC: Island Press.

Laird, R. 1991. The Ethnography of Disaster. Unpublished M.A.Thesis. San Fran-cisco: San Francisco State University.

Maskrey, A. 1993. *Los Desastros NO Son Naturales*. Bogota: La Red/ITDG.

McBane, M. 1995. "The Role of Gender in Citrus Employment: A Case Study of Recruitment, Labor, and Housing Patterns at the Limoneira Company,

1893–1940." *California History* 74, 1: 68–81.

Menchaca, M. 1995. *The Mexican Outsiders: A Community History of Marginalization and Discrimination in California*. Austin: University of Texas Press.

Morrow, B., and E. Enarson. 1996. "Hurricane Andrew through Women's Eyes: Issues and Recommendations." *International Journal of Mass Emergencies and Disasters* 14, 1: 5–22.

OES (California Governor's Office of Emergency Services). 1995. *The Northridge Earthquake of January 17, 1994: Preliminary Report of Data Collection and Analysis, Part A: Damage and Inventory Data*. Irvine and Pasadena: EQE International and Office of Emergency Services.

———. 1997. *The Northridge Earthquake of January 17, 1994: Report of Data Collection and Analysis, Part B: Analysis and Trends*. Irvine and Pasadena: EQE International and Office of Emergency Services.

———. 1986. *The Martyred City: Death and Rebirth in the Peruvian Andes*. Albuquerque: University of New Mexico Press.

Oliver-Smith, A. 1996. "Anthropological Research on Hazards and Disasters." *Annual Review of Anthropology* 25: 303–328.

Palerm, J. 1991. "Farm Labor Needs and Farm Workers in California, 1970–1989." Unpublished report. California Agricultural Studies, Employment Development Department.

Palerm, J., and J. Urquiola. 1993. "A Binational System of Agricultural Production: The Case of the Mexican Baj'o and California," in *Mexico and the United States: Neighbors in Crisis*. Conference Proceedings, University of California Institute for Mexico and the United States (UC MEXUS), California.

Peacock, W., B. Morrow, H. Gladwin. (eds). 1997. *Hurricane Andrew: Ethnicity, Gender, and the Sociology of Disaster*. London: Routledge.

Phillips, B. 1993. "Cultural Diversity in Disaster: Shelter, Housing, and Long-Term Recovery." *International Journal of Mass Emergencies and Disasters* 11, 1: 99–110.

Poniatowska, E. 1995. *Nothing, Nobody: The Voices of the Mexico City Earthquake*, translated by A. Camacho de Schmidt and A. Schmidt. Philadelphia: Temple.

Schulte, P. 1991. *The Politics of Disaster: An Examination of Class and Ethnicity in the Struggle for Power following the 1989 Loma Prieta Earthquake in Watsonville, California*. Unpublished M.A. thesis. Sacramento: California State University.

SSC–Seismic Safety Commission. 1995. *Northridge Earthquake: Turning Loss to Gain*. Sacramento: SSC Report No. 95-01.

Subervi-Velez, F., M. Denney, A. Ozuna, C. Quintero, and J-V. Palerm. 1992. "Communicating with California's Spanish Speaking Populations: Assessing the Role of the Spanish-Language Broadcast Media and Selected Agencies in Providing Emergency Services." *CPS Report*. Berkeley: California Policy Seminar, University of California.

Triem, Judith P. 1985. *Ventura County: Land of Good Fortune.* Chatsworth, Califor-
    nia: Windsor Publications/Ventura County Historical Society.
U.S. Bureau of the Census. 1992. *Poverty in the United States: 1964–1989.* Current
    Population Reports, Series P-60, No. 175. Washington, DC: US Government
    Printing Office.
Vaupel, S. 1992. *A Study of Women Agricultural Workers in Ventura County, Califor-
    nia.* Report to the County, Ventura: Committee on Women in Agriculture, Ven-
    tura County.
Ventura County. 1987. Cultural Heritage Survey. Unpublished report, Ventura County,
    General Services Agency, Recreation Services, Ventura, California.
———. 1996. Piru Community Enhancement Plan. Unpublished report, Ventura
    County Supervisors, Ventura, California.
Wallrich, B. 1996. "The Evolving Role of Community-Based Organizations in Disas-
    ter Recovery." *Natural Hazards Observer* 21, 2: 12–13.
Waterstone, M. 1992. "Introduction: The Social Genesis of Risks and Hazards," in M.
    Waterstone (ed.), *Risk and Society: The Interaction of Science, Technology, and
    Public Policy*, pp. 1–12. Boston: Kluwer Academic.
Watts, M. 1991. "Heart of Darkness: Reflections on Famine and Starvation in
    Africa," in R. Downs, D. Kerner, and S. Reyna (eds.), *Political Economy of an
    African Famine*, pp. 23–54. Philadelphia: Gordon and Breach.
Wisner, B. 1993. "Disaster Vulnerability: Scale, Power and Daily Life." *GeoJournal*,
    30, 2: 127–140.

6

THE NEGATION OF DISASTER: THE MEDIA RESPONSE TO OIL SPILLS IN GREAT BRITAIN

GREGORY V. BUTTON
University of Michigan

Does this kind of thing happen so often that nobody cares any-more? Don't those people know what we have been through? We were scared to death. . . . Is it possible nobody gives substantial coverage to such a thing? . . . Are they telling us it was insignificant, it was piddling? . . . Do they have to have two hundred dead, rare disaster footage, before they come flocking? . . . Everything we love and have worked for is under serious threat. But we look around and see no response from the official organs of the media. . . . Even if there hasn't been a great loss of life, don't we deserve some attention for our suffering, our human worry, our terror? Isn't fear news?

—Don DeLillo, *White Noise*

INTRODUCTION

DISASTERS OFFER THE SOCIAL SCIENCE RESEARCHER A FINE OPPORTUNITY TO study the nature of the social and cultural construction of reality. As Barth (1993: 4) has astutely reminded us, the study of the construction of reality should always be directed at "the here and now." One opportune way in which to examine these processes is to investigate the role the news media play in mediating our perception of reality. In particular, conducting an analysis of the media coverage of such events as the *Braer* oil spill in the Shetland Islands or the *Sea Empress* spill in Wales allows for a fine-grained understanding of how the media contribute to the construction of reality. The analysis lends insight into what is included and excluded in current historical archives.

How the media packages information and participates in the construction of reality informs us of the ideological elements that work to maintain the status quo in the wake of a disaster. They also remind us that disasters are not merely material phenomena, but are grounded in the intensely political world of social relations. This analysis underscores, along with other contributors to this volume, that disasters are not only socially and physically disruptive but are also political events. By necessity disaster research must involve the examination of political power relations among those affected as well as among the various agencies and institutions that are involved in the event, and the victims. Disaster events, whether they are labeled "man-made" or "natural," highlight ongoing power struggles in society. Controlling information, whether in the media or in public discourse, is an attempt to control the social production of meaning. It also is an attempt to define reality in accord with a favored political agenda and, therefore, must be seen as a distinctly ideological process. The struggle over control becomes more pronounced in the wake of a technological disaster.

This paper uses the two oil spills in Great Britain as case studies to examine the role of the press in creating public perception of the events and contributing to the creation of contemporary historical archives. Based on field and archival research, this paper also demonstrates the critical role that framing plays in mediating our perception of disasters and suggests that rather than being unbiased, objective accounts, frames—particularly those influenced by the media—tend to support proestablishment narratives. Consequently, they severely constrain alternative interpretations and influence which interpretations prevail in public discourse and endure in historical consciousness.

The news media play an important role in informing the public, policy makers, politicians, and emergency management officials about any disasters, but especially about technological disasters. Technological disasters, which do not seem to arise from nature, but rather from human error or carelessness, particularly perplex people and leave them to struggle for explanation or meaning. Victims often turn to the media to answer these needs.

In this age of technological disasters, most people treat the news media as their principal source of information about disasters, and it is the language of the media which they experience, unless they are victims. Edelman (1977) observes that people experience the language about a political event rather than experiencing the event themselves. The news media's depiction of these events shapes and mediates our understanding of catastrophes. In the wake of disaster, in the struggle to assign meaning to tragedy, the news media constructs and limits meanings. Media analyst James Fallows notes that the real purpose of news "is to satisfy the general desire for information to have meaning" (1996: 129). The framing process both constructs and reconstructs meaning in a selective manner that legitimizes some accounts while obscuring others, privileging some political agendas and negating others.

The way news stories frame an event strongly mediates how the public thinks about an event. Frames are the packages in which the central focus of a news story is developed and understood. While frames are "largely unspoken and unacknowledged" (Gitlin 1980), they aid journalists in organizing the world; they also strongly shape how we, as readers, perceive the world. Frames create the story line and narrative in which a news event is presented to the public. Frequently, they are unchallenged assumptions about the world that are taken for granted. Rather than appear as the cultural constructions that they are, frames usually appear to both reporters and news consumers as natural. They present seamless, seemingly objective accounts of the world without revealing their underlying subjective selective account of complex events. The contestation over the meaning of a disaster and the struggle to interpret it commonly result in a struggle to frame the event, and that struggle is, in turn, often dependent on access to the media.

Technological disaster frames also tend to focus on individuals as victims. Individualism, the "mainstay of capitalist ideology" (Cormack 1995: 53), obscures the extremely relevant categories of class, race, gender, and age which are essential to understanding and explicating the politics of disaster. This emphasis on the individual accomplishes at least two things. Dwelling on the individual displaces any systemic account of the disaster and its causes, and an overreliance on anecdotal, individualistic accounts serves to decontextualize the larger sociopolitical conditions in which the tragedy occurred. This kind of narrative discourse also makes individuals appear as passive victims and not as active agents struggling politically to redefine events and reframe official accounts of the disaster. This approach is galvanized by the media's tendency to rely mostly on official accounts of the disaster.

News stories are, thus, texts that convey meaning, but the meanings that are conveyed are selective, and, as I shall demonstrate, the selectivity of framing a news event like an oil spill can be contested. In the first place, the response of both the general public and policy makers to disasters is often predicated on perceptions of preexisting disasters reported in the news. The *Braer* oil spill in the Shetland Islands is no exception; neither is the *Sea Empress* spill in Wales. The danger in this dependence is clear, since, as Sahlins (1974) has argued, there is no such thing as an "immaculate perception"; there are also no "immaculate" news accounts.

The *Exxon-Valdez* oil spill, which preceded both disasters in Great Britain, had a tremendous impact on how public officials, "victims," and the news media responded to the events.[1] The influences that the Alaskan spill had on the media and public officials, especially in the wake of the *Braer* spill, cannot be underestimated. In numerous interviews with individuals in the political and emergency response sectors, people stressed the importance of their perception of the earlier spill and the role it played in their decision-making process. By the same token, the *Braer* spill in the Shetland Islands, as it was perceived by public officials, had a significant impact on policy decisions surrounding the United Kingdom's response to the *Sea Empress* spill in Wales. In fact, as we shall see, the influence of the *Braer* spill was both explicit as well as implicit. Before we can explore this, we must first discuss the characteristics of technological disasters.

THE SOCIOCULTURAL CONSTRUCTION
OF TECHNOLOGICAL DISASTERS

Technological disasters are axial events, because "the arrangements of society become most visible when they are challenged by crisis" (Wolf 1990). The study of these disasters provides a quintessential example of the "anthropology of trouble" (Rappaport 1993). In the aftermath of technological disasters, people struggle to make sense of the event by interpreting it and assigning it meaning and significance. Disaster victims ask such questions as "Why me?" "Why here?" "Why didn't the government prevent this from happening?" "Why aren't people being held accountable?"

People need to interpret the disaster event in order to negotiate, manage, and comprehend. They need to locate the disaster within a set of cultural logics that enables them to understand what happened and why it happened. However, the task often becomes conflicted due to a chain of factors. Often the frustrating failure to prevent disasters or ineptitude in responding to them causes people to question the social order. The turmoil that is engendered concerning social arrangements may create radical shifts in people's worldview, particularly regarding issues of justice and equity. Since worldview involves the assignment of sense and import, questioning worldview in turn sends the diagnosis of disaster into ambiguity. An atmosphere of uncertainty and a sense of loss of control emerge, and they carry within them a dispute over the way things are understood. In essence, the very process of meaning-making results in a bargaining about the meaning of reality (Comaroff and Roberts 1981; Rosen 1984).

In the conflict that is born of this process of meaning-making, people's ability to persuade others of their perception and interpretation of the problem hinges on the power and skill to do so (Gusfield 1981; Merry 1990; Edelman 1977). This contestation over the meaning and significance of events prefigures the power struggle inherent in establishing systems of meaning and reveals the social arrangements of society. Our two case studies reveal much about the social arrangements and the role the media has not only in articulating the contestation of meanings, but also in defining which meanings gain currency and which enter the historical record.

THE *BRAER* OIL SPILL IN THE SHETLAND ISLANDS

On January 5th, 1993, the American-owned oil tanker *Braer* went aground at Garth's Ness on the southern tip of the Shetland Islands.[2] Amid a hurricane, the tanker was smashed into several sections and spilled 84,413 tons of Norwegian crude oil into the North Sea. By official estimates, this spillage was approximately twice the amount of the *Exxon-Valdez* oil spill in Alaska. Over twenty million gallons of crude oil were spilled at a cost of over 100 million British pounds sterling in damages; three million farm salmon had to be destroyed as a result of spill contamination; over seven thousand seabirds were killed by the spill; and the spill provided the only known case of oil droplets and dispersants being blown ashore and inhaled. Prolonged psychological uncertainty about the hazardous effects of the spill and the cleanup persisted for months. It was severe by any standard of oil spill magnitude. Nevertheless, the spill would ultimately be portrayed as a nonevent—"a disaster that wasn't," as one publication labeled its final story on the event. The spill narrative, however, began on a more dramatic note.

Sensing a story bigger than even the *Exxon-Valdez* spill, six thousand reporters from all over the world flocked to this remote northern island within hours. The press corps were not the only ones who had the *Exxon-Valdez* on their mind. Shetland Island officials and Scottish Office officials feared a tragedy of the magnitude of the Alaskan disaster as well as criticism similar to the controversies surrounding the *Exxon-Valdez* cleanup effort. Some public officials made off-the-record comments to me that they feared they would be criticized for "letting the spill get out of hand," as was said of some public officials during the *Exxon-Valdez* spill. Another public official told me he felt the press had too much information about the Alaskan spill and that they were fortunate in the United Kingdom in not having the permissive freedom of information statutes that existed in the United States.

As the ferocious winds blew oil vapors and droplets clear across the island, the houses and land of nearby communities became coated with a brown gooey slime. Despite hurricane-force gale winds and rough seas, officials decided to spray over one hundred twenty tons of chemical dispersants by plane on the wreck of the *Braer* within forty-eight hours. While virtually ineffectual on the crude oil along the rocky coast, the dispersants contaminated the island's prime agricultural land, most of the nearby inhabitants, and several thousand sheep and cattle unsheltered from either storm or chemical sprays.

Four communities lie in close proximity to the island's airport and the tip of Garth's Ness. As Royal Navy Air Corps airplanes took off from the runways, they began spraying these toxic chemicals as soon as their wheels were up—that is, at an altitude of thirty feet over the adjacent communities. The three thousand residents of Dunross Parish at the southern end of the island were not warned to stay indoors and were not informed of the times of spraying, nor were they evacuated. By the time the spraying was terminated, almost all the inhabitants on the western side of the island's southern end, including eighteen pregnant women, most in their first trimester, had been exposed to both dispersants and oil.

The public health advisory issued by the Shetland Islands Council and local public health officials simply advised residents to minimize skin contact with oil and dispersants and stay indoors. This advice was difficult to follow for crofters obliged to attend to their animals day and night during the storm. Local schoolchildren who had to wait for school buses twice daily also had trouble heeding this counsel. Many other locals were compelled to go outside to commute to their jobs, and hundreds of airport employees were constantly exposed to the dispersants while at work. Only a small number of residents were provided with proper respiratory masks. For most, staying indoors did little good, since odors permeated homes and lingered for several days, nauseating occupants.

Moreover, during the first ten days of the disaster there was no official clinical monitoring of the residents' health. The assessment of public health was impaired by the lack of necessary equipment for monitoring and measuring pollution levels. Most of the monitoring that was conducted calculated only gaseous hydrocarbon levels. There was no monitoring of oil droplets and no equipment for monitoring chemical dispersants in the atmosphere. The chemical content of the dispersants was unknown to both the people using them and those accidentally exposed to them. For the first forty-eight hours not even the island's health official knew the chemical composition of the dispersants. The content of dispersants is generally a mixture of solvents and detergents, many of which are toxic. However, their level of toxicity not only varies, but in some cases is largely unknown. All of this contributed to a second man-made disaster.

Once Dr. Derek Cox, the local public health official, was informed of the chemicals used in the spray, he withheld the information from other officials and the general public because of "commercial confidentiality." As Dr. Cox would later bemoan, his refusal to release this information, coupled with the chemical companies' insistence on withholding the information from the public, was the largest single factor for the pervasive feeling among the Shetlanders that there was a conspiracy to withhold vital information.

Eventually the high winds and rough seas split the tanker apart, and the oil appeared to wash out to sea, apparently posing little threat to the islands. However, by the time the crisis had seemingly passed, all of the agricultural land and the adjacent salmon farms were condemned because of contamination from both the oil and the dispersants. Several million farm salmon had to be destroyed, and a huge fish exclusion zone was established off the coast. While the international media corps went home disappointed that no story as sensational as the *Exxon-Valdez* emerged, an extended controversy began on the island that was ignored by everyone but the local press. With complaints of too few dead animals to photograph and severe weather that kept most indoors, the world press ignored the human story that unfolded (Button 1994).

Since almost all the early media reports billed the spill as another *Exxon-Valdez*—indeed one that would possibly be more spectacular—a number of reporters who had covered the Alaska spill came with preconceived ideas of what would happen. When the anticipated scenario did not transpire, they became disappointed and frustrated. Since the spill did not conform to the prepackaged notions of their editors and producers, most reporters left the island. The international reporters that I interviewed all voiced disappointment because the spill did not follow an anticipated script. The reporters failed to realize that, while spills do have reoccurring patterns, they seldom, if ever, resemble one another. Since the spill did not resemble the *Exxon-Valdez*, it probably would not sell papers and would not be the kind of momentous event that would further their journalistic careers.

The Harm to the Human Population

The *Braer* spill was framed as an environmental disaster, and, in keeping with that story line, the impacts of the spill and cleanup on the human population were all but ignored, even though the public health effects were perhaps the most distinctive and significant aspect of the disaster.[3] The focus of attention was turned toward oiled marine life and the fury of the North Atlantic, which provided more photogenic drama than the possible invisible effects of chemical contamination.

Almost immediately, hundreds of Dunross Parish residents complained of eye and skin irritation, headaches, and diarrhea. Over forty people experienced severe asthmatic responses. Later more than two hundred fifty people would demonstrate abnormal lung functioning. A smaller number would show test results that demonstrated renal and liver malfunction. When Greenpeace and a Norwegian environmental group disseminated literature criticizing the use of dispersants, residents grew uneasy. The environmentalists cited reports that dispersants were never approved for use around humans and may adversely affect the amount of oil absorbed by the lungs and increase the rate of absorption of toxic oil in the mucous membranes of the mouth and nose.

One of the dispersants used on the spill, Dispolene 34s, was not even licensed to be used in the United Kingdom. Another dispersant had never been approved for use along rocky shorelines. A third dispersant had failed toxicity tests in Norway. It was not until January 21 that Agriculture Minister David Curry admitted these facts, stating finally: "The disclosure of this information underlines that residents of the south Mainland of Shetland were well justi-fied in expressing misgivings about the use of dispersants."

The man immediately immersed in the middle of this controversy was Dr. Chris Rowlands, the general practitioner for the parish. In contrast to Dr. Cox's assurances that all was well, Dr. Rowlands advised school officials not to allow schoolchildren outside during recess. He also advised a public gath-ering that the crude oil contained three chemicals known to cause cancer: butadene, naphthlane, and benzene. He questioned the use of dispersants, telling another public group that government officials were keeping the chem-ical contents of the dispersants a secret even from him, the parishioners' physician. Moreover, he alleged that the government was using an old, out-dated stock of dispersants, and that cleanup personnel were unsure of the dis-persant ingredients because barrels of different chemicals were being mixed. These allegations were subsequently substantiated.

Alarmed over the symptoms many of his patients were presenting, Dr. Rowlands began clinically monitoring his patients two days after the spill, although the national and local health board were refusing to conduct medical monitoring of the residents. Dr. Rowlands took blood and urine samples of the parishioners, especially those who worked outdoors. In an effort to conduct fuller tests, he asked the Scottish Health Board to test all the residents in the exposed regions. According to Rowlands, the health board ran into severe opposition from the Scottish Home Office. However, once the press reported that Dr. Rowlands had conducted tests, the Home Office relented. Unfortu-nately, because of the ten-day time delay, the tests were almost meaningless; moreover, they failed to test for carcinogens like benzene, toluene, and zylene.

Both Home Office and Shetland Islands Council officials pressured Dr. Rowlands to stop making public statements and to stop testing. Dr. Cox made public statements to the press that Dr. Rowlands was using scaremon-gering tactics and creating public hysteria. Amid the controversy, the islanders themselves were very concerned about the lack of testing and the use of dis-persants. A petition signed by several hundred people sent to the Shetland Island Council demanded, among other things, that there be an open investi-gation of the disaster and that all information regarding the use of chemical dispersants be disclosed to the public. According to Martin Hall, director of environmental health, even members of the Shetland Island Council were upset over the use of dispersants. When they protested, the MPCU responded, "I don't care if you like it, we are going to do it." The controversy over spraying dispersants came to a head when residents in a community adjacent to the airport, and several airport employees, threatened to sit on the runways and block planes from taking off. Malcolm Green, the executive director of the Shetland Island Council, then told the Department of Transport that he wanted the spraying discontinued. As a result, a compromise was reached limiting spraying to certain areas and only at certain altitudes (Shetland Islands Council Public Notice 1.10.93).

The official word from the Scottish Home Office from the first day of the spill was that there would be no long-term health effects from the spill or the use of dispersants. This claim was largely unsubstantiated. For one thing, the spill was unique in that it was the first known instance of respirable oil droplets, rather than vapor, being blown ashore, and there were no preexisting studies of the possible health hazards from such an occurrence. To make matters worse, chemical dispersants were being used in unauthorized areas and contaminating nearby settlements. Furthermore, although some studies suggest that dispersants increase the dangers of oil inhalation, there is no scientific knowledge of the effects of the combination of oil and dispersants on the human body. The only givens were that both the oil and the chemicals contained known carcinogens. Under these circumstances accepted scientific practice would require the assumption of a risk, the taking preventative action, and the monitoring the environment and the human population.

THE *SEA EMPRESS* OIL SPILL IN WALES

The second case study, the *Sea Empress* spill, which occurred three years later, lends itself well to analysis, since it also occurred in Great Britain and has direct linkages with the Shetland Islands case. Policy makers in London responded to the spill in Wales with the *Braer* spill still fresh in mind. Indeed, as it will be shown below, the connection between the two spills was formalized when the recommendations made in response to the earlier spill were used in the Welsh event. Both affected spill communities were, furthermore, distinct cultural enclaves struggling outside the pale of London's authority.

On the night of February 15, 1996, the Liberian-flagged, Russian-crewed 147,000-ton oil tanker *Sea Empress* went aground on the rocks in the Mouth of Milford Haven, Wales. By the time the tanker was freed from the rocks six days later and towed into harbor, the ship had spilled over ninety thousand tons of crude oil onto one of Britain's most pristine coastlines. The Pembrokeshire coastline is the only national park in Great Britain. The coastal area is also the location of three islands set aside as preserves for tens of thousands of pelagic and coastal birds.

The spill was approximately twice the size of the *Exxon-Valdez* oil spill and the second largest spill to occur in Great Britain's waters. Ironically, although the spill was larger than the *Braer* spill, it received much less worldwide publicity. Although the *Sea Empress* spill approached the size of the *Torrey Canyon* spill (1967, one hundred thousand tons spilled), which was also headed for Milford Haven and was described in Great Britain as its "largest peacetime threat," the government refused even to recognize the *Sea Empress* spill as a "disaster."

As with previous spills, considerable controversy surrounded the government's response to the spill, although very little of this controversy eventually appeared in the international press coverage. When the tanker first went aground, the local harbormaster, local ships' pilots, and the Countyside Council for Wales recommended that the tanker be towed out to sea for fear that it would continue to leak crude oil on the coastline and might eventually rupture amid rough tidal surges and frequent winter storms. In a classic example of global versus local knowledge and authority, the government's Joint Response Center overruled the advice of those most familiar with local conditions. Six days after the spill, the *Sea Empress* was towed into Milford Harbor, but not before it would leak more than an additional seventy thousand tons of oil. Many local officials felt that this additional spillage could have been prevented, given that during the first forty-eight hours after the ship's grounding, the seas were unusually calm. The conditions were ideal for towing the ship to sea or for off-loading the oil to another tanker, but the government failed to respond during this ideal opportunity, and many local officials and citizens accused the government of being more concerned with saving the tanker than with the threat of a major spill.

Whatever the government's motivations, it lost the race against time because there were not enough tugboats on hand to move the tanker. Ironically, the challenge that the Joint Response Center faced would have been considerably less had the government adopted the recommendations of Lord Donaldson's inquiry on oil tanker safety submitted after the *Braer* spill. Following the *Braer* spill, Lord Donaldson was disturbed that the government had failed to do two fundamentally important things. First, the government failed to declare the waters surrounding Milford Haven a "marine high-risk area." Second, they failed to have major salvage tugs on permanent standby to provide emergency towing in the event of a marine catastrophe (the closest tug of its kind was in Portugal). While the government had allegedly implemented 84 of the 103 recommendations in the Donaldson Report, it had failed to enhance the salvage capacity at one of Europe's largest and busiest oil ports. To many observers, this failure was unthinkable, given not only that Milford Haven ranks as one of the largest harbors in the world, but that the coastline of southwest Wales is the home of a multimillion-dollar fishing industry, is a major tourist region for all of Great Britain, and is one of the largest wildlife sanctuaries in all of Europe.

As the event unfolded, more uncanny parallels appeared. The economy of southwest Wales, like that of the Shetland Islands and Alaska, is extremely fragile. As after most spills, local residents and officials were afraid of the possible long-term effect on their regional economy, which was precarious even prior to the spill. The unemployment rate is 13.8 percent in Haverford-west and 18.4 percent in South Pembrokeshire. Recent closing of military bases had resulted in the loss of fifteen hundred jobs and twenty million pounds sterling a year. Added to that, according to a study conducted by the Cardiff Business School and the Welsh Institute of Rural Studies, the impact of the spill cost the local tourist industry nearly twenty-one million pounds. A further five million pounds were lost as a result of the restrictions imposed on fishing in the contaminated waters. The study declared that the losses were "significant," especially since the area has an estimated gross domestic product of under eight hundred million pounds, only 72 percent of the United Kingdom per capita average. The study dramatized the regional economy by stating that it was more on a par with Portugal's than that of the United Kingdom or other northern European countries.

The regional economy relies most heavily on tourism. Some 1.1 million tourists visit the area every year because of the beautiful beaches and major nature preserves. The spill occurred at the worst time for the economy, since Easter, a major holiday of the year, was close at hand. The Welsh Tourist Board had also just launched a 2.5-million-pound television advertising campaign. As in both the Shetland Islands and Alaska, the tourist industry was greatly concerned about the pervasive, highly visible, environmental damage to their pristine shores. The head of the Welsh Tourist Board was also very concerned about the "worldwide negative images" that were being broadcast and printed. Within days of the spill thousands of reservations were canceled, and tourism all but disappeared until the second week in June. One local hotel owner declared the impact of the spill "absolutely devastating." In an effort to reverse the negative image of the region, the tourist board spent five million pounds in a multimedia campaign and established a tourist "help line" that attempted to quell tourist fears.

The British government delayed putting a fishing ban into effect for more than thirty days. A three-hundred-square-mile zone around the Pembrokeshire coastline was placed off-limits for food gathering when scientists found oil levels in mollusks one hundred times above normal. Much of the near-shore fishery centers around mollusks, crab, lobsters, and crawfish rather than fish. The most lucrative portion of this industry comes from whelks, which are exported to Asia. The fishermen were concerned that the nonfish species ban would last for years, as did similar bans in the Shetlands. There, shellfish bans lasted two years, scallop bans lasted longer, and there is still a ban on prawn and mussel fishing. In contrast, the ban on salmon fishing was lifted by the first week in May, almost three months after the spill.

While fishermen were eligible for compensation from the oil spill funds, many were unhappy over the impact on their industry. As one fisherman stated, he was worried about his "way of life," which he felt was devastated and could not be replaced by compensation funds. Some fishermen were worried about the possible devastation of a two-thousand-year-old tradition. The bans included a doubling of the licensing fee and on men taking their sons to the water to teach them maritime skills. Since coracle fishing was first officially recorded by Julius Caesar, this practice is viewed by many as an important part of the Welsh coastal culture, and some feared the restrictions heralded the end of a way of life. Their concerns were similar to the concerns for local indigenous culture that were expressed by Shetland Islands crofters. Restrictions on fishing following the February spill were gradually eased by September, including the ban on whelks and crustaceans. However, the bans continue on edible seaweed and shellfish.

As in other oil spills, anxieties about public health were given little attention by spill response authorities. In the town of Dyfed the director of public health had to rely on radio and television accounts for information and was not even officially notified of the spill until the day after the accident. Five days into the spill, he had to break into a meeting of the *Sea Empress* response team in order to obtain information. Formal ongoing monitoring of the atmosphere and the ocean did not commence until the third week in March. Local public health directors advised strict supervision of children on the beach and warned people to avoid contact with the oil. People were also warned not to collect or consume local shellfish. In the Milford Haven area residents were warned to stay inside, close their doors and windows tightly, and avoid inhalation of the oil fumes—an impossible task even indoors. A number of local people complained of respiratory problems and other ill effects from the oil. Six weeks after the spill, the Dyfed Public Health Office mailed two thousand questionnaires to area residents about their perception of possible short- and long-term health consequences of the disaster.

All in all, despite some efforts by local health authorities, the actual monitoring of the event was insufficient and much too late of be of any significance. By the time the oil stopped spreading, one hundred miles of Welsh coastline were saturated, as were several miles of the nearby coast of Ireland. Estimates of bird casualties ran as high as forty-five thousand. The fishing and tourist industry all but came to a halt. There was widespread public criticism of the government's handling of the spill response, but the Joint Response Center would not comment on its handling of the situation prior to an official inquiry. Members of the Response Center were given a gag order and told they were not allowed to use the word "disaster." Despite repeated pleas from a broad sector of Welsh society, the government refused to recognize the spill as a national catastrophe. Many local people were distrustful of the government's role from the first week of the calamity. Stephen Mulholland, chief of the Royal Society of Birds, expressed sentiments that were shared by many when he stated, "It is already clear that the spill is substantially larger than so far stated by authorities and that its effects will be considerably greater than any present official predictions. The carefully stage-managed press briefings by officials were either naive or designed to mislead." Indeed, there was a pervasive sense among many that the government had totally mishandled the situation and distorted the true extent of damage. The crisis was compounded, in part, by the fact that the region was contending with another disaster, "mad cow" disease, about which the people felt the government was less than forthcoming. Given the years of official denial and the reluctance to declare the mad cow disease a crisis, the credibility of the government was further weakened in the wake of the *Sea Empress* spill.

When it was announced that the official inquiry into the spill and the government's handling of it would be conducted in-house by the Department of Transportation (which was in charge of the spill response), there was widespread dissatisfaction. Over thirty different groups representing various segments of the country banded together and collected one hundred thousand signatures calling for an independent inquiry to be conducted by Lord Donaldson. The government refused, and massive protests followed.

How the Events Were Framed by the Media

Many of the above-mentioned events from both oil spills were excluded from most of the international newspaper accounts. In fact, public health accounts and political controversies appeared in very few published news stories and were only mentioned in passing several paragraphs below lead paragraphs. Nor were any of the controversies I have mentioned used to frame the disaster. Furthermore, no systemic explanatory accounts of the oil spill or the resulting disasters were used.

In an effort to examine how the spills were reported, I examined the accounts published in both the local and international press. My survey of the *Braer* spill included the week following the spill, the period that coincides with the time in which the *Braer* went aground and broke up and the departure of the international press corps. Few international newspapers published any accounts after this date. Since the events surrounding the *Sea Empress* spill unfolded more slowly, I examined the news coverage for two weeks following the tanker first going aground, which again corresponds with the period in which the disaster received international coverage. In analyzing the newspaper accounts, I examined how the media framed the stories, how they constructed the events, who were used as the primary informants, what informants were underutilized or excluded, and what causal logic was used to account for the events.

The international press reports that were examined in the case of both spills all adhered to the same frame. The international account of the *Braer* spill can best be summarized thusly: In the fury of the North Sea an oil tanker was forced aground. The spill had the potential to be every bit as dramatic as the *Exxon-Valdez* oil spill. The government of the United Kingdom valiantly tried to save the almost pristine environment of the Shetland Islands. While the government struggled against the sea and storm, thousands of birds and tens of thousands of fish were killed by the spillage of the crude oil. The rugged Shetland Islanders, united by the threat of the calamity, joined forces with the United Kingdom to wrest the *Braer* from the rocks and protect their homeland. When the storm's ferocity increased and the breakup of the tanker neared, a tragedy was averted when Mother Nature's forces miraculously washed the oil cargo out to sea.

The international accounts of the *Sea Empress* spill displayed many of the same themes. A supertanker went aground along a pristine coast during a ferocious storm and threatened a major wildlife habitat. Ultimately, the damage was not as bad as first feared. Heavy seas were responsible for breaking up the oil and saving the environment from considerable harm. However, the United Kingdom was portrayed in a somewhat less positive light, largely because of the failure to adhere to the Donaldson Report's recommendation to have salvage tugs on hand. Still, although it was subjected to more criticism than in the *Braer* spill, the government largely succeeded in downplaying the actual size and impact of the spill by withholding crucial information from the media until the major focus of the international press was lessened by time. The government also succeeded in underplaying the actual extent of the public criticism that existed not only in Wales but in all of Great Britain. In both instances the framing of the stories centered around Mother Nature being largely responsible for both the disasters and the protection of the environment from their potentially devastating impact.

Although the Texaco corporation was the owner of the oil aboard the *Sea Empress* and was to some degree liable for damages, mention of the company was conspicuously absent in press accounts. While there were several questions about whether the corporation had acted responsibly, Texaco was undoubtedly eager to avoid public attention for a number of reasons, including the recent worldwide scandal involving the corporation's behavior in oil extraction in Ecuador. Texaco had already been severely criticized in many quarters for what was perceived as its callous disregard for both the environment and the welfare of indigenous people.

The framing of the spill in Wales was also influenced by the allegations made during the *Braer* spill that nongovernment organizations were guilty of scaremongering tactics in order to raise money. As one NGO spokesperson told me, "The press comes to NGOs to define whether it [a spill] is a disaster. . . . They eagerly try to get NGOs to make calamity statements and then blame us later if it turns out the spill wasn't the disaster they depicted." Greenpeace was especially singled out for harsh criticism by a columnist for the conservative *Sunday Telegraph*. When the environmental impact of the *Braer* spill was not quite as devastating as Greenpeace spokesperson Paul Horsman had predicted, he was sharply criticized. In reality, Horsman's statement was reasonable at the time it was made. Furthermore, the judgment of whether ultimately a spill is a disaster is always narrowly defined in strictly environmental terms, rather than in terms of economics, politics, or the impact on human populations. Environmentalists, politicians, and the press are responsible for constructing this narrow standard of judgment.

The harsh criticism that Greenpeace was subjected to in the press by some columnists after the *Braer* catastrophe made the representatives of the organization very reluctant to make any statement about the spill in Wales. One Greenpeace official told me off the record that "[the criticism] was the reason we were slightly more cautious this time. If anyone was going to define the disaster, it wasn't going to be us." Greenpeace officials were afraid that if they made such statements "they [Greenpeace] would become the issue rather than the spill itself becoming the issue." Since this fear had a chilling effect on a major international environmental group, it made other, smaller organizations reluctant to make assessments of the spill, according to other NGO representatives that I interviewed.

The frames the local media presented resembled the frames of the international press in many ways. However, they also stressed the controversies surrounding the United Kingdom's cleanup and the uncertainties and anxieties centered around the public health issues. Local press printed far less emphasis on collective solidarity and much more emphasis on social conflict. United Kingdom officials and their cleanup teams were often portrayed as unwelcome outsiders. For centuries both regions, which are culturally distinct from England, have resented and resisted the intrusive authority imposed by London. The contestation between local and national authority was underscored by these communities' historical, cultural, and political-economic locations within the larger orb of Great Britain. In the instance of the *Sea Empress* spill, one influential regional paper, *The Western Telegraph,* actually became involved in organizing a protest against the United Kingdom's reluctance to conduct an independent inquiry of the disaster. However, social conflict and unrest were not systematically or consistently explored. In terms of explanation, local frames again resembled those of the international media, despite proximity to the local perspective. Local opposition expressed during the disaster was all but muted, thereby silencing the substance of their opposition which is so pertinent to our understanding of the event.

One major difference between the coverage of the local and the international media is that the local media, as might be expected, continued to have extensive coverage of the spill for months after the international media departed and all but abandoned the story. Thus, local coverage proved to be both more highly nuanced and extensive. However, in keeping with the news coverage of other technological disasters, the media, with few exceptions, failed to discuss the possible long-term health effects of the spill and the cleanup effort.

There was, however, one disturbing similarity between the way in which both the local and nonlocal media reported the stories. The majority of the sources cited were from the power elite. The journalists relied to a disturbingly large degree on government sources. On one level this was surprising, since other studies indicate that local coverage often provides more balanced sources of information (Molotch and Lester 1975). This propensity of reporters to depend on government sources is in keeping with news media's reporting of other technological disasters, including the Santa Barbara and *Exxon-Valdez* oil spills, and Bhopal.

In the case of the two United Kingdom spills, overreliance on government sources gave the government power to define the stories and to serve its own interests. The differential access to the media further prevented other groups from providing competing accounts of events. The consequence was that some accounts, namely the government's, were valorized while others were marginalized.

Although the spills were presented as environmental disasters, few scientists or environmentalists—who could potentially have explained the spills in more objective context—were actually quoted. Other sources, such as local residents, were seldom cited, even by the local press. The people who were at greatest risk and harmed the most by the spills and cleanups were the fishermen, crofters, and people in the tourist industry; in other words, people who may legitimately be labeled the actual disaster victims. The failure to record the voices of disaster victims, who bear a disproportionate share of the risk and harm that results from a technological disaster, is a common oversight of the press in its coverage of these events.

ANALYSIS: THE MEDIA RESPONSE TO DISASTER

News becomes the contested terrain in which a struggle for meaning is often encountered. The media play a significant role in both informing people about events and influencing what they think about events. While some argue that the media may not tell people what to think, the media does hold the power to tell people what to think about (Wallack and Dorfman 1993). News reports have the power to influence and shape our perception of disasters and define them.

The media literally have the ability to create a disaster or dismiss it as a nonevent, as they did with the *Braer* spill. More often than not, when the media do construct a catastrophic event as a disaster, they seldom construct the frame from the victim's perspective. As stated in the introduction, the media's ability to define a situation lends them ideological power. Public perception of a disaster is largely determined by the way in which news stories frame the event. Although these frames often appear as natural constructions about the world, they are decidedly cultural constructions that have great potential to deceive and distort the reporting of events. This social production of meanings by the news media often results in contestations of interpretation. The victims, those most harmed by a disaster, often must struggle to establish their interpretation of the event against the ideological frames generated by the status quo and replicated by the media. The victims' ability to resist or overcome these frames is constrained by the differences in relative power and ability to manipulate imagery and text. The disaster narrative frames employed by the media vary surprisingly little from one disaster to another, drawing upon existing broad underlying themes which serve as templates for cultural constructions of reality.

TECHNOLOGICAL DISASTER NARRATIVES

Disaster narratives that journalists employ in their descriptive accounts often reiterate a standardized story that can fit a wide array of calamities. Accounts of previous influential events—as evidenced by the way the *Exxon-Valdez* spill colored subsequent reporting of other spills—also shape narratives. When reporters are struggling to decide what angles to emphasize in the early hours of a story, they are further influenced by the kind of story their editor expects of them and what other reporters are writing about the story (Smith 1993). The "myth" of a story—that is, the decision on what a story is to be— unfolds quickly in the early hours of the days of an event and is seldom later challenged by reporters (Smith 1993: 24).

While there may be practical organizational reasons why reporters select a compelling narrative, the origins of these narratives do not lie solely with the urgent need to process and make sense of large amounts of information quickly. If the construction of news is situated in a broader arena than the newsroom and is seen through Gramsci's notion of hegemony, the decisive role of the political/economic influence of certain interest groups emerges (Ryan 1991). As one observer has argued, "the ultimate impact of framing is pro-establishment" (Iyengar 1991). In other words, the underlying cultural logic of disaster narratives tends to reinforce the hegemonic forces of society. It is unavoidable, then, that the discourse about disasters becomes a discourse about the politics of disasters. Consequently, the extremely political processes of controlling access to information and of the construction of meaning must lie at the center of any analysis of man-made or natural disasters.

While technological disaster narratives vary from incident to incident, there are certain recurring themes that emerge, reinforcing the hegemonic forces of society. In so-called environmental disasters such as oil spills, the focus is generally on the effects on the ecology and not on the effects on human communities. This is an attempt to naturalize the disaster. It is often taken a step further when the disaster narrative also places the spill outside human control. This, in effect, removes oppositional discourse about responsibility and blame from both government agencies and corporate entities. The response to disaster is depicted as a valiant, and often futile, struggle with Mother Nature—a scenario that places much responsibility outside human control. The resultant reification makes the event appear all the more like an accident and less the result of human negligence (Tuchman 1978).

Finally, routinized disaster narratives ignore the long-term continuum of a technological disaster and tend to report on the event in an episodic fashion typical of the news media. Thereby they ignore the longitudinal evolution of the disaster and serve to reinforce the neglect of systemic forces and the long-term effects of disaster on human communities. This results in little nonlocal follow-up as the disaster story continues to unfold over the coming months or even years. Most stories that appear after the initial event are framed around "anniversary" stories rather than in-depth, follow-up features. The media treat technological disasters as they do most news stories. Stories become dated very quickly and are abandoned for other "breaking" stories. Obviously this precludes any systemic analysis of long-term social or health problems. In the case of technological disasters, this treatment is most unfortunate, since the continuum of these particular phenomena, unlike that of many disasters, often unfolds slowly, and it can take years for many of the effects to become manifest.

CONCLUSION

As witnessed in the Shetlands and Welsh accounts, in the aftermath of technological disasters people struggle to make sense of the catastrophe by assigning it meaning. What follows is a bargaining about the meaning of reality. The ability and power of people to advance their competing accounts are increasingly contingent, in large part, on their access to the news media. Thus, the news becomes one of the central arenas in which this contestation of meaning is played out. The subtle frames that the news media use to depict and narrate the disaster determine, to a significant degree, which interpretations will prevail and which may endure in the historical record.

The media accounts of a disaster are more than a mere collection of narrative stories. They are social relations mediated by narratives that are produced and reproduced by hegemonic forces which seek to present a unified view of social reality. Moreover, they are decidedly not stories that disaster victims "tell themselves about themselves" (Geertz 1973: 448). They are altogether too often stories that perpetuate the disjunction between "our" history and "their" history. Examining these media narratives allows us in the "here and now" to witness firsthand how "a people without history" (Wolf 1982) is possible.

NOTES

1. For an in-depth exploration of the *Exxon-Valdez* oil spill, see Button (1993).

2. The Shetlands are an island archipelago approximately two hundred fifty miles west of Bergen, Norway, and over two hundred fifty miles north of Aberdeen, Scotland. They are governed by the Scottish Home Office. For a more extensive analysis of this spill, see Button 1995.

3. For a discussion of the tendency to overlook the impact of "environmental" disasters on human populations, see Button 1994.

BIBLIOGRAPHY

Barth, F. 1993. *Balinese Worlds.* Chicago: University of Chicago Press.

Button, G. 1993. *Social Conflict and the Formation of Emergent Groups in a Technological Disaster: The Exxon-Valdez Oil Spill and the Response of the Residents in the Area of Homer, Alaska.* Unpublished Ph.D. dissertation. Waltham, MA: Brandeis University.

———. 1994. *The Exxon-Valdez Oil Spill: An Environmental or Human Disaster?* Paper presented at the annual meeting of the American Public Health Association, Washington, DC, November 1, 1994.

———. 1995. "'What You Don't Know Can't Hurt You': The Right to Know and the Shetland Islands Oil Spill." *Human Ecology* 23, 2: 24–258.

Comaroff, J., and S. Roberts. 1981. *Rules and Processes.* Chicago: University of Chicago Press.

Cormack, M. 1995. *Ideology.* Ann Arbor, MI: University of Michigan Press.

DeLillo, D. 1985. *White Noise.* New York: Penguin Books.

Edelman, M. 1977. *Political Language.* New York: Academic Press.

Fallows, J. 1996. *Breaking the News.* New York: Pantheon Books.

Geertz, C. 1973. *Interpretation of Culture.* New York: Basic Books.

Gitlin, T. 1980. *The Whole World Is Watching.* Berkeley: University of Calfornia Press.

Gusfield, J. 1981. *The Culture of Public Problems*. Chicago: University of Chicago.

Iyengar, S. 1991. *Is Anyone Responsible?: How Television Frames Political Issues*. Chicago: University of Chicago Press.

Merry, S. 1990. *Getting Justice and Getting Even*. Chicago: University of Chicago Press.

Molotch, H., and M. Lester. 1975. "Accidental News: The Great Oil Spill as a Local Occurrence and a National Event." *American Journal of Sociology* 81, 5: 235–260.

Rappaport, R. 1993. "The Anthropology of Trouble." *American Anthropologist* 95: 295–303.

Rosen, L. 1984. *Bargaining For Reality*. Chicago: University of Chicago Press.

Ryan, C. 1991. *Prime Time Activism*. Boston: South End Press.

Sahlins, M. 1974. *Culture and Practical Reason*. Chicago: University of Chicago Press.

Smith, C. 1993. "News Sources and Power Elites in News Coverage of the *Exxon-Valdez* Oil Spill." *Journalism Quarterly* 70, 2: 393–402.

Tuchman, G. 1978. *Making News*. New York: The Free Press.

Wallack, L., and L. Dorfman. 1993. *Media Advocacy and Public Health*. Newbury Park, CA: Sage.

Wolf, E. 1982. *Europe and a People Without History*. Berkeley: University of California Press.

———. 1990. "Facing Power: Old Insights, New Questions." *American Anthropologist* 92: 586–596.

IV

VARIETIES OF CULTURAL RESPONSE

The social and cultural responses of individuals and groups to catastrophe alter in relationship to the problems that face both during the often lengthy evolution of a disaster: through warning, impact, emergency, relief, recovery, and reconstruction. Communities may fragment and coalesce many times around specific problems crucial to survival and well-being. Many people will see disaster and reconstruction as an opportunity for major changes in the way things are done, to improve conditions both in the society and in their own individual lives. On the other hand, many others want nothing more than to continue with the status quo, to reestablish a degree of consistency and continuity with the past. How resources are mobilized, and on whose behalf, often brings conflict.

Ultimately, people's responses to disaster pivot on the crucial elements of their multiple social identities in the various stages and their negotiation of the issue of the changes that disasters present. The separation and coincidence of individual and societal concerns at different times can ultimately become crucial to the continuity of both in traditional terms.

THE WORST OF TIMES, THE BEST OF TIMES: TOWARD A MODEL OF CULTURAL RESPONSE TO DISASTER

SUSANNA M. HOFFMAN
Independent Researcher

A GREAT MANY MORE PEOPLE SURVIVE CATASTROPHES THAN ARE KILLED BY them. When the dust settles, the water recedes, and the ashes take flight in the wind, the survivors are left in pieces. A world that was solid has turned friable. A milieu that functioned has disassembled into silos without seed, roads without terminus, homes no longer standing. A set of meanings and explanations that offered sense has dissolved into detritus as much as has levee and promenade, edifice and avenue.

People's recovery in the aftermath of disaster constitutes the Janus face of a major catastrophe, the social countenance laid over the physical reality. It can be a time of not just material but social devastation, fragmentation, and despair. For many, it can also be, quite remarkably, a time of social cohesion, purpose, and almost glory. Recently much anthropological research has taken place among people who have survived major calamities. The misfortunes described are as different as the survivors' faces. The locales of the calamities are as diverse as survivors' languages. The anthropologists' foci in studying the calamities have been as serendipitous as the discipline allows. Yet, among the cacophony of place, event, and topic, a certain order generally emerges. For those suspended between havoc and wholeness, by and large a process ensues. Its steps are many and complex, yet they are almost as predictable as crawling, standing, and walking.

There has been debate about whether the experiences disaster victims encounter are universal. Certain scholars say the steps of recovery do not always occur or that the order of phases is not necessarily consistent. I step in to add my considerations to the controversy. I speak from a research platform of rare intensity even for an anthropologist. Anthropologists undergo day-to-day participant observation, often in less-than-pleasant conditions. I went through day-to-day disaster recovery as witness and victim that was decidedly harrowing. The Oakland firestorm, in which I lost my every material posses-sion, was not a disaster one would expect to produce the phases I am about to describe. It never involved the ghettoization of disaster victims. No survivor camps or tent cities ever stood. Few victims needed much material help, though all that arrived was appreciated, and most required eventual financial settlement to rebuild homes. Aid agencies became a fixture for a time, but the Federal Emergency Management Administration largely offered only the potential for funds few victims in the long run used. Other agencies aided more with problems and paperwork than with goods. None stayed so long or was so important as insidiously to build dependencies among the victims. Nonethe-less, the Oakland firestorm survivors passed through recovery phases in almost the clockwork order and parallel characteristics that researchers have described for other populations.

Because of that and the consequent research I have been drawn to, I risk compiling a general scheme of disaster recovery. The model stems from my own data in combination with material garnered from other researchers. The process I describe may not be utterly universal nor the steps exact for all peo-ples, but it is highly pervasive. The model is ideal in nature, though the word "ideal" seems misplaced when it comes to disaster, a situation where every-thing is all too real. The periods outlined in the scheme may blend one into another. They may take place earlier or later and occur to greater or lesser degree than I outline, and the particulars of a people's experience may vary. Not all phases are experienced by all disaster survivors. By schematizing, I mean not at all to trivialize the catastrophe or the sufferings of anyone. Being one who has traveled the time line and endured firsthand the paradigm, I would not do that. But I do believe that for a more complete understanding of disaster's effects on human communities, for those who suffer the phenome-non, study it, or tender aid, the beginnings of a synthesis concerning the process of disaster recovery is called for.

A BRIEF SYNOPSIS OF THE OAKLAND FIRESTORM

On Sunday, October 20, 1991, the residents of Oakland and Berkeley, Califor-nia, were struck by a tremendous firestorm sweeping down the hills behind them. Traveling at sixty miles an hour, the raging fire tore through block after city block, reducing most of the houses it met to two feet of ash. When the flames were finally quelled, miles of community lay in ruin. Nearly four thou-sand dwellings had been destroyed, twenty-five people had died, and some six thousand residents were left homeless. Since the temperature of the fire reached over two thousand degrees Fahrenheit, most survivors had lost almost every possession they owned.

The inhabitants of the devastated zone could in general be described as middle to upper middle class. Most were well educated and relatively affluent. They held such jobs as professor, doctor, lawyer, teacher, social worker, nurse, business owner, and artist. Despite elevated occupations, though, most were dependent on regular salaries, and many strained to make ends meet. The majority were white, but many Asians, a considerable number of African Americans, and a Joseph's coat of ethnicities lived in the fire zone. Among the victims were a number of notables: a federal congressman, a state senator, a former mayor, a famous sports star. As the community was primarily familial, most of the victims were married. About one fourth of those rendered homeless were children. Single individuals and unmarried couples both hetero- and homosexual also lived among the area's homes and flats, and residing here and there were students attending several nearby colleges.

Living so near a renowned university and distinguished city, most of the victims could be said to follow socially progressive tenets. Most gave heed to racial, gender, and age equality. Many were highly committed to political causes. Most socialized with a network of friends in preference to extended family ties. Most, though not the students and some misguided elderly, had home insurance, although almost all quickly discovered that their insurance was seriously deficient.

Albeit middle class, affluent, and sophisticated, the Oakland firestorm survivors were still disaster victims, and the destruction they suffered was devastatingly total. In the following months and years, they, like disaster victims everywhere, faced the enormous task of reconstituting their lives from residence to relationship, pots and pans to understanding. These people were far from parochial, yet among them ritual immediately arose. They built shrines, invented ceremonies, and told sagas. A newspaper with fire-related news, columns, and fire-inspired poetry and fiction sprang to life. A book of disaster writings and shows of firestorm art appeared. Interaction among the survivors and between them and others went through an intricate social pavan of unification and segmentation.

As both victim and social scientist, I participated in the reconstitution of Oakland's charred world. I attended community meetings and gatherings. I belonged to my and other emergent neighborhood groups. I organized and led a group of those who held policies with my same insurance company. These groups included survivors of both genders, every age, race, and ethnicity. I also participated in a large women's group organized by the area's women architects, and I belonged to a small support group of twelve women that still occasionally gathers. As is almost universally the case, most of the survivors

returned to dwell again in the disaster zone. Some scattered to nearby locations, a few to distant ones. What the Oakland firestorm survivors underwent
and how they behaved does not differ greatly from survivors of other disasters.

Because of the circumstance of my research, in this article I cannot avoid
that I myself represent a number of "voices." To separate them I have chosen
to use the pronoun "they" and an occasional "we" to mean the victim
survivors of the firestorm, despite the fact that I am one of them. I use "I" to
designate my own experiences and impressions. I give ethnographic data, but
my approach is largely analytical, and much of my reportage is correspondingly through that screen. I hope that my various voices are not muddled in
this narrative. It is not the easiest chore to be ethnographer, ethnologist,
and subject.

THE CRISIS—RECOVERY'S PRIMARY PHASE   1ˢᵗ phase = crisis

Beginning almost immediately after a major catastrophe, be it hurricane, tornado, cyclone, fire, earthquake, volcanic eruption, flood, avalanche, or a technological calamity, generally there follows a period, usually quite short in   immediate aftermath
duration, when victims are propelled into a circumstance of extreme individuation (Turner 1961; Wallace 1956a, 1957a; Erikson 1976). This dramatic
phase occurred in Oakland, too.   And they are alone

Social form and fabric have dissolved, and survivors find themselves on
their own. Given the social nature of human life, this constitutes an abnormal,
disconcerting situation, often frightening for the victims. Wallace aptly paints   b/c social structure absent
the condition as survivors being "left naked and alone in a terrifying wilder-
ness of ruins" (1957b). As one survivor of Cyclone Tracy in Darwin, Australia,
describes,

> I thought there'd be nobody alive in the morning, including us. We
> were still all huddled together as it gradually died down and the
> dreadful noise stopped and the banging and breaking glass and the
> rest of it. Then there was a tap on the outside louvres and a male mid-
> dle-European voice said, "Is there anyone alive in there?" He said,
> "I'm looking for my wife and family," and he just moved off into the
> grey rainy dawn. (Bunbury 1994: 41)

> There was no warning, no evacuation order, no police, or coordina-
> tion. We were all on our own to save ourselves. Then when it was
> over, people wandered back like solitary ghosts, not knowing what to
> do. You could see them prowling like shadows in the still-smoking
> ashes. (An Oakland firestorm survivor)

This primary individuation marks the beginnings of victims' "liminality," a state where survivors have little sociocultural context and, thus, little identity. Disaster victims are cast into a transition not unlike that of a rite of passage, and though uninvited, the transition will likewise mark those affected throughout the process of recovery, if not forever (Turner 1961; Wallace 1956a; Oliver-Smith, this volume, chapter 8). As a victim of the Mexico City earthquake of 1970 related,

> I think it had to do with a new way of looking at things because of our experience. You can call it like mystical, philosophical, or Marxist, what the heck, Jesus, I don't know what it is, but it was a new state of awareness, something like cathartic, a constant catharsis, you know what I mean? (Poniatowska 1995: 139)

Survivors of the Oakland firestorm frantically took autonomous action as the flames encroached upon their homes. People leaped into cars and attempted to drive out of the fire's path by a number of escape routes. One that was narrow and blocked led to most of the deaths. Husbands and wives tried to locate one another. People threw belongings into vehicles and, in one case, a swimming pool. Some, fearing for family, pets, and belongings, crazily tried to reenter the flames. People were propelled by extreme states of anxiety into self-determined, self-saving actions. As is often the case in disaster, stories of this time made up most of the told and retold tales that later gave victims their sense of distinction (Adler 1992). Individual acts in the first dramatic moments offer a peak experience and defining mark in the total disaster episode. People in my support groups recounted their stories numerous times.

Despite the individuation that characterizes the critical early hours and days of disaster recovery, almost simultaneously two behaviors emerge that are highly communal in nature and that sow the seeds of a unity and emotional climate to come. While personal survival and economic self-interest may characterize action during the actual event, in the dawning aftermath victims save and aid one another no matter what their predisaster differences. As Redfield pointed out, quite pan-globally human societies emphasize life and the preservation of it over death. This basic rule takes precedence over cultural divisions of religion, class, ethnicity, or race. Indeed, it defines the essential nature of the group, the membership or who the people are called "us," and reasserts shared humanity and community (1962). Thus, from the first urgent moments, disaster victims reassert unity and identity with others. In Thera, Greece, villagers told me that after the 1956 volcanic earthquake, islander assisted islander across kin, religious, and occupational lines.[1] In the Oakland firestorm, those fleeing in cars gathered up those on foot. People canvased homes for one another's children, elderly parents, tenants, and pets. Those attempting to reenter the flames were often joined by friends and strangers so as not to enter alone.

Most primary credos also call for fellowship between compatriots, and disaster victims in the early aftermath further provide one another essential sustenance. They sacrifice their own goods to feed others, pool clothing, take in the lost. Oliver-Smith states that in the terrible days before aid arrived after the avalanche in Yungay, Peru, survivors donated vegetables and precious livestock to provision the gathering crowd of homeless (1992: 77–83). In Homestead, Florida, after Hurricane Andrew, victims pooled their clothing so that all were clad. In Kobe, Japan, earthquake survivors took in the disoriented even though they were strangers. The morning after Cyclone Tracy a Chinese man in a truck showed up at the shattered homes of many survivors distributing cigarettes and brandy he had taken from a shop (Bunbury 1994: 51). In all these actions, disaster victims exchange with one another, sending out the tentacles of bonding (Mauss 1967). A transition from atomized to community takes place.

In rapid succession, many disaster victims accordingly traverse a trinity of profound and provocative engrossments; life promoted over death, survival overwhelming the pull of possessions, and aid evolving into commonality. Various authors have attested that this succession brings about among disaster survivors a state something akin to euphoria (Wallace 1957b; Fritz 1961). I find it more a sense of purity derived from having come in touch with core tenets of existence, and, in fact, the term purity was much used to depict the sense that pervaded survivors of the great Chicago fire (Smith 1995: 35). Along with the other experiences, survivors have as well defeated danger, the shock of which imparts a peculiar, often remorseful, sense of hallowedness. Amidst the tragedy a state somewhat like exultation, humble but dignified, with profound closeness to others, sweeps over many survivors. Its overflowing sensibility constitutes what is later recollected as "the best of times." It lasts varying amounts of time, depending on how promptly complications and discord overtake recovery.

Initial responses at first link disaster victims to the peripheral community, those persons next to or nearby the calamity but not suffering loss. They, too, are life savers and aid givers and they, too, feel elation. They have escaped harm and surfaced owning the luxury of charity. They play a part in recovery that continues in ongoing counterpoint with those who bear more conspicuous injury.[2] Through the early days of the Oakland firestorm, the extended community united to help those devastated by the fire, donating apparel, money, and goods. "We camped out with a friend whose house was just beyond the fire zone for the first three days. We had no money, no clothes, the car had melted. I picked up clothes from the boxes people brought. Later I got toys, pots, and pans that people brought in," said one survivor. Local churches and synagogues provided dinners and put together emergency baskets of such necessities as spices, candles, and detergent. Volunteers rushed in to save pets (Zompolis 1994).

This sense of unity and community with disaster victims in the first recovery days often extends to far reaches. Smith describes that after the Chicago fire of 1871, "If the fire purified Chicago by burning away all but what was best within it, the challenge of the relief worked a similarly miraculous renewal and reunification of mankind elsewhere. In responding to Chicago's needs, the rest of the country forgot its petty artificial divisions and rediscovered its finest collective self" (Smith 1995: 44). More recently, Americans from coast to coast sent goods and money to victims of the Northridge earthquake, the Mississippi and Grand Forks floods, the East Coast icestorm and El Niño–driven California mudslides and Florida tornadoes.

In abrupt disasters the individualization, rescue, and sharing follow the occurrence of the calamitous event. In longer-developing disasters, such as chemical pollution of the soil, according to Erikson (1994), these actions tend to take place upon the discovery of damage. In either case, the initial responses set up two elements that continue to characterize the survivors: The most important help victims receive generally comes from among themselves, despite what outside aid might arrive later (Zaman 1989); an aura of purpose, almost a higher purpose, arises and immerses victims.

Victims begin to cohere into a group. "We headed for the school and set up there and found a lot of people had converged there with the same idea. We all calmed down. We organised ourselves into the school and set up quite quickly with what we needed to get though the next couple of days," stated one victim of Cyclone Tracy (Bunbury 1994: 54). In Oakland as they discovered their homes were lost, victims began to assemble under the freeway, where police and firemen had set up central headquarters, and to organize their first community meetings.

With invisible compulsions amidst visible dilemma, the first individualized survivors embark on what soon becomes a communal ship of demos over person. Despite questions of causes, faults, and failures, they begin to foster what in due course grows into a double nimbus of redemption—a drive for recovery combined with a sense of validity and deservedness. This two-pronged sentiment, which sometimes evolves into righteousness or martyrdom, helps give definition to later estrangement.

Meanwhile, as if a kaleidoscope turned, the pattern of what was the victims' worldview begins a shift from former design into a new one. If denial of risk was in place, it has crumbled. If vulnerability was part of the ideology, it is now manifest. As a result, the lives of survivors, their perspective and understandings, become permanently altered, never to recapture completely the convictions once held. Erikson calls it a new sense of truth, that the environment, both social and natural, in which all takes place has proved to be brittle and full of caprice.

Human beings are surrounded by layers of trust, radiating out in concentric circles like the ripples in a pond. The experience of trauma, at its worst, can mean not only a loss of confidence in the self but a loss of confidence in the scaffolding of family and community, in the structures of human government, in the larger logics by which humankind lives, and in the ways of nature itself. . . . They (disaster victims) look out at the world through different lenses. And in that sense they may be said to have experienced not only (a) a *changed sense of self* and (b) a *changed way of relating to others* and (c) *changed worldview* altogether. (1994: 240–242)

Kalsched also offers some insight into the changed sense of self, way of relating, and worldview. He finds that, once traumatized, the psyche continues to be self-traumatizing and that the victims of trauma continually find themselves in life situations where they are retraumatized (1996: 5). A Cyclone Tracy survivor said: "It helped me to realize that even the best set out and most orderly lives can so easily be overturned or destroyed by a cyclone or a flood or a bushfire" (Bunbury 1994: 143). I understand as well. My experience has proved that nothing lasts forever, nothing is trustworthy, not a house, not alliances, not intentions, and I operate daily under this new conception.

THE AFTERMATH NEXUS—SECONDARY PHASE

As the pitch of the actual critical event wanes and leaves the extent of devastation clear, a second, more prolonged phase of disaster recovery replaces the first. Its length depends on the place, the disaster, and the particular circumstance, but generally it lasts from some months to some years. The nexus of it—and I use this term because the events are as interlinked as they are sequential—incorporates occurrences both internal and external to the survivor group. The euphoria of the first phase, if experienced, carries over for a time, but in the secondary phase, as Erikson points out, the state of "utopia" and the euphoric sentiment experienced immediately after the crisis prove to be short-lived (1994: 234–236).

The onset of the second stage of disaster recovery could be defined as starting when the individuated survivors merge into the union described above, and when they consolidate, at least for a while, into a unity. Survivors come to the realization that as both individuals and a set, they are the lambs of the catastrophe and on this terrible foundation they cleave. The sudden commonality they share becomes a common bond. Such cohesion takes place among all disaster victims, no matter where or what the catastrophe. Button points out that even in areas of chronic disaster, where prior thought held that continuous crisis kept the population fragmented, unification occurs (1995).

A new definition, a ruler to describe status and mark membership, arises that is at once inclusive and exclusive. Some certain amount of loss, some measured degree of damage, comes to herald who is and is not calamity's true sufferer. In Oakland the criteria became whether or not the *whole* home was destroyed. Those whose homes were only partially damaged were not accepted as the same sort of victim as those who had lost everything. Oliver-Smith states that victims of the Yungay avalanche acquired a different status from survivors of the earthquake only. The differentiation took on increasing importance in the social life of the survivor society after the emergency had passed (1992: 81).

Whatever the definition, group sentiments ferment and spread. In Yungay, by the time the government started efforts to move them, survivors refused to relocate from their refugee camps. Unity and mutuality as victims were solidifying (Oliver-Smith 1992). In Oakland, group cohesion started in diverse meetings and gelled into unity when a single disaster center was demanded and opened. Though living sites were scattered, the center served as a focal point where survivors found comradery and the collective agendas that propelled them.

Individually, but also as part of the newly unified group, disaster survivors in the secondary phase begin the effort to regather and reconstruct their lives. It is within this stage that disaster victims enact, and the disaster researcher sees, the reformulation of the social and cultural edifice. The specifics of the disaster victim responses arise from all levels of their prior cultural context, including ethnohistory, political ecology, local social structure, political organization, and economics. Chairetakis found that prior political systems and affiliations affected the recovery of Italian villagers devastated in an earthquake (1995). Bolin and Stanford depict the different recovery of rural communities due to such factors as citizenship, home ownership, education, and language (see this volume, chapter 5). In Oakland, undoubtedly victims' affluence and political power led to successful financial recovery. Still, in general the recovery process rolls for most disaster survivors much like a tram hurtling over the cultural landscape.

Immediately, gatherings in Oakland were marked with the motto and statement of purpose that the community would rebuild and be again as it had been. These same words are commonly the early motto, commonly those spoken at first among all survivor groups. "We will rebuild. We can. We must. We will grow stronger," read a sign on a Florida City church after Hurricane Andrew (Gore 1993: 37). These words were echoed at Yungay and after the *Exxon-Valdez* oil spill. They were uttered by the victims of the Mississippi and Grand Forks floods. The idea of return to what was, to replace things that had been as they were, becomes a driving aim. The will to adapt to change has to overcome an impulse to restore the past, states Marris, and in their early cohesion disaster survivors reflect the universal conservatism and resistance all people exhibit when faced with new and altered circumstance (1974: 5). Also attesting to the unity and group adhesion among the survivors is the use of the pronoun "we" combined with statements of purpose.

Part of the first "gathering element" disaster victims experience in this second stage is the generation of ceremony. The rapidity with which rites and rituals appear gives credence to just how essential they are to human existence. The rites disaster victims fashion acknowledge the event, give vent to grief, settle questions, and perhaps, as Chapple proposes, operate as a vehicle to enable necessary change (1970). While marking the event, however, they also give survivors ownership of it and constitute the first maneuver to lift the calamity to the abstract and restamp it in a cultural fashion. Ceremony classifies the calamity; simultaneously it launches an interpretation of it, one of numerous "framings" to come.

Survivor rites sometimes replay forms and acknowledge beliefs that are cultural standards. Sometimes they apply new content to old forms. Sometimes they represent totally new creations. Whichever, many manifest another element. In the face of the undeniable physical basis to existence, they remarry, if only for the passing moment, nature and culture—at least in those cultures that abstractly separate the two realms. Disaster victims' observances almost inevitably take place near or upon the devastated turf and focus on environment. People in Yungay gathered on the avalanche scar. They brought flowers to the muddy wash and adorned it with crosses of wood and stone. The four palm trees that survived the onslaught and remained atop the flow were turned into a chapel. The town moved its commemoration ceremonies to take place there, so that the physical remains of the event evolved into a culturized, sacred monument (Oliver-Smith 1992: 192–195). People in Oakland gathered for their convocations as near the burn site as possible. What was left of nature within the burned-out area was placated with cultural gifts. Surviving people turned surviving trees into cultural altars. They bedecked whatever hardy dendra still thrived with vases of cultivated flowers, man-made trinkets, and messages. Some transformed their charred property into semi-chapels and meditation sites.

Within their conclaves survivors cast themselves into the identity and lot of survivors, and they recommunalize society in ways other than through ceremony. Survivors become engulfed in practices and immersed in a litany of concerns related to their circumstance. They blanket themselves in a coating of new alliances, in essence initiating a nascent subsociety and culture within their larger traditions. New devotions and new aims overrun their lives, alienating them from the commonality they held with kin, ally, and neighbor before the calamity. Soon they feel they cannot deal with those who did not share their trauma. As if being swirled into an eddy off the mainstream of a river, disaster survivors spin into separate life ways. Isolated in space, departing in the interests that absorb them, swept away in time by their idiosyncratic involvements, they evolve into a set of social marginals.

In contemporary disasters, outside agencies arrive during this period, an element that contributes to the complexity of recovery. "Outside arriving forces now enmesh the process of recovery," Dyer and McGoodwin remark (this volume, chapter 11). The actions of external respondents to the disaster can allow for successful reformulation of patterns within a disaster community or they can result in what constitutes a secondary disaster. External authorities carry everything from doughnuts to dogma on their relief trays. When their ideas diverge from survivors' traditions, they depress both client and recovery process. Furthermore, external relief often conflicts with survivors' continuing self-help. Self-help relies on the ability to mobilize resources, and those resources usually depend on old sociocultural institutions. In Bangladesh these were kinship and associations (this volume, chapter 10). In Oakland they were kinship, community clubs, and religious organizations. Survivors also used their professions to organize advice "fairs" replete with tax specialists, lawyers, psychologists, and other experts to counsel fellow survivors.

Step by step the marginalization, exclusion, and self-involved interests of survivors evolve into their social estrangement. To begin with, the survivors of many disasters are bivouacked in spatially separate encampments. Even without separate camps, as in Oakland, assembling together evolves into a theme, and from theme to self-imposed social isolation. As Erikson states it, it is as if survivors are persons without home, citizenship, or niche, invited to gather in a quarter set aside for the disfranchised, a ghetto for the unattached (1994). What once defined stranger and friend snakes into new boundaries. Survivors begin to see themselves not only as a group distinct from the community surrounding them but adversarial to it. It is, in fact, adversity to the outside community that adds the final fix to disaster victims' cohesion. Segmentary opposition and the concomitant cleaving it evokes pops up as aftergrowth to disaster like mushrooms shadow rain.

The line demarcating association on the one side and contention on the other is often twofold. First, survivors develop a divergence from those unharmed around them, and vice versa. We in Oakland soon found that our sentiments and actions were so foreign to those "unsinged" surrounding us that we isolated our social relations to fellow survivors. Second, disaster victims inevitably seize upon a particular faction they come to deem the enemy. The perceived foe is generally whatever agency brings or embodies, and consequently controls, restricts, or denies, restitution. Most commonly, as in Yungay (Bode 1989; Doughty 1986; Oliver-Smith 1992) and Thera, Greece, it is the government. It can also be the main relief agency or possibly the empowered upper class. After Cyclone Tracy the Australian government forced evacuation of women and children from the disaster site and sent in first the Navy and then the state police. The government and police became the adversary. "They weren't allowing people in. . . . To us it didn't make a lot of sense to us that they wouldn't allow us back. We were residents of the place. Surely we could get back in," quoted one survivor (Bunbury 1994: 106–107). Among the Oakland firestorm survivors, as echoed by Hurricane Andrew's, the enemy that emerged was America's great collective Goliath, the insurance companies. While most firestorm survivors thought they were fully insured, they had been misled by wording and other insurance policy manipulations. The square-footage rates for rebuilding homes had been vastly underestimated. The insurance agents who sold the policies were shockingly ill informed. Typical of insurance industry practice, when disaster struck, victims were assailed with a bevy of rotating adjustors—most survivors had to deal with as many as twelve—who were often reticent to inform them of rights and were wantonly inconsistent in their treatment of claims. In consequence, survivors united to battle the insurance companies in allied groups. I, for example, advertised, discovered, and eventually led thirty-five persons insured with my same company to settlement. Claimants of other insurers did the same. Never before had the insurance companies faced united leagues of policy holders.

Correspondingly, the outside community and the relief or government agencies slide from initial compassion into an oppositional stance of their own, particularly as the victims' conditions continue. The community surrounding disaster survivors, once sympathetic, begins to react rigidly against the new class among them. Disaster victims by their circumstance threaten change, and in the face of that potential, the larger community retrenches. Having early on embraced disaster victims, now outsiders tag survivors as users and abusers who, if they receive aid, are "getting something for nothing." Negating the disaster, they begin to view the victims' circumstance as the result of their own failings, a consequence of sin, idleness, or indigence. The outsiders also feel betrayed by the victims. Once comrades, they now find themselves excluded from arriving aid. Their sense of unity with victims turns to resentment and jealousy. We in Oakland were told we didn't deserve new houses. We were robbing insurance companies and committing fraud. At the same time we were frequently met with such comments as: "I wish my house would burn down so I could have a new one." Victims are hard put to understand the resentment. As outsiders see survivors as the great unwashed, survivors see outsiders as the great unscathed.

Conflict is a powerful organizing principle of behavior, simplifying and clarifying immediate purposes, says Marris. Conflict also functions as a way to work out grief (1974: 98). Ideologies of conflict enable those overwhelmed by the confusion of change to take their bearings and lean toward strategy for reconstruction. These conflicts, however, thereafter tend to maintain themselves and become part of what is conserved (1974: 98–103).

At this point in disaster recovery, what occurs is a series of events that no survivor, agency, or neighbor is prepared for. A near-to-full bag of cultural tricks, including categorization, name-calling, social isolation, resistance, and occasionally combative actions—all the devious truck of segmentary opposition—drops down to divide, devalue, and dehumanize. Disaster survivors come to view the surrounding community as languorous, merciless, and selfish, their particular foe as deprivational, duplicitous, and wanton. The outside community and agencies likewise rigidify against the new class among them. Syllogisms that facilitate breakdown erupt. Most commonly each groups labels the other "takers." The taker—in essence "thief"—is an efficacious metaphor. Through it each accusing group declares itself the possessor of superior principles not held by the other. Each becomes the good against the bad. The taker, after all, takes goods. The goods are as tangible as brick and mortar and as intangible as dignity and honor. Other accusations are cast as well, all of them constituting a form of attack that rids one of obligation (Douglas 1970; Lewis 1983). And that is what occurs. Between outside community, aid giver, and disaster victim duty is forsaken. Reciprocity in every way diminishes.

"I do remember quite vividly having resentment against some of the interstate police," said a Cyclone Tracy survivor. "(My nephews) got heavily harassed by the police who believed they were stealing." Another characterized the police as "like storm troopers" (Bunbury 1994: 97, 98). In Oakland, survivors accused insurance companies of withholding insurance payments and of thievery in accepting premiums but not fulfilling claims. Insurance companies in Oakland called survivors who pursued their claims "greedy." Members of the community seemed to feel the victims should accept their lot and not pursue their claims to the fullest. Local merchants and builders were making considerable money on survivors' needs, and survivors, well aware of it, decried them. Meanwhile friendships dissolved for all, as nonvictims belittled victims' suffering and told them how well off they were to get new things.

Consequently, there arrives between disaster victim, outsider, and agency a new code of behavior. From behind oppositional boundaries, only trickery allows for success (Douglas 1970, 1978). Deceit, often fraud, and a potent cocktail of double-edged betrayal and denouncement follow. About cyclone Tracy one victim stated:

Darwin citizens wishing to return to their home to rebuild their lives and make their future . . . were told unless they had a permit they couldn't come back. Now these permits were issued by petty bureaucrats who would ask questions as to where were you going to live. At this stage I was involved in that system. I was handing out addresses of houses which were habitable so people could say, "Oh well, I'm staying at 26 Smith Street," or whatever until they woke up that all of a sudden there were hundreds of people giving the one address, but we were deliberately finding ways around the system. (Bunbury 1994: 107)

In Oakland, insurance companies required that in order to receive funds to replace destroyed personal items that policies covered, victims provide them with lists of items, the original date of purchase, purchase price, and present-day cost of replacement. On top of that, one of America's most renowned insurance companies demanded rosters of wedding guests of victims married twenty or more years as proof that destroyed belongings were gifts. The effort psychologically, but also in terms of labor, was daunting. In reaction, those who found themselves able to compile lists provided theirs to those who could not. The same lists with the same items were, therefore, used any number of times.

Agencies' agendas differ from survivors', further firing conflict. A Cyclone Tracy victim said:

But of course, what happened after the cyclone was the planners (the Cities Commission from Canberra) . . . they saw a clean slate, now here was a flattened town and they could maybe implement some of the interesting things that they thought would be good for Darwin, and so they made these plans. Now the people who stayed here, well they immediately got very possessive about what they were going to do with their own plot of land, and they wanted a very strong say in any changes that were going to take place. Resident action groups sprang up all over the place. (Bunbury 1994: 131)

During this phase disaster survivors often pass further from the sort of victims who were injured to the sort who are prey. "For just about every aircraft going out full of evacuees [one] was coming back full of consultants, building system designers, etc. It was staggering the number of opportunists who flocked into the place" (Bunbury 1994: 132). The same phenomenon was reported in Yungay after the avalanche, in Florida after Hurricane Andrew, and in Oakland after the fire. Architects and builders from far-flung communities arrived to take advantage of the destruction, many of them deserting unfinished houses when they took on yet other houses to build or their estimates were incorrect. Architects from across the country flew in to find prospective clients. Arriving by the hundreds, carpenters, bulldozer drivers, tree removers all worked both for survivors and against them with insurance companies.

Meanwhile, internal to the ostensibly unified disaster group, another set of processes in disaster recovery unfolds. For various reasons the survivor group turns fractious. This happens sometimes in rapid order, sometimes over a more prolonged period. Often the point of fission occurs when outside aid or matters of resettlement arise. It is then that prior rules of inequality, alliance, and allegiance come back into play. As a survivor in Darwin stated, "You felt closer to people because you'd shared an experience very few people probably have shared. You felt very united for quite a while. It changed later. . . . " In Yungay, as housing was assigned, middle-class mestizo survivors did not want to live near Indians in government-built housing (Oliver-Smith 1992).

Once goods start to flow, every economic principle in the textbook—true and false scarcity, formal and informal markets, the difference between principle and practice, discord over and between production and distribution, reciprocity, redistribution, and exchange—crops up. Economic strain arises over food, housing, and land (Hirschleifer 1987). In the political realm, issues of leadership arise. Recovery leaders are frequently new leaders as the situation opens avenues for command previously closed or undeveloped, or old leaders prove unsatisfactory. Emergency alone provokes new helmsmen; so do a deprivational aftermath and rising factions. Individuals and groups previously quiet take opportunity. After the Chicago fire, great concern reigned for the aristocracy and landowners that they see restitution, but not for the poor. Political ferment started that ran on through the rest of the century (Smith 1995). In Oakland, internal quarrels were not economic, but quietly political. All the leaders of neighborhood and insurance groups were newcomers to leadership. As recovery efforts dissolved and recovery leaders faded away, old political leaders, however, took credit for the recovery. Since the city of Oakland and much of its population demonstrated little concern for its affluent neighborhood, a movement for the area to separate from the city of Oakland and form its own polity ensued, but failed.

The combination of economics and political control invariably produces a tremendous struggle for hegemony. The fray takes place among coteries within the victim set and between survivors and the external parties. Definitely no utopia or euphoria now, for many disaster survivors the recovery turns raveled, strife-ridden, debilitating, and sometimes stalemated. Moreover, a scuffle over "framing"—whose definition of disaster, victimization, need, and other matters—trails every juncture of disunion. Disaster is a social construction in which not all concerned paint the event, or even what constitutes a calamity, similarly. Frequently victims, neighbor, agent, government, and media entertain different pictures of the occurrence, even as to whether it happened or not. All vie for ideological domination (Button 1995 and this volume, chapter 6). In Chicago resurrection led to insurrection. Modernizers and moralizers arose among and surrounding the survivors (Smith 1995; Sawislak 1995). Those who built big houses in Oakland have faced condemnation by those who felt the integrity of the area was destroyed. "We were supposed to build it like it was," said one survivor to me. "These mega-houses take up every inch of their lots. There's no room for landscaping. It's horrible and I want to move." Others embrace the new constructions for the architectural or economic worth they may someday entail.

In the meantime, while reconstructing a new sociocultural framework, overwrought survivors experience a backlash of old cultural themes. Codes, roles, and expectations decades, even millennia old, sweep down despite whatever modern changes might have transpired in survivors' lives. The themes concern gender, kinship, other relationships, institutions, religion, and customs (Shaw 1992; Hoffman 1994, 1995 and this volume, chapter 9; Zaman 1989). As recent sociocultural changes both desired and undesired disappear, survivors are left as much at sea in understanding as they are awash in mud.

PASSAGE TO CLOSURE—THE THIRD PHASE

No sharp line indicates when the third stage, the passage to closure, occurs in recovery from disaster. Some view this shift in disaster recovery as coming when victims return to the physical site of the calamity once more, but in technological disaster, with its spoiled earth, that sort of end is not forthcoming. In general, victims have achieved some sort of settlement in place, desirable or not. By and large aid has left and a more or less fixed pattern of life has again taken over from what was, for many, freefall (Turner 1961; Wallace 1956a, 1956b).

In Oakland in about four years, most, but not all, survivors had settled in rebuilt or purchased houses, or they were awaiting the completion of houses in construction. Still, by March 1997, almost six years later, Kirp notes some houses stood in a state of perpetual incompletion. Other occupied houses had no steps, unlandscaped yards, unfinished exteriors (1997: 53). Most, but not all, survivors had returned to jobs. Most, but not all, had insurance settlements. In Thera, Greece, ten years after the earthquake, though all the villagers were permanently settled in government-built or repaired homes, they were still churchless. They attended services in the graveyard chapel, a place that is anathema to Greeks. In both sites there were many adjustments to come, but they were of more subtle nature now.

As both Doughty and Oliver-Smith point out, the aftermath of a disaster and the changes it brings can take decades to unfold (Doughty, this volume, chapter 12; Oliver-Smith 1992). Bunbury states about Cyclone Tracy that it would be weeks, months, and for some, years before people fully realized what they had lost, and much of that loss was not material. Many inhabitants never returned, especially the old and those less rooted. Many of the survivors' marriages broke up. The cyclone blew away far more than buildings and treasured possessions. "Tracy," says Bunbury, "blew away hopes" (1994: 79, 110).

However, once survivors are more or less "grounded," a gradual termination of recovery operations takes place and dissolution of survivor unity occurs. Purpose is slowly abandoned. Victims to one degree or another reintegrate with the whole society. Segment and opposition within the community attenuate. Except for occasional anniversary observance, ceremonies that acknowledge the calamity fade away and rites revert to traditional edifice and customary concern. Economic channels that grew out of the disaster gel into routine practice. Occasionally, new leaders retain significance. More likely they vanish with the ebbing incident, and power brokers from before reappear. Survivors come to a reframing of their lives, including an explanation of the calamity. They overlay old ideologies and explanations with revisions (Bode 1989). They arrive once again at a construct of identity and formulate a picture of their vulnerability. They emerge from liminality. "We just got back together. We re-established our garden, we re-established our household . . . ," said a Cyclone Tracy survivor (Bunbury 1994: 136).

In Oakland my insurance group dissolved as each person settled, bought, or began to build a home and dropped out. At the end only three were left. Neighborhood meetings dwindled after four years, though they continue today with skeleton membership. Survivors as a whole get together only on anniversaries, and that in ever fewer numbers. Stores devastated by the loss of customers have been replaced. People now drive new but regular routes to and through the fire zone. Religious services have returned to formula. Friends gather and socialize, perhaps in new alliances, but as before.

In Thera the earthquake, now forty years past, is rarely spoken of. The town's worst scar, the village square filled with rusted building materials for the unbuilt church, was finally cleared and the new church erected about ten years ago. Not only are people who survived the earthquake housed, but so are the survivors' daughters and some granddaughters. Electricity came twenty years ago; running water came six years ago. The village still contains only one wired telephone, though several individuals have cell phones. The village thunders with the roar of motorcycles and small cars. Many significant, though scarcely visible, changes occurred during the period from rehousing to present, though, and it remains to be seen what ongoing shifts will eventuate. (see Hoffman, this volume, chapter 15).

Resentment, however, lingers through the third phase and beyond. In Darwin, Australia, anger at the government's forced evacuation of women and children from the disaster scene remains. "I now realize what a dreadful thing the Pied Piper did to Hamelin when he took the children because a society ceases to exist," said one survivor (Bunbury 1994: 107). Although the Oakland survivors at one point had hopes of changing America's insurance industry, that notion disappeared. The power of the enemy was too large. Yet, deep resentment of the insurance industry abides with all survivors. Some still actively lobby against the industry. "With every California calamity, it becomes clearer that the state insurance commissioner should have more clout. The insurance companies continue to rip people off, contorting coverage, resisting payment. I call victims of every disaster and tell them how to fight their insurance company," a fellow survivor recently told me. The disparaging characterizations of the oppositional groups continue as well. Suspicion and antagonism are long in dissolving (Watzlawich 1984).

The question of change is a complex one (see Hoffman, this volume, chapter 15). Sometimes a calamity is a bridge to change, even great change (Stephens 1995; Paine 1992). Sometimes, to quote a famous children's book, it is only "a wrinkle in time," with prior culture ending up pervasive and little *can lead* change perceivable (Doughty 1986; Chairetakis 1995). At other times changes *to change* meld together, with timeless practices providing only new content for old for- *but* mats. If little else, disaster usually spurs increased political awareness. Some- *also can* times the calamity results in reinforced authority of a certain segment over *worsen* others, and in the long run conditions for survivors worsen. Sometimes emer- *conditions* gent groups bring significant change (Button 1992). Do better safeguards result? A pamphlet published at the time of the ferocious fire that swept across Berkeley, California, on September 17, 1923, states:

> The protection of the city against future fires presents many angles of interest. . . . Differences of opinion as to method are less important than the fact that there is unanimous agreement regarding the central purpose. It is safe to say that every possible safeguard will be made against a recurrence of this disaster, which, in respect to material damages at least, must be numbered among the most destructive fires of modern times. (Cerny and Bruce 1992)

In most zones of chronic disaster people make adjustments materially and conceptually to survive their environments (Moseley, this volume, chapter 3; Sheets, this volume, chapter 2). However, California seems to have failed.

Among some people the calamity produces an enshrinement of the past. Almost all disaster victims fall prey to some enshrinement, at least for a while. They set up reliquaries of items found in the catastrophe's detritus, haunt old locales, enshroud past practices. In Oakland almost all the rental homes of the early phases of the recovery contained shrines of burned items that recalled the destroyed house. Some survivors hung large photographs of their old homes on walls. A few new homes continue to have such shrines. Some people take such enshrinement into mummification. Their loss too great to overcome, they ridigify former ways until they occupy a moribund island out of time and clouded in collective melancholy (Foster 1985; Steward 1992). They continue old pageants *sans* government, perpetuate former practices that no longer avail them, keep up old status systems though part of different societies.

At other times the occurrence provides survivors with a new horizon. The rapture drawn from an almost archaic sense of community and purpose glides into a sense of spirituality and self. Long after the event, survivors continue to share the particular intangibles they developed and recollect the aura they felt. These remain an invisible asset even when the group disperses. The luster of purity elapses into a feeling akin to baptism that outsiders lack, and the illusion of once-embraced homogeneity lingers like a reverie. ". . .when a cyclone comes near the old Tracy veterans, if I can call them such, they say, 'Oh this will be a fizzer compared to Tracy,' " said a Cyclone Tracy veteran (Bunbury 1994: 138). Victims also almost always see their inner lives as different, even when their outer circumstances revert to much the same. "Material things were no longer as important because they blew away," said a Tracy survivor. Another vowed he would "only own six knives and six forks, that number of plates. . . . I would never more have possessions that kept me in place" (Bunbury 1994: 136). Many Oakland firestorm survivors claim a detachment they cannot overcome and a longing for the sensibility and direction attachment gave, yet some feel they are freer to experience more of life than their former attachment allowed them. They have lost their social-cultural "legs," in a sense. They are amputees. Yet, almost every Oakland firestorm survivor, though their lives are different and many wish they had never rebuilt, feel their lives are enriched spiritually and in other ways due to the disaster.

They have overcome the worst of times and the best of times and come out in some way whole.

Models have the power to generate meaningful theories and research. They resolve puzzles and lead to answers. They help the social scientist to understand human commonalities that span across many social and cultural worlds. They aid in the assay of what motivates human behavior, how and why individuals interact in social realms, and how and why they produce social behavior. The scope of one model's principles can further often be extended to other situations.

The seemingly parallel phases and processes—emotional, psychological, and social—disaster survivors cross-culturally pass through offers just such a powerful model. It contributes, I believe, not only to our understanding of society and culture, but to what is common to all peoples, especially those egregiously injured. Through the phases that those who travel through "the worst of times and the best of times" endure, perhaps come insights that in the long run might provide to all the hope of ongoing, less disruptive, more evenly exalted good times.

NOTES

1. For further description of Thera's disaster recovery, see chapter 15, this volume.

2. Dudasik (1980) describes four sorts of disaster victims: event victims—those who are killed, harmed, or damaged by the event; context victims—those around the impact who are disrupted or directly affected by the event, such as members of the surrounding community; peripheral victims—those with strong ties or connections to the community or event victims, not on the scene, but therefore affected, such as relatives and associates; entry victims—those who come to the impact scene, such as relief workers and aid agents.

BIBLIOGRAPHY

Adler, P. (ed.). 1992. *Fire in the Hills: A Collective Remembrance*. Berkeley, CA: 24 Avalon Ave.

Bode, B. 1989. *No Bells to Toll: Destruction and Creation in the Andes*. New York: Scribner's.

Bunbury, B. 1994. *Cyclone Tracy: Picking up the Pieces*. Fremantle, Australia: Fremantle Arts Centre Press.

Button, G. 1992. *Social Conflict and Emergent Groups in a Technological Disaster: The Homer Area Community and the Exxon-Valdez Oil Spill*. Ph.D. thesis. Waltham, MA: Brandeis University.

———. 1995. " 'What You Don't Know Can't Hurt You': The Right to Know and the Shetland Islands Oil Spill." *Human Ecology* 23: 241–257.

Cerny, S., and A. Bruce (eds.). 1992. *The Berkeley Fire: Memoirs and Mementos*. Berkeley, CA: The Berkeley Architectural Heritage Association.

Chairetakis, A. 1995. *The Two-Sided Mirror: A Theory of Culture and Crisis Response in Complex Societies*. Presented at the 94th Annual Meeting, American Anthropological Association, Washington, DC.

Chapple, E. 1970. *Culture and Biological Man*. New York, Holt, Rinehart Winston.

Doughty, P. 1986. "Decades of Disaster: Promise and Performance in the Callejon de Huaylas, Peru," in A. Oliver-Smith (ed.), *Natural Disasters and Cultural Responses*, pp. 35-80. Williamsburg: College of William and Mary.

Douglas, M. 1970. *Witchcraft: Confessions and Accusations*. London: Tavistock.

———. 1978. *Cultural Bias*. Occasional Paper No. 34 of the Royal Anthropological Institute of Great Britain and Ireland.

Dudasik, S. 1980. "Victimization in Natural Disaster." *Disasters* 4: 329–338.

Erikson, K. 1976. *Everything in Its Path*. New York: Simon and Schuster.

———. 1994. *A New Species of Trouble: The Human Experience of Modern Disasters*. New York: Norton.

Foster, H. 1985. *Recordings: Art, Spectacle, and Cultural Politics*. Port Townsend, WA: Bay Press.

Fritz, C. 1961. "Disaster," in R. Merton and R. Nesbet (eds.), *Contemporary Social Problems*, pp. 651–694. New York: Harcourt Brace.

Gore, R. 1993. "Andrew Aftermath." *National Geographic* 183, 4: 2–37.

Hirschleifer, J. 1987. *Economic Behavior in Adversity*. Chicago: University of Chicago Press.

Hoffman, S. 1994. "Up From the Embers: A Disaster Survivor's Story." *Clinical Quarterly* 4, 2: 15–17.

———. 1995. *Culture Deep and Custom Old: The Reappearance of a Traditional Cultural Grammar in the Aftermath of the Oakland-Berkeley Firestorm*. Presented at the 94th Annual Meeting, American Anthropological Association, Washington, DC.

Kalsched, D. 1996. *The Inner World of Trauma*. London: Routledge.

Kirp, D. 1997. "There Goes the Neighborhood." *Harpers* 294, 1762: 45–53.

Lewis, I. 1983. *The Language of Ethnic Conflict: Social Organization and Lexical Culture*. New York: Columbia University Press.

Marris, P. 1974. *Loss and Change*. London: Routledge.

Mauss, M. 1967. *The Gift*. London: Routledge.

Oliver-Smith, A. 1992. *The Martyred City: Death and Rebirth in the Andes*. Prospect Heights, IL: Waveland Press.

Paine, R. 1992. "Chernobyl Reaches Norway: The Accident, Science, and the Threat to Cultural Knowledge." *Public Understanding of Science* 1: 261–280.

Poniatowska, E. 1995. *Nothing, Nobody: The Voices of the Mexico City Earthquake*. Philadelphia: Temple University Press.

Redfield, R. 1962. *Human Nature and the Study of Society*. The papers of Robert Redfield. M. Redfield, ed. Chicago: University of Chicago Press.

Sawislak, K. 1995. *Smoldering City*. Chicago: University of Chicago Press.

Shaw, R. 1992. "'Nature', 'Culture' and Disasters: Floods and Gender in Bangladesh," in E. Croll and D. Parkin (eds.), *Bush Base: Forest Farm*, pp. 200–217. London: Routledge.

Smith, C. 1995. *Urban Disorder and the Shape of Belief*. Chicago: University of Chicago Press.

Stephens, S. 1995. "'Cultural Fallout' of Chernobyl Radiation in Sami Regions: Implications for Children," in S. Stephens (ed.), *Children and the Politics of Culture*, pp. 292–321. Princeton: Princeton University Press.

Steward, K. 1992. Nostalgia—A Polemic," in G. E. Marcus (ed.), *Rereading Cultural Anthropology*, pp. 552–566. Durham: Duke University Press.

Turner, V. 1961. *The Ritual Process*. Chicago: Aldine.

Wallace, A. 1956a. "Revitalization Movements." *American Anthropologist* 58: 204–281.

———. 1956b. "Mazeway Resynthesis: A Biocultural Theory of Religious Inspiration." *Transactions of the New York Academy of Sciences* 18, 7: 626–638.

———. 1957a. "Mazeway Disintegration: The Individual's Perception of Sociocultural Disorganization." *Human Organization* 16, 2: 23–27.

———. 1957b. "Tornado in Worchester." *Disaster Study Number Three*, Committee on Disaster Studies, National Academy of Sciences-National Research Council.

Watzlawich, P. 1984. *The Invented Reality.* New York: Norton.

Zaman, M. 1989. "The Social and Political Context of Adjustment to Riverbank Erosion Hazard and Population Resettlement in Bangladesh." *Human Organization* 48: 196–205.

Zompolis, G. 1994. *Operation Pet Rescue: Animal Survivors of the Oakland, California, Firestorm.* Exeter, NH: Townsend Publishing.

8

THE BROTHERHOOD OF PAIN: THEORETICAL AND APPLIED PERSPECTIVES ON POST-DISASTER SOLIDARITY

ANTHONY OLIVER-SMITH
University of Florida

WHEN CHARLES DICKENS PENNED THE MEMORABLE LINES "IT WAS THE BEST of times, it was the worst of times . . . " to begin *A Tale of Two Cities*, he effectively captured in few words the sense of the great selflessness and rampant selfishness that prevail in the climate of social crisis. Dickens was referring to the frequent appearance of noble, self-sacrificing acts and to the equally frequent instances of mean and egotistical behavior in periods of great stress. In case after case in crisis situations, a form of spontaneous social solidarity emerges that temporarily enables people to put aside self-interest and come together in common effort. And equally recurrent, this solidarity proves fragile and gives way to intense expressions of self-interest. Understandably, Dickens's memorable lines have often been used to characterize the social climate of disasters (see Hoffman, this volume, chapter 7).

Although social solidarity is well documented and has received considerable theoretical scrutiny, consideration of post-disaster solidarity has, for the most part, been frequently noted but only briefly tapped for its theoretical potentials (Wallace 1956; R. Turner 1967; Barkun 1974). Recently, some researchers have explored the appearance of prosocial behavior under conditions of stress, particularly for its relevance to practice and policy (Pennebaker and Harber 1993; Sampson 1991; Schumaker 1993; Sugden 1993; Wright et al. 1990). A disaster constitutes a form of challenge, and people, individually and in groups, often respond very constructively to such an encounter. This fact was repeatedly impressed upon me during a ten-year period of fieldwork in Peru after the massive 1970 earthquake. The disaster, the worst in the history of the Western hemisphere, killed seventy thousand people in an area roughly the size of Belgium, Holland, and Denmark combined. Central to the tragedy was the avalanche loosed from Peru's highest peak by the earthquake. The avalanche buried the provincial capital of Yungay, killing 90 percent of the population. Although I was not in the region during the actual impact, I began my research with survivors of Yungay shortly after the disaster and continued my study through various field trips throughout the decade (Oliver-Smith 1992).

In this chapter, I outline a path for further theoretical exploration of post-disaster solidarity and place in consideration issues of possible relevance for social policy and practice. It is in the matter of community solidarity and counterposing individual need that the lines of theory and application most profoundly intersect in the social sciences. Thus, it is both appropriate and necessary that theoretical and policy-oriented projects be closely linked. If policies are not based on a solid understanding of human behavior in general and cultural behavior specifically, their success in terms of how they respond to human needs is jeopardized. By the same token, policy and practice can form the testing ground for theory. In broader terms, then, my goal in this chapter is to use disasters to address both theory and practice in anthropology.

FIRST, BROTHERS . . . THEN UNEQUAL . . . NOW UNITED

On the afternoon of May 31, 1970, a massive earthquake rocked the north central coastal and Andean regions of Peru. The earthquake was measured at 7.7 on the Richter scale and unleashed forces that caused the worst natural disaster in the history of the Western hemisphere. Approximately 86 percent of all the structures in an area of about eighty-three thousand square kilometers were destroyed. The earthquake triggered an avalanche from Mount Huascarán, the highest peak in the Peruvian Andes, which buried the city of Yungay, a provincial capital of some forty-five hundred inhabitants in the intermontane valley known as the Callejón de Huaylas. Approximately forty-five hundred of Yungay's inhabitants perished. With the exception of a few houses in outlying neighborhoods, less than four minutes after the initial shock waves virtually nothing of the city remained.

The moments following the death of Yungay are described by survivors as a ghastly silence disturbed only by the distant and receding rumble of the avalanche-swollen river rushing northward toward further destruction. While some survivors were immobilized by shock, within minutes others had turned to aiding the injured and searching for wounded in the frigid mud of the avalanche. In the four days of isolation before the fate of Yungay was known to the outside world and aid was sent in, the survivors from both the city and the surrounding peasant hinterland clustered in a field not far from the avalanche path and fended for themselves. There, they formed a number of committees for the acquisition of food, the construction of shelter, and the care of the injured. Many surviving owners of animals and other foodstuffs simply donated them to the common pots being organized. Indian peasants descended from hillside hamlets with donations of food from their own meager surpluses.

In effect, in the periods of immediate postimpact and isolation in the Yungay area, social relations were characterized by numerous acts of altruism and considerable social solidarity and cooperation. Concepts of individual private property temporarily submerged, a situation common to many disasters. The crisis also had an immediate status-leveling effect on the nascent community of survivors it had created. A sense of brotherhood, bonded in pain and grief, with little reference to class or ethnicity, prevailed as Indian and mestizo, lower and upper class, collaborated in the collective efforts to obtain immediate necessities and survive harrowing conditions. Representatives of the two surviving local authorities stated that in this initial period of two to three days, there was a great respect for their offices and a heightened spirit of unity and common identity. "We are all brothers" *(Todos somos hermanos),* was the characteristic self-description during this time, and the degree of organized purposeful activity on behalf of the community was ample demonstration of the survivors' adherence to this perception. Such behavior is not at all atypical of disaster victims in many cultural contexts.

The scope of the Yungay disaster was not known to the outside world for several days. Finally, on the fourth day, the dust thrown up by the earthquake cleared sufficiently for helicopters and other aircraft to get a view of the area around Yungay and begin landing to rescue injured people and deliver the first assistance supplies. By the fifth day, seventy tons of emergency supplies had been parachuted into the entire valley. With the arrival of substantive forms of aid, the spirit of brotherhood across class and ethnic lines waned. The distribution of aid reawakened the sharp lines of class and ethnic differentiation between Indian and non-Indian peasants and middle- and upper-class urban survivors.

In the aftermath of the catastrophe the survivors had taken shelter on a hillside some seven hundred meters north of their buried city, and there they formed a refugee camp. This camp became an aid center, attracting more and more rural people whose homes had been destroyed in the earthquake. Within weeks, the camp was a sprawling tent city composed of rural and urban survivors of multiple class and ethnic identities. The trauma, dislocation, and loss suffered by virtually everyone now created an environment characterized by various well-documented sequelae of disasters, including substance abuse and class and ethnic feuding.

The urban Yungainos initiated their efforts to ascertain the origin of everyone in the camp in order to differentiate in the distribution of aid between survivors *(sobrevivientes)* and refugees *(damnificados)*, signifying a return to traditional social relations. The initial efforts of the emergency aid period and many of the continuing efforts for rehabilitation and recovery were in partial violation of the traditional status arrangements, and, as a result, they produced and exaggerated the class and ethnic tensions and friction which had already existed within the system. The internal social conflict in which class and ethnic group interests sharply split Yungay society increased throughout the distribution of food, clothing, and household articles, finally reaching its peak during the distribution of the two-year provisional housing program.

The Peruvian Ministry of Housing organized a plan for two-year provisional dwelling structures, most of them measuring six by thirty meters, divided by quarter-inch plywood sheets into eight to ten "I"- or "L"-shaped dirt-floored rooms for a maximum of sixty residents per structure. No plumbing or electricity was provided. The registration and assignment of the provisional housing caused great dissension in the community. Social workers assigned to the project distributed the housing on an egalitarian, first-come, first-served basis which immediately conflicted with traditional patterns of ethnic and class stratification and status preferentiality. The issue was brought to a crisis when a local official of some importance informed the social workers that he did not want any peasants (Indians) in the encampment and that he himself wished to choose the location of his dwelling. He was told that he would receive a unit where there was a vacancy and that all those people with documents certifying their refugee status would receive a house in similar fashion, whether they were peasants or Indians or not. "We are all equal in the eyes of God," a social worker told him. Outraged, he responded, "We are not equal!" Whenever the social workers indicated the essential equality of all human beings in response to complaints of proximity to people of lower class or lesser-valued ethnic origins, the response by urban survivors was invariable. *"No somos iguales!"* (We are not equal!) was adamantly repeated again and again (Oliver-Smith 1992).

These difficulties receded into the background when a new challenge confronted the population in the form of a government plan to resettle the town some fifteen kilometers to the south for reasons of geologic safety. The response to this initiative was an immediate and vehement rejection. A variety of reasons, including economic values and deeply felt emotional ties to the buried city, mobilized the population to combat what they perceived as still another threat to their survival, not only as individuals, but as a community. To survive as a sociocultural entity and as the principal urban center for the province became the *raison d'etre* of the population. The relocation project constituted a challenge and a threat to identity. Consequently, the conflict with the government once again united a seriously divided population in a common cause. Together they resisted a resettlement project which in their view would have torn them from their roots and turned them into a dependent, artificial, administrative creation rather than a community.

The government, in proposing relocation, became the new adversary, the new disaster, in the perception of the community. In effect, the crisis of the disaster had been reactivated in the rehabilitation period by the new challenge to the existence of the community. There was a concerted, highly organized effort on the part of the town leaders to recover all the administrative, educational, economic, religious, and governmental institutions of the old city before the relocation project could be activated. The goal was to confront the government's resettlement project with the *fait accompli* of a reestablished and firmly rooted provincial capital inhabited by an equally rooted and determined population. Although it took them more than two years, they succeeded. In no sense would it be unreasonable to attribute the rapid growth and recovery of Yungay at least in part to the challenge posed by resettlement. That purpose, sparked by the threat of relocation, was demonstrated repeatedly in solidarity and cooperation on projects relating to reconstruction and reinstitutionalization of the provincial capital in new Yungay (Oliver-Smith 1992). In sum, the people of Yungay responded to both disaster and conflict in extremely constructive ways.

DISASTERS, SOLIDARITY, AND SOCIAL ORGANIZATIONAL THEORY

How do we account theoretically for such a rapid shifting of social identities, symbols, and interactional patterns? The most encyclopedic review of disaster research documents the large literature on emergent groups after disasters but laments the lack of insight into the dynamics of their internal social processes (Drabek 1986). Is it enough simply to take the situations at face value, that is, to say that in crises people give help to get help and, when things stabilize, return to their normal behavior? If things are in fact so practical and instrumental, why then do people suddenly become "brothers"? Does the ascription of brotherhood represent just a cynical manipulation of symbols to achieve goals that benefit individuals? When people give up their property for the common good, their actions could be seen as a form of investment with some payoff expected in the future. It potentially follows a straightforward rational-choice theory analysis and, at some level, can probably be reduced to such a calculus (Douty 1973; De Alessi 1975; Hershleifer 1987). However, I think that cost-benefit forms of analysis miss some important aspects of the quality of social interaction that have relevance for both theory and social policy.

Post-disaster solidarity is frequently assigned to that field of study known as collective behavior. Anthropology does not explicitly identify the field of "collective behavior" as within its purview. Collective behavior is usually considered to be the sociological and social psychological study of crowds, mobs, panic, mass hysteria, and other phenomena associated, I think erroneously, with the irrational dimensions of human behavior. However, anthropologists study many instances—cults and social movements, for example—that fall under the category of collective behavior. Indeed, since anthropology's major theoretical concept is culture, which refers to those understandings a human collectivity holds in common, thus making up a society, we tend to seek cultural roots or explanations for many forms of collective behavior.

Social and behavioral sciences have explained or theoretically accounted for collective behavior and social solidarity in a number of ways. Although collective behavior encompasses a vast array of human actions, one topic, social movements, stands out as a principal focus of research, and it is around social movement research that the fundamental debates on reason and sentiment, as well as on solidarity, have been met. The dominant model in the theoretical toolkit on solidarity in social movements centers on explanations derived from the application of rational choice theory. The core issue in this approach is the commitment of individuals, who are assumed to be rational, self-interested actors, to common group goals and purposes. The tension between the individual and the group, which is the focus of an enormous philosophical and social scientific literature, lies at the core of such varied concepts involving solidarity. They include the invisible hand (Smith 1976), alienation (Marx 1964), mechanical versus organic solidarity (Durkheim 1949), substantive versus formal rationality (Weber 1947), and *Gemeinshaft* versus *Gesellshaft* (Tonnies 1988), to name only a few classics. Much of the theoretical discourse on social solidarity is devoted to explaining how individual and group concerns must or can be reconciled or how individuals are threatened, coerced, sanctioned, rewarded, cajoled, or deceived into supporting or producing public goods or goals. Although social solidarity or group solidarity to some sufficient degree must be present in all societies for them to hold together, the locus of much research on the issue has been the examination of social movements. Social movements are smaller than entire societies and permit the identification of group and individual boundaries more easily than large, somewhat more amorphous forms of association.

The most dominant theoretical approach on social movements, the resource mobilization school, based on rational-choice theory (Hechter 1987), holds that it is irrational, or at best nonrational, for an individual to contribute to a collective cause from which he or she will derive no benefit, either material or nonmaterial. In correlation, it is considered irrational for an individual to contribute to a public goal if that individual will derive the benefits of that public goal anyway, the so-called free rider problem (Olson 1965). Free riders or not, people form or become members of solidary groups because they judge that it is in their individual interest to do so. In sum, an explicit individual calculus of cost-benefit is said to exist in social movements. People will associate themselves with social movements when they calculate that individual benefits outweigh the costs of joining (McAdam et al. 1988). It may seem somewhat obvious to remark that the ascendence of the resource mobilization approach (RMA) probably derives as much of its popularity as an analytical framework from its conceptual isomorphism with reigning cultural models in contemporary Western society as it does from its explanatory power (Aguirre 1994: 258).

RATIONALITY AND EMOTIONALITY IN COLLECTIVE BEHAVIOR

Indeed, as RMA rose to eminence and its adherents worked to affirm that individual actors rationally calculated their chances of achieving specific goals by affiliating with social movements, they tended to discredit other approaches, principally those based on a collective-behavior approach, subscribing to theories of irrationality and emotionality (Killian 1994: 276). One of the most persistent issues in the discussion is the tension between the rational calculus of individual self-interest and the affect or bonds of sentiment and other *Gemeinshaft* emotions in the formation of solidarity groups. Affective conceptions of solidarity have been generally rejected as providing the best explanations of solidarity group formation in favor of more empirically testable behavioral approaches such as rational-choice theory (Hechter 1987). Indeed, there is a distinct impression that in discovering or laying bare the rational basis individuals have for joining social movements, resource mobilization theorists establish the worthiness of such movements and give their members true scientific justification as rational human beings; meanwhile they consign those for whom no rational calculus of cost-benefit can be discovered to a kind of emotional, immature, or primitive state of confusion.

However effective rational-choice theory may be at explaining or imputing a rational calculus to some forms of solidarity, any understanding of the power of expressed affect, such as common identity, to motivate people collectively to action is lost in them. In a sense, there may or may not be a rational cost-benefit equation for the mobilization of resources that accounts for solidarity, but such an equation also may or may not provide sufficient energy to coalesce individuals. Nor may such a calculation always move people to action. More fundamentally, rational choice may provide the reason for solidarity, but reason may not always move people to action. A recognition of this feature is now reflected in the shift from the resource mobilization model (rational-choice theory) toward "social constructionist" approaches which emphasize meaning, affect, cultural content, and social context in research on social movements (Mueller 1992: 5). Failure to understand and factor into its analysis the power of emotion to mobilize people undermines the explanatory power of RMA.

Disasters are clearly periods in which people experience a vast spectrum of intense emotions—anxiety, fear, terror, loss, grief, gratitude, anger, frustration, relief, and resignation—in all their shadings and intensities. These emotions color their experiences of preparation (if any), the event itself, and the aftermath of a disaster for indefinite periods of time. They further help to shape their responses in regularly patterned ways, including organizing to carry out important tasks and tackle often insurmountable problems in the midst of enormous obstacles. However, the problematical construction of emotion in the current sociological analyses of collective behavior, of which response to disaster is but one example, has led to a focus on a more instrumental approach. Anthropological theory can correct this flaw and lead to better understanding of the interplay between sentiment and rationality in societies dealing with disasters and other crises, and in social life in general.

As both Ferree (1992)and Killian (1994) have pointed out in dealing with social movements, RMA falsely dichotomizes reason and emotion. There is a distinct tendency, even in the choice of issues studied, to equate emotionality with irrationality and to denigrate as irrational those forms of collective behavior in which emotions prevail in orienting action and setting goals. Indeed, many forms of collective behavior, other than social movements assessed as motivated by reason in RMA, are often characterized as irrational or emotional and are frequently associated, as Ferree mordantly notes, with "women and the lower orders of men"(1992: 42). Rational-choice theory and RMA tend to contrast sentiment against rationality in ways that not only devalue emotion but also obscure the important relationship between deeply rooted feelings of community, place, commonality, and self-interest (Ferree 1992: 42). In point of fact, reason and emotion may coincide or reinforce each other in many instances. For example, the deeply felt emotions of brotherhood expressed across class and ethnic lines in Yungay, and producing acts of great altruism, were in the interest of everyone's survival. Emotion clearly does not undermine purposeful, organized activity. Indeed, there are many contexts in which sentiment and self-interest are virtually inseparable.

Sentiment and value as well as concrete, individual self-interest all play an important role in the kinds of solidarity that are expressed in the aftermath of disasters, as well as in other forms of collective behavior, including social movements. People affirm who they are, and where they belong in the world is expressed far more through value and emotion than pure material interest.

Jaggar proposes that "emotions provide the experiential basis for values. If we had no emotional responses to the world, it is inconceivable that we should ever come to value one state of affairs more highly than another" (1989: 153, as quoted in Ferree 1992: 42–43).

INTERACTIONAL FORM, STRUCTURE, AND ANTISTRUCTURE IN CRISIS

There is clearly a major difference between the social solidarity emerging from considered assessment of common economic, political, and social interests and the intense bonding that takes place in crises, however similar short-term outcomes may be. Rational-choice theory does not explain all kinds of patterned, constructive human behavior.

To explore solidarity in the context of both disaster and conflict, we need to examine briefly the relationship that sometimes exists between crisis, ritual, and action. Certainly the starting point for any discussion of social solidarity must be Durkheim's *The Division of Labor in Society*. Durkheim was concerned in his discussion of the division of labor with showing the differences between primitive and modern societies in terms of the kind of solidarity that each displayed. Primitive societies were described as having a very simple division of labor. Everyone performs essentially the same acts, procuring food, teaching children the traditional roles, and executing other tasks with insignificant or only slight variation. Such societies were said to be characterized by "mechanical solidarity" founded on the ideology of a common cultural identity. Since there is little differentiation based on the division of labor, solidarity is a function of an overarching cultural identity.

Primitive societies with their mechanical form of solidarity are contrasted with modern societies that have larger populations and more complex divisions of labor. Modern societies are characterized by "organic solidarity." In modern societies with complex divisions of labor, individuals have many different tasks, do not share as many common characteristics with others, and yet are interdependent with one another. The society functions not because everyone shares a common identity but, rather, because of common interdependence and an implicit contract that each will perform according to culturally constructed expectations. Durkheim, however, did see mechanical solidarity as continuing to exist along with, or perhaps as a substratum of, organic solidarity in modern societies.

This idea of a substratum of mechanical solidarity is informative in understanding disasters. When a disaster strikes, suddenly enveloping everyone in its destruction, one of the first casualties may be the division of labor. Everyone's normal tasks, with the possible exception of emergency workers, are put on hold, at least until the obligations associated with the individual's other roles—spouse, parent, child, etc.—have been attended to. In effect, the division of labor is suspended while people attend to the more immediate necessities of individual and familial well-being (R. Turner 1967). Everyone experiences the same stresses and hardships, and everyone has now assumed the same or similar tasks.

In disasters, modern societies may revert to that substratum of mechanical solidarity, their common human identity at some fundamental level, since the division of labor with all its differentiation and hierarchy has been rendered temporarily inoperative (R. Turner 1967). For relative periods of time disasters reduce the vast majority of people to one relevant status, that of victim, and in many instances this sudden equality of status is reflected in a great deal of assistance and rescue activities rendered across class, ethnic, and other boundaries. As we saw in Yungay, until aid arrives, and sometimes even after that, people seem to recognize only another's need and basic humanity. Even the most deeply held prejudices and fears are suspended. Only after a working mechanical solidarity—that is, some profound sense of shared identity that unites an otherwise differentiated people—is in place do people see the need for the division of labor to be reestablished and to return to organic solidarity (R. Turner 1967: 62).

Anthropological research on ritual also provides important insights for understanding social relations in crisis conditions, particularly in enabling people to negotiate and adapt to change (Chapple 1970). Chapple contends that rituals are biologically necessary to allow human beings to negotiate and adapt to change, in that certain kinds of rituals are social forms that help people vitiate the psychological and biological stress that particular forms of change create.

For Chapple, "the consequences of man as an animal are perhaps best seen in the ways in which his culture and, in particular, the dimensions of communication are biologically (emotionally) affected or possessed" (1970: 294). Emotions trigger both psychological and physiological responses, which are then expressed through and mediated by social and cultural forms and contexts. Human biology and social behavior interact not in any deterministic, sociobiological sense but, rather, in the way biological and social features and processes interact in dealing with the events of human life. Forms of social interaction affect and are affected by the physiology of emotional responses to specific events or conditions. Ritualized interactional forms mitigate the low-level stress occasioned by the constant changes in context and situation in daily life. Chapple posits that, particularly in situations of strong emotional content, "the autonomic-interactional systems short-circuit logic"(1970: 293). People under acute stress will behave according to autonomic-interactional systems rather than some abstract logic of individual self-interest. The strong emotions occasioned by stress trigger a social response which will resemble a ritualized interactional form, and the endowed symbol system ("*todos somos hermanos*"—"we are all brothers") associated with that form takes on particular power for facilitating particular types of adjustment, such as the alleviation of emotional stress or the building of transactional relationships (Chapple 1970: 293).

The work of Victor Turner complements these ideas from the purely social perspective when he speaks of "a type of dialectical social process that involves successive experience of . . . homogeneity and differentiation, equality and inequality"(1961: 97). Turner's work dissolves the dichotomy between reason and emotion constructed by RMA. The human need for ritual is not based on rationality but on sentiment, and the actualization of ritual is founded on culturally rational constructions of reality. Turner posits that social life entails a continual, if not consistent, alternation between two polarized or contrasting forms of human interaction he terms "structure" and "communitas." In "structure" human relationships and interaction may be seen as a network of specific and concrete statuses and roles, and of differentiated political, legal, and economic positions assigning value to individuals.

"Structure," the form of impersonal, status-determined interaction, is contrasted with the vision of society as an unstructured community of equal individuals bound together. This vision not of an organized system of statuses but of a communion "between concrete, historical and indiosyncratic individuals" confronting one another as human beings with whom something is shared forms a spontaneous consciousness of "we," not unlike Durkheim's conception of mechanical solidarity. This model of social interaction is known as "communitas," and usually emerges in a period or place separated from normal modes of structured social action. Such separate or "liminal" periods constitute an important stage in the universal rituals of passage or transition, in which individuals are separated from an earlier status or condition, enter into a marginal or ambiguous (liminal) state stripped of their normal structural characteristics, and ultimately pass on to another status or condition whereupon they rejoin society with new or altered identities. During the liminal period, in which the initiates lack both their previous status or condition and those they will ulitmately assume, their social interaction with fellow initiates is a structureless, shared consciousness of common identity, without rank, property, or insignia. It is a condition of communitas.

The similarity between Turner's portrayal of the structure of rituals and much of the behavior that marks crises is striking. The immediate postimpact stage of crises and catastrophes seems to evoke a kind of liminal state, in which victims have been violently separated from their previous social, economic, and political identities with their normal modes of interactions. The disaster has cast them into an emotionally charged, relatively unstructured common consciousness, involving a general reduction of status, or at least a decreased recognition of rank and property. This common consciousness, perhaps a "brotherhood of pain," arises spontaneously from the "transformative experience" which goes "to the root of each person's being and finds in that root something profoundly communal and shared" (V. Turner 1961: 138). The liminal period and its spirit and consciousness of communitas are symbolically expressed and enacted in interactional forms, persisting in varying degrees for varying amounts of time, and often empowering people to undertake extraordinary efforts on their own behalf. However, ultimately the condition of communitas will succumb to the need to return to a less spontaneous, more predictable, organized form of behavior to carry out long-term tasks. In disasters, this return to structure characterizes the end of the emergency period and the beginning of relief and reconstruction. Frequently, people express amazement or even nostalgia for the solidarity they experienced in the crisis. Indeed, on one occasion a friend of mine in Yungay expressed the idea that the year following the disaster, a period of great physical misery and emotional pain, was also beautiful:

> How we all suffered! How we all suffered together! How beautiful that life. How beautiful that life of suffering! Of brotherhood! We suffered together; even though it was terrible, it was also beautiful. (Oliver-Smith 1992: 260)

Other forms of crisis also serve as catalyst and context for the emergence of solidarity. Fantasia's discussion of class consciousness among American workers proposes that crises suspend the customary practices of daily life and require a "new repertoire of behavior, associational ties and valuations" (1988: 14). He asserts that while consciousness of class identity may not be particularly high among workers, when they are drawn into industrial conflicts over layoffs, low wages, or union busting, their responses may involve actions which, in opposing management, allow for the alignment of common symbols and meanings which create "cultures of solidarity." Challenges require action, and consciousness is generated and changed by social action (Fantasia 1988: 8). It is out of the associations and actions required of people challenged in crisis that solidarity groups, based not only on mutuality of interest but on common identity, are formed, generating an ideology that actively arises "in conflict, creating and sustaining solidarity in opposition to the dominant structure" (Fantasia 1988: 19).

OPERATIONALIZING COMMUNITAS

As a final consideration, the frequent appearance of communitas during or in the aftermath of crises warrants attention for its relevance to social policy.

The matter might be phrased in terms of whether social policy makers and practitioners wish to address the potentialities of action and change which crisis-induced solidarity represents. It might also be rephrased in terms of whether policy makers and practitioners merely wish to contain those potentialities. To express the issue in Victor Turner's terms, what are the potentialities in operationalizing communitas?

The importance of crisis-induced solidarity can be addressed on a level of practice and on a level of theory/policy. In practice, the question deals with how social policy responds to communities afflicted by a crisis such as disaster or involuntary resettlement. The usual response has been to assuage the situation with waves of material assistance of varying kinds at various stages of the crisis. As we saw in the case of Yungay, the arrival of aid tended to dissolve the bonds of solidarity which had been created in the immediate aftermath of impact. It was not until a further challenge appeared that those bonds were reawakened, this time to confront and reject a regional reconstruction policy and to impose their own intentions. The Yungay case suggests that, while certain forms of aid in disasters are absolutely necessary, the continuation of other kinds of aid may have very deleterious effects. The Yungay data further suggest that much aid also is characterized by a fairly consistent underestimation of the internal resources and capacities of communities to respond to crisis. Perhaps there needs to be less consideration toward the delivery of more aid and more attention devoted to devising culturally appropriate ways to nurture the potentials represented by post-disaster solidarity.

In that light, it follows that there is no development-neutral aid. Aid either enhances or undermines development in communities (Anderson and Woodrow 1989). After the Mexico City earthquake of 1985, a destroyed neighborhood with little prior organization or sense of community was challenged by a local NGO with the requirement to organize into self-help groups before any housing assistance would be provided. The self-help groups were formed, and in the process of constructing houses, sufficiently cohesive bonds of solidarity were formed to enable the people to move on to other areas of joint enterprise, including a cooperative laundry and bakery (Anderson and Woodrow 1989: 19). In effect, the challenge obligated them to become actors rather than be acted upon by aid programs.

After the 1989 Loma Prieta earthquake in California, the local Mexican immigrant population in Watsonville learned from relatives or from their own experience of the 1985 Mexico City earthquake about the politics of aid. This information enabled them, as it did the Mexico City survivors, to focus public and media attention on the issue of affordable housing, which they achieved by invading public land (Johnston and Schulte 1992). It is out of such experiences that dependency can be vitiated and genuine forms of empowerment can be nourished. However, methods must be developed to distinguish between those communities that will confront a challenge and those that will be further eroded. The contrasting responses of Native-American communities, for example, to centuries of insult should inspire caution in the issuing of challenges (Khera and Mariella 1982; Shkilnyk 1985).

At the level of policy making and theorizing, crises represent moments or spaces for new options. In the specific crises of disasters or resettlement, policy makers may become more receptive to the negotiation of new options out of governmental concern for public image or genuine sympathy for disaster victims or resettlees. In effect, crises create moments of flexibility for elaborating new policies and practices. However, if the crisis is systemwide, rather than local or regional, that responsiveness may be short-lived as the government works to solidify control of the situation. In the immediate aftermath of the 1985 Mexico City earthquake, the federal government responded so slowly and inadequately that emergent neighborhood groups began taking major roles in aid and assistance, ultimately mobilizing a significant threat to the party in power. The reigning party recovered its hegemony only by appropriating and manipulating aid distribution, particularly of housing, after more than three hundred thousand people were left homeless by the disaster (Robinson et al. 1986).

Finally, it is out of crisis-induced solidarity groups that emergent cultures of resistance are often produced, which in turn challenge hegemonic models of society and development through confrontations over specific policies or practices (Oliver-Smith 1992). In both Brazil and Mexico the recent national debates over involuntary resettlement of communities due to infrastructural development projects, such as dams and highways evolved out of specific community-level resistance movements formed by people challenging involuntary relocation (Bartolome 1992; Oliver-Smith 1996). These debates involve the questioning of development models that require such projects. In Brazil, the Movement of Dam Affected People (Movimento de Atingidos de Barragems—MAB), a coalition of many small resistance groups, now negotiates with Eletrobras, the national power company and major resettlement agent, over the formation of social policy on resettlement and development at the national level (Oliver-Smith 1996).

Unfortunately, the potentials which might be realized in the contexts of postcrisis solidarity generally go unperceived, particularly in disasters where the tendency is to use institutionalized distributional mechanisms rather than interface with community resources for community capacitation. In resettlement-induced crisis, resistance movements are more often seen as obstacles to policy rather than as expressions of potential empowerment and productive collaboration. In developed and developing societies where communities have been weakened or eroded today, we should not ignore the potentiality of renewed community and empowerment which lies in postcrisis solidarity.

CONCLUSION

Solidarity that is born of crisis is not based on a purely rational calculus but is profoundly embedded in our social nature, in that realm of emotion and thought in which we as individuals are created and recreated through time. In the final analysis, however, the problem is not "either-or" between reason and emotion, or for that matter between individual and group, but when and under what circumstances or conditions these dimensions of human behavior emerge. Chapple's work suggests that our solidarity responses in crises are deeply rooted in social interactional forms and their associated symbolic expressions. They are sufficiently emotionally rooted to override any individuated logics under conditions of stress, helping us to defuse emotional impacts and build alliances to deal with stressors. Turner's work on ritual teaches us not to think in terms of dichotomized forms of behavior such as reason versus emotion but rather in terms of a continuum of behavior that allows insight into the power of affect for social organization in stressful conditions and underscoring the importance of the social emotional realm in how people respond to crisis. The solidarity that appeared in Yungay, Mexico City, and Watsonville, California, created social movements in which disaster victims mobilized to take a role in their own reconstruction, and more significantly, in their own development. Disaster assisters who recognize this potential can foster rather than obstruct an empowerment process that can have implications for the development of the community long after the disaster has passed.

For a long time, there was a rather facile maxim in disaster research, that disasters stripped away the epiphenomenal cultural layers and revealed the essentially human. Now we understand that there is no essentially human without culture, nothing that is not given expression and reality through culture. That conclusion notwithstanding, we can still search through cultural process and expression for that which is common to all cultures and, therefore, to all human beings. Research into forms of solidarity in crisis promises to disclose further dimensions of our fundamental human sociability. These issues are key to understanding the deepest roots of the social nature of human life. This understanding should also enable us to help each other when that help is most needed.

BIBLIOGRAPHY

Aguirre, B. 1994. "Collective Behavior and Social Movement Theory," in R. Dynes and K. Tierney (eds.), *Disasters, Collective Behavior and Social Organization*, pp. 257–272. Newark: University of Delaware Press.

Anderson, M., and P. Woodrow. 1989. *Rising from the Ashes: Development Strategies in Times of Disaster.* Boulder: Westview Press.

Barkun, M. 1974. *Disaster and the Millenium.* New Haven: Yale University Press.

Bartolome, L. 1992. "Fighting Leviathan: The Articulation and Spread of Local Opposition to Hydrodevelopment in Brazil." Paper presented at the 41st Annual Conference of the Center for Latin American Studies: Involuntary Migration and Resettlement in Latin America. University of Florida, Gainesville, FL.

Chapple, E. 1970. *Culture and Biological Man: Explorations in Behavioral Anthropology.* New York: Holt, Rinehart and Winston.

De Alessi, L. 1975. "Toward an Analysis of Post-Disaster Cooperation." *American Economic Review* 65: 127–138.

Douty, C. 1973. "Disaster and Charity: Some Aspects of Cooperative Economic Behavior." *American Economic Review* 62: 580–590.

Drabek, T. 1986. *Human System Responses to Disaster: An Inventory of Sociological Findings.* New York: Springer-Verlag.

Durkheim, E. 1949. *The Division of Labor in Society.* Glencoe, IL: The Free Press.

Fantasia, R. 1988. *Cultures of Solidarity.* Berkeley: University of California Press.

Ferree, M. 1992. "The Political Context of Rationality: Rational Choice Theory and Resource Mobilization," in A. Morris and C. Mueller (eds.), *Frontiers in Social Movement Theory,* pp. 29–52. New Haven: Yale University Press.

Hechter, M. 1987. *Principles of Group Solidarity.* Berkeley: University of California Press.

Hershleifer, J. 1987. *Economic Behavior in Adversity.* Chicago: University of Chicago Press.

Jaggar, A. 1989. "Love and Knowledge: Emotion in Feminist Epistemology," in A. Jaggar and S. Bordo (eds.), *Gender/Body/Knowledge: Feminist Constructions of Being and Knowing,* pp. 145–171. New Brunswick: Rutgers University Press.

Johnston, B. R., and J. Schulte. 1992. "Natural Power and Power Plays in Watsonville, California and the US Virgin Islands." Paper presented at the 51st Annual Meeting of the Society for Applied Anthropology, Memphis, TN.

Khera, S., and P. Mariella. 1982. "The Fort McDowell Yavapai: A Case of Long-Term Resistance to Relocation," in A. Hansen and A. Oliver-Smith (eds.), *Involuntary Migration and Resettlement: The Problems and Responses of Dislocated Peoples,* pp. 159–178. Boulder, CO: Westview Press.

Killian, L. 1994. "Are Social Movements Irrational or Are They Collective Behavior?" in R. Dynes and K. Tierney (eds.), *Disasters, Collective Behavior and Social Organization,* pp. 273–280. Newark: University of Delaware Press.

Marx, K. 1964. *The Economic and Philosophical Manuscripts of 1844.* New York: International Publishers.

McAdam, D., J. McCarthy, and M. N. Zald. 1988. "Social Movements," in N. Smelser (ed.), *Handbook of Sociology.* Newbury Park, CA: Sage.

Mueller, C. McC. 1992. "Building Social Movement Theory," in A.D. Morris and C. McC. Mueller (eds.), *Frontiers in Social Movement Theory,* pp. 3–25. New Haven: Yale University Press.

Oliver-Smith, A. 1992. *The Martyred City: Death and Rebirth in the Andes*. (2nd edition). Homewood, IL: Waveland Press.

———. 1996. "Fighting for a Place: The Policy Implications of Resistance to Resettlement," in C. McDowell (ed.), *Understanding Impoverishment: The Impacts of Development Induced Resettlement*, pp. 77–97. Providence: Berg.

Olson, M. 1965. *The Logic of Collective Action*. Cambridge: Harvard University Press.

Pennebaker, J., and K. Harber. 1993. "A Social Stage Model of Collective Coping: The Loma Prieta Earthquake and the Persian Gulf War." *Journal of Social Issues* 49: 125–146.

Robinson, S., Y. Franco, R. Mata Castrejon, and H. Bernard. 1986. "It Shook Again—The Mexico City Earthquake of 1985," in A. Oliver-Smith (ed.), *Natural Disasters and Cultural Responses*, Publication # 36, Studies in Third World Societies, pp. 81–122. Williamsburg, VA: Department of Anthropology, College of William and Mary.

Sampson, R. 1991. "Linking the Micro- and Macrolevel Dimensions of Community Social Organization." *Social Forces* 70: 43–65.

Schumaker, P. 1993. "Estimating the First and (Some of the) Third Faces of Community Power." *Urban Affairs Quarterly* 28: 441–462.

Shkilnyk, A. 1985. *A Poison Stronger than Love*. New Haven: Yale University Press.

Smith, A. 1976. *An Inquiry into the Nature and Course of the Wealth of Nations*. Oxford: Clarendon Press.

Sugden, R. 1993. "Thinking as a Team: Towards an Explanation of Non-Selfish Behavior," in E. Paul, F. Miller, Jr., and J. Paul (eds.), *Altruism*. New York: Cambridge University Press.

Tonnies, F. 1988. *Community and Society*. New Brunswick, NJ: Transaction Books.

Turner, R. 1967. "Types of Solidarity in the Reconstituting of Groups." *Pacific Sociological Review* 10, 2: 60–68.

Turner, V. 1961. *The Ritual Process*. Chicago: Aldine Press.

Wallace, A. 1956. "Revitalization Movements." *American Anthropologist* 58: 264–281.

Weber, M. 1947. *The Theory of Social and Economic Organization*. Glencoe, IL: The Free Press.

Wright, K., R. Ursano, P. Bartone, and L. Ingraham. 1990. "The Shared Experience of Catastrophe: An Expanded Classification of the Disaster Community." *American Journal of Orthopsychiatry* 60: 35–43.

9

THE REGENESIS OF
TRADITIONAL GENDER PATTERNS
IN THE WAKE OF DISASTER[1]

SUSANNA M. HOFFMAN
Independent Researcher

ON OCTOBER 20, 1991, A DRY, HOT DAY WITH UNUSUAL, TURBULENT WINDS, a spark from a fire of the previous day that the tranquil residents of Oakland and Berkeley, California, were totally unaware of, reignited. From that spark developed a ferocious firestorm which swept down from the hills, leaped two multilane freeways, and, although the fire burned for two more days, within essentially four hours destroyed 3,356 homes and 456 apartments.

The Oakland firestorm was the largest urban fire that the United States has ever witnessed. In the aftermath the area devastated—block after block, acre after acre, once filled with homes, yards, streets, and avenues—looked like Dresden after the bombing, just as razed, but with less debris. With temperatures over two thousand degrees Fahrenheit, nothing remained of the homes but incinerated foundations, nothing stood but chimneys and blackened tree trunks.

Twenty-five people died, a number remarkably small. Six thousand people were left homeless. Ninety-five percent of them lost virtually every possession they owned, for the fire had moved faster than sixty miles per hour. Most people received no warning and got no evacuation order. Those who did had little time and rarely the presence of mind to gather any belongings.

I am one of the survivors. In the fire I lost my home and all my possessions. I lost my clothing, furniture, photographs, heirlooms, artwork, beloved objects, one car, and two pets. Since my office was in my home, I also lost twenty-five years of anthropological research, seven manuscripts not yet in to publishers, all my other writings, ideas, projects in development, the slides and photos of travels, lectures and course notes, and my entire library.

Though thankfully I lost no family, no friends, no people, still to describe the devastation, both physical and psychological, of this kind of loss is like trying to define eternity or infinity. It defies words, evades phrase, and renders mute any and every euphemistic catchall. I will say these things.

I had no salt. By this I mean I had no salt to put upon my food, and also that I had no salt left for tears. My weeping depleted every grain from my being.

I had no thread. By this I mean I had no thread to stitch my daughter's hem, and also I lost the thread of my life. The pattern of my days, my plans, my routines were irrevocably ruptured. The warp of my past was torn from the weave of my future. Who I am, what I was, what I intended to do, the fabric of my life, utterly unraveled.

I had no numbers. I lost all the addresses and phone numbers of everyone I knew or had ever known. I further lost all my accounts, my journals, records, and calendars, the numbers of my days. I lost my vita, and while some might find this refreshing, without it and the rest of my numbers I lost both my connections and the equations that lead to opportunity.

I had no paper, no sheets, no warm, wooly sweater, no lights. By this I mean no light bulbs, no work lamp, no flashlight, candles, matches, but also no light*ness*. No joy crept into my days for a lengthy while. Happenstance banished the happy-go-lucky, seemingly forever.

As for my anthropology, it was a rapid introduction into deconstructivism.

Rapid, but not long-lasting. I found that although I was in an annihilating situation, I was also in a most amazing one. While standing amid the rubble of my home, I also stood amid the rubble of a social and cultural system. An entire community and its trappings, both physical and metaphysical, had been dismantled, and while no people are ever totally without culture, I was seared as close as any anthropologist ever comes into a cultural void. In the days, weeks, and now seven years to follow what occurred has been as fascinating as the calamity was ravaging. I have born witness to the reformulation of a social and cultural milieu. More incandescent still, with it I have seen played out the evidence for anthropological discourses of many decades. To use, I think, an apt metaphor, in the starkness of disruption as a people recover and reconstruct, they expose the foundations of their cultural structure, the framing of their ties, the joists beneath their cultural character, the divisions by which they organize space, time, and objects, the doors of their conflicts, and the elevation of the ideology. All of it lies open to the ready observer.

To my awe as an anthropologist—though it may not be the case with every disaster—what appeared first among the survivors of the Oakland firestorm was not the reconstitution of the life lived immediately prior to the conflagration but rather the regeneration of old, deeply rooted cultural patterns.

Though the community had long stood as a vanguard of cultural progressiveness, in the fury of the fire recent cultural innovations burned away like so much patina. The phoenix that arose renewed wore the feathers of a social order far older than the California hills settlement in which the flames raged.

One of the primary and most startling expressions of the conservative regeneration entailed gender. Indeed, a gender division resurfaced that was fleshy enough, archaic enough, and poetic enough to make Levi-Strauss, Griaule, Foucault, and a long list of feminist theorists dance an "I told you so" jig.

A great deal of research in recent years has focused on the fact that in disasters certain populations are, or have been made, more vulnerable than others, and that various segments of society recover differentially in calamity's aftermath (Hewitt 1983; Dudasik 1980; Torry 1978, 1980). Factors leading to such variability can include race, ethnicity, class, poverty, and age. Numerous studies have also shown gender to be one of the factors (Wiest et al. 1992; Blaikie et al. 1994; Enarson and Morrow 1998). Shaw, for example, details the particular effects of disaster on women in purdah in Bangladesh (1992). What I was not expecting was that gender could be such a criterion in disaster response and recovery in a consciously progressive community such as Oakland.

I base my observations on a considerable amount and range of material. As well as being a survivor of the Oakland firestorm, I participated in the recovery in ways that gave me much access to the persons and processes involved in response and recovery. I organized and led a group of survivors who carried home insurance policies with my same insurance company. The group consisted of twenty-five individuals and couples. We met every two to three weeks, starting several months after the fire and continuing for about a year, with considerable telephone communication between meetings. Meetings were attended by men and women alike, with somewhat more men than women. Both parties of a couple frequently attended together, although sometimes just one or the other came. One husband always came alone because his wife was too distraught by the loss to suffer the insurance details. Single policy holders were both male and female. One woman regularly attended for her aged mother who was the actual policy holder, although the mother came to the final party. The age range spanned from the thirties to the eighties. The group dissolved when most members achieved their insurance settlements and stopped appearing. At the time I disbanded the group, only three policy holders remained uncompensated. I also met with the leaders of all the other insurance groups.

As well as the insurance group, I participated in several of the many neighborhood associations that sprang up in response to the calamity. Through one of these associations I served on a panel investigating why the water for the fire hydrant system failed. The association for my street involved only about twenty members from households stretched out along several blocks. Since the fire had stopped its westward course at my street, not all the houses had burned and some were only partially damaged. The group included people whose homes still stood, along with those whose houses were but heaps of cinders. Again both men and women, couples and singles, and all ages were party to the group. Meetings took place about once a month. Beyond my street's group, I also participated in two larger neighborhood associations for my area. Each consisted of over one hundred members, single and coupled, male and female, all ages. Meetings were held every two to three weeks, growing more widely spaced as time passed. Topics at first focused on immediate fire issues, such as debris removal, building policies (both city and county), and water, but later broadened to include wider matters of neighborhood concern, such as arranging safer traffic (and escape) patterns, limiting construction noise, installing underground utility wiring, and so on, as people returned.

In addition to the insurance and neighborhood groups, I belonged to two specifically women's groups. One was organized by the women architects of the area when they realized women survivors were having particular problems with the loss of their homes. The problems spanned not only the loss of the house and belongings, but also insurance, finance, tax matters, emotions and alliances, and rebuilding decisions. Some sixty-five members belonged, although actual participation was often double that or more. Meetings usually, but not always, entailed guest experts who offered advice on various issues; grief and mourning, how to invest insurance money in the short term while waiting to rebuild, what the IRS demanded, sources for appliances and furnishings, decor, and post-disaster illness. The architectural process was also addressed, not only for new homes, but also for the reconstructive drawings of destroyed houses—a painful requirement of the insurance companies. There were vivid group discussions and interactions as well. Included in this group were women whose husbands or other family members died or were injured in the fire.

I was also a member of a small self-organized women's support group that had twelve members. The group was started when several women realized their concerns and griefs were divergent from those of the men in their lives and that they wanted the empathy of other women. Of the members, ten were married and two single. Nine were white, one was African-American, and two were Asian. The group included one preschool teacher, two kindergarten/first-grade teachers, one nurse, one travel agent, one psychologist, one social worker, one pianist, one woman who owned her own skin care business, one physical therapist, one homemaker who was also an artist, and one anthropologist. The group met every Monday for over three years at different women's homes. Meetings were leaderless and had no specific topics, but an incredible range of issues was covered. Each of us was recruited by a friend or acquaintance, but we by no means all knew one another. Unanimously we decided to limit our number to twelve so that a single discussion group would prevail and talk would not fray into small side conversations. The group was so important to the women that attendance was almost total every Monday for over three years.

In addition to particular groups, I attended all the general meetings of all the survivors and was a frequent patron of the relief center where I spoke to numerous other survivors and various officials. Represented there were persons from various bureaus and agencies, including aid programs, utilities, employment, building permits, debris removal, post office, and so on. I also lost pets, so I interacted with the pet rescue hot line on a regular basis. As best I could, considering my trauma and all I needed to do, I kept notes on all the groups, the needs, and issues, and, of course, I was experiencing all the difficulties and issues personally.

Before the fire it would be fair to say that the Oakland firestorm survivors to a large degree represented the pinnacle of modern sexual definition, or better put, nondivision. The women of the community were independent, men equitable, couples by and large egalitarian. People of both genders occupied the same segments of space, public and private arenas, hours of day and night. But for many, progress in carving out new gender behavior suffered a fifty-year setback after the firestorm. In the shock of loss, both men and women retreated into traditional cultural realms and personas. Men launched into command and took action. Assuming the family helm, they proceeded to exercise autonomous decision making. For example, the husband of one woman in my support group would not let her speak to the insurance adjustor, architect, or contractor and refused to allow her input on the design of their new home, including the kitchen, despite the fact that he never cooked.

With the domicile *gone*, women on the other hand found themselves thrown into utter domesticity. Whether they worked in the outside world or not, women drowned in a veritable sea of intestine, homely detail, towels, toothbrushes, underwear, Spaghetti-Os. Women's caregiving roles expand dramatically at all stages of disaster response, say Enarson and Morrow. As primary household managers responsible for obtaining, preserving, and distributing food and household supplies, women's taken-for-granted skills help prepare and maintain their households in times of crisis, and they are depended upon and exploited (1998: 4). Bari, for instance, noted that in Bangladesh, because of women's financial situation and household duties, coping with disaster is much more difficult for women (1992: 58). This proved utterly true in Oakland, even when previously a family had established, at least superficially, an equal and non-sex-based division of labor. To women, immediately and for the course of several years of the recovery, fell almost all the childcare chores, the soothing, clothing, feeding, tending, chauffeuring of the young. Women became ensnared in an almost unbearable tangle of child-rearing duties, particularly burdensome if they also worked outside the home. Women again found themselves responsible for all food "gathering" chores, the obtaining, preparing, and serving of meals, often without the benefit of pots, pans, plates, tables, or chairs. A constant topic in my women's group was how to deal with food needs, where to get meals, what to feed the family, how to maintain some semblance of a proper balanced diet. Women further fell unwittingly into old habits of compliance. As men picked rental houses and very often commandeered family finances, money allocation, the filling out of paperwork, the choice of professionals, and all other decisions, even down to new telephone numbers, women retreated in silence and acquiesced.

What had happened?

The deep grammar of Western society employs a very basic division to sort out people and define the rules, roles, and behavior. It is based on the distinction between male and female. We eschew borrowing symbols from our environment and grouping people according to totems of, say, bear, eagle, and wolf. We superficially note, but little heed, less environmental, more literary categories such as occupation, caste, or family name to delineate people's place and define their actions (Levi-Strauss 1964). Rather, our core organizational principle, the one that says who's who and what they should do, operates according to sex (Hoffman 1973, 1976, 1997). The employment of gender to categorize and circumscribe people arises from sensory perception. The fact of two sexes is a phenomenon that exists in nature, a phenomenon that can be heard, touched, and most importantly, seen. It is then lifted from sensory perception, from its actual physicality, and used in an abstract or "cultural" way to sort all manner of matter that are not connected and not gendered in actuality at all. Nature does not declare who wears a shirt and who a skirt, who chops wood and who cooks, who is a C.E.O. and who an R.N. But, because gender as the basis for defining division derives from nature, and because the distinction is so close at hand, so readily visible, it seems constantly justifiable and results in a very tenacious pattern. The use of gender as a device to define grouping and declare action is long fixed and very pervasive in our culture, and it is what surfaced once again in the duress of the calamity.

The resurgence of old gender roles after the Oakland firestorm overlapped with another traditional cultural division, that of public and private arenas. Most men among the disaster survivors immediately reclaimed the public world. Calling on the prerogative of work, they lifted themselves out and away from the coals and drove away daily. Men further allied with public persons, attorneys, architects, contractors, and the other titled people who arrived on the scene. To the contrary, many women *quit* their jobs or took extensive leaves. Women could not reconcile their now-massive domestic chores with their outside occupations (Lamphere et al. 1993). They went to the Bed and Bath Superstore and dealt with clerks. Their lives became confined to the fire area and coffee klatches with one another. The work they gave up or took leave from was not merely manual or service chores. They retreated from careers such as social work and hospital administration. Some eventually returned, but some did not. Moreover, a matter of "big" chores versus "small" entered, with women taking up all small tasks, making the phone calls, waiting for deliveries, while men took the large, attending meetings, hiring crews, and overseeing removal of foundations and trees. Internal to homes, the private space sacrificed in rental homes was often women's private space, so that women were unable to separate themselves from others. Extra room became men's exclusive workspace, with first objects bought frequently being men's computers and equipment. In reinforcement from an outer, male-oriented industry, many insurance companies issued checks for homes in men's names alone, despite the community property nature of the houses, and husbands could not understand their wives' objections.

The return of old behaviors and the loss of new was so swift, so engulfing, and so unconscious that few understood what occurred. Many unions, long and short, broke apart. In my small support group of twelve alone, two marriages and one long nonmarital relationship broke up, and I know of many other breakups outside this group. That ratio, between one fourth and one third of unions dissolving, is typical for disasters. One marriage and the nonmarital relationship in my group had been troubled before, and the stress of the recovery proved the proverbial straws that broke the camel's back. The breakup of the second marriage struck the unsuspecting wife as yet another calamitous jolt. Though she was virtually the first of us to buy and furnish a home, wishing to tackle problems head on and have them done with, it was, as Shaw describes for Bangladesh (1992: 210) as if her work had been undervalued by her husband and she was nonetheless somehow, in some way perceived as a burden. She was deserted. Bangladeshi women are often deserted after a disaster as well.

Individuals felt like overturned snails crawling back to former upright circumstance. "The first three years there was no light at the end of the tunnel. Everything was so grim, so tiring, so endless. I would go to bed at eight at night, not get up for twelve hours, anything to not face the next day. The next two years I saw light at the end of the tunnel, but I couldn't get there. People kept saying that I would emerge from this and when I did, that I'd come out glad I experienced it. What a cliche. I'm better now, but still not over it. I don't know if I ever will be," one woman said to me. Male survivors, having maintained access to the public realm and to the concomitant approval that sphere garners, more quickly claimed they were fully recovered. The majority

of men returned to their work within a week of the fire, and meetings to
include them had to be scheduled for evenings and weekends. Men bought
adequate enough clothes and equipment to cover their basic requirements,
and devalued other household needs. Their roles as major money makers
aided this. "I recovered," said a man in my insurance group, "after about six
months. It happened. It's over. I don't know why my wife is still disturbed."
"I don't see the point of your women's group," another said. "You just get on
with things. But if you need it, hey." Meanwhile, the women, uprooted from
or severely diminished in their venues, outwardly suffered more depression
and longer recovery periods. The Alameda Health Department tallied a far
greater use of health services and recommendations for therapy and therapy
groups for women than men among firestorm victims (personal communication, March 1998).

In a second development that stunned the survivors and survivor anthropologist, new and innovative American kinship revealed its shallow underpinnings and dissolved, while there returned from a seeming grave old bilateral
consanguineal kinship. Though both of these developments were general,
they affected women far more than men.

Oakland firestorm survivors had marched well into the brave new world
of social alliances. Extended families had long given way to nuclear. Many
nuclear families were broken down yet further, and most victims felt their
closest ties lay with nonrelated friends. Friendships are the key associations in
most women's lives today, certainly with modern urban women such as lived
in Oakland. It was mostly women's friends in Oakland who were their close
associates, their main companions outside of conjugal unions, and the persons with whom they, as individuals and with partners, socialized. But our
new bonds, mere decades rather than millennia old, disclosed their lack of
shared and culturally reinforced rules. Friendships bear no understood schedule of obligations, no course of expected action, no set of proscribed emotions. As a consequence, while some friends proved themselves "Rocks of
Gibraltar," virtually every survivor suffered wrenching shifts in former associations. Friends did not, or could not, offer aid or comfort. Friends grew impa-
tient, proved unsympathetic, disappeared. I, for example, lost three of my
closest friendships. My "best" friend did not come to my aid nor call for
months, then blithely passed off my trauma as "that's the breaks." Another, a
colleague as well as close friend, said to my old college roommate, "I don't
know why Susanna is so upset about losing her field notes. She wasn't using
them anyway." (I was, in fact, in the middle of writing a book based on them,
and they were spread out on my desk, although that is not the point.) She did
not come to my aid in any fashion and urged another important person in my
life to end our relationship. A third, perennially swept away with her own

problems, simply had no time or words for mine until the friendship withered. The loss of these salient, not-kin relationships became so dire, especially for women, that the Alameda County Health Department issued a bulletin advising survivors of the prevalence of friendship loss after a disaster and advising on ways to manage it.

What were maintained for most were the links that lie more deeply rooted in our society: blood kinship ties. Like clans gathering, mothers, fathers, sisters, brothers, cousins arrived. Relatives sent family heirlooms. A cousin replaced my vaporized silver vase, a gift from my father's long-dead, beloved cousin, with a creamer and sugarer of her mother's, though her mother was not my blood kin. Siblings returned borrowed property, sent money, and took in children. My sister, in the face of all the utilitarian items I required, decided to cheer me up with something utterly frivolous. She bought me a lingerie set decorated in peonies, my favorite flower. With little time when I'm relaxed enough to wear it still, I've considered framing it. Extended families, such as they were, embraced their own, stood up and were counted in both presence and presents.

But the return of kinship also immediately became, as it had customarily been in our traditional society, women's job to facilitate. It is true that soothing benefits flowed from the return of blood kinship—gifts, support, identity. Still, even good kinship relations require mediating, and not all go smoothly. Onus often tags along with aid, and troublesome aspects of kinship ties that many survivors, both men and women, had disengaged from, like the ubiquitous Cat in the Hat, came back. In the dust of the dead embers, as women became the reestablishers of household circumstance, it fell to them to sort and store the items, material and immaterial, that arrived from relatives. "My mother-in-law and her daughters nagged me to death. They harangued me to get a bread maker, a mixer, to get curtains. I don't use any of that," said a neighbor as we shopped for plates. But her in-laws bought for her the items she was shunning, and they rest dusty on her shelf today. A woman in my small group hated her boxy, ill-maintained rental house so much she called it "the Holiday Inn with holes," yet, she said, "My mother, who is the bane of my existence, won't let up on me. She loves this house. She wants me to buy it." Many found themselves constrained to accept undesired clothes, pots, chairs, tables, and other items. The paraphernalia that arrived was sometimes battered, sometimes not, yet women could neither refuse items nor throw away what they received, since kin brought them. "I turned down that dining room table ten times," a woman in my insurance group said. "Now I've got it for keeps." Another's sister, many times larger than she, sent her new clothes, but, as if in spite, in sizes many times bigger than the survivor wore. Another recently told me, "My mother-in-law keeps checking to see if I still have what she gave me. I'll never be allowed to forget how she 'helped.'" In conse-

quence, women could not control the accoutrements nor the aesthetics of
their living environment. Indeed, they could hardly control their family's or
their own demeanor. These were areas which, before the fire, women governed, and the loss of that governance further increased women's sense of
powerlessness. As Enarson and Morrow point out, women's paid and unpaid
caregiving responsibilities position them emotionally and materially to sustain
kin and community throughout the experiences of disaster recovery. A gendered division of labor makes many women frontline responders in moments
of extreme crisis and long-term caregivers to disaster-impacted family members (1998: 3).

As culturally defined keepers of kinship, women could also not send relatives packing, and they were—or certainly felt they were—constrained to submit to the visits as much as to the dictates and opinions of parents, aunts,
uncles, siblings, and in-laws. For married women, the arrival of a husband's
family brought the strain that accompanies in-law courtesies. The majority of
relatives that turned up, however, bore the invisible matrilineal stamp Schneider (1969) so well deciphered in American kinship. Thus, it was often a
woman's own mother, sisters, and aunts who docked on the charcoal shores.
While this might manifestly seem to have offered a woman ease, it also meant
that at a time when playfulness and humor were short and gestures to reaf-
firm their position were beyond most women's ability, who was covertly
Alpha-female of the female line, who the Beta, the Gamma, and so on, came
into contestation. One woman's younger sister who had waited years to claim
the right to make Christmas at her house went off with all the survivor's new
platters. Another's several sisters unloaded their children on her for care, since
she "wasn't working now." All together, women had difficulty reestablishing
prior familial authority and their own independence. Women underwent pressures in dealing with kin that men, who had removed themselves from the
domestic scene, did not. Many women experienced considerable discipline
problems with children. With no routines, no family dinners, no space to
do homework, no orders were followed. Indeed, in no time flat, women
survivors felt like they had been through the heavy soil cycle of a scorched
Maytag.

Undeniably, the disintegration of friendships severely crushed women,
certainly more so than men whose associations were often at or through their
work. Women in our society, as part of our domesticity, act as the social con-
nectors. We are to a large extent the "linesmen" of our ties and the "bonds-
men" of our everyday social circles. We form and maintain the family's
intimate network. Di Leonardo points out that women are the persons who
knit kinship and the social world together in most cultures (1987). Most of us
also construct supportive coteries of our own, clasping into sisterly closeness
pals and allies whom we very much rely on. We love our friends, and the dis-

solution of those friendships rends our milieus more badly than those of men. Women in the Oakland firestorm suffered greatly over the loss of friendships.

But while the loss of friendship was wrenching, it seems that loss of blood kin was worse. Though I am aware of other instances, I intimately knew three women who lost kinship ties. One of the women was in my small support group, another was in the architect groups, and one was a prior friend who unfortunately also ended up a disaster survivor. In the first two cases the survivors' mothers asked them to hand over their insurance money. One mother wished to give the money to a ne'er-do-well brother, despite the fact that her daughter was patently homeless and needed the money desperately to build and buy objects again. Her mother told her that the brother needed it more. Since turning her mother down, the woman's entire family has not spoken to her. The second mother felt the money should be "shared" by all, though other family members had lost nothing, and in the third situation, a well-off brother who lived at some distance, sent clothes, toys, and household goods to his sister in a seemingly wonderful gesture, unasked. However, he followed up the package with the bill for all the items. These two women have not spoken again to mother or brother. These women have suffered particularly great pain, and their emotional recovery decidedly lags behind others. The shifts in both friendship and kinship alliances profoundly affected women survivors. Social worlds from before the fire have never been the same.

To add to the domestic and household problems, around our nest of ashes a new, as-ever dichotomous rendition of segmentary opposition—factions uniting due to contention and contestation with one another (see Evans-Pritchard 1940)—complete with concomitant ideology, texts of terms, and ensuing psychological warfare, sprung forth. It occurred between survivors and outside community and also with the outside "others" we had to deal with. Segmentary opposition pops up from disaster zones like jonquils from frozen ground. Typically every survivor group seizes upon a particular "outsider" enemy. Usually it's the government or an aid agency, such as the Red Cross (Oliver-Smith 1992: 75–114). Ours was the insurance companies. None of us would ever marry one of their sons or daughters again. As soon as the insurance companies arrived with their forms, but more so their tactics, denials, and delays, the survivors became the "us." Insurance agents became the "them." In short order survivors delineated, fixed, and stereotyped insurance personnel into a scurrilous mob. The insurance companies termed us as "difficult," the modern-day equivalent of "witch."

The insurance camps especially applied this epithet—or versions of it—to the women who confronted their ranks of adjusters and agents. Almost to a man, all the insurance adjusters and executives were male, and here again women survivors were confronting the public arena of official and titled persons. As Douglas points out, accusations of witchcraft are an instrument to break down relations, a form of attack that rids one of obligation, which is exactly how the insurance company agents rancorously behaved toward us, unobliged and unobliging (Douglas 1970; also see Lewis 1983). The more insistent women were with insurance officials, the more we were promoted to the category of "difficult" and then on to the second level of the "difficult" category, the one known by the repellent and insulting term (forbidden in my family)—"bitch." By deeming women "difficult" or more, of course, one removes them from individuality and places them in a set whose complaints are deemed meaningless and thus dismissable. We were in a situation where complaints were legion, yet we were lumped in a bunch such that our requests were rendered inconsequential. One of my insurance company adjusters baldly told a woman in my group that she was "just a greedy woman." Another was asked, "Just what do you want?"—shades of Freud!

As the leader of an insurance group, I particularly fell under the epithet "difficult," a word I never heard applied to a man. "Oh, her, don't listen to what she says," another of my group heard, and "she's a lot of trouble." I was told falsely by an adjuster that I could not get displacement-from-home funds my policy included unless I rented a home of equal size and value. On that statement I signed a lease on a house far larger than I needed or wanted in my crisis state. When I found out I had been led astray and demanded reimbursement for the lease, I was stalled for a year and accused of being "demanding." The insurance company eventually paid in full. Indeed, my "difficulty" succeeded for all those under my leadership, and when I saw all but three of my insurance group to settlement, and then went into negotiations for my own, the company penned off on every dotted line. Of course, by then they had held everyone's payments for a year, earning whatever interest the money accumulated.

By and large, in all dealings and associations, I saw what is true of other societies, that women after the disaster are economically and politically disadvantaged in getting disaster compensation and proper treatment. Already by the second or third month of the aftermath, Oakland's women were less well treated than men and received less monetary compensation. Insurance companies, for example, were supposed to give insurees immediate small checks to ease them over the first hurdle of recovery. Single women specifically did not readily get those checks. Numerous women told me their insurance adjusters treated them as "stupid." They patronized them and stalled on payments by making them review all details, acting as if the women were illogical and did not understand policies or as if the woman's demands were outrageous and beyond policy scope when they were not. Many women were seemingly purposefully driven to tears, and a number, even one in my own insurance group and against my advice, were driven to settle with insurance companies quickly and for less compensation than due, just to end their dealings with insurance agents. Enarson and Morrow point out that in all forms of disaster relief, be it from government agency or private organization (or in Oakland from insurers), women receive less (1998: 1–5).

Over time not only insurance officials, but architects, contractors, and the many workers who entered the scene stereotyped Oakland women in an old cultural fashion and devalued our voice. We were in a situation where we absolutely had to deal with men and over a large variety of matters. There were not enough women architects and contractors. Indeed, there was only one company of female contractors in the town. Emergency management, building code inspectors, utilities workers, and cleanup crews were largely male. Perhaps the situation revealed into how narrow a scope of endeavors women have marched and how little integration we have actually achieved. Our egalitarian world only seemed egalitarian because the range of our usual and daily contacts was so limited. A neighbor of mine found that though she gave up her work to be on hand for the rebuilding process, her contractors would not heed her. She had to wait for her husband's return from work, tell him what she wanted, and have him tell the contractors to get accomplished what she wanted, although she had earlier informed the workers of the same requests. "I resented terribly being put in that position again," she said, "having to tell a man what I wanted and having to have him handle it for me." Her anger still simmers.

In rather rapid course, disaster victims were also grouped into oppositional category by the wider, neighboring outside community, and we disparaged and withdrew from them. This occurred especially as waves of jealousy overtook neighbors, acquaintances, storekeepers, and others, and as we were soldered into unity by the extenuated aftermath of our blistering catastrophe. At first the outside community saw us with sympathy. Eventually, when recovery took longer than the day, week, or month they envisioned, they came to view us as greedy whiners and undeserving receivers of pots of gold. We, perceiving instantly their adversity, adopted equally separating, and in due course dehumanizing, conceptualizations to mark them. They, too, were avaricious whiners, but of their own form. They were insensitive narcissists who sashayed on in sublime comfort. As the community divided itself and jealousy erupted, it was often once more the women who bore the brunt of it. Since it was the women survivors who daily dealt with the community's realtors, salespersons, clerks, it was women who largely heard and dealt with the comments. Targets of wanton envy, we were each more than once informed that, as we had all new things and did or would have new houses, we were "lucky." Of course, since ancient times the brimstone of criticism in our culture has been directed more at women than men. More venerated men are rarely swiped at with petty assaults, and with their more decorous business ties, male survivors scarcely endured aspersion. Women survivors had little

choice but to turn inward and seek solace among those who were devoid of
envy—other survivors—and thus isolate themselves further (see Erikson 1994
on the ghettoization of disaster survivors). "I've given up talking to people
who didn't lose their homes," said one mainstay of my support group. "They
don't understand. I find I'm safer if I only see other fire victims." "I didn't
believe what my wife was saying until one day I was near her in a store. She
ran into old acquaintances and they accused her of getting more things. One
asked her when she'd ever be satisfied and another said it would be nice if her
house would burn too so she could get new things. It was unbelievable. No
man ever said anything to me like that," a husband in one of my neighborhood groups told me. As we limited our associations to one another and
rarely saw outsiders, we meanwhile embraced an illusion that we were homo-
geneous. We took on an aura as if we, as a group, were sacred, almost purified by the fire. Outsiders were the "unbaptized" who "could not understand."
No one who had not suffered the fire could understand. In a book of fire
writings, a woman writes: "Since the fire, I have rarely allowed myself ordinary pleasures. Indeed, I make every attempt to be alone, to be away from
noise, the ordinary sounds of modern life. . . . I do not watch the news. . . . I
will do everything to avoid driving or even being with any people, except
some fire survivors" (Adler 1992: 183). In a 1997 magazine article, accusations of survivors' voracious greed by an outsider continued (Kirp 1997). But
Berkeley and Oakland are shrewd communities, and women, men as well,
soon became cognizant of their tumble back in time. It was when the women
architects of the area realized how disenfranchised women victims were
becoming that they formed their women's group, and the numerous individual support groups for themselves also emerged. Now seven years later, my
small support group still occasionally meets. Women are victimized by disaster, states Enarson, but they are also survivors and responders whose capacities and recovery resources need investigation. A number of case studies
illustrate women's active disaster responses, from the simple act of replanting
crops and rebuilding homes to sophisticated political organizing, community
mobilization, and research-based workshops on gender, development, and
disaster (1997: 23).

Enarson and Morrow also point out that women's formal and informal
networks are central to household and community recovery (1998: 4). In
Oakland it was women among survivors who pushed for events and processes
that reinforced community and provided a sense of achievement over time. It
was largely women who tatted neighborhoods together like so much lace.
While men in general led insurance groups dealing with adjusters and so on
(all but three were led by men), women played major roles in neighborhood
associations and have been ongoing forces for neighborhood improvements

such as the installation of stop signs. They largely did the writing for the post-firestorm and now small neighborhood newspapers that emerged. Women were the driving force behind the commemorations and ceremonies that took place. Women organized the rituals and today assemble the anniversary celebrations. These are clothed in the success of our survival rather than the grief of our loss. Women organized the art showings and contributed a majority of the disaster writings that appeared in books and the newspaper. Women conceived of the firestorm memorial, that it was to be formed of individual tiles designed by the victims. They oversaw the production of the tile mural and procured the site. Meanwhile, everywhere surviving trees were turned into inspiring shrines. I didn't witness exactly who turned trees into living icons of our return, nor did I spot exactly who left talismans on burned-out lots. But since most of the ornaments left at these sites were flowers and jewelry, I have my sneaking suspicion what the gender was of those who did it.

These often women-inspired events and processes reinforced community as opposed to individualization. Meetings that took place at regular intervals, rather than occurring randomly, provided the survivors an almost archaic sense of shared cyclical time. Anniversaries—one week, one month, one year—were public, known to all and celebrated by all. The content of meetings was repetitive and thus unifying, not fragmenting. In women's as well as other groups, survivors repeated a common litany of lists and chores that had sameness and reemphasized both the mundane and shared truck of life, the commonweal as opposed to atomic. Only in about the fourth year did individual interests and postmodern fragmentation return to Oakland.

"Gender is a pervasive division affecting all societies, and it channels access to social and economic resources away from women and towards men," state Blaikie and colleagues. "Women are often denied the vote, the right to inherit land, and generally have less control over income-earning opportunities and care within their own households. Normally their access to resources is inferior to that of men. Since our argument is that less access to resources, in the absence of other compensations to provide safe conditions, leads to increased vulnerabilities, we contend that in general women are more vulnerable to hazards" (1994: 48). In their groundbreaking compendium on disaster vulnerability, Blaikie and colleagues also point out that women have different coping abilities with respect to disaster. Household framework places women in situations of taboo, in a sexual division of labor that restricts or overwhelms them, or puts them behind men and children in sharing goods. Yet the resources that aid recovery are women's as well, their jewelry or small crafts. Women and children frequently bear the brunt of disasters because of the discriminatory allocative power of male members of the household, a state which continues in disaster camps and shelters. They have less entitlement (Torry 1986). Despite the mutual economic and emotional support they provide, families may break up because of individual survival drive, and when they do, the breakdown of obligations is revealed through the abandonment of women, children, and the elderly. Women have the responsibility of caring for suffering children. Women and poverty combine. Those women with better placement in society often have the ability to recover more completely than those with worse placement, but better placement is generally achieved through marriage. Women's lives are almost always more constrained and difficult than men's. Women are more prone to post-disaster disease. Women tend to lose conflicts over scarce resources. Time and place patterns of daily and seasonal activities often place women in more risky positions. They are frequently in the home, not outdoors, and isolated when disasters strike. After disasters, in many societies women are more likely to end up on government handouts or permanently dependent on aid. The elderly are vulnerable, but among them particularly widows. Yet, women's support networks aid survival as does their often neighborhood-based self-help activity. Blaikie and colleagues go on to assert that more attention in disaster mitigation and aid needs to be paid to women. Women need more access to aid money, to loans, to political and other organizations. (For a set of policy guideposts for the disaster treatment of women, see Enarson and Morrow 1998: 224–230.) Blaikie and colleagues as well as others acknowledge that the women's movement has made an enormous contribution in understanding women's vulnerability as well as environmental degradation (1994: 13–24, 488, 113–133, 205–237).

Women in Oakland were largely products and adherents of the woman's movement. They had come much of the "long way." Nonetheless, though the constraints were less visible, women in this affluent community still had less access to resources, especially those now needed from what has clearly remained a man's world. Despite often good incomes, Oakland women produced less earnings than men, and old cultural traditions demanded they give up their sources of income when faced with the burden of old gender-based domestic roles. The vulnerability Oakland women suffered was, as Blaikie and colleagues describe, basically cultural. Women's continuing vulnerability in the Oakland firestorm cost them, however, in more than just cultural ways. More than half those who died in the flames were women. At least two of these were, as Enarson warns, isolated in their homes (1997: 10).

As devastating as the disaster was, I was gratified to see the strands of cultural DNA that lie behind the lives of people caught up, until then, in the everyday. We inch to a new order it seems, but the old is not far buried. Doesn't the bride's family at a wedding still sit on the sinister side of the church? Don't we continue to hear arguments that women should remain at home and only men should venture into the workplace, that women should raise children, not handle money or hold office? We continue to employ a division of cultural items according to gender and claim that division arises from the fact that the sexes are "by nature different," in short, on sensory perception. Certainly the fire in Oakland revealed who is still the more empowered. Enarson and Morrow state that the less economically and politically empowered a person is and the more isolated, the greater their suffering (Enarson and Morrow, 1998). In Oakland to all outward appearances the women flourished financially and held considerable political clout. Yet they differentially suffered. I aver that in Oakland, women suffered more. Cultural empowerment lags behind the other forms.

The whole event brought me to yet one more concern of anthropology and one that is a seeming mystery of human life. Except for some words from an occasional psychological or biological anthropologist, few have found any satisfying explanation for place attachment. Though I have left the scene of the disaster (I felt I must in order to see it; as Levi-Strauss declares, an anthropologist is forever an amputee), a very large percentage of the Oakland firestorm survivors—like survivors of other disasters—have not only returned to the site they occupied before, they have rebuilt almost virtually the same house. It was often men who wanted the same lot; women who wanted the same house. They shook in fear at recent close fires and earthquakes, yet there they are. In this facet, the genders seemed equal. I realize the comfort of the familiar far too well. Nothing I owned carried the aroma of my family for at least a year, and for a long while I thought I had checked forever into Hotel California pretty much as described in song. So I ponder. Were male survivors attached so well to the hunting ground of their jobs that they could not wander? Were the women loath to leave the locations of nuts and grass in the local Safeway? I'd like an answer to what holds people to a "there," even a there where, as Gertrude Stein said of her birthplace, Oakland, "there is no there there."

The firestorm was a devastating occurrence to me and to all the victims. I would not wish what I went through on anyone (not even a sociologist). Still, I must say that the clarity I obtained in seeing the operative tenets pulsing behind the facades and pressure of modern life was matchless. I was singed into a living laboratory where I could observe the molecules of our society reaggregate from cultural atoms. It turned out that two of the atoms are still Adam and Eve.

NOTE

1. Parts of this chapter appeared in E. Enarson and B. Morrow, *The Gendered Terrain of Disaster: Through the Eyes of Women*, Westport, CT: Greenwood Publishers, and are reprinted with the publisher's permission.

BIBLIOGRAPHY

Adler, P. (ed.). 1992. *Fire in the Hills: A Collective Remembrance.* Berkeley, CA: 24 Avalon Ave.

Bari, S. 1992. "Women in the Aftermath," in H. Hossain, C. Dodge, and F. Abel (eds.), *From Crisis to Development: Coping with Disasters in Bangladesh.* Dhaka: University Press Limited.

Blaikie, P., T. Cannon, I. Davis, and B. Wisner. 1994. *At Risk.* New York: Routledge.

Di Leonardo, M. 1987. "The Female World of Cards and Holidays: Women, Family and the Work of Kinship." *Signs: Journal of Women in Culture and Society* 12: 440–453.

Douglas, M. 1966. *Purity and Danger: An Analysis of Concepts of Pollution and Taboo.* London: Routledge and Kegan Paul.

———. 1970. *Witchcraft: Confessions and Accusations.* London: Tavistock.

Drabek, T. 1986. *Human Systems' Response to Disaster: An Inventory of Sociological Findings.* New York: Simon and Schuster.

Dudasik, S. 1980. "Victimization in Natural Disaster." *Disasters* 4: 329–38.

Enarson, E. 1997. "His and Hers Disaster: New Questions for Disaster Social Science." Paper delivered at the National Hazards Workshop, Denver, CO, July, 1997.

Enarson, E., and B. Morrow (eds.). 1998. *The Gendered Terrain of Disaster: Through the Women's Eyes.* Westport, CT: Greenwood.

Erikson, K. 1994. *A New Species of Trouble: The Human Experience of Modern Disasters.* New York: Norton.

Evans-Pritchard, E. 1940. *The Nuer: The Political Institutions of a Nilotic People.* Oxford: Clarendon.

Hewitt, K. (ed.). 1983. *Interpretations of Calamity.* New York: Allen and Unwin.

Hoffman, S. 1973. *Kypseli—Women and Men Apart: A Divided Reality.* Film, distributed by Extension Media Center, University of California, Berkeley, California.

———. 1976. "Kypseli: A Marital Geography of a Greek Village." In *Lifelong Learning* 45, 58. April 5, 1976. Berkeley: University Extension, University of California.

———. 1994. "Up from the Embers: A Disaster Survivor's Story." *Clinical Quarterly* 4, 2: 15–17.

———. 1997. "Bringing the 'Other' to the 'Self': Kypseli—the Place and the Film," in S. Parman (ed.), *Europe in the Anthropological Imagination,* pp. 44–59. Englewood Cliffs, NJ: Prentice-Hall.

Kirp, D. 1997. "There Goes the Neighborhood: After the Berkeley Fire, an Architectural Disaster." *Harpers* 294, 1762: 45–53.

Lamphere, L., P. Gonzales, and P. Evans. 1993. *Sunbelt Working Mothers: Reconciling Family and Factory.* Ithaca: Cornell University Press.

Levi-Strauss, C. 1964. *Totemism.* London: Merlin.

———. 1966. *The Savage Mind.* Chicago: University of Chicago Press.

Lewis, I. 1983. *The Language of Ethnic Conflict: Social Organization and Lexical Culture*. New York: Columbia University Press.

Marris, P. 1974. *Loss and Change*. London: Routledge and Kegan Paul.

Oliver-Smith, A. 1992. *The Martyred City: Death and Rebirth in the Andes*. Prospect Heights, IL: Waveland Press.

Sapir, J. 1977. "The Anatomy of Metaphor," in J. Sapir and J. Crocker (eds.), *The Social Use of Metaphor: Essays on the Anthropology of Rhetoric*, pp. 3–32. Philadelphia: University of Pennsylvania Press.

Schneider, D. 1969. "Kinship, Nationality and Religion in American Culture," in V. Turner (ed.), *Forms of Symbolic Action*, pp. 115–125. Proceedings of the 1969 Annual Spring Meeting of the American Ethnological Society.

Shaw, R. 1992. "'Nature,' 'Culture' and Disasters: Floods and Gender in Bangladesh," in E. Cross and D. Parkin (eds.), *Bush Base: Forest Farm: Culture, Environment and Development*, pp. 200–217. London: Routledge.

Torry, W. 1978. "Natural Disasters, Social Structure and Change in Traditional Societies." *Journal of African Studies* 13: 167–183.

———. 1980. "Urban Earthquake Hazard in Developing Countries: Squatter Settlements and the Outlook for Turkey." *Urban Ecology* 4: 317–327.

———. 1986. "Morality and Harm: Hindu Peasant Adjustments to Famines." *Social Science Inf.* 25: 125–160.

Turner, V. 1961. *The Ritual Process*. Chicago: Aldine.

Wallace, A. 1956. "Mazeway Resynthesis: A Biocultural Theory of Religious Inspiration." *Transactions of the New York Academy of Sciences* 18, 7: 626–638.

———. 1957. "Mazeway Disintegration: The Individual's Perception of Sociocultural Disorganization." *Human Organization* 16, 2: 23–27.

Watzlawich, P. 1984. *The Invented Reality*. New York: Norton.

Wiest, R., J. Mocellin, and D. Motsisi. 1992. *The Needs of Women and Children in Disasters and Emergencies*. Winnipeg: University of Manitoba.

10

VULNERABILITY, DISASTER, AND SURVIVAL IN BANGLADESH: THREE CASE STUDIES[1]

MOHAMMAD Q. ZAMAN
Independent Researcher

INTRODUCTION

DISASTERS RESULT FROM A COMPLEX MIX OF BOTH NATURAL HAZARDS AND sociopolitical and economic processes in any society. Yet, a review of disaster research worldwide indicates that many studies do not adequately address the social processes in their accounts of calamity (Oliver-Smith 1996). Geophysical and other natural processes, such as drought, floods, tropical storms, or earthquakes, receive a great deal of attention at policy-making levels while the social and economic processes involved are often ignored, resulting in largely unsustainable technical solutions for disaster preparedness, management, and mitigation. The United Nations International Decade for Natural Disaster Reduction (1990–2000) took a similar narrow view of hazard and hazard reduction by focusing concern solely on physical "risks" and promoting mitigative policy measures derived from natural science and techno-engineering knowledge (Mitchell 1990; Zaman 1994a). Disasters, when and where they occur, however, are identified by government agencies, the media, and others *only* in terms of social and economic impacts like loss of life, disruptions of livelihoods, and destruction of properties. Hence, geophysical or natural events like floods or hurricanes are seen or defined as disasters only in how they affect peoples and communities. The irony in the contrast between the research focus and the definition of disaster reveals the essence of the problem. The geophysical or natural events are the "trigger" events whose impacts *cause* disasters. Disasters can be better understood and explained in relation to and as a product of the larger economic and political systems in which they occur (Hewitt 1983; Torry 1979). This means that disasters do not simply happen; they are products of preexisting social and economic forces within the society.

This chapter presents case studies of three types of natural disasters in Bangladesh—flood, erosion, and coastal cyclone—and focuses on the nature of physical, economic, and social processes that determine vulnerability of populations. It examines how people in Bangladesh cope with life in disasters and crisis and illustrates the role of sociocultural factors such as kinship, friendship, community, and/or patronage networks in adjustment strategies. The examination is followed by a review of the disaster preparedness and management policies, which reveals inadequate attention to various indigenous technological, material, and social resources people utilize at both individual and community levels. Lastly, a number of policy prescriptions are presented for adoption of a more sustainable disaster preparedness and development policy in Bangladesh.

VULNERABILITY: THE CONCEPT AND THE APPROACH

To conduct this analysis, this paper approaches the issue of disaster from the point of view of vulnerability. Early studies of natural disasters (White 1974; Kates 1971; Mileti et al. 1975; Burton et al. 1978) assumed that disasters were departures from "normal" social functioning—kinds of "breaks in pattern" and "isolated and annoying interruptions" (Wallace 1956) and that recovery meant a return to normalcy. Disasters are viewed merely as "natural" phenomena requiring some technological fixes to modify and/or control the geophysical processes. This research orientation among both geographers and sociologists from the 1950s through the 1970s resulted, according to Hewitt (1983), in the development of a distinctively "technocratic" approach for mitigating hazard losses in the form of disaster preparedness, emergency evacuation plan, relief and rehabilitation efforts, and in generally ignoring the issue of vulnerability.

In recognition of the failings of the conventional and technocratic approaches to address the social dimensions of vulnerability, an alternative approach emerged in the 1980s which puts greater attention on predisaster social issues in disaster analysis. The approach, variously known as the sociohistorical, political economy, or vulnerability approach, does not deny the significance of natural hazards as trigger events, but focuses largely on the structural and systemic causes that generate disasters by making people vulnerable. Many recent studies (Zaman 1989; Winchester 1992; Varley 1994; Blaikie et al. 1994) have spotlighted how disaster impacts are compounded by patterns of resource control, landownership, local stratification, and inequalities that define everyday lives of disaster victims. The vulnerability approach to disaster considers most natural disasters as *unnatural*. Indeed, in many instances, disasters happen when a natural hazard strikes a people whose everyday conditions are difficult to distinguish from the conditions suffered under disasters.

Central, then, to the vulnerability approach is the relationship between natural hazard or crisis and everyday conditions. As a concept, vulnerability refers to the social and economic characteristics of a person, a household, or a group in terms of their capacity to cope with and to recover from the impacts of a disaster. In many developing countries, due to the underdevelopment and inequalities in the totality of social life, situations of crisis exist every day for most people. In such circumstances, the physical vulnerability of populations, in, for example, the cyclone disaster area of coastal Andhra Pradesh in India, is a symptom of economic fragility within the society; the cyclone or flood disasters only accentuate existing conditions of vulnerability (Winchester 1992). Vulnerability evolves over a long period of time and involves a combination of physical as well as socioeconomic factors that determine one's ability to resist or recover from risks by events in nature or society. Since individuals' ability to resist or recover from the same extreme natural phenomenon vary depending on their losses vis-à-vis control over resources, material assets, and political linkages, people suffer differentially in disaster context (Winchester 1992; Zaman 1989). Table 1 presents various types of vulnerability and their components.

As evidenced in Table 1, the various types of vulnerability are interconnected as a process. Physical vulnerability, like exposure to risks and settlement in hazard-prone areas, is a symptom of economic vulnerability. In the case of Bangladesh, for instance, due to land scarcity coastal dwellers are compelled to settle in extremely vulnerable lowlands along the coastline. The impact of coastal cyclones makes their already tenuous existence more precarious. Economic vulnerability, thus, shapes social and environmental vulnerability as well. The colonial legacy of landownership, the social structure of inequality, and overpopulation in contemporary Bangladesh have created such economic and social conditions that many poor people today are pushed into the most fragile and risk-prone areas, making them yet more vulnerable. Over 50 percent of the rural households in Bangladesh are landless, and nearly two thirds of the population live under the official poverty line. In actuality, it is poverty—an all-pervasive fact of life in Bangladesh—that leads to much of the disaster impacts. A large majority of people in both rural and urban areas cannot meet the basic needs of their lives: food, clothing, shelter, and essential services like health and medicare. For instance, in Bangladesh daily calorie intake per capita is 1,804 (as against 3,682 in the United States); 17 percent of the population do not have a minimum of two pieces of clothing; only 15 percent of the population live in durable houses; 25 percent of the population live in thatched single structures, while another 10 percent are completely shelterless (Rahman 1992). The devastation caused by natural disasters in Bangladesh is, therefore, more a function of the social and economic characteristics of Bangladeshi society than of the actual physical repercussion of the catastrophe. The impacts and responses to erosion, flood, and cyclone disasters presented here provide compelling illustration of this point.

TABLE 1. *Vulnerability types, components, and indicators.*

Type of Vulnerability	Components	Indicators
Physical vulnerability	Exposure to risks; human settlement in hazard-prone areas; poor-quality housing; inadequate physical protection	High death tolls; damage to crops, animals, buildings, and properties; disruption of normal life
Economic vulnerability	Loss of livelihoods and income opportunities; economic status; loss of assets and savings; need for recurrent aid	Low income; poverty, unemployment; unequal land distribution; landlessness; relief and rehabilitation
Social vulnerability	Disintegration of social organization; incidence of female-headed households; health status	Social helplessness; apathy; ethnic/social crisis; poor health and diseases; marginalization
Education/ informational vulnerability	Forecasting; early warning and evacuation systems; training for emergency responses	Lack of information; poor preparedness and evacuation; ineffective information diffusion
Environmental vulnerability	Land-use and environmental degradation; deforestation; increasing risks of hazards	Rapid population growth; rapid urbanization; migration to risk-prone uninhabitable areas

Sources: Cannon 1994; Lavell 1994; Winchester 1992.

ANTHROPOLOGY AND DISASTER RESEARCH

Natural disasters have profound and long-term social and economic consequences for the people and communities inflicted by such disasters. As such, any understanding of disaster impacts and local adjustments to disasters requires in-depth studies to develop a better perspective of adjustment strategies as well as to generate the kinds of data needed for theory building and effective analysis. Through the anthropological lens, "...*theories about disasters are inherently theories about communities,* that is, community continuity and change" (Torry 1979: 43, italics in original). Hence, studies of disasters are in effect studies of society and culture and of how people respond to and manage crisis situations to reestablish their communities in post-disaster periods.

As a discipline, anthropology provides a unique opportunity to observe how people live with disaster and crisis and make sense of things simply by virtue of "being there." It is a way of seeing, observing, and documenting events through the power of basic anthropological modes of investigation—participant observation methods. Furthermore, the anthropological tradition and practice of seeking to immerse oneself within fieldwork situations help to understand the folk knowledge or models of adjustment and encourage the development of a holistic perspective on social and community life (Zaman 1994b). The anthropological holistic description of events and cultural processes, the link between microlevel situation and macrolevel forces, and analytical techniques and explanations are, in a number of respects, beyond the methodological charters or capabilities of other disciplines. Finally, by working at various levels within the study communities and organizations and with local/national governments and/or development agencies, anthropologists can assist in the development of community-based and sustainable mitigation measures for policymaking and institutional development in disaster management. Thus, the holistic, developmental, and comparative nature of the discipline as a whole are useful tools to understand and integrate ethos and worldviews of people in developing any analytical framework in disaster studies.

DISASTERS IN BANGLADESH: A BRIEF OVERVIEW

It is often said that Bangladesh is a country made for natural disasters (Bingham 1989). The geography and climate have made Bangladesh prone to periodic flood, drought, and coastal cyclone. Too much rainfall during the monsoon season (May–October) causes large-scale floods affecting farmland and other property, while too little rainfall brings drought. Cyclones, which sweep into this low-lying deltaic country from the Bay of Bengal, create the most devastating disasters in terms of death and destruction. In November 1970, a severe cyclone storm associated with high tidal waves in the southern coastal areas swept away an estimated half a million people overnight. The 1985 cyclone killed ten thousand people and damaged more than ninety thousand homes; the cyclone also destroyed nearly four hundred kilometers of coastal embankment (Heitzman and Worden 1989). The 1991 cyclone killed an estimated two hundred thousand people; millions of houses were washed away, and road transport networks and other infrastructures were severely damaged. In addition to these periodic disasters, riverbank erosion caused by continuous shifting of channels within the major rivers—Brahmaputra-Jamuna, Ganges, and Meghna—particularly during high floods, displaces an estimated one million people annually and causes much distress in the country. People lose their land, homes, and sources of livelihoods. Riverbank erosion is considered one of the principal contributors to the process of

impoverization and marginalization of the rural peasantry (C. Haque 1988; *result in poverty & marginalization* [handwritten margin note]
Zaman and Haque 1989).

Since 1960, the incidence of natural disaster in Bangladesh has been on the rise. According to one source (M. Haque 1994, Table II.2), there were eighteen major disaster events between 1960 and 1969; the number increased *↑ disaster since 1960* [handwritten margin note] to thirty-seven during 1970–1979 and then doubled to seventy-seven between 1980 and 1989. Some scholars (Bingham 1989; Holt 1992) consider that global warming or greenhouse effects may be responsible for increased weather-related disasters in Bangladesh and may even bring more cyclones in the future. Further, it is claimed that if the sea level were to rise by another one meter, already predicted by some climatologists for the coming century, nearly one third of Bangladesh would be permanently flooded. This would mean less land available for people to grow food—a calamity of much higher intensity for this already overcrowded country of one hundred twenty million people with a rural density of twenty-one hundred persons per square mile.

Bangladeshi accounts of flood and cyclone disasters, particularly by the government and the media, attribute their origins to nature; disasters are viewed as "acts of God" and "savagery of Nature." The human suffering caused by disasters is considered as misfortune and a "curse" on the country (*Dhaka Courier*, May 16, 1991). To some extent, international donor agencies also share this interpretation of disasters (Dove and Khan 1996). As a

TABLE 2. *Major natural disasters in Bangladesh (1963–1991).* *

Year	Event	Approximate Death Toll
1963	Tropical cyclone	22,000
1965	Tropical cyclone	17,000
1965	Tropical cyclone	30,000
1965	Tropical cyclone	10,000
1970	Tropical cyclone	500,000
1974	Flood	2,000
1984	Flood	2,000
1985	Tropical cyclone	10,000
1987	Flood	2,000
1988	Flood	3,000
1988	Tropical cyclone	3,000
1989	Tornado	2,000
1991	Tropical cyclone	200,000

* This table does not include *all* disasters that occurred during the period covered. Also, the death tolls for various events often vary from one source to another.

Sources: Rattien 1990; Brammer 1990; Zaman 1994b.

result, government policies regard cyclone vulnerability as a function of the exposure to "nature's onslaughts" and struggle of "man against nature" (*The Bangladesh Observer,* May 8, 1991). These "images" of disasters are then used to explain the economic and social hardship of disaster victims in the post-disaster period and are further reinforced by the exclusive focus on "misfortune" and its relief in all disaster operations and cyclone preparedness policies (e.g., M. Haque 1994). Current Bangladeshi practices—for example, mapping risk-prone areas, impact assessment, emergency planning, and construction of permanent shelters in the coastal regions—generally ignore the social and economic dimensions of vulnerability and adjustment, and in doing so, oversimplify the essential reality.

ADJUSTMENTS AND SURVIVAL: THREE CASE STUDIES

In this section, I briefly present responses and adjustments to three types of disasters—riverbank erosion, flood, and cyclones—particularly focusing on the traditional or indigenous methods which are practiced to minimize and/or adjust to losses in disaster and crisis. Some of the adjustment strategies are related to social organizations and relationships defined by kinship and community ties; others are associated with material responses at an individual level.

Case Study 1:
Riverbank Erosion and Population Displacement in Kazipur

Erosion and population displacement in Bangladesh is an annual phenomenon. Currey (1979) identified 66 out of 495 *upazilas* (subdistricts, now renamed *thana*) in the country as affected and/or liable to annual bank erosion (see Figure 1). There are few riverine areas in the world that have such unstable river courses (Coleman 1969). It is said that the Brahmaputra-Jamuna has never been in the same course for two successive years in the past one hundred fifty years (Ahmad 1968). The annual flooding and the massive flow of water from the upstream Himalayas, where the river systems originate, cause extensive bankline erosion and channel migration due to substantial siltation of riverbeds forming mid-channel islands—locally called *chars*—which further amplify flood risks and erosion.

According to one estimate (Hossain 1984), over thirty thousand people were displaced in Kazipur *thana* alone between 1972 and 1982. In 1978, eight bankline villages and the headquarters of the Kazipur *thana* were literally washed away almost overnight by the sudden shift of the main west channel of the Brahmaputra-Jamuna river. The *thana* offices were later shifted to local "flood shelters," originally built to accommodate the flood victims and those affected by erosion. Using Landsat imagery data, C. Haque (1987) estimated that out of its total land area (143 square miles or 32,662 acres, including existing water bodies), Kazipur lost 5,776 acres (18 percent) and regained (through the process of accretion and deposition) 3,744 acres (12 percent) between 1968 and 1981. The fact that Char Chashi (pseudonym), the village where I carried out my study in 1984 and 1985, was virtually

FIGURE 1. *Major rivers and areas liable to erosion in Bangladesh.*

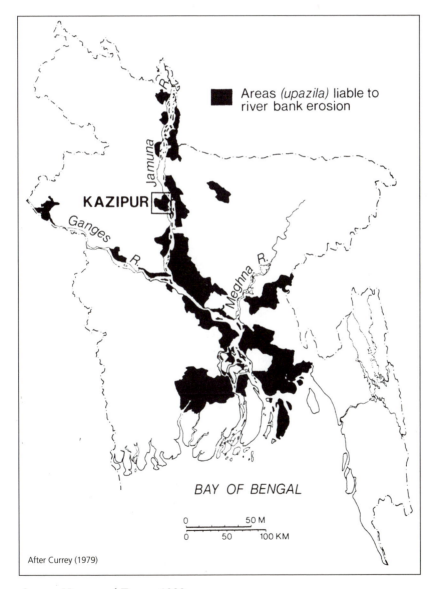

Areas *(upazila)* liable to river bank erosion

KAZIPUR

Jamuna

Ganges R.

Meghna R.

BAY OF BENGAL

0		50 M

0	50	100 KM

After Currey (1979)

Source: Haque and Zaman 1989.

devoured by the Brahmaputra-Jamuna in 1986 further attests to the capricious nature and extent of erosion, in effect, in the floodplain.

In Kazipur, the extent and frequency of displacement at the individual and household levels is phenomenal. According to the Kazipur Household Survey (KHS) carried out in eight (two mainland and six *char*) villages, a total of 394 (64 percent) of the 619 sample households reported to have been displaced by erosion at least once; of them, over 80 percent reported multiple displacement, the mean average being seven times! Both incidence and frequency of displacement are higher in *char* villages than in the mainland. One possible reason for this high frequency of displacement is the fact that people tend to move only short distances after displacement. According to KHS data, nearly 50 percent of the displaced households remained within half a mile of their previous homes; 30 percent moved between half a mile to one mile and the rest up to five miles. The survey found very little evidence of long-distance migration even after repeated displacement.

The pattern of limited and localized migration and adjustments to displacement in the floodplain has been conditioned historically by cultural, social, economic, and political factors. First, the floodplain inhabitants view the river as a symbol of fertility and life. For Hindus, the river, despite the misery and its ferocity, is sacred, and they perform many *pujas* (prayers to *jol devota*—the water deity) in their annual cycle of rituals. During my fieldwork in Kazipur, Moslem villagers told me stories about Khwaj Khizir—the "*zinda pir*" ("spirit" of a dead preacher)—believed to inhabit the river system and to be responsible for all hardship caused by erosion. According to local myth, the outraged spirit is the powerful "king" of all waters and shall live as long as the river flows. To pacify the spirit, local villagers in Kazipur offer sweets, milk, and puffed rice with the hope that Khwaj Khizir will stop eating away their farming land and homes. This view is fairly widespread in Bangladesh. In Kazipur a poster announcing a religious gathering for prayer to check erosion in Daulatkhan *thana* in the coastal areas read: "*Allah* is all Powerful. Biggest ever Mass Prayer (and recitation from the Holy Koran) in Daulatkhan. Please join by Thousands. Donations Welcome. Kindly note three preselected sites to drop *tabiz* [talisman in the form of small bundles of sacred papers with verses from the Koran] into the river to stop erosion. Meetings organized by the People of Daulatkhan thana." Such religious attitudes to erosion hazards coincide with lack of any active physical measures to control bank erosion.

Second, the majority of the displacees have a strong belief that their land will reemerge soon from the riverbeds, which does occur within two to five years in most instances, allowing them to return to their place of origin in the near future. Finally, many poor peasants cannot afford to move greater distances because of their economic inability to bear the necessary transport costs and other initial expenses involving such long-distance migration.

It is precisely for these reasons that displacees generally move short distances. The adjustment choices in the floodplain are further products of a complex set of factors including 1) the availability of land for resettlement, 2) support from friends and *gusthi* (patrilineage) people, 3) the possibility of maintaining closer ties with the *samaj* (local corporate group based on kinship and patronage), and 4) whether or not displacees have committed themselves to such patronage as sharecropping for free use of land for homestead (locally called *uthuli*) from relatives and/or locally powerful *jotedars* and *talukdars* (classes of rich peasants and large landowners) who head *samaj* organizations.

Table 3 lists the various reasons given for moving to the present place of residence by 322 displaced households after previous displacement. The single most important factor in choosing the present destination is the presence of friends and patrilineal relatives (55 percent). This confirms that kinship remains an important factor in migration and adjustment decisions. Existence of residual land (27 percent), *khas* (unused government land) or rented land (19 percent), and free use of land provided by relatives/patrons were some of the important factors for moving to the present place of residence. About 11 percent of all respondents considered it important to remain within, or to maintain closer ties with, their traditional *samaj* organization prior to resettlement after displacement. As a local political and religious community, the *samaj* is the primary arena within which members interact and participate in social and ceremonial networks (Zaman and Haque 1982). Therefore, any

TABLE 3. *Reasons given for resettlement in the present place of residence.*

Reasons	Frequency of Responses*	% of Households Stating Reason
Had residual land	88	27
Availability of *khas*/rented land	66	19
Free use of land provided by relatives	35	11
Returned to depositional land	45	14
Hoped land would reemerge	29	9
Support/presence of *gusthi* people and relatives	176	55
Closer ties with *samaj*	34	11
Had no money to move elsewhere	30	9
Had no time for alternative options	49	15
Others	29	9

* Respondents could indicate and rank more than one response.

Source: Zaman and Haque 1989.

detachment or separation from *samaj* puts the displaced households in a relatively difficult situation, entailing loss of both membership and support of the *samaj* group. Out of the total 322 households, 141 (44 percent) reported separation from their respective *samaj*. So far as is possible within the hazardous situation, the general principle found among the displacees in Kazipur villages is to cluster together with their kin and *samaj* group in their new place of residence.

little extend support

In terms of institutional support for erosion victims by national and local government agencies, compared with flood and coastal cyclones, there is very little assistance offered to displacees. A Kazipur *thana* officer told me that the local government does not have the necessary resources, either material or human, to respond to this ongoing and recurrent event. The response of national government agencies to erosion and dislocation remains to date limited to expensive engineering schemes such as embankment, town protection works, and construction of temporary relief facilities and shelters. Immediate relief and rehabilitation programs are almost nonexistent. According to Kazipur survey data, while 21 percent of all displaced households received assistance and support primarily from relatives and friends, only 6 percent mentioned receiving some assistance from local government and relief agencies (Haque and Zaman 1989).

Case Study 2:
The 1988 Flood Disasters and Responses

Because it is a delta country, flood occupies a unique position in the economy and culture of Bangladesh. The traditional agricultural economy is largely dependent on the annual normal or moderate flooding *(borsha)* for its replenishment; rice and fish—the main staples of the people—need tremendous amounts of flood water to grow and flourish. In general terms, Bengali peasant life in the floodplain is well adjusted to this predictable annual event that benefits crop cycles and virtually rejuvenates rural life. Only high or abnormal floods *(bonna)*, which in the past occurred once in every ten years or so and are associated with widespread damage to crops and properties and loss of human life, are viewed as calamities or disasters. Thus, flood as a natural phenomenon holds dual significance in the Bangladeshi society.

The 1988 flood is considered the most disastrous to have occurred in the Bangladesh region in the last seventy years. Instead of a decadal event, it followed the severe floods of 1984 and 1987, which had already caused damages of millions of dollars. In 1988, nearly 66 percent of the land area was inundated, some three thousand people died, and an estimated forty-five million people were temporarily dislocated. Major cities, including the capital city of Dhaka, were under flood water for weeks, and the Dhaka International Airport was closed for five days due to flooding of the runways. Important transportation networks such as railroads, highways, and bridges were largely wiped out. Over seven million houses were destroyed or damaged, and about two million tons of *aman* rice—the main crop of the year—were lost, leaving a three-million-ton shortfall for the year. In sum, the flood brought the entire country to a virtual standstill for nearly a month (for more on this, see Brammer 1990; Haque and Zaman 1993).

Following the 1987 and 1988 floods, flood control became a highly charged political agenda in Bangladesh, and what was often referred to as "floods of aid" for Bangladesh poured in from other nations and international agencies (Bingham 1989). A number of flood studies were commissioned by bilateral and multilateral agencies in collaboration with the Bangladesh government in order to find a permanent solution to the misery of catastrophic floods. The studies prepared by USAID (United States Agency for International Development), France, UNDP (United Nations Development Program), JICA (Japan International Cooperation Agency), and SAARC (South Asian Association for Regional Cooperation) resulted in a wide variety of viewpoints, ranging from "living with floods" to expensive structural engineering "megaplans" that called for construction of massive embankments on major rivers throughout the country and the dredging of rivers to obtain lower water levels. In 1991, under the leadership of the World Bank, a multiyear internationally funded Flood Action Plan (FAP) proposal was undertaken primarily to conduct various feasibility studies of the technical, socioeconomic, and environmental aspects of the FAP to prepare ground for structural measures to embank the rivers to control future flooding. This "technological fix" approach has been criticized by many scholars (Rogers et al. 1989; Rasid and Paul 1987; N. Islam 1990; Haque and Zaman 1994; Zaman 1993) because such measures may be hugely expensive for a country like Bangladesh; furthermore, it is incompatible with the hydraulic characteristics of the river systems of the country.

The structural or technological fix approach tends to overlook the fact that floodplain villagers have traditionally organized, produced, and survived within the constraints imposed by flooding. In other words, the floodplain users have long been familiar with flooding and have historically adopted numerous strategies to cope with flooding and reduce crop losses (Paul 1984; Rasid and Paul 1987). These strategies, known as "nonstructural" measures in the flood literature, are culturally informed local adaptive practices. In order to explore these indigenous adjustments and measures, a postflood survey was carried out in December 1988 in Sreenagar *thana* in Munshiganj district (Haque and Zaman 1993). The survey, which followed a random sampling procedure, covered 280 households. Nearly half of the families were functionally landless. The heads of households were interviewed. Of the 280 households, 136 (49 percent) of household heads had memberships in some local organizations such as agricultural cooperatives, credit unions, integrated rural development program, women's groups, and nongovernment organizations.

The survey results show (Table 4) that the majority of respondents took some corrective measures to minimize their flood losses. More than 71 percent of the respondents had reduced their losses to flood by selling land, livestock, or belongings; some moved house structures, livestock, and family members to safer places. It is evident that the flood victims opted for a number of responses aimed at reducing their potential losses through deliberate measures. Although most of the villagers received some assistance from various sources to cope with flood hazards, less than 12 percent were recipients of support from the local and national government sources. As indicated in Table 5, the principal sources of assistance to adjustment efforts are relatives (79 percent) and other community members (33 percent). Assistance received include moral support, free shelter and accommodation, free labor at the time of move, and cash loans and food. Nongovernment organizations (NGOs) provided a great deal of support to the affected households in flood mitigation efforts. More than 50 percent of the sampled households received food and clothes, housing materials, seeds, and loans from NGOs to regain their predisaster status.

The field data provide further evidence of the benefits of institutionalized networks in the mitigation of flood losses (Tables 4 and 5). In terms of

TABLE 4. *Distribution of adjustment measures taken by respondents during the 1988 flood in Sreenagar (%).*

Types of Adjustment Measures Taken (multiple responses possible)	All Households (N=280)	No Membership in Institutional Groups (N=144)	Membership in Institutional Groups (N=136)
Sold land	2	4	–
Sold livestock	17	26	7
Sold belongings	26	33	18
Mortgaged land	4	6	3
Dismantled housing structures	39	31	47
Borrowed money	39	65	11
Spent previous savings	24	44	3
Moved family to safer areas	66	79	52
Moved livestock and belongings to other areas	26	21	32

Source: Haque and Zaman 1993.

TABLE 5. *Sources of assistance received by the flood victims during the 1988 flood in Sreenagar (%).*

Sources of Assistance (multiple responses possible)	All Households (N=280)	No Membership in Institutional Groups (N=144)	Membership in Institutional Groups (N=136)
Relatives	79	86	71
Other villagers	33	32	34
Local government	7	8	6
National government	4	4	4
Relief agencies/NGOs	51	18	87

Source: Haque and Zaman 1993.

both preparedness and coping ability, the households which had membership in institutionalized groups demonstrated a better performance compared to the nonmembers. This suggests that the development of social and institutional networks can effectively lessen hazard impacts.

Case Study 3:
The 1991 Cyclone Disaster and Responses

Cyclone disasters cost more lives than floods in Bangladesh. The 1988 flood was unprecedented, but the loss of life, although high at roughly three thousand, is dwarfed by the mortality attributed to the 1991 cyclone. The 1991 cyclone was responsible for the death of an estimated two hundred thousand people (some accounts put the figures as high as three hundred thousand), and the cyclone of 1970 killed five hundred thousand in the southern delta and was perhaps the deadliest tropical storm in history. Figure 2 identifies some of the major cyclone storm tracks since 1960 across coastal Bangladesh.

The 1991 tropical cyclone hit the coast of Bangladesh at midnight on April 30, with winds gusting up to 234 kilometers per hour. According to national news reports (*The Bangladesh Observer*, May 1, 1991), the storm was associated with tidal surges up to six meters high in the offshore islands. The cyclone left ten million people homeless. It also destroyed 197 kilometers of coastal embankment, 30,000 hectares of crop, and over 900,000 head of cattle (*Asiaweek*, May 31, 1991). The cyclone also cut off all communication links between the coastal districts, the offshore islands, and the capital city of Dhaka. Furthermore, the cyclone battered the port city of Chittagong—the industrial base of the country. The loss of property and crops alone, according to initial estimates, was over U.S.$4 billion.

Early warnings were issued on April 25, when the storm was in its formative stage, through the national radio stations and HF/VHF radio networks

FIGURE 2. *Flood and cyclone vulnerability (1960–1991).*

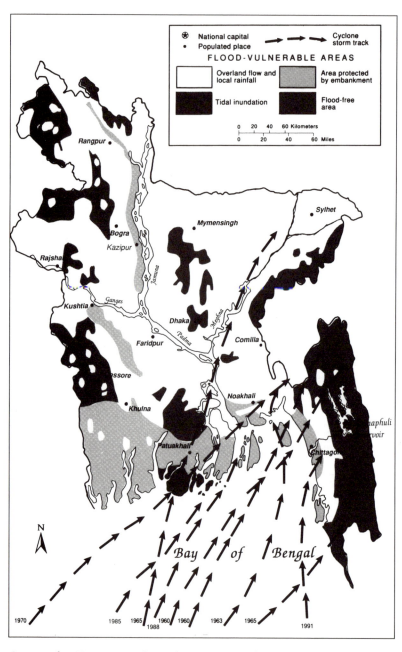

Source: after Heitzman and Worden (1989, modified).

for the coastal zone (Haque and Blair 1992). The warning systems, operated jointly by the Bangladesh government's Cyclone Preparedness Programme (CPP) and the Bangladesh Red Crescent Society (BRCS), advise coastal residents of impending cyclone threats and encourage people to take refuge in cyclone shelters or on raised grounds/embankments. The CPP was established following the disastrous cyclone of 1970 to draw up plans to protect the coastal areas. In the 1970s, considerable funds were also allocated nationally for building shelters for cyclone victims.

Available reports provide mixed assessment of the effectiveness of the preparedness and emergency evacuation plans for the 1991 cyclone disaster. The early warnings about the cyclone perhaps reduced the number of casualties, but emergency evacuation and relief operations were the least coordinated (Rahman 1992). The 302 shelters, with a total capacity of only about half a million people, were unable to provide refuge to the massive number of people who needed shelter. A large number of people reportedly did not leave their homes because of fear of burglary and disbelief in the warnings (Haque and Blair 1992). Rahman (1992) reported that nearly all, or some 80 percent, of the people who lived close to the coastline were killed, whereas death tolls were limited to 5 to 10 percent in villages that were seven to eight kilometers inland. Sevenhuysen (as cited in Haque and Blair 1992) estimated that 40 to 50 percent of the people living on the unprotected offshore island were killed, as were 30 to 40 percent of those on islands protected by coastal embankments, and about 20 to 30 percent in the affected mainland areas.

As we look at the coastal regions and the offshore *char* settlements in the southern delta, which have experienced an enormous death toll and suffering by storm surges for the past thirty years, one can logically ask why so many people—currently estimated at twelve million—live in those fragile and disaster-prone areas. The answer is simple and clear. Land scarcity, coupled with population growth, pressure on land, and acute poverty have forced poor people to migrate to the vulnerable low-lying areas. They have nowhere else to go but to those "islands of death" (Hossain et al. 1992: 376). The fertile land in the newly formed islands or *chars* along the coastline attracts both settlers and seasonal migrants. Poor farmers from the mainland who migrated to the newly formed *chars* have contributed to the enormous death toll in the 1991 cyclone. According to one source, most of the 7,331 people confirmed dead on Hatia island were landless settlers who were pushed outside the coastal embankment and were living in the tidal flats (*International Herald Tribune*, May 9, 1991). Many newly formed *chars* are barely above the sea level and are, thus, uninhabitable. They are, however, an irresistible temptation for millions of poor families desperate for a piece of cultivable land. Despite the fact that it is nearly suicidal to live on those *chars*, thousands move there every year from the overcrowded mainland and try to scratch out a living. What all these issues suggest is that there is "a fundamental associa-tion of poor rural migrants to cyclone victims" (Dove and Khan 1996: 13).

DISASTER MANAGEMENT IN BANGLADESH:
LOOKING BACK AND AHEAD

It is abundantly clear that the vulnerability of a social system to natural disas-ter is determined *not* by physical or natural factors alone, but also by the complex socioeconomic characteristics of the population. This means that disaster is a *social* process that is created largely by the *interaction* between natural events and the social conditions of human organization. From this perspective, disaster may be seen largely as a social product. If so, what should constitute disaster prevention, mitigation, and preparedness? In Bangladesh, current disaster mitigation programs are mostly geared toward preparedness—to provide "protection" from natural disasters and to mini-mize human and material losses. Cyclone preparedness programs such as early warnings, rescue, relief, and rehabilitation plans are built around the "event" that triggers disasters. When predisaster social vulnerability is so high and poverty forces poor rural migrants to become flood or cyclone victims, there is a need to revisit disaster policies and address social vulnerability issues on a national basis. This is critical, since social vulnerability plays a crucial role in determining both the range of destruction and number of deaths, as well as mitigative options in the aftermath of the events.

Since erosion, flood, and cyclones occur every year in Bangladesh, we should perhaps look at these events as "normal." Floodplain and coastal resi-dents do not perceive these events as unexpected. They are also aware of the risks involved and have shown resilience to them, both individually and col-lectively, over the years. The cultural and social adjustment strategies dis-cussed earlier provide ample evidence that the floodplain and coastal inhabitants are not passive victims of disasters; the extraordinary and heroic achievements of the ordinary people in "living with disasters" have been rather impressive. It is then, perhaps, more useful to think of erosion, flood, or cyclone disasters as extensions of everyday events. This perspective shifts our orientation away from disasters as random events or sudden onslaughts of nature that disrupt normal life and necessitate assistance through short-term relief operations, and turns the focus to long-term development pro-grams for building economic infrastructures of the rural poor and other vulnerable groups, such as women, to reduce their vulnerability.

A recent development concerning the future of FAP signals a change in the current thinking in disaster preparedness and management, particularly of

flood and erosion disasters. After a careful evaluation of the results of the feasibility studies, some of the major structural projects originally envisaged by
the FAP have now either been dropped or scaled down substantially in favor
of a sustainable, long-term development perspective. However, at this writing,
no specific details of the long-term strategies are available. Certainly, the
search for a single, conclusive solution—for example, embankment protection
for flood control—has ceased in Bangladesh. A strategy from a structural
approach to a combination of both structural and nonstructural measures
should now constitute the basis for future disaster preparedness and management. Given the geography and hydraulic characteristics of the river systems
in Bangladesh, there is a clear need for preparedness in terms of improved
techniques of flood forecasting and development of measures for flood loss
reduction. These measures, however, should be complemented increasingly by
an integrated approach to floodplain and coastal development, taking into
account some of the social, demographic, and economic aspects of life in the
delta. Further, disaster mitigation policies should spend more resources for
studying and promoting many indigenous ways of "living with flood." In my
view, disaster management policies should address more economic and social
processes, for example, land reform and redistribution, improved tenurial systems, alternative employment, local economic diversification, and reinforcement of indigenous techniques of adjustment through village-level planning
and development. Such a strategy would enhance economic well-being of the
population and would further promote local technologies and traditional
social adjustment networks that people utilize to cope with disasters. More
importantly, this strategy would allow community and NGO participation in
reconstruction and development in the post-disaster period. In sum, disaster
planning in Bangladesh should form the basis of all kinds of vulnerability
reduction—natural, social, political, economic, and environmental.

NOTE

1. This chapter incorporates ideas, issues, and findings of research I conducted
together with C. Emdad Haque (Zaman and Haque 1991; Haque and Zaman 1989,
1993, 1994). I am indebted to my co-author for his contributions. Many other friends
and colleagues, notably K. Maudood Elahi, Bimal Kanti Paul, John R. Rogge,
Anthony Oliver-Smith, and Raymond E. Wiest, have been of great help over the years.
I wish to thank them all for their support.

BIBLIOGRAPHY

Ahmad, N. 1968. *An Economic Geography of East Pakistan.* Oxford: Oxford University Press.

Bingham, A. 1989. "Floods of Aid for Bangladesh." *New Scientist* 1693: 42–46.

Blaikie, P., T. Cannon, I. Davis, and B. Wisner. 1994. *At Risk: Natural Hazards, People's Vulnerability, and Disasters.* London: Routledge.

Brammer, H. 1990. "Floods in Bangladesh I: Geographical Background to 1978 and 1988 Floods." *Geographical Review* 156: 12–22.

Burton, I., R. Kates, and G. White. 1978. *The Environment as Hazard.* New York: Oxford University Press.

Cannon, T. 1994. Vulnerability Analysis and the Explanation of 'Natural' Disasters," in A. Varley (ed.), *Disasters, Development and Environment,* pp. 13–30. London: John Wiley.

Coleman, J. 1969. "Brahmaputra River: Channel Process and Sedimentation." *Sedimentary Geology* 3: 129–239.

Currey, B. 1979. *Mapping Areas Liable to Famine in Bangladesh.* Ph.D. dissertation. Honolulu: University of Hawaii.

Dove, M., and M. Khan. 1996. "The Discourse of Disaster: Contested Dimensions of the April 1991 Bangladesh Cyclone." Unpublished paper, Program on Environment, East-West Centre, Hawaii.

Haque, C. 1987. "Impact of Riverbank Erosion in Kazipur: An Application of Landsat Imagery." *Riverbank Erosion Impact Study Newsletter* #3, Savar, Bangladesh: Jahangirnagar University.

———. 1988. *Impacts of Riverbank Erosion in the Brahmaputra-Jamuna Floodplain: A Study of Population Displacement and Response.* Ph.D. dissertation. Winnipeg, Canada: University of Manitoba.

Haque, C., and D. Blair. 1992. "Vulnerability to Tropical Cyclones: Evidence from the April 1991 Cyclone in Coastal Bangladesh." *Disasters* 16, 3: 217–229.

Haque, C., and M. Zaman. 1989. "Coping with Riverbank Erosion Hazard and Displacement in Bangladesh: Survival Strategies and Adjustments." *Disasters* 13, 4: 300–314.

———. 1993. "Human Responses to Riverine Hazards in Bangladesh: A Proposal for Sustainable Floodplain Development." *World Development* 21, 1: 93–107.

———. 1994. "Vulnerability and Responses to Riverine Hazards in Bangladesh: A Critique of Flood Control and Mitigation Approaches," in A. Varley (ed.), *Disasters, Development and Environment,* pp. 65–80. London: John Wiley.

Haque, M. 1994. "Relief in Full Swing," in H. Hossain, C. Dodge, and F. Abed (eds.), *From Crisis to Development: Coping With Disasters in Bangladesh,* pp. 27–54. Dhaka: University Press Limited.

Heitzman, J., and R. Worden. 1989. *Bangladesh: A Country Study.* Washington DC: Library of Congress.

Hewitt, K. (ed.). 1983. *Interpretation of Calamity*. Boston: Allen and Unwin.

Holt, J. 1992. "Bangladesh: Land and Water." *Asian Affairs* 12, 1: 44–48.

Hossain, M. 1984. "The 1984 Flood and Population Displacement in Serajganj District." *Riverbank Erosion Impact Study Newsletter* #2, Savar, Bangladesh: Jahangirnagar University.

Hossain, H., C. Dodge, and F. Abed (eds.). 1992. *From Crisis to Development: Coping with Disasters in Bangladesh*. Dhaka: University Press Limited.

Islam, A. 1987. "Bhola Island: Some Impressions from Field Experience." *Riverbank Erosion Impact Study Newsletter* #3, Savar, Bangladesh: Jahangirnagar University.

Islam, M. 1989. "Floods in Bangladesh: Causes, Consequences and Adjustments." Paper presented at the International Conference on Bangladesh Floods, May 11–12, 1989, Montreal, Canada. May 11–12, 1989.

Islam, N. 1990. "Let the Delta be a Delta: An Essay in Dissent on the Flood Problem of Bangladesh." *Journal of Social Studies* 48: 18–41.

Kates, R. 1971. "Natural Hazards in Human Ecological Perspective: Hypothesis and Models." *Economic Geography* 47: 438–451.

Lavell, A. 1994. "Prevention and Mitigation of Disasters in Central America: Vulnerability to Disasters at the Local Level," in A. Varley (ed.), *Disasters, Development and Environment*, pp. 49–64. London: John Wiley.

Mileti, D., T. Drabek, and J. Hass. 1975. *Human Systems in Extreme Environments: A Sociological Perspective*. Boulder: IBS, University of Colorado.

Mitchell, J. 1990. "Human Dimensions of Environmental Hazards," in A. Kirby (ed.), *Nothing to Fear: Risks and Hazards in American Society*, pp. 131–175. Tucson: University of Arizona Press.

———. 1986a. "Disaster Context and Causation: An Overview of Changing Perspectives in Disaster Research." *Studies in Third World Societies* (Special Issue: Natural Disasters and Cultural Responses) 36: 1–34.

———. 1986b. *The Martyred City: Death and Rebirth in the Andes*. Albuqerque: University of New Mexico Press.

Oliver-Smith, A. 1996. "Anthropological Research on Hazards and Disasters." *Annual Review of Anthropology* 25: 303–328.

Paul, B. 1984. "Perception of and Agricultural Adjustment to Floods in Jamuna Floodplain." *Human Ecology* 12, 1: 3–19.

Rahman, A. 1992. "Disaster and Development: A Study in Institution Building in Bangladesh," in H. Hossain, C. Dodge, and F. Abed (eds.), *From Crisis to Development: Coping with Disasters in Bangladesh*, pp. 351–373. Dhaka: University Press Limited.

Rasid, H., and B. Paul. 1987. "Flood Problems in Bangladesh: Is There an Indigenous Solution?" *Environmental Management* 11, 2: 155–173.

Rogers, P., P. Lydon, and D. Seckler. 1989. *Eastern Water Study: Strategies to Manage Flood and Drought in the Ganges Brahmaputra Basin*. Arlington VA: ISPAN.

Rattien, S. 1990. "The Role of Media in Hazard Mitigation and Disaster Management." *Disasters* 14, 1: 36–45.

Torry, W. 1979. "Anthropology and Disaster Research." *Disasters* 3, 1: 43–52.

Varley, A. (ed.). 1994. *Disasters, Development and Environment*. London: John Wiley.

Wallace, A. 1956. "Human Behavior in Extreme Situations: A Study of the Literature and Suggestions for Further Research." NAS-SRC Disaster Study #1.

White, G. (ed.). 1974. *Natural Hazard: Local, National, Global*. New York: Oxford University Press.

Winchester, P. 1992. *Power, Choice and Vulnerability: A Case Study in Disaster Management in South India*. London: James and James Science Publishers.

Zaman, M. 1989. "The Social and Political Context of Adjustment to Riverbank Erosion Hazard and Population Resettlement in Bangladesh." *Human Organization* 48, 3: 196–205.

———. 1993. "Rivers of Life: Living with Floods in Bangladesh." *Asian Survey* 23, 10: 985–996.

———. 1994a. "Disaster Research, Management and Mitigation: Past Trends and Future Agenda." *Canadian Journal of Development Studies* 15, 1: 101–108.

———. 1994b. "Ethnography of Disasters: Making Sense of Flood and Erosion in Bangladesh." *Eastern Anthropologist* 47, 2: 129–155.

Zaman, M., and C. Haque. 1982. "Corporate Groupings, Religious Ideology, and Community Leadership in a Village of Bangladesh." *South Asian Anthropologist* 3, 2: 39–45.

———. 1988. *The Socioeconomic and Political Dynamics of Adjustment to Riverbank Erosion Hazard and Population Resettlement in the Brahmaputra-Jamuna Floodplain*. Ph.D. dissertation. University of Manitoba, Winnepeg, Canada.

———. 1989. "The Social and Political Context of Adjustment to Riverbank Erosion Hazard and Population Resettlement in Bangladesh." *Human Organization* 48, 3: 196–205.

———. 1991a. "Working Together: Reflections on Collaborative Research in Bangladesh." *Canadian Journal of Development Studies* 12, 2: 387–403.

———. 1991b. "Social Structure and Process in Char Land Settlement in the Brahmaputra-Jamuna Floodplain." *Man (N.S.)* 26, 4: 673–690.

11

"TELL THEM WE'RE HURTING": HURRICANE ANDREW, THE CULTURE OF RESPONSE, AND THE FISHING PEOPLES OF SOUTH FLORIDA AND LOUISIANA[1]

CHRISTOPHER L. DYER
University of Rhode Island

and

JAMES R. McGOODWIN
University of Colorado

INTRODUCTION

DISASTERS ARE EVENTS THAT CAN SEVERELY DISRUPT THE IMMEDIATE BIO-physical and social environments of human communities, threatening the ability of impacted cultural systems to adapt and survive (Fritz 1961; Barton 1969; Dyer forthcoming; Oliver-Smith 1996). As such, disasters provide opportunities to understand responses of individuals, communities, and institutions in crisis, allowing anthropologists to penetrate the core of culture systems, as people recover, restore, and reinvent themselves in the post-disaster environment. Also revealed by disaster is the influence of the political ecology on response, in ways that can determine when, where, and how much aid might be directed at a particular area, population, subculture, or minority group.

Political ecology also exposes competing interests in contested interpretations of power (control of resources). In disasters the struggles of communities to maintain power come to the fore. Power relationships work themselves out within the place and space—the territories or environments—of communities. Communities that primarily depend on natural resources for survival are closely linked to the ecosystem in that the health and sustainability of the economy, or community power, are tied to the renewability of the natural resource base. However, since territorialization of community space seldom follows the natural contours of ecosystems, political entities often do not control key elements or parts of the ecosystems upon which they depend. If an ecosystem is pulverized by a disaster event, the territorial (community) space can lose both economic and ecological viability, and recovery can be difficult or impossible without external assistance. Thus, response to disasters involves the political ecology and ethnohistory of human populations under disaster conditions. It is further impacted by social and economic factors, all of which combine to create what can be identified as the "culture of response" (Dyer 1995).

The culture of response emerges from underlying traditional structures that have evolved as adaptations to disaster. Torry (1978) points out that many adaptations—or maladaptations—of the culture of response can influence the recovery process. Examples include administrative inefficiency which retards recovery (Baldassaro 1975; Nugent 1973; Levine 1995), fatalistic belief systems that jeopardize life (Sims and Baumann 1972; Kates 1971), and alien technology introduced to regulate hazards that pose new sources of danger (Flannery 1972; Dyer forthcoming; Lees 1975; Reidinger 1974; Van Der Schalie 1974; Obeng 1977; Torry 1979). The culture of response is also tempered by political economics when power relationships dictate access to disaster recovery resources.

Vulnerability to disasters can be increased by the culture of response as well, particularly for marginal communities. Marginality is defined by relative lack of control over resources and, thus, over power. Coastal communities and populations that rely on renewable natural resources are currently being transformed, losing power to gentrifying forces (Gale 1991). Gentrification threatens the resource base—in this instance, coastal fisheries resources—of natural resource communities (NRCs) (Dyer 1993). A natural resource community is defined as a population of individuals living in a bounded area whose existence depends upon the utilization of renewable natural resources (Dyer et al. 1992). Natural resource communities are unique in their dependence on the immediate environment. In coastal NRCs extraction of fishery resources defines the cultural cycles and priorities of the community. The relationship between community cultural activities and resource utilization provides a dynamic pattern that links human behavior to the ecosystem. However, fisheries-dependent NRCs are particularly susceptible to both natural and technological disasters. Hurricanes, in particular, represent natural disaster events that can have severe consequences to coastal fishing communities.

For coastal fishing NRCs, economic welfare and sociocultural identities are articulated with, and dependent upon, certain marine resources. In this sense, a "fishing community" may include peoples living in a named, nucleated settlement that has a great deal of fishing industry, such as coastal Louisiana, as well as one having dispersed commercial fishers here and there along a coastline who do not live in any particular settlement, such as coastal south Florida. The fishers in either situation have much in common. Both share patterns of articulation with the wider cultural community. This involvement can vary depending on how the wider society values the NRC lifestyle. If the values and traditions of the NRC are shared by the wider society and recognized in the political decision making of local leadership, then the culture of response after a disaster event can be expected to be timely and appropriate to the local needs of NRC communities. If not, the external cultural articulation can threaten the sustainability of these communities made vulnerable by a disaster event.

The form of incorporation into the wider society is particularly threatening to NRCs when intrusive market forces put prices on selective parts of the ecosystem without regard to their ecological importance but, rather, in terms of demand for such commodities (Gale 1991). Furthermore, because of the complex ways governmental policies and regulations are enforced, decisions affecting ecosystem-embedded communities such as fishing NRCs are seldom made by the local populations that have the greatest stake in the ecosystem's preservation. As coastal areas are transformed, wetlands are filled, and gentrification intrudes, often little control of resources is left for fishermen and their families. As a result, even when governmental policies and regulatory efforts work to strike a balance between preservation of NRCs and competing economic interest groups (e.g., recreational fishers and beach condominium developers), these policies and decisions can be compromised by disaster events in ways that increase the vulnerability of fishing communities and allow for other interests to step into the power vacuum and accelerate demands for gentrification.

In the post-disaster environment, fishing communities can, thus, find themselves in a position of marginality. In consequence, they can suffer further severe impacts that often go unmitigated, with outcomes ranging from impoverishment through both economic and cultural unemployment to complete community dysfunction, or "community death." As Oliver-Smith (1996) asserts: "As local communities come to grips with increased vulnerabilities, they enter into new relationships with both the environment and larger social contexts, inevitably affecting the pace of social and cultural change."

Ultimately, it is some decision-making authority that determines the impact of disasters on marginal communities. Adams (1965) notes that understanding the specter that haunts communities under stress requires explanation of the failure of repair and replacement to keep pace with entropic events that undermine community integrity. Failure to recover in NRCs may be a signal that a community's resource base has become inaccessible to resource users. This happens when community authority dissolves or has been absent from the onset.

Community collapse is most likely to occur then, when under disaster conditions, the natural resource base is compromised, external recovery assistance is misdirected or withheld, and the post-disaster political economy of the region hinders restoration of traditional patterns of human-environment interaction. Collapse is counteracted most effectively when the natural resource base is uncompromised, external agencies aid community recovery, and the political economy of the region does not unconsciously or purposefully hinder the recovery process.

This chapter explores the culture of response of two polities—Florida and Louisiana—in terms of the post-disaster needs of fishing communities after Hurricane Andrew (McGoodwin and Dyer 1993). We demonstrate that differences in the culture of response of these two states can be framed by differences in the economic organization of natural resource exploitation. As Oliver-Smith, following Harvey (1996: 174), states: "Interpretations of the relation to nature are simultaneously interpretation of society, often involving the use of identical metaphors." For Louisiana, the articulation of society and resource utilization is based upon commonly shared metaphors of Napoleonic origin attuned to the hunting-fishing cultures of bayou communities (Din 1988; Dyer and Leard 1994). In Florida, marginalized fishing communities are virtually ignored in an environment where tourism and recreation (the "Disney World" metaphor) dominate the local political economy at the expense of commercial fishing.

To explore these differences in the culture of response, we begin with a review of the impacts of Hurricane Andrew on local natural and fisheries resources and their associated NRCs.

THE DISASTER EVENT AND INITIAL PERCEPTIONS

Hurricane Andrew slammed into south Florida's coastline early in the morning of August 24, 1992. It continued across the state of Florida and hit Louisiana the following day. This category-four hurricane (sustained winds from 131 to 155 mph) left fifty-two dead in Florida, Louisiana, and the Bahamas and caused over $20 billion in damages. The storm damaged 125,000 homes and apartments (of which 63,000 were completely destroyed), and left 160,000 homeless throughout the area (Anonymous 1993: 1). More than 82,000 business enterprises in the region were badly damaged or destroyed. Damage to the fisheries, from estimates made four months after the event, totaled in the hundreds of millions of dollars in lost fishing boats, gear, and dead fish (Louisiana Department of Wildlife and Fisheries 1992).

Shortly after the event, we applied for and received a rapid response grant from the Natural Hazards Center in Boulder, Colorado. Our purpose was to investigate the impacts of the disaster on south Florida's commercial fishing peoples. Being maritime anthropologists, we focused on this sector in an attempt to gauge the response of local agencies to the needs of peoples whose livelihood arose directly from the natural environment—an environment that had been, we assumed, severely modified in the wake of the hurricane. The project was an exercise in post-disaster human ecology focusing on the occupational sector of commercial fishing.

We received our grant to do fieldwork in October 1992, just two months after the hurricane struck. Prior to leaving for the field, we reviewed an article published in *National Fisherman* (Fee 1992: 12), the journal of record for much of the commercial fishing industry. Fee characterized the storm's impact on the south Florida commercial fisheries as being more like a "20-mile wide, two-hours-long tornado," than the extensively destructive storm we assumed it had been from our exposure to television and print news. Fee quoted a biologist from Florida's Department of Natural Resources (DNR) as saying "I had the impression this was not *the* storm," that this was not "the big one," that everybody for years had predicted would eventually hit south Florida. Furthermore, the article went on to say:

> Because wind damage, rather than water damage, was Hurricane Andrew's claim to fame in Florida, and because the effects were serious along such a narrow corridor, most of south Florida's commercial fishing industry was untouched by it. From Key West to Marathon, and westward past Flamingo to the southwest coast's Everglades City, commercial fishermen were wide-eyed over their good luck. (Fee 1992: 12)

Upon arriving in Florida, we met with state and federal officials whose concern is the region's commercial fisheries, as well as with scientists at the region's major marine-research institutions. They included the National Marine Fisheries Service (NMFS), the Florida Department of Natural Resources (DNR), and the Rosenstiel School of Atmospheric and Marine Sciences (RSMAS). This last institution is a component of the University of Miami and is mostly supported by the Sea Grant Research Program of the National Oceanographic and Atmospheric Administration. Other organizations consulted included the Federal Emergency Management Agency (FEMA) and the Small Business Administration (SBA).

Of these organizations, only RSMAS had planned to investigate impacts on the marine environment. However, the planned research was limited to the storm's impact on marine organisms and marine ecology, physical and chemical oceanography, and other traditional oceanographic and ocean science concerns, with no inclusion of human-ecological impacts. While one section of the RSMAS proposal was elaborated under the subheading "The Boating Community," this referred only to the extent to which recreational fishing boats sunk during the storm contributed to coastal pollution by leaking fuels and lubricants into the region's harbors and bays.

In discussions with NMFS regional staff, they expressed the opinion that few commercial fishers or fish marketing businesses were to be found in the impacted region and that overall losses suffered by this sector were "insignificant." The only community of commercial fishers in the area of any significance was noted to be a group devoted to catching spiny lobsters. Their docks were along the Miami River in downtown Miami. However, the NMFS staff was quick to point out these docks were located considerably north of the storm's destructive path, and as a result the fishers had suffered no loss of life or any damages to their vessels. Instead, they assured us, these fishers "came through just fine." Yet, when asked whether this information was based on communication with these fishers, they replied that no one had spoken to them because, as one staffer joked, "No, how could we? None of us speaks Cuban."

REALITY OF THE IMPACT—FLORIDA

Despite the initial claims that impact on fisheries in south Florida was minimal and that, in fact, there was little significant fishery activity and marketing in south Florida, our fieldwork and our follow-up in which we used secondary sources proved otherwise. In practically every aspect of our research we encountered evidence of widespread and severe impacts on the region's commercial fishing peoples and others involved in the fishing industry. A port agent from Monroe County, Florida, recorded the following on August 27, 1993, three days after Andrew struck:

> Hurricane Andrew has severely limited all fishing in the keys beginning on the 22nd when warnings were first posted. Although the keys were spared a direct hit, the storm still dealt a blow to the fishing industry. In the upper keys, early reports indicated some craft and many lobster traps were destroyed. And, the shoreside infrastructure that escaped damage was still non-functional due to power outages and transport problems. Even fishermen in the lower keys were idled by Andrew. That was because most dealers held their boats at the dock until logistics with those few buyers still operational were arranged late Wednesday. (Florida DNR 1992)

In Florida, loss of fishery resources was tied to loss of important marine fisheries habitat, including destruction of marine habitats and commercially important marine species. Artificial reefs, for instance, which are deployed along the southeast Florida coastline, are important to the region's commercial fishers, as well as to components of the state's recreational sector, particularly the diving industry. Quality fish from these reefs supply many fish markets and restaurants throughout the region, and were a major source of income for the seafood processing and retail industry. Many of these artificial reefs consist of sunken vessels or other man-made structures, such as oil rigs, and they greatly increase the productivity of marine life in nearshore waters.

Among the twenty-six major artificial reefs situated in the region impacted by Andrew, twenty-two were damaged, fifteen severely (*Miami Herald,* October 17, 1992). Those severely damaged included the Arida (flattened and crushed), the Almirante (turned upside down), the Miracles Express (reduced to rubble), and the Tarpon. Attesting to the fury of the hurricane, the Belzone Barge disappeared completely. Concerning this reef, Ben Mostkof, artificial reef coordinator for the DNR in south Florida, stated:

> This was a barge two-thirds the length of a football field. It was so large that it took five minutes to swim its length. It's not the kind of thing you would think would just disappear. (*Miami Herald,* September 1, 1992)

The artificial reefs which had been placed off the Dade County coast from the Broward County line to the city of Homestead are the backbone of a local diving industry, which has important recreational and commercial components. Some of the more important species of marine life to be found around these reefs are jackfish, snappers, sea basses, and groupers. The devastation wrought on artificial reefs offers clear evidence that seafloor configurations were drastically altered by the force of Hurricane Andrew in the impacted area, a finding which is clearly opposite to that which was reported in *National Fisherman* shortly after the storm. Robert Arnove, a Miami dive captain for eleven years, in discussing the Tarpon, a 165-foot sunken vessel, asserted:

> Everything that was alive on that reef was picked clean. It was alive with soft corals, sea fans, and sponges, and now nothing is there. It has been ripped right out of the bottom. I swam way north and south along the reef and it's all the same. It's just devastated. Looking to the future, you have to wonder if it will ever be a viable dive site again. (*Miami Herald,* September 1, 1992)

Similarly, the destruction of natural coral reefs in south Florida also hurt the local diving industries, both commercial and recreational. Again, this impact was not quickly appreciated by local officials, even though later studies of the impact of the hurricane on primary productivity of reef systems by the Florida DNR and the RSMAS followed. Other ecosystem impacts included destruction of mangroves and seagrass, particularly along the stretch of coast close to ground zero near Black Point (see Figure 1). Mangroves are crucial to the reproduction of many fish species, whose juveniles grow and mature in these sheltered habitats.

In our rapid-response field research we encountered three elements of the fishing industry, making up the diffuse (open) natural resource communities (Dyer and Leard 1994) of south Florida that were heavily impacted by Hurricane Andrew. These included the seafood processors, the spiny lobster fishery, and the bait fishery.

Many seafood processors suffered heavy losses in the hurricane, including losses of product supply, business infrastructure, and clientele. Impacts to regional infrastructure of the region also delayed recovery for months, driving some processors out of business. The complete loss of electrical power, not only in the region directly affected by the storm's path, but, indeed, all the way down to Key Largo, more than thirty miles south of where the eye of the

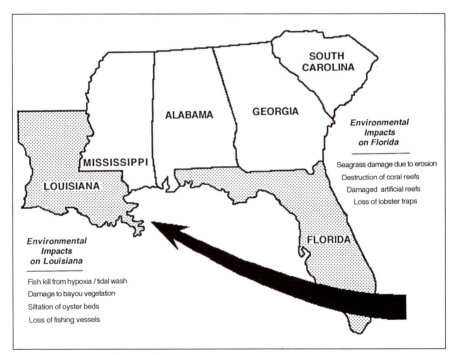

FIGURE 1. *The path of Hurricane Andrew across Florida and Louisiana, and significant environmental impacts affecting the fishing communities of each state.*

hurricane made landfall, seriously affected these businesses. A few processors were given priority in having their electrical services restored and in return for supplying ice to the regional populace at a preestablished price, but many others whose facilities had come through with only minor damages were otherwise unable to resume operations for several months. However, many of those damaged suffered complete destruction of their facilities. In February 1993, nearly four months after we returned from our field study, the Florida DNR sent us information concerning the 113 fish processors in the south Florida region. By DNR regulations, the region's processors are required to make monthly reports concerning what types of fish products, and in what quantities, they have processed and sold during the required reporting interval. There is a "comments" section at the bottom of each report, which we analyzed. We subsequently determined that 67 percent (64) of the 113 processors who had sent reports to the DNR had reported suffering severe impacts from the storm. Typical comments included these: "lost everything," "destroyed by Andrew," "we're only now getting back into operation," "we'll never re-open," and "we're still out of business." Many processors whose facilities were situated directly in the storm's path suffered such severe damages that it is doubtful that they will ever resume operations. Beyond these problems, the massive disruption of the local economy in the region left even those processors who were able to resume operations with few customers. Local demand for seafood, they noted, had dropped considerably since so many people in the region were living on relief funds. Others had moved away (Dyer 1995).

Another component of south Florida's fishing industry that suffered severe impacts was the spiny lobster fishery, particularly the lobster fishers located in downtown Miami along the Miami River. These people fish exclusively for spiny lobsters, a high-value export item, by deploying baited traps in relatively shallow waters offshore. It is precisely this group which NMFS officials had told us had come through practically unscathed. When we met with these fishermen, we learned that all twenty-five boats involved in the fishery had, in fact, come through the storm in good condition, and all the nearly one hundred fishermen who work on these boats, most of whom are either Cuban immigrants or descendents of Cuban immigrants, had experienced no loss of life or any serious injuries. Nevertheless, we quickly learned of two especially severe impacts these fishermen had suffered as a direct result of Hurricane Andrew. First, they all had a large number of lobster traps deployed when the first storm warnings were announced and were able to recover only around 20 percent of these prior to the storm's arrival. Overall, the fleet lost around 80 percent of its lobster traps, amounting to an average loss per fishing boat of around $16,000. Moreover, these fishermen explained, their fishing success was heavily dependent on their ability to intercept lobsters along certain predictable migration routes. These routes, they explained, are imprinted when the lobsters are still young by magnetic fields along the seafloor. Now that the storm had greatly disrupted bottom configurations in the areas they customarily fished, the lobsters were not appearing in their usual numbers, and catches had dropped considerably. Thus, fishermen were unable to maintain predisaster production levels due to lost lobster gear and the displacement of lobster stocks.

Power relationships in the south Florida commercial fishery are based on a centralized "command and control" model of management by which regulators decide on fish stock quotas and regulations without seeking the input of the users of the stocks (Dyer and McGoodwin 1994). This unbalanced control of resources was one of the sources of the frustration and anger Miami River lobster fishermen showed toward the Florida DNR and NMFS over their inadequate response to fishers' post-disaster needs. In fact, fishermen claimed that these management agencies had not shown any concern at all for them after the disaster. Similarly, they expressed critical sentiments concerning the Small Business Administration (SBA), which they felt had not provided them with adequate loans to help them replace the lobster traps they had lost. Several offered the opinion that the Florida DNR had secretly urged the SBA not to provide loans sufficient to restore their traps to prestorm numbers. Before the storm, they said, the DNR had for many years been trying to limit the number of traps a boat could deploy, and over the past several years had progressively raised license fees on traps to discourage any increase in their numbers. Thus, the storm had accomplished for the DNR what it had been unable to accomplish on its own: a significant reduction of the number of traps being utilized in the fishery. Fishers also disputed the DNR's attempts to limit the total number of traps being utilized in the fishery in the interests of conserving resources. They felt that the DNR was showing undue favoritism to the recreational diving industry, which also targets spiny lobsters. The DNR denied urging the SBA to drag its feet in providing loans to replace lost lobster traps, but otherwise feels it is healthy for the fishery that the total number of traps now being utilized by the commercial fishers is considerably less than what it was before the storm (McGoodwin and Dyer 1993).

The bait fishing sector of the industry also suffered severe impacts from the hurricane. South Florida's bait fishers catch shrimp for sale to recreational fisheries in the region. We met with bait fishermen at the large marina at Coconut Grove in the south end of greater Miami and at the marina at Black Point, situated nearly twenty miles down the coast, squarely in the path of the storm's eye. The storm's impact on Coconut Grove bait fishers was unexpected. They reported no loss of life, no serious injuries, and no loss of any fishing gear. Instead, they said, because of the extensive losses of recreational fishing boats, whose owners, generally speaking, were either not as skilled or not as interested in securing boats in advance of the storm, local demand for bait shrimp had dropped considerably. Several of these fishermen feared they would go out of business if demand did not increase soon.

At the Black Point marina, on the other hand, which had experienced the full fury of the hurricane, the situation for commercial fishers was much worse. There almost all of the recreational boats that used the marina had been severely damaged, with many completely destroyed. Many of the commercial bait boats had suffered severe damage as well. The result was a total collapse in demand for bait shrimp caught by commercial fishers working out of the Black Point marina. Consequently, when we visited the Black Point marina, two months after the hurricane had gone through, only two of its seventeen bait boats had resumed operations. The fishermen working on these boats told us that despite the availability of good quantities of shrimp and corresponding good catches, they were experiencing insufficient demand for their production to justify continuing operations. Moreover, all of the fishermen we met at Black Point expressed uncertainty over their ability to remain in business in the future. Several doubted they could maintain sufficient capital to make necessary repairs on their boats, and nearly all said that while there currently seemed to be a lot of shrimp immediately offshore, they worried that the extensive destruction of the mangroves around Black Point—the main rearing grounds for the shrimp—might mean a collapse of these stocks several months in the future. Sentiments were expressed that the NMFS, the agency of the U.S. government that they felt should be concerned for them, had done nothing. "Tell the fisheries service we need help," one group repeatedly urged us.

REALITY OF THE IMPACT—LOUISIANA

After striking Florida, Hurricane Andrew continued west into the Gulf of Mexico. In the Gulf, offshore oil platforms sustained damage from the high winds, and at least one platform suffered a blowout resulting in a ten-mile-long oil slick. Gulf fishing and shrimping activities there were brought to a standstill before, during, and after the hurricane. Hurricane Andrew then made landfall in Louisiana at Cypremont Point, St. Mary Parish, on August 25, 1992, a day after hitting south Florida. Although not packing the punch it had in Florida, it still retained wind speeds of over one hundred forty miles per hour.

The Louisiana fishing communities that lay in the path of Hurricane Andrew differ markedly from Florida fishing communities. Concentrations of families living in rural bayou fishing villages, oyster camps, and coastal bay boat communities dominate the cultural and ecological landscape in St. Mary and South Terrebonne Parish, areas heavily hit by the storm. Thus, while

Florida commercial fishermen are spread out in a narrow band across the coastline of the state, Louisiana fishers are embedded in a complex ecosystem of bayous, estuaries, and rivers yielding a bounty of natural resources and providing many millions of dollars in annual revenues. Unlike the marginalized fishing peoples of south Florida, these Louisiana fishing communities are much more critical to the political economy of the state (Dyer and Leard 1994; Din 1988).

Although they provided an existence markedly different from the more suburban Florida setting, overall, the fishing, hunting, and trapping activities of these rural NRCs, when added to the conveniences of modern life, allowed people to enjoy an equivalent quality of life:

> A significant difference between the rural inhabitants of the past and the people who today choose to live in the countryside is that the latter are able to enjoy most urban conveniences—electricity, running water, and modern plumbing. Moreover, with highways, automobiles, and television antennae or satellite dishes, isolation belongs to the past, and country living can be favorably compared to life in the suburbs. Today's rural inhabitants of Louisiana, as most of those elsewhere in the nation, can take advantage of the best in both worlds. (Din 1988: 195)

However modern, the commerce of rural Louisiana still depends on commercial and recreational fishing, hunting, and trapping. When Hurricane Andrew made landfall in Louisiana, it seriously disrupted the resources and well-being of numerous NRCs, with Cypremont Point in St. Mary Parish suffering the most serious damage. Impacts to fish processing facilities in St. Mary Parish included structural damage, product loss, loss of electricity and refrigeration capacity, loss of product suppliers, lost capital (e.g., boats and traps contracted to specific processors), lost income from downtime repairing facilities, and total destruction of facilities. At least ten local seafood houses lost large amounts of shrimp and frozen seafood products. The local health department and USDA condemned seafood products ruined in the storm. Several large wholesalers dealing exclusively in finfish products received extensive damage, and at least three were totally destroyed. Crab, oyster, and menhaden plants were also damaged, with the most severe *immediate* impact being lost downtime in production. Oyster camps were decimated, boats stranded and sunk, and oyster beds silted over from the tidal surge of the storm.

As opposed to Florida, however, local media coverage of impacts to fishing communities was widespread, and political leaders such as Louisiana Senator Tauzan called on massive relief for fishing families and communities. Poignant stories covering the plight of the fishing industry covered the pages of the *Picayune Times* and other media sources. And, while the Florida DNR was unaware of the extent of losses to fishers and communities many months after the storm, the Louisiana Department of Wildlife and Fisheries (DWF) rapidly deployed agents in the field to assess the extent of damages to fisheries (Louisiana Department of Wildlife and Fisheries 1992). Their activities included assessment of lost and damaged gear and fishing vessels and fish stocks (assessed from fish kill counts). Fish kills occur when bottom sediments are mixed in the water column by a storm surge, driving out oxygen and suffocating millions of commercially valuable fish. For example, initial DWF estimates of freshwater fish kills in the Atchafalaya Basin were valued at $159,900,500. Saltwater fish were also killed by being washed inland, suffocated in silt, or stranded in mud flats. By August 31, one week after Hurricane Andrew hit the Louisiana coast, saltwater fish kills in South Terebonne Parish were approximated by the DFW at 9.4 million fish dead from suffocation. This figure includes 198,000 spotted seatrout, 922,500 Atlantic croaker, and 5,740,000 Gulf menhaden, the mainstays of Louisiana's commercial fishing industry. The estimated value of these and other lost saltwater fish resources is over $7.8 million. A significant fact in this accounting of these lost fishery resources is that the accounting occurred at all. In Florida, no detailed estimates were collected by the DNR on fisheries or gear or catch losses other than what was reported by fish processors and collected by us in our fieldwork.

Public and leased oyster beds were also a casualty of the storm. The oyster leasing system is one that was established at the turn of the century with the collaboration of the state and Acadian immigrants. This co-managed system provided stability for hundreds of oyster fishing families over the century and is one of the most stable and productive shellfisheries in the world. When the oyster camps were impacted, a ripple effect traveled from the back bayous to the seafood restaurants of New Orleans that contributed to the actions and concerns of public officials. Overall estimates of losses to the public oyster reefs alone were $3.5 million. Oyster fishers, oyster shuckers, truck drivers, processors, and tourist-filled restaurants in the French Quarter saw no oysters from the region for months after the impact. The price of oysters from St. Mary and South Terrebonne parishes also increased due to lack of supply (personal communication, Louisiana DFW agent, Baton Rouge, 1992).

Another significant natural resource impact was to the trapping and hunting sector. Andrew made landfall in one of the most productive recreational and commercial hunting areas of the state. Trapping and hunting are important components of the lifestyle of residents in the impact area. They provide additional income as well as subsistence resources to the diet of settlements in the disaster impact region. Losses to hunting, fur (e.g., muskrat), and alligator (skins and meat) trades totaled some $500,000. Overall, a conservative estimate of total fishery, hunting, and trapping losses for the six-month period following the hurricane amounted to approximately $270 million.

DISCUSSION—THE CULTURE OF RESPONSE

Interpreting the differences in impacts, knowledge, and concern for natural resource losses for the fishing communities of Florida and Louisiana can be examined through the state and federal "culture of response" to community needs in the two states. Prior to leaving for the field we assumed that the principal agencies that are involved in fisheries in south Florida and Louisiana would be responsible for assessing the hurricane's impact on the regions' commercial fishing peoples, as well as for developing relief efforts. This assumption was correct for Louisiana, but incorrect for south Florida. In Florida, there are no legislative mandates or standing operating policies at municipal, county, state, or federal levels which require any of the agencies to take such responsibilities. Instead, these agencies' legislative mandates and current operating policies are almost exclusively directed toward marine-ecological and marine-conservation issues, and not people.

Under disaster conditions such as Hurricane Andrew, there is legislative authority for NMFS response, but it is limited to providing for the restoration and replacement of marine habitats and marine natural resources and has no provisions for providing relief to the fishing industry per se. This legislation, which is known as the Interjurisdictional Fisheries Act (1987, P.L. 99-695, Title 3, Section 308[b]), enables an NMFS response to natural disasters, with a focus on assessment and compensation for damages and restoration and replacement of marine natural resources. The Louisiana DFW was aware of this and provided, as shown above, detailed accounting of the losses and values of fisheries from the disaster zone. In response to the DFW accounting and under the provisions of this act, the NMFS provided $4.1 million to the state of Louisiana for the restoration and replacement of marine natural resources. However, no such funds were provided to Florida *even though such funds were potentially available.*

Why did Louisiana receive such significant funding, which provided, in part, for making assessments of damages to important commercial fish stocks and for their restoration, while south Florida did not? First, and simply, Louisiana requested funds under the act, while Florida did not. The act stipulates that the U.S. Congress has to appropriate funds under the act and that the state receiving such funds has to both request the funding and be willing to meet it by 25 percent in matching funds. Secondly, the situation in Louisiana fisheries and fishing communities as described above is quite different from that in south Florida. As indicated, Louisiana has a large, concentrated, economically significant, highly visible fishing industry integrated with the wider urban seafood-restaurant economies of New Orleans and Baton Rouge; south Florida, on the other had, does not. As a result, Louisiana's commercial fishing sector had sufficient political clout to persuade state legislators to seek relief funds under the federal act mentioned above, as well as to provide the requisite matching funds.

Commercial fishers in south Florida, while more numerous than the NMFS officials suggested, are ethnically marginalized and geographically dispersed. They do not comprise a large number of people relative to the rest of the total populace in the region, and they are economically much less significant in the region's economy as compared with their counterparts in Louisiana. They therefore have far less political clout. Unlike in coastal Louisiana, there is no highly visible natural resource "fishing community," that is, no small towns, villages, or harbor areas which might be identified as commercial fishing towns, villages, or sites. Instead, south Florida's commercial fishers are intermingled with the surrounding urban, suburban, and ex-urban populace. Nevertheless, there is still a substantial commercial-fishing populace scattered along south Florida's coastline, which, as mentioned earlier, we were helped to locate and analyze by the concept of the natural resource community. Overall, we estimate this dispersed "community" to consist of around two hundred primary producers, plus several times that number of ancillary people who supply and support the fishing industry, a significant chunk of humanity whose welfare following the storm was woefully neglected.

There is another crucial difference between the situation in Louisiana and that in south Florida that significantly contributes to differences in the culture of response. While both states have notable recreational-fishing sectors, in south Florida the recreational sector of the fisheries has historically overshadowed the commercial sector in terms of its economic importance, political power, and corresponding ability to influence fisheries-management policy. Both Meltzoff (1989) and Durrenberger (1992: 196) have discussed the preeminence of the recreational fishing sector in south Florida (and in the Florida Keys), and particularly its ability to dominate fishery policy against the interests of the commercial sector. For example, in the 1930s, when Ernest Hemingway was catching marlin and idling at *Sloppy Joes* in Key West, the south Florida recreational fishing sector was already well established and economically significant. Durrenberger describes how "fishing for fun" has supplanted "fishing for exchange" in south Florida's fisheries, noting that these fisheries have become "playgrounds for the rich," and he criticizes this as an aspect of the state's "Disney World" mentality (Durrenberger 1992: 196).

Finally, questions of class and ethnicity possibly have a bearing on the indifference of fishery managers to the plight of fishermen in Florida after Hurricane Andrew. It was apparent in discussions with NMFS that they rarely communicated with the "Cuban" spiny lobster fishers on the Miami River, and had no intention of documenting their losses after the hurricane. This stands in sharp contrast to the many weeks of fieldwork put in by Louisiana DFW agents in their attempts to account for the losses of fish stocks and fishermen's losses in the aftermath of the disaster. In addition, the wider cultural view of fishers by Floridians has been documented to follow denigrating stereotypes (Meltzoff 1990). Commercial fishers are typically viewed by tourists, retirees, and state agents as "dirty, polluting, and disorderly in nature" (Meltzoff 1990: 13). Sympathy is also not shown by recreational fishers, who perceive commercial fishers as privileged competitors for "their" fish, or by Florida-based environmental organizations such as the Center for Marine Conservation, who portray commercial fishers as environmentally destructive and greedy.

CONCLUSION

This chapter has introduced the concept of the culture of response to explain differences in how state and federal agencies in Louisiana and Florida reacted to the needs of fishing communities impacted by Hurricane Andrew. We have shown that despite the existence of clear and measurable impacts in both states, agencies, political leaders, and natural resource managers in Florida did not react to the damage to fishers and the marine resources on which they depended. In fact, they were ignorant of the extent and nature of these impacts in the seafood processing sector, the spiny lobster fishery, and the shrimp bait industry. The factors behind this apathy have been related to the lack of a political presence and geographic concentrations of fishers in south Florida, and to a political economy that has historically favored the recreational and tourist sector over commercial fishing interests. Because of the "control and command" nature of the fishery management system in Florida and elsewhere in the United States, fishers often have little power and can find themselves marginalized and vulnerable when facing a natural disaster. At present, NMFS has no mandate to help commercial fishers through natural disasters such as hurricanes, and, correspondingly, no direct discretionary funds for their recovery. A year after the disaster event, interviews with select key informants in the fishing sector indicated that nothing was ever done to assist in the recovery of the three highlighted areas, and that many commercial fishers have been unable to resume fishing, their preferred lifestyle. There has also never been any assessment by a government agency of the overall impact of the hurricane on the region's fishers, nor was help, such as technical assistance, ever provided for their recovery.

By contrast, we demonstrated a focused concern for the Louisiana fishing communities caught in the path of a natural disaster. The political economy of the state of Louisiana is attuned to the needs of its fishing peoples, who provide hundreds of millions of dollars in fresh seafood product from the rivers, bayous, and coasts surrounding their natural resource communities. This concern was manifest in a request for federal funding assistance under the Interjurisdictional Fisheries Act by state authorities. No such assistance was sought for fisheries in south Florida, even though they were eligible. Furthermore, the fishing culture and communities of Louisiana are in a more central position to the culture and economy of the state. In the Louisiana case, the culture of response to a powerful hurricane was to commit state resources to restore the natural resource base of the damaged communities.

NOTE

1. We especially thank Gilbert F. White, Director, and Mary Fran Myers, Project Manager, at the Hazards Research and Applications Information Center, University of Colorado, Boulder, for their advice and support with this project. Susanna Hoffman and Anthony Oliver-Smith are to be thanked for their editorial support in the preparation of this manuscript. Gerald Krausse, Department of Marine Affairs, University of Rhode Island, is thanked for his assistance in preparation of Figure 1 .

BIBLIOGRAPHY

Adams, W. 1965. "The Dead Community: Perspectives from the Past," in A. Gallaher, Jr., and H. Padfield (eds.), *The Dying Community,* pp. 1–23. Santa Fe: School of American Research.

Anonymous. 1993. Untitled editorial. *Aide* 24, 1: 1–8.

Baldassaro, L. 1975. "Sicily's Earthquake Zone: Waiting in the Wreckage." *Nation* (September 13): 239–242.

Barton, A. 1969. *Communities in Disaster: A Sociological Analysis of Collective Stress Situations.* Garden City, NY: Doubleday.

Din, G. 1988. *The Canary Islanders of Louisiana.* Baton Rouge: Louisiana State University Press.

Durrenberger, E. 1992. *It's All Politics: South Alabama's Seafood Industry.* Chicago: University of Illinois Press.

Dyer, C. 1993. "Tradition Loss as Secondary Disaster: The Long-Term Cultural Impacts of the *Exxon-Valdez* Oil Spill." *Sociology Spectrum* 13: 65–88.

———. 1995. *Assessment of the Economic Development Administration's Post-Disaster Recovery Program after Hurricane Andrew.* Bethesda, MD: Aguirre International.

———. Forthcoming. "Punctuated Entropy as Culture Induced Change: The Case of the *Exxon-Valdez* Oil Spill," in S. Hoffman and A. Oliver-Smith (eds.), *Culture and Catastrophe.* Santa Fe, NM: School of American Research.

Dyer, C., and R. Leard. 1994. "Folk Management in the Oyster Fishery of the United States Gulf of Mexico," in C. Dyer, C. McGoodwin, and J. McGoodwin (eds.), *Folk Management in the World Fisheries: Lessons for Modern Fishery Management.* Boulder: University Press of Colorado.

Dyer, C., and J. McGoodwin (eds.). 1994. *Folk Management in the World Fisheries: Lessons for Fisheries Management.* Boulder: University Press of Colorado.

Dyer, C., D. Gill, and J. Picou. 1992. "Social Disruption and the *Valdez* Oil Spill: Alaskan Natives in a Natural Resource Community." *Sociology Spectrum* 12: 105–126.

Fee, R. 1992. "Hurricane Andrew: A Narrow Swath Cut Through Florida." *National Fisherman* 73, 7: 12.

Flannery, K. 1972. "The Cultural Evolution of Civilization." *Annual Review of Ecology and Systematics* 3: 399–426.

Florida DNR (Department of Natural Resources). 1992. September Fisheries Newsletter. Tampa: Florida Department of Natural Resources.

Fritz, C. 1961. "Disaster," in R. Merton and R. Nisbet. (eds.), *Contemporary Social Problems,* pp. 651–694. New York: Harcourt.

Gale, R. 1991. "Gentrification of America's Coasts: Impacts of the Growth Machine on Commercial Fishermen." *Society and Natural Resources* 4: 103–121.

Harvey, D. 1996. *Justice, Nature and the Geography of Difference.* Cambridge: Blackwell.

Kates, R. 1971. "Natural Hazard in Human Ecological Perspective: Hypotheses and Models." *Economic Geography* 47: 438–451.

Lees, S. 1975. "Oaxaca's Spiraling Race for Water." *Natural History* (April): 30–39.

Levine, I. 1995. "A View from the Field: Operation Lifeline Sudan," in *Retrospective DHA 1995: Coordination of Humanitarian Assistance,* pp. 10–12. New York: United Nations Department of Humanitarian Affairs.

Louisiana Department of Wildlife and Fisheries. 1992. DWF Newsletter, September 11, 1992. Baton Rouge: Louisiana Department of Wildlife and Fisheries.

McGoodwin, J., and C. Dyer. 1993. "Hurricane Andrew and South Florida's Commercial Fishing Peoples: Impacts and Immediate Needs." *MAST* 6 (1/2): 205–219.

Meltzoff, S. 1989. "Politics of Conservation in the Florida Keys," in E. Durrenberger, L. Maril, and J. Thomas (eds.), *Marine` Resource Utilization,* pp. 125–132. Mobile, AL: Mississippi-Alabama Sea Grant Consortium.

———. 1990. "The Cross-Currents of Ethnicity and Class: Conflict and Conservation in the Florida' Keys." Unpublished manuscript. Miami: University of Miami.

Nugent, T. 1973. "After Buffalo Creek: Bureaucracy of Disasters." *Nation* (June 18): 785–788.

Obeng, L. 1977. "Should Dams be Built? The Volta Lake Example." *Ambio* 6, 1: 46–50.

———. 1998a. "Global Changes and the Definition of Disaster," in E. Quarantelli (ed.), *What Is a Disaster: Perspectives on the Question.* New York: Routledge.

———. 1998b. "Disasters, Social Change, and Adaptive Systems," in E. Quarantelli (ed.), *What Is a Disaster: Perspectives on the Question.* New York: Routledge.

Oliver-Smith, A. 1996. "Anthropological Research on Hazards and Disasters." *Annual Reviews in Anthropology,* pp. 303–328. Palo Alto: Annual Reviews Inc.

Reidinger, R. 1974. "Institutional Rationing of Canal Water in Northern India: Conflict between Traditional Patterns and Modern Needs." *Economic Development and Cultural Change* 23, 1: 79–104.

Sims, J., and D. Baumann. 1972. "The Tornado Threat: Coping Styles of the North and South." *Science* 176 (June 30): 1386–1392.

Torry, W. 1978. "Bureaucracy, Community and Natural Disasters." *Human Organization* 37: 302–308.

———. 1979. "Natural Disasters, Social Structure, and Change in Traditional Societies." *Journal of Asian and African Studies* 13, 3–4: 167–183.

Van Der Schalie, H. 1974. "Aswan Dam Revisited." *Environment* 16, 9: 18–26.

V

AGENCIES, SURVIVORS, AND RECONSTRUCTION

WHEN A DISASTER OCCURS, VERY FEW PLACES ARE LEFT TO RECOVER ON their own. Disasters commonly elicit rapid local, state, national, and international aid. They call private and public organizations into the area with personnel and materials. This convergence of people and goods, often foreign or strange to the local population, may ultimately be as great a source of disturbance as the disaster agent and destruction themselves. In large-scale devastation, the recovery may last almost indefinitely. It often evolves into development programs such that experts and their work become almost permanent features of the social landscape. While humanitarian aid initially focuses on alleviating the emergency conditions of victims, longer-term recovery and reconstruction assistance is as much designed to further the political agendas of, usually, the state and its agencies as it is to reconstruct the community. In fact, assistance programs and their implementation frequently impose conditions on communities that vary significantly from community desire, thus becoming focal points of contestation.

The state's performance in assistance often becomes an important yardstick for assessing the validity of state programs and competence of personnel. In fact, post-disaster assistance constitutes a unique opportunity for establishing more effective relationships between state and local contexts for enhancing community empowerment and development and for reducing risk and vulnerability that, unfortunately, is only occasionally taken advantage of by the state and its agencies.

12

PLAN AND PATTERN IN REACTION TO EARTHQUAKE: PERU, 1970–1998

PAUL L. DOUGHTY
University of Florida

MAY 31, 1970

IT WAS A TYPICAL SUNDAY AFTERNOON IN THE CALLEJÓN DE HUAYLAS, A valley high in the Peruvian Andes. Soccer teams played, farmers tended their chores, markets were closing, children's parties entertained the young, and strollers enjoyed the plazas as the sun reflected brilliantly off the vast snow peaks of the Cordillera Blanca. In five minutes the bucolic setting was shattered as an earthquake of 7.7 magnitude on the Richter scale convulsed the earth, precipitating enormous avalanches and floods, destroying nearly two thousand cities and villages, killing over seventy thousand persons, and injuring twice as many. Eight hundred thousand, about 6 percent of Peru's citizens, were left homeless in an eighty-three-thousand-square-kilometer area stretching from the Pacific Ocean across the Andes to the upper Amazon basin, 5 percent of the nation's territory. In terms of death it was the largest natural cataclysm in Western hemisphere history. Today, people still curse the event and its aftermath, the consequences of which are felt almost three decades later.

THE HUMAN RESPONSE TO "ACTS OF GOD"

Aside from legendary cosmological events like the biblical "great flood," natural perturbations leading to human disasters are rarely commemorated in history. Instead, small plaques are affixed to walls indicating the high-water marks of a flood or etched on gravestones, although few events so capture our attention, so terrify and enthrall us simultaneously. Natural disasters, however destructive, cannot compete with wars. Earthquakes produce few identifiable heroes, but rather, faceless martyrs lost to the "acts of God." Neither commemorated on postage stamps nor formally concluded with treaties, disasters fade from memory and their impacts are largely forgotten.

The proclivity to distort or dismiss things that are inconvenient for one's theories or comfortable routines seems universal. Such neglect links disaster recovery with development programs and affects them similarly, especially in poor nations like Peru. The lament of many in development work is that responsible institutions, despite their bureaucratic redundancy, have poor to nonexistent memories when it comes to benefiting from experience. The gaps between past experience, policy creation, and implementation are difficult to bridge when administrative and policy changes and personnel mobility leave only longtime members of secretarial staffs to remember. Associated with the inability to utilize past experience effectively in either development or post-disaster contexts is a lack of interest in evaluating the results (Jones 1997: 116–118).

Aside from their sensational aspects, the human conditions that result from calamity receive little continuing attention despite the fact that it is exactly these conditions that actually define the disaster. Volcanic explosions, earthquakes, and "El Niño" are ongoing natural processes of the planet— episodes in earthly evolution. They become disasters only by human definition when they produce direct, deleterious impacts on individuals, society, and culture. An earthquake becomes a cultural artifact as people place it in societal context to cope with its effects over many years. In Peru, the people affected by the May 31, 1970, earthquake understood the human role in creating a disaster culture from the very beginning, when they cynically remarked after the event: "First the earthquake, then the disaster!" To what degree and how do natural processes necessarily become human disasters?

DISASTERS AS HUMAN EVENTS

Three basic "measures" are used to describe the severity of earthquakes: the loss of life, the loss of property, and the points registered on the Richter scale. These, however, are insufficient to understand the sociocultural effects or the complexity of damage to human society. Along with comprehensive disaster impact on population, property, and wealth, institutions, affective relationships, and community must be taken into account to achieve a wholistic approach to a reasonable recovery. Failure to do this will certainly prolong and even deepen the disaster.

The comprehensiveness of Peru's 1970 earthquake and the effectiveness of the response are seen by: 1) the degree of victimization and effects on the normal operation of social institutions; 2) the duration of this impact and related developments; 3) the speed with which society recuperated; and 4) how much society improved its capacity to handle future perturbations. Following any event, some of these points can be quickly evaluated; others may require a generation or even a new catastrophic episode to access. Such time depth is especially important because major earthquake disasters are profoundly comprehensive, disrupting and modifying societies in ways that are not revealed in a one- or even five-year period of assessment (Oliver-Smith 1996: 312–321). Yet, with greatest attention focused on immediate emergency concerns, long-term studies of disasters are hard to find.

Many questions merit attention in the long-term study of earthquake effects. These include the concepts and theories about social processes, human needs, and behavior that can be of future use. Unfortunately, despite their pertinence, the insights drawn from these queries rarely seem to inform or serve as guidelines in the development of institutional policies or actions. Unstated theoretical assumptions about policy, method, and the nature of the human society, however, did lie behind the actions and results of earthquake recovery operations in Peru. These can be noted as follows: 1) centralized authoritarian administration is the most efficient method of operation; 2) local leaders and citizen groups are not competent to make important decisions, which are best left to the experts; 3) most needs are largely of an infrastructural nature, and sociocultural issues will take care of themselves; 4) assistance should be provided in accord with the hierarchical structure of society; and 5) the poor require less assistance because their needs and wants are fewer. Such assumptions led to the actions taken by the managers of relief and recovery agencies after the 1970 earthquake. They precipitated far-reaching consequences over this long period[1] throughout the Callejón de Huaylas and in the three cases cited here: the regional capital of Huaraz, the provincial capital of Yungay, and the district of Huaylas.[2]

THE CALLEJÓN DE HUAYLAS, PERU: 1970

Ancash Department is one of the most mountainous and geographically partitioned regions of Peru, with valleys running from south to north on either side of the great Cordillera Blanca (see Figure 1). The westernmost valley is the 125-mile-long Callejón de Huaylas flanked by the massive El Huascarán, Peru's tallest mountain at 6,746 meters, and dozens of other snow peaks (Kinzl and Schnieder 1950; Ricker 1977). The arid west side of the valley, more sparsely populated, is bounded by the snowless Cordillera Negra. Born in glacial waters, the Santa River flows northward through the Callejón de Huaylas, dropping from four thousand to eighteen hundred meters, where it slices through a deep defile called the Cañon del Pato and falls rapidly to the Pacific at the industrial city of Chimbote.

The sides of narrow valley rise above the river over rough foothills. The

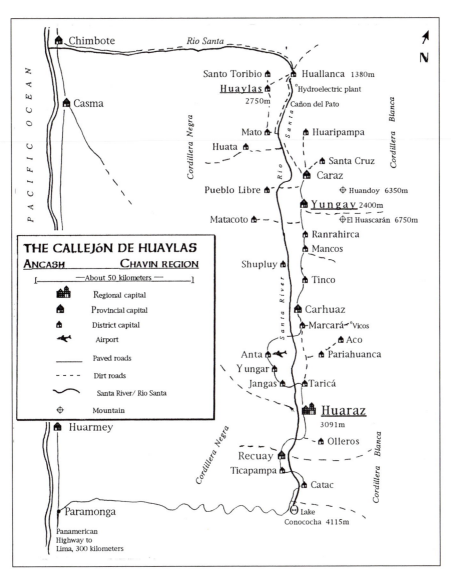

FIGURE 1. *Map of Callejón de Huaylas, Peru.*

main towns, established there by the Spanish in the late sixteenth century, are set well above the riverbed. Because many are located on preconquest cere- monial and town sites, these old settlements and the hamlets surrounding them have cultural roots that nourish a strong sense of local identity. The peo- ple of the valley broadly classify themselves in cultural terms as being *indí- gena, cholo,* or *mestizo,* gradients that reflect the relative presence of the indigenous or Hispanic creole culture and language in each individual's behavior and identity. In the past, *mestizos* dominated all important eco- nomic and official affairs of society, and indigenous peoples were kept in place through their institutionalized exploitation as peons. They were denied access to schooling and their rights as citizens (Stein 1961; Dobyns et al. 1971). Prior to 1970, however, many changes were occurring, prompted by political changes and extensive migration to the urban coast.

On the eve of May 31, 1970, Peru fervently aspired to modernize and overcome long-standing frustrations. A self-styled "Revolutionary Govern- ment of the Armed Forces" energetically pursued policies to reorganize the nation through land reform, community restructuring, nationalization, and cooperativization of certain industries (McClintock and Lowenthal 1983; Stepan 1978). Change was the *leitmotif* of the regime. Guided by "Marxian" assumptions and inspired by European socialism, Peru moved rapidly through new societal landscapes with stern military authoritarianism. The government attempted to erase colonial legacies, reorient the capitalist pat- terns, and design a new national society. As never before, government hands reached into every hamlet.

The military rulers had unquestioned confidence in their technical capaci- ties, absolute power, faith in authoritarian methods, and certainty that their views about Peru's needs were correct. Conditions conducive to change were everywhere: the expectation of change, a dependence upon authority, a col- laboration of effort, a sense of relative deprivation, and the increasing flow of new ideas and knowledge (Barnett 1953: 39–96). Unhappiness generated by the previous regime's failures contributed substantially to this situation after it had spurred desires for self-improvement, mobilizing Andean highlanders to build needed schools, roads, water systems, and bridges (Belaunde 1965). Highland communities strove to manipulate policy and resources of the national government in their favor, and many communities became skilled lobbyists in a highly competitive atmosphere (Doughty 1986; Smith 1989). By 1970, the promise of important institutional and material changes quickened the lives of most Peruvians.

Without presenting the details of the many disaster events well described elsewhere (Oliver-Smith 1977, 1979, 1982, 1986; Dudasik 1976, 1980; Bode 1989; Doughty 1971, 1986), the ensuing summary outlines developments in the Callejón de Huaylas and provides a context for the case studies that follow.

CHRONOLOGY OF EARTHQUAKE HISTORY: 1970–1998

May 31, 1970:   An earthquake of 7.7 magnitude on the Richter scale strikes an area of twenty thousand square miles, encompassing all of the department of Ancash and adjacent areas. Over a million people, about 8 percent of the nation,[3] are affected, with damages equivalent to 30 percent of national expenditures that year. A concomitant avalanche from El Huascarán obliterates the small city of Yungay and wrecks a major hydroelectric plant. In Ancash almost two thousand cities, towns, and hamlets are damaged, some losing all of their buildings. Local emergency committees are rapidly formed.

June 1, 1970–1972:   The Commission for the Reconstruction and Rehabilitation of the Affected Zone (CRYRZA) is created in Lima to manage relief and redevelopment, headed by an air force general and military staff; international relief supplies, organizations, and personnel descend on the region to take charge. In late 1971, CRYRZA moves to an administrative center at Vichay outside Huaraz; emergency aid rises to U.S.$44 million, almost double the average yearly amount of foreign economic aid. Most debris is removed from larger cities by 1972; a "disaster boom economy" energizes Huaraz.

1972–1973:   CRYRZA is reorganized to become ORDEZA (The Regional Organism for the Development of the Affected Zone); bureaucracy expands; paving begins on main road; several villages and towns are relocated; major attention is given to infrastructural investment in damaged coastal cities and the regional capital, Huaraz; a new airport is constructed near Huaraz at Anta; housing projects begin in some cities.

1978:   ORDEZA is reorganized to become ORDENOR (The Regional Organism for the Development of the North), with an administration somewhat "friendlier" to local concerns; school reconstruction is underway; the main road from the coast through the Callejón is fully paved; rebuilding of Huaraz and Yungay advances. Many are still housed in emergency quarters; the hydroelectric plant resumes operations, and a rural electrification program is initiated. Slow pace of redevelopment and lack of assistance at the family level lead many to migrate to the coast or Lima. A permanent memorial is raised at the former Yungay city site, now called the *Campo Santo* (Holy Field). By 1980, the average yearly development aid to the region over ten years is 287 percent more per year than prior to the quake.

1982:   ORDENOR is reorganized to become CORDEANCASH (The Corporation for the Development of Ancash). Regular government agencies have reassumed full operations; activities of the post-disaster agencies and NGO operations are greatly reduced with the exception of U.S. Food for Peace projects. The roadway paved by ORDEZA is in need of constant repair due to faulty construction; nonetheless, travel is facilitated and regular flights to the airport cease. Now rebuilt, Huaraz grows while Yungay remains incomplete. Other towns continue reconstruction work. Emergency housing remains in use in many places; most families have rebuilt their homes without any assistance.

1986:   CORDEANCASH is cut back, and the complex of administrative buildings at Vichay becomes headquarters for the new regional government; the administrative housing evolves into a new suburb of Huaraz, which now bears little resemblance to the old colonial town, exceeding its prequake population and importance.

1997:   The pilgrimage site of the Campo Santo features a monumental altar, family shrines, and flowers. Emergency housing remains in regular use in several places; earthquake debris remains visible in many districts; reconstruction slowly continues without assistance; Huaraz is an important tourist center, attracting international mountaineering teams, trekkers, and thousands of Peruvian holiday visitors.

With the clarity of hindsight, these developments are neither surprising nor unpredictable. On the other hand, there was no clear vision on the part of CRYRZA or its successors of the goals sought, aside from the large-scale infrastructural projects. Few projects sought to develop the local economies, and none was aimed at bolstering local governance. Rhetorically, the agencies involved in recovery operations spoke of avoiding the "reconstruction of underdevelopment," but their activities to this effect were uninspired. In a country whose yearly per capita income was about three hundred dollars, such goals were modest in the extreme, with accessible resources being greater than the total normally available to the entire country.

ANTICIPATING THE COURSE OF ACTION AND RESPONSE

One could expect that well-organized communities would benefit from the availability of multiple resources, assuming as well that the agencies charged with recovery management would follow their customary bureaucratic procedures. In the immediate aftermath, this occurred. The energetic communities such as Huaylas flew into action with initiatives that surprised relief workers. In contrast, government and international agencies, having little or no familiarity with the region, plunged ahead with authoritarian and paternalistic fervor. What happened is illustrated in three cases from different areas of the Callejón de Huaylas: the regional capital of Huaraz, the provincial seat of Yungay, and the northern district of Huaylas (see Figure 1). Although all suffered terribly, the disaster experience in each place was notably different, as were the outcomes.

HUARAZ, "PRETENSIÓN"

#1

Nowhere did post-earthquake developments produce greater changes than in the departmental capital. Huaraz was a rustic colonial town with corresponding behaviors, the center of provincial elitism and home to a landlord class which dominated regional economy and society. In local lore its people were thought "pretentious." At 10,500 feet beneath snow-capped mountains, with narrow cobbled streets and out-of-plumb, balconied adobe buildings, Huaraz was picturesque. Homespun-clad Indians and self-important *mestizos* jostled each other for narrow sidewalk space. From its gracious plaza, the view northward to the vast white peaks of El Huascarán sixty kilometers away was awesome.

Disaster struck Huaraz in 1941, when a flood of mud and water from the mountains poured through the city, killing a reported five thousand persons and leaving a rocky scar through the middle of the city. This time it was different. In less than two minutes, the panorama was obscured by immense dust clouds of collapsing adobe as the city imploded amidst screams of frightened and dying people.[4]

Bulldozers took more than a year to clear the area. Rows of emergency barracks (*modulos*) made from metal braces, fiberboard, and corrugated roofing served as homes for several thousand persons for over five years while new housing slowly rose along newly arranged residential streets. In the old plaza, the undamaged trees, gardens, and fountain were unceremoniously scraped away as well. Enlarged to twice its former size, the plaza is now paved and treeless, with a large (dry) fountain in its center. The plaza area is only partially complete, with unfinished sidewalks and large vacant lots that formerly held the cathedral, banks, and restaurants. There is a new church with a colored glass roof that was designed without local input and is despised by native Huarasinos who use it reluctantly. Highlighting this disdain is a monument replicating the old cathedral's cupola situated prominently on the main thoroughfare. The center of Huaraz religiosity, the church of the Señor de la Soledad, in the hands of local committees was quickly reconstructed and lavished with adornments (Bode 1989).

With 92,385 people, Huaraz is three and a half times its predisaster size, despite the fact that over ten thousand persons there perished in the quake. Huaraz remains the capital of Ancash Department and is now the seat of government for the newly created Chavin Region, part of Peru's attempt at national decentralization. It is the center of banking, communications, and commerce, and is also the seat of the dioceses, with convent and religious schools along with the largest and best-equipped public high schools in highland Ancash. In 1977, the first university in the department was founded, converting Huaraz into a student mecca, something which had never before been the case. Huaraz, thus, became the undisputed center of regional activity.

Tourism developed rapidly once the roads into the valley were paved, permitting visitors to arrive on air-conditioned, nonstop buses. Numerous hotels were built, and the city now offers many consumer services for tourists, with businesses, small industries, and a vigorous regional market whose daily activity far surpasses its former weekly level (Babb 1989). Socioeconomic differentiation is more complex and the opportunities for mobility greater, a major contrast to the old Huaraz society. Whereas Huaraz before played a key role in suppressing regional change by maintaining a caste-like atmosphere as far as the large indigenous population was concerned, the destruction of the "colonial" city by the earthquake created an opportunity for socioeconomic transformation.

These consequences of post-disaster assistance were not cleverly induced by strategic policy, however. While the main commercial street with its pleasant arcades is a popular development, as are the new, solidly built private homes owned by a diverse population, the deficiencies in the redevelopment process are serious and destined to perpetuate earthquake-derived problems into the twenty-first century. Blocks of ever-expanding street commerce and informal vendors surround the badly designed central market; the lack of a central bus terminal produces serious traffic problems; the lower-class neighborhoods which sprang forth unplanned from the barracks-like emergency housing continue to grow, with limited sewer and water systems giving promise of environment problems, costly future solutions, and a host of other conditions to come. The site of the 1941 flood is also filling with houses and businesses, all located in the path of past, and probably future, inundations. All of these problems could have been anticipated and mitigated by effective planning, direction, and local participation.

The Huaraz post-earthquake experience highlights at least two important features. The first is the unanticipated impact of a disaster boom economy on the city and region. After almost three decades it is clear that it has produced effects substantially altering Huaraz. Elsewhere the people did not experience this continuous economic jolt. Huaraz has also benefited from the presence of bureaucratic operations, with eighteen hundred employees whose above-average salaries were spent in Huaraz for over twelve years. This has energized commercial activity by circulating capital at levels never experienced in the Callejón.

The second feature stems from the Peruvian proclivity to concentrate wealth, power, and other values in one place toward which all else is oriented. This primacy principle assured that Huaraz would develop as it has, dominating all spheres of regional life in a fashion that mirrors the national pattern exemplified by Lima (Doughty 1979, 1997). Knowing this propensity, it was predictable that the areas outside Huaraz province would not only receive less aid, despite the devastation they suffered, but that they would receive dispro-portionately less as well. Moreover, the distribution of projects directly reflects the political clout of the places receiving them (Doughty 1986: 63). Recognizing this would have provided an opportunity to devise strategies for more equitable distribution of development investments, assuming this was a goal of the agencies. As matters unfolded, however, decisions followed old patterns, and Huaraz province received a total of 45 percent of all projects undertaken in the valley.

The relocation of the airport from its better site at Caraz to a narrower space at Anta, near Huaraz (see Figure 1), illustrates this. Although designed to serve the imagined needs of the regional capital and endowed with paving and control tower, its utility lasted only five years. Modern buses plying the newly paved highway and offering low fares and fast, comfortable rides from Lima were its demise. Although one of the more expensive projects under-taken, the airport serves only occasional VIP and emergency functions, and is essentially abandoned.

The primacy pattern is also manifest in the new regional demography outlined in Table 1, illustrating the influence of place and policy in the demo-graphic process. Places in Huaraz province increased an average of 153 per-cent in population since 1970, whereas those outside Huaraz grew by only 35 percent in the same period. A similar pattern emerges with respect to the divi-sion of the valley into the Cordillera Blanca side, with its glacial waters, and the arid Cordillera Negra side, whose towns have averaged far less growth since the disaster.

YUNGAY, "BEAUTY" # 2

The picturesque town of Yungay and 90 percent of its residents disappeared entirely in less than five minutes.[5] *Yungay hermosura* was gone, buried under an avalanche of millions of cubic meters of mud, rock, and ice that descended from Huascarán.

The Yungay experience demonstrates not only the resilience of its few survivors but the logic of local demands in the face of the poorly considered policies, inadequate consultation, and lost opportunities for making invest-ments to support local initiatives when resources were readily available. There are few excuses for these errors. This catastrophe was not a new expe-rience for Yungay province, as house-sized boulders deposited there over mil-lennia evidence. Indeed, a glacial avalanche provoked by storms swept down from El Huascarán in 1962, killing three thousand and obliterating the dis-trict capital of Ranrahirca only a few kilometers from Yungay city. The con-fused response to that tragedy led to eight years of delays, planning mistakes, nasty conflicts among survivors, and the misappropriation of development

TABLE 1: *Principal urban population centers of the Callejón de Huaylas, 1961–1992.*

City	Valley Location	Political Rank	Estimated Damage	°1961	ᵉ1970	°1972	°1992	% Change 1970–1992
Catac	R B	D	4	908	1153	1640	2150	87+
Ticapampa	R N	D	2	784	925	1649	1639	77+
Recuay	R N	P	2	1755	2071	2165	3044	47+
Olleros	H B	D	3	353	417	1871	1623	289+
Huaraz	H B	R	4	20300	27700	31382	92300	244+
Jangas	H N	D	2	333	393	484	1216	209+
Taricá	H B	D	4	460	542	550	933	72+
Pariahuanca	C B	D	3	387	456	515	840	84+
Yungar	C N	D	3	194	229	540	480	109+
Anta	C N	D	2	233	276	225	455	65+
Marcará	C B	D	2	843	995	1035	1000	1+
Carhuaz	C B	P	3	2175	2567	2453	4448	73+
Tinco	C B	D	1	300	354	589	797	125+
Shupluy	Y N	D	4	188	222	231	210	12-
Mancos	Y B	D	3	872	1029	1635	1211	21+
Ranrahirca	Y B	D	3	417	492	752	598	22+
Matacoto	Y N	D	2	210	248	96	153	38-
Yungay	HyB	P	5	3543	4181	1537	4646	11+
Caraz	HyB	P	2	4033	4759	5663	9636	139+
Santa Cruz	HyB	D	1	215	304	369	508	67+
Pueblo Libre	HyN	D	4	255	301	366	327	9+
Huata	HyN	D	3	483	570	440	238	58-
Mato (Sucre)	HyN	D	1	446	526	748	526	0
Huaylas	HyN	D	4	1258	1484	1072	1179	21-
Huallanca	HyN	D	3	491	579	934	701	21+
Averages								
*Cordillera Negra**				552	652	746	847	47+
*Cordillera Blanca**				560	1527	1558	2505	95+
Callejón de Huaylas: total, all areas				155602	186722		238191	54+

The settlements are listed in geographical order, from south to north as the Santa river flows. °Census years; ᵉ—estimated; Valley Location: Province: R—Recuay; H—Huaraz; C—Carhuaz; Y—Yungay; Hy—Huaylas; B— east side, Cordillera Blanca; N—west side, Cordillera Negra; Rank: R— regional/department capital; P—provincial capital; D—district capital. Estimated degree of earthquake damage in 1970: 1—10% or less; 2—10–25% of buildings heavily damaged; 3—major damage to 25–50% of homes and public buildings; 4—50–80% destroyed or severely damaged; 5—100% destroyed or severely damaged. *Omitting Huaraz, the two sides of the valley are compared only in terms of provincial and district capitals.

funds. Partially rebuilt next its former site, Ranrahirca was still vulnerable in 1970 when the same *aluvión* that struck Yungay demolished its new school and some houses, leaving still-unused streetlight posts protruding like the heads of cobras above the two-meter-thick cap of mud.

Clearly, there were lessons here for making a better response to the new but identical provincial catastrophe. Noteworthy were the resistance of survivors to being relocated and the ill-informed, misguided efforts of redevelopment agencies that exacerbated local factionalism, leading to delays and general mismanagement. The lack of consultation with residents by external authorities intensified the aforementioned conditions. The earlier Ranrahirca episode never received research attention, although anecdotal information was readily available which could have warned of potential difficulties. Neither CRYRZA administrators nor their successors profited from that experience in failed disaster management five kilometers away from Yungay.

New Yungay reestablished itself near the avalanche zone when the three hundred surviving inhabitants refused relocation in order to remain close to loved ones buried by the *aluvión* (Oliver-Smith 1982). The survivors were soon joined by refugees from the surrounding area, who gathered to take advantage of emergency housing, to create a new community of fate and interest, and to militate against relocation. "Yungay stays here!" signs appeared along the highway. After the provincial government resumed operations from tents amidst a fast-growing conglomeration of shacks and barracks, it was continuously in conflict with CRYRZA policy and fighting for resources.

The Yungay case showed that despite the horrific nature of the disaster, people were not loath to exploit socioeconomic opportunities even as the dust cleared. As elsewhere throughout the valley, opportunists sprang into action, seeking to profit from momentary scarcity and need, producing a dynamic socioeconomic environment. The avalanche surgically excised the conservative, urban, *mestizo* elites who had previously controlled affairs For the new Yungainos, it was a unique opportunity for social mobility in a frontier-like scenario. The reestablishment of the provincial capital offered advancement to persons whose prospects were limited in preearthquake times. Yungay completely replaced and surpassed its preearthquake population.

Assisting Yungay's renewal was the reemergence of its produce market through which thousands of farmers commercialize their crops, providing opportunities for employment and investment. The market was an essential feature of the old city, and after the quake it was important for the distribution of foodstuffs and material goods. Yungay's strategic location along the main highway, market functions, attractiveness to refugees, and reemergence of provincial government over the objections of CRYRZA illustrate how central place theory can predict events. Had planners recognized this from the onset, redevelopment could have begun more effectively and rapidly.

Yungay hums with the indigenous and *mestizo* farmers from the upland villages bringing their produce for daily sale. Government, regional hospitals, and new central high schools further stimulate the movement of people. The reestablishment of the schools restored Yungay as an educational center, continuing its strong education ethic and supporting the pattern of local leadership coming from the ranks of school teachers.

Yungay is radically different in layout from its former appearance. The new plaza and municipal building are embraced by hillsides, out of sight of and presumably protected from the "traitorous" mountain, El Huascarán. Rows of new houses rise up like an amphitheater from the plaza along terraced and unpaved streets. There are few sidewalks, and a dusty frontier-like quality pervades the city. Residences consist of concrete, brick, and adobe buildings, with a hundred prefabricated wooden houses sent by the Soviet Union providing a distinctive touch. Although a painting of the old church and plaza, with its palms and rose garden, on the facade of the municipal building is all that remains of old Yungay, a flourishing rose garden in the plaza replicates the old one. The eighteenth-century church was replaced by a round structure of wood and steel, but remains uncompleted despite a large subsidy from the president's office in 1997. It is not a popular design.

Yungay is an evolving community still coping with the aftermath of the disaster while inventing new traditions, even at the expense of the old. An example of changing customs is the celebration of the patronal feasts. The traditional means of observing the annual patronal feasts of Santo Domingo and Santa Rosa—celebrated largely by the indigenous population—has been rendered impossible by the new streets and buildings. Formerly these August fiestas reaffirmed the social and ritual division of the province in that the special alignment of the central plaza, adjacent streets, and church entrance demarcated preconquest moiety boundaries between the *waranqas* or barrios of Huambo and Mitmaq. In 1980, the fiesta was vastly diminished, and by 1997, observances had all but disappeared except in the upland villages.[6]

HUAYLAS, "HARVEST"

The district of Huaylas[7] nestles in a compact hanging valley of the Cordillera Negra at the northern head of the valley which bears its name. Huaylas was heavily populated and farmed before the rise of the Chavin culture around 1000 B.C., and its ancient irrigated terraces and fields surround large temples and ruins that are adjacent to modern settlements (Doughty 1986; Burger 1992; Thompson 1962). The district's massive colonial church had persisted through the centuries, and there were many houses whose original structures were built more than one hundred fifty years ago. Continuity was

taken for granted by a people who referred to their district as "Atun Huaylas," "Great Huaylas," its ancient name.

Prior to 1970, Huaylas was regionally famous for its high level of success
in achieving developmental goals that included attaining the highest levels of
literacy and electrification in all of Peru's rural highland districts; a strong
agricultural economy based on independent small farms; high levels of technological skills; and effective linkages to the Lima power bases in the min-
istries and congress (Doughty 1986).

The earthquake shattered this romance. All the houses of Huaylas suffered damage, and for 75 percent destruction was total or nearly so. Over two
hundred people were killed among a district population of about five thousand; hundreds were injured, with most casualties in the town. The two roads
entering the district were closed by landslides, as were the irrigation canals
(Doughty 1971). As the suffocating dust clouds settled, refugees climbed up
to Huaylas from the hydroelectric plant in Huallanca. Located forty kilometers from Caraz, with blocked roads, Huaylas was "out of sight" of the
authorities. Quickly organized work parties built an emergency landing strip
and cleared the roads by hand, permitting relief supplies to enter and
CRYRZA to reach the badly damaged hydroelectric plant and begin its
repair.[8] For the next eight years, despite precarious roads, vehicles passed
through Huaylas to reach the northern parts of Ancash because the main road
through the Cañon del Pato remained closed and the railroad from Huallanca
to Chimbote was destroyed. Despite their appalling situation, however,
Huaylinos obtained little significant assistance from CRYRZA and its successors. More debilitating still were the agency's reconstruction regulations, pro-
hibiting urban reconstruction without approved plans, something which
never happened despite requests (Doughty 1986).

Huaylas did receive volunteer assistance, however, from the U.S. Peace
Corps, a Soviet clinic whose small staff offered general medical services for
about two years, and four Dutch volunteers using Huaylas as a base from
which they provided engineering assistance over a large area outside the district. Nevertheless, like the Huaylinos themselves, the volunteers became frustrated over the lack of official activity in this part of the valley.

Huaylinos were, therefore, slow to recuperate their sense of well-being
and lamented the loss of political linkages under the military regime and the
unresponsive reconstruction bureaucracy in Huaraz. With most debris shoved
into convenient gullies by bulldozers, Huaylas appeared forlorn, as dust bil-
lowed in the wake of vehicles traversing the town en route to Huallanca and
beyond. Once the road through the Cañon del Pato was cleared in 1978, traffic through Huaylas virtually ceased, and the town was sadly tranquil. By
then, aside from several primary schools and a new municipal office, hope
that there would be more aid forthcoming from ORDEZA or other agencies

diminished. Moreover, the urban water system installed by ORDEZA was faulty and eventually had to be replaced. After 1979, the Huaylas migrant colony in Lima successfully raised funds to build a new church, and by mid-1980 work was underway with local volunteers and a few municipally paid laborers. Hopes brightened when a new engineer at ORDENOR proved to be a Huaylino who helped significantly in beginning the new church and in maintaining the roads.

For the most part the redevelopment agencies not only failed to provide support or technical assistance but managed at the same time to disempower local organizations and leaders. Over twelve years, Huaylas changed from a progressive and competent district to one which appeared stagnant and inept. Abetting this change were demographic changes: a 21 percent loss of population as discouraged individuals and families departed for the coast following well-established migration patterns (Doughty 1997), and a 41 percent drop in birth rate, the consequence of socioeconomic difficulties affecting everyone.

A typical phenomenon was the struggle over the distribution of limited resources in the absence of coherent management. In 1971, the Organization of American States offered to build forty houses in Huaylas at a time when about four hundred were needed. With no mechanism in place to make a fair selection of recipients, CRYRZA's ineptness led to bitter disputes that disrupted social cohesion. Huaylinos' demoralization was exacerbated when CRYRZA arbitrarily decided to place half of the "OAS" houses in another district. In 1980, there were still people living in the "temporary" modular multifamily housing in Huaylas, and remaining debris had hardened in vacant lots where houses once stood. Although the plaza and three adjacent streets were paved in stages during the 1980s, other streets show old cobblestoned portions in poor condition next to widened areas comprised of hardened earth.

During the first decade after the earthquake, some rural areas of Huaylas received considerable assistance from a fundamentalist Protestant group which sought to establish itself by offering agricultural services. Their proselytizing achieved little, however, and by 1984, their mission withdrew, leaving behind a very small congregation. Catholic Huaylinos were quick to comment that they "were already faithful Christians." The patronal feasts of the district were not held after the earthquake in 1970 (in July and August) because everyone was in mourning. The following year saw massive and impassioned participation, however, as the fiestas regained their central role in local culture and identity.

By the end of the second postquake decade, Huaylas remained dispirited, little resembling the vibrant cultural and social environment it had once been. The only noticeable progress being made was on the new "mother church," an ambitious concrete structure with twin towers, far larger than its predecessor. Its initial stages of construction were made possible by grants from a German bishops' fund and the continued contributions of the Huaylas migrant colonies in Lima and Chimbote. The project is planned and controlled by Huaylinos with parish priests playing minor roles.

Huaylas's decline in political effectiveness after the 1968 military coup was worsened by the autocratic redevelopment bureaucracy in Huaraz. The national paralysis caused by the threats and actions of the Shining Path (*Sendero Luminoso*) movement after 1983 further distorted political life, although the movement was not directly active in the district. In 1990, due largely to weakened political capability and the sour effects of the disaster, Huaylas was partitioned to create the new district of Santo Toribio—a move previously thwarted by the lack of local support and national influence (Doughty 1986: 243). Returning a last-minute favor, however, outgoing President Allan Garcia capriciously divided Huaylas, creating two smaller, antagonistic, and politically even less important places.

A NEW CATASTROPHISM

Although Huaraz province received the largest percentage of projects and assistance, after almost three decades ripple effects of the catastrophe had penetrated every domain of regional society, creating new problems on top of old ones. Such an earthquake produces wholistic impacts on society. It interrupts, destroys, and despoils life in many communities simultaneously, showering its effects on all sectors of the society. Its comprehensive impacts made it unrealistic to think that things would quickly be corrected. The old culture was destined to change significantly, however much some wished to restore it. The infrastructural components seem an easy place to start for any development project; how to strengthen and create viable sociocultural institutions is less clear and far more difficult. Thus, the propensity to give short shrift to sociocultural elements is commonplace in development activity, even though the failure to meet such needs produces frequent, well-documented problems and undesirable side effects over several years.

The nation and the world focused upon the dramatic impact of the quake and responded to it, seeking quick results. Of the U.S.$800 million spent on relief and recovery, 60 percent was expended during the first three to four years, leaving little for long-term redevelopment programs (Doughty 1986: 62). The comprehensive nature of the catastrophe throughout the valley was beyond the competence and resources of the regional authorities to manage, and led to significant changes in the power structure. The weaknesses of government were exacerbated by conditions, and local authority was usurped by national interests in the coordination of relief and rehabilitation tasks. Through its surrogate CRYRZA and its successors, the national government became more dominant in local affairs than was customary, assuming almost absolute control over the region for almost a decade, relocating populations, controlling reconstruction, and allocating all resources. The agencies also delegated the management of some programs and places to NGOs, further diluting the power and roles of legitimate local authorities.

Such policies resulted in badly relocated settlements in several districts; poor design and construction of buildings; and investments in unwanted or ill-advised projects. Over the long term they undermined the cohesion of several districts besides Huaylas. Despite governmental rhetoric about public participation, outsiders controlled and manipulated decisions at many levels. In Huaraz, a massive influx of eighteen hundred technicians and bureaucrats produced lasting repercussions in local political affairs. In Huaylas, where agency ineptness produced an extended liminal state, frustrations continued for years. In no case did the rehabilitation administration appreciate the need to fortify or create municipal organization as being critical to the recovery process, or, indeed, as part of a future mitigation strategy. Because Callejón society was so completely disrupted and disoriented, the absence of appropriate specialists in community development and institution building was a major omission in both the short- and long-term contexts.

Compounding the lack of support for local institutions was the intense competition over resources among needy communities and families, an upshot that should have been anticipated. In a poor nation with profound problems stemming from antagonistic ethnic, social class, and economic conditions, the victims were quick to apply "zero-sum game" principles to struggles over the "limited goods" in the form of relief and recovery supplies, as happened with the OAS houses in Huaylas. What one person received, others could not; one group or person was seen to benefit at the expense of others, since there was not enough for all. As a corollary, people further suspected that relief agencies and "authorities" were stealing and misappropriating resources, a belief that remains strong even today. The government's inability to deal effectively with this enormous catastrophe took considerable luster from the military "can-do" image. For example, the engineering battalion stationed in Caraz built a much-heralded bridge over the Santa River at Shupluy, only to have it virtually collapse a few months later. More importantly, the disaster forced the unplanned commitment of resources to the region amidst intense pressures from regional representatives.[9]

In organizational terms, municipalities are no more effectively equipped to deal with future earthquakes now than they were in 1970. Instead, because of the many struggles over resources, managerial ineptitude, and other failings real and imagined, public expectations for future success at mitigation are low. Unfortunately, this attitude conforms with long-standing negative perceptions of governmental efficiency and integrity held throughout the provincial areas of the nation, where failure to fulfill political promises is legendary.

Evidence accumulating over the decades indicates that communities which combined their resources with critical outside assistance on their own terms managed to recover with relatively rapid success. The people in the case studies cited tried, but were largely unable to do this. Mancos, adjacent to Yungay and Ranrahirca, did so. Often bypassed by officials en route to the avalanche zone and left largely to their own devices, the well-organized Mancosinos were energized to pursue their own recuperation, obtaining materials in an opportunistic manner from ORDEZA and restoring their homes and community. Of the badly damaged towns, Mancos stands out as retaining its character and the "flavor" of its predisaster ambience.

RECOVERING WELL-BEING

The well-being of individuals, families, and communities vies with property damage as the greatest concern in disaster contexts. After counting the dead and treating the injured, the sociopsychological stresses among survivors due to the loss of loved ones, lack of shelter, privacy, food, and information, pervasive insecurity, and diminished self-respect and authority lead to a questioning of beliefs and inability to predict what each day will bring. Numbed by grief, many after Peru's massive quake were helpless and dependent, living in a liminal context in which resort to excessive amounts of alcohol was commonplace, and entrepreneurs quickly met the demand (Oliver-Smith 1986: 103–104). The earthquake created many of the conditions known to be conducive to the formation of revitalization movements (Wallace 1956). That none developed was due perhaps to the available alternative of migration, and, whatever their faults, to the programs undertaken being sufficient to obviate a total breakdown of society. Many of the NGOs entering the scene during the early months represented religious organizations that probably provided a sociopsychological outlet for many on a temporary basis, as was the case in Huaylas.

Communities throughout the Callejón, however, carefully preserved the spiritual symbols of their collective identities. The need for community, as well as individual psychological well-being, concerned everyone, but psychoreligious needs were not encompassed in policies pursued by official agencies. These did not assist churches, although in the "premiere" disaster sites of Huaraz and Yungay, architects could not resist the opportunity to "make a statement." Elsewhere, this was not the case: People scrupulously salvaged the saints and religious paraphernalia and built temporary sanctuaries.

Emergency housing came in the form of modular barracks, tents, styrofoam "igloos," and sheet-metal roofing distributed throughout the Callejón. Intended to last for two to three years, over twenty-eight years later some of these structures and materials, even tents, are still in use. Extensive public housing projects were undertaken in Huaraz, Yungay, Taricá, Jangas, Carhuaz, and Catac, but in most places families were left to build their homes without credit facilities or advice in constructing safer structures. Apart from the use of reinforced concrete when affordable, most families rebuilt with adobe in the traditional manner. Redevelopment agencies might have given workshops to retrain builders and correct traditionally faulty construction practices.[10] Unfortunately, cultural and class biases among the agency's professionals precluded such thoughts: Improvements had to be the domain of qualified architects and engineers. Alas, these worked only with public housing projects or wealthy families.

On the positive side, the earthquake destroyed woefully inferior medical facilities, which were replaced by services and equipment that had been previously unavailable in the region arriving as part of relief donations. In particular, the Soviet Union's teams offered much-needed general medical treatment for two years after the emergency phase and left their equipment and hospitals for continued use in Huaraz, Yungay, and elsewhere. People eagerly used these services for all endemic health needs which had little to do with the quake. By the end of the first decade, greatly improved health facilities coming from international donations existed in all the provincial capitals, and many districts as well.

TWENTY-EIGHT YEARS LATER: A RETROSPECTIVE VIEW

Throughout the valley many projects begun by the four recovery administrations rest in partially completed states; some are functional, others not, and some are abandoned entirely. A fish hatchery in Marcará lay incomplete and abandoned for over a decade before local people made it productive. Similarly, some of the housing projects foundered before eventually being reorganized and occupied. The hog and ham project, funded by USAID in three communities, was too grandiose and inappropriate for local conditions to succeed. The expensive buildings were put to other uses or abandoned entirely within five years of their construction, remaining as monumental concrete curiosities.

Rebuilding and improving the avalanche-clogged roads stretching from the Pacific coast to the Callejón was a high priority for recovery. By 1978 the road from the coast to Caraz was widened and paved with asphalt, a vast improvement over the serpentine preearthquake dirt road that climbed the Andean wall and connected valley towns. The ruined Huallanca–Chimbote railroad was replaced by an unpaved road over the rail bed. Since then, the increase in vehicular traffic throughout the region has been constant, and the airport remains closed because of continued excellent bus service. The better roads also enhanced agricultural and general commerce and led directly to a continuous rise in tourism in the valley, with its associated services. As part of the redevelopment process, most of the Cordillera Blanca became part of Huascarán National Park in 1975, a centerpiece for the burgeoning international "eco-tourism" industry featuring high-altitude climbing, trekking, and nature tours. Today, Huaraz caters to the cosmopolitan needs of thousands of tourists who are radically transforming its old conservative ambience.

Along the highway near the city of Caraz on the site of the former airport, foreign entrepreneurs began flower production for export, made feasible by the paved highway. This industry has spread, providing wage employment for rural people, especially women, and playing an important, if serendipitous, role in the economy of the Callejón. Its emergence, however, was not forseen by redevelopment policies. The new road was pivotal in opening the valley to change, and, thus, it was the most successful investment of post-disaster dollars—proof of the old adage that "one good road is worth all the bureaucrats and their programs." Nevertheless, the road was never quite finished: The emergency Bayley bridges were replaced with modest concrete spans, and at the north end of the valley dirt roads remain poor and hard to maintain.

CONCLUSIONS

Great catastrophes can and do alter society, but it is obvious that their lessons are quickly lost. The colossal Mississippi floods of 1927, whose repercussions reoriented southern American agrarian society, economy, and national politics, are a case in point (Barry 1997). Could the experience of Peru's earthquake, whose national impact was even greater in its context, be remembered and taken into account to mitigate the effects of future earthquakes? Unlike most natural disasters, the 1970 earthquake is commemorated with significant monuments in Yungay and Huaraz, as well as thousands of tombs calling attention to the tragedy. There is a gap between the memories of the experience and actions to escape its repetition.

Avoiding inconvenient precautionary measures, people willingly accept risks by overpopulating the shores of rivers which regularly flood, living on the flanks of active volcanoes and on geological fault lines, and refusing to accept evidence of pending tragedy. They continue to pollute the air, land, and water with abandon. People seem resigned to "acts of God" despite the fact that human decisions constantly deepen the consequences of natural environmental processes, converting perturbations into cultural events as human disasters, that can, therefore, alter society profoundly, even mythically, for generations. As time passes, recovery efforts operate with less fervor and diminishing policy commitments. There is only a narrow window of opportunity in which to act before declining budgets and interest doom redevelopment programs.

Comprehensive events like the Peruvian earthquake of 1970 illustrate the need for commensurate action to mitigate forces that impact all domains of value in society, offering new options while closing old ones. The cases here illustrate that the management of power produces significant impacts on well-being, respect, wealth, and all other institutional areas. Programs that can bring about equity in access to and distribution of these items in post-disaster situations constitute a true measure of recovery success. Because disaster assistance often marks a zenith in the availability of development aid, it is scandalous that it should not be well managed and effective. Lack of attention to sociocultural and equity issues is an irresponsible act toward both victim nations and aid providers alike.

NOTES

1. Data come from my research in the Callejón beginning in 1960 and eleven times since 1970, most recently in 1997. From 1970 to 1975, with colleagues Anthony Oliver-Smith, Abner Montalvo, Brian Beun, and Rodomiro Vazquez, I coordinated a modest village-level assistance program in about fifteen different places using donations from anthropologists and others who knew the area prior to the quake.

2. There are five levels of political hierarchy in Peru: nation, region, department, province, and district, each with its own capital. Ancash Department, now part of the Chavin Region, includes the Callejón de Huaylas valley with its five provinces, thirty-three districts, and over twelve hundred small settlements.

3. The magnitude of Peru's disaster is appreciated in perspective to the United States, where proportionately it would have affected 14.5 million persons: over a million dead, 2.25 million injured, and 12.2 million homeless.

4. Barbara Bode's *No Bells to Toll* (1989), Marcos Yauri Montero's *Tiempo de Rosas y Sonrisas. Tiempo de Dolor y de Muerte* (1971), and Stephan Dudasik (1976, 1980) provide excellent analyses of Huaraz after the earthquake.

5. Yungay is capital of the province, with eight districts and sixty-eight villages. Yungay city is often wrongly reported as having twenty thousand inhabitants killed in the avalanche. Oliver-Smith gives a riveting account of the disaster in his book (1986) and in other writings (1977, 1979, 1982). Roberta Goldman also analyzed aspects of post-disaster development (1985).

6. I am indebted to Phillip Williams for his observations of the 1997 event.

7. The town of Huaylas is capital of the district of Huaylas, located in the Province of Huaylas, whose capital is Caraz.

8. Repair of the hydroelectric plant located in the 4,500 foot deep Cañon del Pato of the Santa river had high priority because it serves Chimbote and Trujillo (Doughty 1987).

9. Military government programs of land reform and industrial reorganization led the United States and others to halt or reduce assistance, forcing Peru into debt with new lenders such as the Soviet Union.

10. Adobe houses are made of four- to six-inch-thick, twelve- by twenty-inch rectangular dried mud blocks made on the house site. These are laid over stone footings with mud mortar and usually not held at the top by stringers and virtually never by trusses to hold the roof in place. Future earthquakes will produce the same effect as in 1970: The walls will move in separate directions; the heavy ceiling and roof will push downward from the center, forcing the adobe walls to collapse outward onto the street and crushing anyone present. Inside, the roof will fall on the occupants.

BIBLIOGRAPHY

Babb, F. 1989. *Between Field and Cooking Pot.* Austin: University of Texas Press.
Barnett, H. 1953. *Innovation: The Basis of Cultural Change.* New York: McGraw-Hill.
Barry, J. 1997. *Rising Tide: The Great Mississippi Flood of 1927 and How It Changed America.* New York: Simon & Schuster.
Belaunde, T. 1965. *El Perú Construye: Mensaje del Presidente de la República al Congreso Nacional, 28 de Julio, 1965.* Lima: Editorial Minerva.
Bode, B. 1989. *No Bells to Toll: Destruction and Creation in the Andes.* New York: Scribners.
Burger, R. 1992. *Chavin and the Origins of Andean Civilization.* New York: Thames and Hudson.
Dobyns, H., P. Doughty, and H. Lasswell (eds.). 1971. *Peasants, Power and Applied Social Change: Vicos as a Model.* Beverly Hills: Sage Publications.
Doughty, P. 1971. "From Disaster to Development." *Americas* 23, 5: 25–35.
———. 1976. "Social Policy and Urban Growth," in D. Chaplin (ed.), *Peruvian Nationalism,* pp. 75–110. New York: Transaction Books.
———. 1979. "A Latin American Specialty in World Context: Urban Primacy and Cultural Colonialism in Perú." *Urban Anthropology* 8, 3–4: 383–398.
———. 1986. "Decades of Disaster: Promise and Performance in the Callejón de Huaylas, Peru," in A. Oliver-Smith (ed.), *Natural Disasters and Cultural Responses: Studies in Third World Societies,* pp. 35–80. Williamsburg, VA: College of William and Mary.
———. 1987. "Engineers and Energy in the Andes: An Update," in H. Bernard and P. Pelto (eds.), *Technology and Social Change,* pp. 111–136, 369–373. Prospect Heights, IL: Wavland Press.
———. 1997. "Revisiting Lima's Migrant Regional Associations," in T. Altamirano and L. Hirobayashi (eds.), *The Regional Cultures of Latin America.* Society for Latin American Anthropology, Washington, DC: American Anthropological Association.
Doughty, P., with M. Doughty. 1968. *Huaylas, An Andean District in Search of Progress.* Ithaca: Cornell University Press.
Dudasik, S. 1976. "Community Response to Shared Tragedy: An Essay on the Disaster Utopia in North Central Peru," *The Florida Journal of Anthropology* 1, 2: 9–15.

———. 1980. "Victimization in Natural Disasters." *Disasters* 4: 329–338.

———. 1982. "Unanticipated Repercussions of International Disaster Relief." *Disasters* 6, 1: 31–38.

Gainesville Sun, "Earthweek: Diary of the Planet," p. 2D, November 11, 1997.

Goldman, R. 1985. *Planning and Development in a Post-Disaster Situation: The Reconstruction of Yungay, Peru.* Unpublished M.A. thesis. Gainsville: University of Florida.

Jones, J. 1997. "Development: Reflections from Bolivia." *Human Organization* 56, 1: 111–120.

Kinzl, H., and E. Schnieder. 1950. *Cordillera Blanca: Peru.* Innsbrück: Universitat-Verlag Wagner.

McClintock, C., and A. Lowenthal (eds.). 1983. *The Peruvian Experiment Reconsidered.* Princeton: Princeton University Press.

Oliver-Smith, A. 1977. "Disaster Rehabilitation and Social Change in Yungay, Peru." *Human Organization* 36: 491–509.

———. 1979. "The Yungay Avalanche of 1970: Anthropological Perspectives on Disaster and Social Change." *Disasters* 3: 95–101.

———. 1982. "Here There Is Life; The Social and Cultural Dynamics of Successful Resistance to Resettlement in Post-Disaster Peru," In A. Hansen and A. Oliver-Smith (eds.), *Involuntary Migration and Resettlement: The Problems and Responses of Dislocated People,* pp. 85–104. Boulder: Westview Press.

———. 1986. *The Martyred City: Death and Rebirth in the Andes.* Albuquerque: University of New Mexico Press.

———. 1996. "Anthropological Research on Hazards and Disasters." *Annual Review of Anthropology* 25: 303–328.

Ricker, J. 1977. *Yuraq Janka: Guide to the Peruvian Andes, Cordilleras Blanca and Rosko.* Part I. The Alpine Club of Canada and the America Alpine Club. Seattle: Pacific Press.

Smith, G. 1989. *Livelihood and Resistance: Peasants and the Politics of Land in Peru.* Berkeley: University of California Press.

Stein, W. 1961. *Hualcán, Life in the Highlands of Peru.* Ithaca: Cornell University Press.

Stepan, A. 1978. *The State and Society: Peru in Comparative Perspective.* Princeton: Princeton University Press.

Thompson, D. 1962. "Additional Stone Carving from the North Highlands of Peru." *American Antiquity* 28, 2: 245–246.

Wallace, A.F.C. 1956. "Revitalization Movements." *American Anthropologist* 58: 204–281.

Yauri Montero, M. 1971. *Tiempo de Rosas y Sonrisas. Tiempo de Dolor y de Muerte: Testimonio del Cataclismo Ocurrido en la Zona Norte del Perú el 31 de Mayo, a las 3 y 25 de la Tarde. . . , y de las experiencias y demás circunstancias desgarrantes, derivados a raiz de su brutal estillido, narrados por un sobreviviente de Huarás.* Lima: Editorial Ultra, S.A.

13

BHOPAL: VULNERABILITY, ROUTINIZATION, AND THE CHRONIC DISASTER[1]

S. RAVI RAJAN
University of California, Santa Cruz

ON THE NIGHT OF DECEMBER 2–3, 1984, A GAS LEAK FROM A FACTORY owned by the Union Carbide Company killed thousands of people in Bhopal, India.[2] For those who survived, the disaster has during the past fourteen years metamorphosed from a sudden calamity to a chronic cancer. According to some estimates, about half a million people continue to suffer today and remain in conditions of acute vulnerability (Kumar 1993; Mukerjee 1995; Dhara 1992; Cullinan et al. 1996).[3] This unrelenting social suffering, has, however, largely receded from public attention.[4] Barring the ritualistic reports datelined Bhopal in the first week of December every year, the potent malignancy of the chronic disaster is ignored by almost everyone but the survivors. The remembered Bhopal disaster is the gas leak from a pesticide factory run by a multinational company, not the day-to-day misery of half a million survivors. A state of affairs that should seem distastefully pathological, therefore, somehow appears normal, routine, and for the most part invisible.

This paper seeks to understand the processes that have normalized the pathological and erased the enduring disaster from public notice. It explores why Bhopal has gone from being the potent political issue that it was on December 3, 1984, to a private nonissue today, the exact opposite trajectory that many other disasters have traversed (Reich 1991). It also attempts to understand the factors that have produced and exacerbated vulnerability. It asks, in particular, why the relief and rehabilitation efforts in Bhopal failed so colossally despite the presence of trained scientific and medical personnel, a bureaucracy that in recent years has responded adequately to natural disasters, and a seemingly potent and active civil society.

The paper begins by considering the safety record of the multinational company, Union Carbide Company, its role in the creation of the accident, and the strategic politics that defined its responses at different stages. It then goes on to examine the state administration's economic and medical relief and rehabilitation efforts in the aftermath of the calamity. Finally, it explores the nature of the various civil society initiatives, including those by nongovernmental organizations, social movements, and anthropologists.

THE COMPANY

The Union Carbide Company was founded in 1898. The company entered India at the turn of the century and by 1983 had fourteen plants in the country, manufacturing an assortment of products including dry cell batteries, chemicals, and pesticides, with sales of $180 million. The company's Indian operations were conducted by its subsidiary, Union Carbide India Limited (UCIL). The parent U.S. company held 50.9 percent of UCIL's stock and exercised managerial control through its eastern division headquartered in Hong Kong (Dembo et al. 1990: 12–21).[5]

Union Carbide established its Bhopal plant in 1969 to formulate a range of pesticides and herbicides derived from carbaryl, a base chemical. The process of manufacturing this compound involves setting up a reaction between methyl isocyanate (MIC) and alpha napthol. Union Carbide initially imported these ingredients (Morehouse and Subramanian 1986: 3). In 1979, however, the company built an MIC unit within the existing Bhopal facility, which was located next to a densely populated neighborhood and a heavily used railway station. In doing so, it violated the 1975 Bhopal Development Plan, which had stipulated that hazardous industries such as the MIC plant be located in the northeast end of the city away from and downwind of the heavily congested areas. According to M. N. Buch, one of the authors of the development plan, UCIL's initial application for a municipal permit for the MIC plant was rejected. The company, however, managed to procure approval from central governmental authorities and proceeded to build the MIC unit in the midst of a dense urban settlement (CSE 1985: 216).

The risks already involved with such a siting were compounded by design and commissioning decisions the company then took. During the planning process, at least two basic issues came to the fore. One concerned the size of the proposed factory. Many in the UCIL preferred a relatively small plant adequate for the company's needs at that time, rather than something as big as the Union Carbide MIC plant in Institute, West Virginia (Dembo et al. 1990: 87). A second issue concerned the method of ingredient storage to be adopted. Again, many in the UCIL argued for a design that demanded only nominal storage of MIC determined by downstream process requirements on grounds that such a facility was inherently safer (Dembo et al. 1990: 87). The design engineers of Union Carbide in the United States, however, insisted on large-scale storage, a less expensive process, but one that was substantially more prone to risk (Dembo et al. 1990: 87).

According to Eduardo Muñoz, a senior executive of Union Carbide who had spent a decade in India, the company made its decisions concerning size and storage for a combination of three reasons. The first of these was strategic. Building a big plant meant that the company would, by virtue of having a large capacity, attain a comparative advantage over potential competitors seeking to enter the Indian market. Secondly, company executives usually delegated decisions about design to the engineers. The latter, however, had a penchant for designing plants that were large in scale and size. Thirdly, there was very little opposition to the design in India, in sharp contrast to France, where a similar design proposed by the same company had been retracted as a result of strong public protest.[6] The net outcome was that the plant built in Bhopal was large, with MIC storage tanks of a capacity of fifteen thousand gallons each (Dembo et al. 1990: 87).

Having decided to build such a plant, the company neglected to put in place many of the safety features that were present at a similar facility in West Virginia (CSE 1985: 207–208, 215–216). This was compounded by a management culture that did not pay much attention to safety, a point that was underlined by three Carbide experts who undertook an internal investigation in May 1982 (CSE 1985: 207–208, 215–216). Largely in response to an unsafe work environment, between half to two thirds of the engineers who had been hired when the plant was commissioned had resigned by December 1984 (CSE 1985: 207–208, 215–216).

As a result of the reduction in operator strength, the company was forced to use underqualified and underpaid workers to operate highly complicated and risk-ridden technological systems (CSE 1985: 216; Chouhan et al. 1994: 23–38, 55–60). While hiring these workers to undertake specialized and hazardous jobs, Union Carbide obligated itself formally to providing them specified amounts of advanced training. In practice, however, the company reneged on this. Several workers, realizing the hazards involved in running complex plants, therefore protested, insisting that the company meet its contractual obligation to provide adequate training (Chouhan et al. 1994: 30-35). At the same time, there was also a litany of accidents, some involving fatalities (Dembo et al. 1990: 86–101; Chouhan et al. 1994: 23–42). During this period the local press carried several articles predicting an impending disaster (CSE 1985: 216). There were also a string of worker protests demanding better and safer working conditions. The company's response to the protests, however, was to use strong-arm tactics to dispel what it saw as routine labor struggle (Chouhan et al. 1994: 31–38).

Why were better safety systems not put in place by the company? A com-

prehensive answer to this question demands an ethnography of Union Carbide's corporate culture, which has, thus far, proved difficult to conduct.[7] The
company's safety record, however, is public knowledge and provides some
important insights. The Union Carbide Company has a long record of environmental negligence in every part of the world throughout its corporate history. Among its worst excesses are some of the most infamous environmental
crimes of the twentieth century, including the Hawk's Nest tunnel incident in
the 1930s (Cherniack 1986), the Oak Ridge mercury contamination problem
from the 1950s (Dembo et al. 1990: 32–45), the Temik poisonings on Long
Island in the 1970s (Dembo et al. 1990: 46–52), and the Kanawaha Valley
pollution controversy in the 1970s and 1980s (Dembo et al. 1990: 53–68).
Union Carbide Company was also implicated in several other cases of environmental respect, in countries including the United States, Puerto Rico,
Indonesia, Australia, France, and India (Dembo et al. 1990; CSE 1985:
213–214). In the words of David Dembo, Ward Morehouse, and Lucinda
Wykle, "Bhopal was only the worst manifestation of 'callousness toward
human life.' In one tragic event after another throughout its history, its social
performance has reflected a similar callousness" (Dembo et al. 1990: 132).

There is a wider context to the company's negligence. There was, in
almost every case of negligence, a direct correlation between economic class
and vulnerability to the risks created by the company's safety procedures
(Dembo et al. 1990: 12–81). Furthermore, that vulnerability was reflected in
a lack of political power among affected communities to address the dangers
through institutionalized formats. In Bhopal this phenomenon was reflected
in the fact that Union Carbide workers did not have the wherewithal to mobilize adequate political support to ensure better and safer work conditions in
the plant (Chouhan et al. 1994: 31–38). Moreover, the company had acquired
a great deal of political power locally by employing or providing illegal favors
to the relatives of a number of powerful politicians and bureaucrats (CSE
1985: 216). Consequently, the state government often looked the other way
when Union Carbide violated environmental regulations or cracked down on
the worker protests (CSE 1985: 216).

The operational decisions taken by the plant management in Bhopal
thus preyed upon the political marginality of the community surrounding the
plant, putting into practice a risk regime that routinized their vulnerability.
The company's behavior in the aftermath of the gas leak further elaborated
upon this trend. To begin with, most people in India and abroad viewed the
accident as an aberration. The *Wall Street Journal* on December 10, 1984,
while expressing sorrow about the disaster, thus urged its readers to see
Bhopal as a blip in an otherwise great success story of the green revolution
and industrial agriculture. Such a perspective had a long genealogy. During
the period in which worker agitations and local news stories drew attention

to safety problems in the Carbide plant, the state labor minister, Tara Singh Viyogi, dismissed demands for relocation, stating that the factory was "not a stone which I could lift and place elsewhere. The factory has its ties with the entire country" (CSE 1985: 216).

In the absence of strong and widespread public pressure to act in the interest of the gas victims, the Union Carbide Company had a number of options on how to react to the gas disaster. It could have responded to the great human suffering with an attempt to contribute in some meaningful way to the rehabilitation effort. The company, however, decided that its principal responsibility was to its shareholders and that the disaster it needed to react to was not that of the survivors, but the threat of financial decline (Kurtzman 1987: 193–223). It is in part this decision of Union Carbide that led to the transformation of Bhopal from an acute calamity to a chronic disaster.

There appears to be a moral economy of pain that explains the company's decision to choose the shareholder over the victim. Although some of its executives might well have empathized with the suffering of the gas victims of Bhopal, as Eduardo Muñoz seemingly did, their corporate decisions appear to have a clear economic and moral logic. According to this, there are social mechanisms to deal with suffering, along with socially constituted methods of calculation and compensation. Institutions such as courts, in this view, can be seen as markets in which the price of pain gets negotiated and formalized into a settlement package by a range of agents including company executives, victims, lawyers, activists, the media, and governments. From the company's point of view, such a system is clearly advantageous in that it helps shift discussions about retribution from absolute and individual responsibility, as in death penalty cases, to a wider societal process of calculation involving not just the corporation but a host of other actors. Once moral blame is in this sense rendered fluid and negotiable, and when the various parties agree to enter such a market, a company can move to do what it knows best—minimize risk and maximize profit for its shareholders. The issue of morality itself is taken care of by the socially sanctioned market mechanism underlying the structure of negotiations between the various agents involved.

If one examines the impact of such settlements on the victims of disasters, however, a different picture emerges. The history of Union Carbide's other disasters indicates that the price of pain, as indicated in postaccident settlements following such a process, has generally not been decided on the basis of the quantity of absolute suffering. What has mattered instead is the relative economic and political clout of the various agents involved in the market of pain. Indeed, this market has worked for the company and against the victims whenever its opponents have been poor and weak. The lower the victim is on the power gradient, the less the settlement figure has historically been (Dembo et al. 1990: 12–80).

In the Bhopal case, the market of pain was formally entered into once the various parties decided to negotiate within the legal system. This process commenced when U.S. personal injury lawyers attempted to obtain the rights of representation from individual Bhopal victims (CSE 1985: 216–218). Subsequently the Indian government filed a lawsuit, following the passage of the parentis-patria act that gave it the sole right to represent the gas victims. Once the legal process began, the Bhopal story began to unfold in exactly the same way that many of Union Carbide's other cases had. The company began to act as a rational agent, focused on regaining viability in Wall Street. It therefore put in place a systematic response strategy toward this end, enacting a series of stock purchases, bond retirements, and personnel and salary adjustments (Lepkowski 1994: 29–30). The company, furthermore, emerged with a new leadership, not only young and energetic, but psychologically distanced from the accident and its implications (Lepkowski 1994: 29–30). The net result of these divestitures and management changes was that Union Carbide became, in its own words, "a more focused company—simpler in structure, more efficient and cost-effective, and a more aggressive and determined competitor" (Lepkowski 1994: 29).[8]

The restructuring of Union Carbide, however, had a clear impact on the gas victims. By all external criteria, UCC and its managers benefited from the Bhopal incident, as did UCIL. They had justification to close a burdensome plant, make aggressive moves to restructure both companies, and enhance management benefits. The irony was that a disaster such as Bhopal left its victims devastated but corporate stakeholders better off (Lepkowski 1994: 29–30).

The company's legal strategy was designed to complement its economic recovery plans. The framework of the approach was clear by the time Union Carbide officers met their shareholders in the spring of 1985. The company would reject any responsibility for the accident, implicitly attributing any technical and managerial problems at the Bhopal plant to its Indian affiliate. It would maneuver to have the trial shifted to India from the United States and, when that happened, aim for an early and inexpensive settlement. To this end, it hired a fleet of top corporate lawyers in addition to some of India's best attorneys. Moreover, a special unit was assigned the full-time job of overseeing Carbide's corporate and public relations strategies (Lepkowski 1994: 28).

Thus began a process of systematic erasure and denial, following a pattern Union Carbide had set in responding to other accidents in the United States and elsewhere (Dembo et al. 1990: 46–52). The company would first of all deny any responsibility for the accident. The strategy of denial soon evolved into a claim of employee sabotage, a claim so vacuous that it was subsequently abandoned (Chouhan et al. 1994: 61–70). It must be noted, however, that the company continues to this date to invoke the sabotage theory as the explanation of the accident in its dealings with the media and the public in the United States and elsewhere.

As a second aspect of its campaign of erasure, Union Carbide began to put the accident "in perspective" and blame the victim. As the Union Carbide works manager told the media barely fifteen days after the accident, "MIC is only an irritant, it is not fatal. . . . We don't know of any fatalities either in our plant or in other Carbide plants due to MIC" (CSE 1985: 206). The company subsequently claimed that the large mortality was due to a combination of undernourishment and a lack of education among the people affected. It also claimed that the persistent morbidity had to do with baseline diseases such as tuberculosis in the gas-affected areas and that the victims afflicted their plight on themselves by maintaining poor standards of public hygiene. Union Carbide also downplayed the potency of the gas in the media and in courts. Moreover, it sponsored research and data-gathering on the toxicological impact of the gas on the physiology of the Bhopal survivors, to counter the data of state hospitals and other NGO clinics.[9]

Union Carbide's third tactic of erasure was to divide public opinion by effective image management. It hired public relations companies, including Burson-Marsteller (B-M), the largest independent public relations company in the world and one with an impeccable track record for handling companies involved with disasters over the last forty years (Greenpeace 1992). This Washington-based giant with offices in more than ten countries was the company picked by Babcock and Wilcox in the aftermath of the Three Mile Island nuclear accident. It was also the company that had assisted A. H. Robins in its problems with the Dalkon Shield contraceptive device, Eli Lilly with the controversy over Prozac, and Exxon after the *Exxon-Valdez* oil spill, among many other such examples. It has, furthermore, been called upon by governments needing "issues management," such as the regime of Nicolae Ceausescu and the generals of Argentina (Greenpeace 1992; B-M internet website, http://www.bm.com).

With the help of agencies like B-M, Union Carbide launched a massive media campaign denying liability and blaming a host of others, ranging from workers to the Indian government and the gas victims themselves. It also managed to mobilize the U.S. media in this effort. The program *60 Minutes* in 1988, for example, portrayed Union Carbide as a victim of Indian politics (Lepkowski 1994: 37). Today, Union Carbide's internet site portrays the company as an epitome of the responsible corporate citizen while making almost no reference to either Bhopal or India (http://www.unioncarbide.com).

Union Carbide also employed political campaigning as part of its recovery strategy. When lingering criminal and civil cases continued to attract support from environmental, labor, and consumer movements internationally,

Union Carbide hired several prominent politicians to mitigate the political impact of these initiatives and to lobby the Indian government to settle without a protracted legal case. An important argument given in favor of a quick settlement was that it would send strong signals to the international corporate community that India offered a favorable business environment.

Union Carbide's post-disaster strategy paid off in February 1989. Against the spirit of an earlier attempt to settle the Bhopal case out of court, and without any consultation with victims or their representatives, the government of India offered a settlement package to Union Carbide. The terms totally favored the latter. In the aftermath of the accident, victims' organizations in Bhopal registered an injury claim of U.S.$10 billion, based on standards in the United States. The Indian government meanwhile claimed $3.3 billion. Union Carbide's initial offer was $300–$350 million, and the final settlement was $470 million. The ultimate cost to Union Carbide came to a mere 43 cents a share. In its annual report following the settlement, Union Carbide boasted: "The year 1988 was the best in the seventy-one-year history of Union Carbide, with a record $4.88 earnings per share which included the year-end charge of 43 cents a share related to the resolution of the Bhopal litigation" (Union Carbide Annual Report, 1988). The parent company then proceeded to sell its entire 50.9 percent shares in UCIL to the Calcutta-based McLeod Russell India Ltd., clearing the way for it to exit India without any further involvement with Bhopal (Chouhan et al. 1994: 174).

It has been argued by a number of scholars that the Union Carbide Company could have acted differently in responding to the Bhopal gas disaster. As Wil Lepkowski put it, "To Carbide, the settlement was a closure that allowed it to walk away from India, to evade the fuller atonement that moral responsibility implies. Bhopal could have been an opportunity for Union Carbide to display legal and moral innovation: a disaster one company decided not to back out on. Instead, it negotiated not a commitment to continuing stewardship at Bhopal, but an uncreative, even antiquarian, way of notarizing its moral responsibility for what was (and is) a unique ongoing tragedy" (Lepkowski 1994: 37).

Yet, the story of Union Carbide in Bhopal is not just a case of a multinational company gone wild. As argued earlier, there appears to be a deep structural logic to each of its actions, and this logic is embedded in a very specific culture that defines the social role of a corporation. A very good example of what this culture entails is in a paper by Harold Burson, chairman of Burson-Marsteller, in which he argues that: "being the professional corporate conscience is not part of the job description of other executives. It is part of the job description of the chief public relations officer" (Burson n.d.). Burson goes on to add that: "A corporation cannot compensate for its inadequacies with good deeds. Its first responsibility is to manage its own affairs profitably," and that:

"We should no more expect a corporation to adopt a leadership role in changing the direction of society than we should expect an automobile to fly. The corporation was simply not designed for that role" (Burson n.d.). Moreover, as Lepkowski points out, "There is a form of dishonesty, or perhaps more properly structural self-deception, built into the process of corporate reparation in a industrial disaster. Such a posture . . . may be unavoidable because liability is always just around the corner in any chemical operation. But it exists nonetheless, supported by two kinds of institutional pressure . . . the need to put the best face forward to shareholders . . . (and) the unavoidably litigation resisting character of the modern U.S. corporation which translates into the position 'we can make no mistakes that can be admitted to'" (Lepkowski 1994: 37).

Union Carbide thus acted according to established cultural practice of absolving itself by participating in the market of suffering. The fact that it could do so, that such a culture is in place to begin with, has to do with issues beyond just the company. It has to do with, among other things, the wider politics of corporate power in contemporary society, the weakness of citizens groups and governments, the global green-washing industry, and the politics of forgetting that the market of suffering engenders. The impact of all this on Bhopal, however, as had happened several times before in Carbide's history in the United States, was that the issue of the disaster was publicly closed in terms that favored the company and its shareholders. For the gas victims, though, it resulted in the perpetration of the chronic disaster.

THE REHABILITATION BUREAUCRACY

While corporate politics and the wider social structures in which they were embedded were important determinants in the production of vulnerability in Bhopal, they do not in themselves explain the chronic disaster. To understand why more than half a million people continue to suffer without any sign of hope, one must also systematically examine the governmental relief and rehabilitation effort in the aftermath.

One of the first issues such an examination reveals is the lack of capacity within the government to deal with a disaster such as Bhopal. To begin with, no obvious contingency planning existed to cope with an event such as a gas leak. There was no systematic governmental operation to evacuate people (CSE 1985: 209). On the contrary, it took no less than forty hours for the government to arrange the first coordination meeting of secretaries and heads of departments (CSE 1985: 218). The government also failed to ensure basic public health. Among other things, carcasses of dead animals were not disposed of effectively for up to three weeks after the gas leak, bringing a well-founded fear of a mass epidemic (CSE 1985: 218).

The government also failed to mitigate panic and communicate effectively with the people. On the night of the disaster, there was no attempt to inform the populace, either through the radio or other means, on how to react to the gas or what precisely to do. In the days that followed, the state radio began proclaiming normalcy instead of providing accurate information (CSE 1985: 218–220). In a context in which most people were acutely concerned about the air, the water, and the food they consumed, this led to a rapid loss of faith in the credibility of governmental information, creating an atmosphere in which rumors flourished and panic took root.

The governmental lack of capacity is, however, perhaps best illustrated by its inability to innovate while designing relief and rehabilitation programs. In the immediate aftermath, the government announced ex-gratia payments to the victims' families to help get them through the immediate crisis. It also arranged for the distribution of clothes, food, blankets, and other material goods. Such measures typify the established response to natural disasters in India. A few months after the accident, though, it became clear that standard governmental disaster management efforts were not going to suffice in Bhopal. Unlike floods or cyclones, which, although they are catastrophic events, are, however, amenable to stabilization and the restoration of normality by consolidated and rehearsed state intervention, the disaster in Bhopal refused to go away. It lingered beyond the first week and month and manifested itself in several persistent ways. Unlike floods or cyclones, the Bhopal survivors were permanently injured physically. This meant a crisis for the city's medical infrastructure, which was simply not designed for such large-scale morbidity. Furthermore, the continuing calamity posed a problem which the Indian bureaucracy's disaster management paradigm had never had to face on this scale before: to devise an economic rehabilitation strategy that was ergonomically viable and economically feasible. In short, the onset of the chronic disaster was a test of the government's ability to innovate.

The bureaucracy responded about eleven months after the disaster with a long-term strategy. Central to this was a program of economic rehabilitation. There were three broad aspects to the plan. Firstly, the government would attempt to attract firms to the Bhopal area and thereby create more jobs for the gas-affected. Secondly, it would set up production centers with the view of employing the victims in industries like garment-making, with the export market in mind. Thirdly, it would attempt to adapt for Bhopal a version of a stock governmental poverty alleviation scheme, the Special Training and Employment Program for the Urban Poor (STEP-UP), itself a derivative of the Integrated Rural Development Program (IRDP), the standard governmental poverty elimination scheme for rural areas. The STEP-UP program envisaged small loans for individuals to help them start businesses in either the retail or service sectors. The government would serve as a guarantor and a provider of training in skills, where needed (GMP 1985a; GMP 1985b).

These programs were, however, launched without without any realistic appraisal of what it took to attract capital, absorb labor in the production process, or market products. As a result, the economic program unraveled slowly but surely. The attempt at attracting firms failed right at the outset. The production facilities, too, quickly ran into trouble. Clearly, the government had overestimated, or had been plainly optimistic about, the market viability of these centers, a point that was soon driven home to the agencies that ran these facilities (Rajan 1988: 10). The STEP-UP program, too, failed for a set of related reasons. To put it simply, the local economy was not geared for this new spate of economic activity. To begin with, IRDP and STEP-UP schemes were not designed to be effective in contexts such as Bhopal, where there was an enormous number of claimants concentrated in a small geographical area. In a context where there was little or no buying power because livelihoods had been debilitated by the disaster, and with little other industrial or economic activity in the city and in its immediate hinterland, the small retail units and other businesses began to collapse and close down one after the other.

There were other reasons for the failure of the STEP-UP program. Foremost among these were the divisions between the rehabilitation bureaucracy and the gas victims engendered by economic and social class differences between these two communities. One illustration of the consequence of these divisions is the behavior of many bank officers. Already biased against poor people, they began to perceive the gas victims and the sheer volume of loan applications they had to process as needless and rewardless work inflicted upon them by the whims of bureaucrats and politicians. Among other things, bad debt recovery would mean a slow track for their own career trajectories. As one bank manager argued, "Tell me, whose disaster is this, theirs [the gas victims] or mine? I have enough work to do as it is. All these ignorant people keep pestering me without satisfying the procedures. If I am to attend to each of their queries, I shall be inviting a disaster" (Rajan 1988: 16).

Another reason for the failure of the STEP-UP program was corruption. An informal market sprung up around the entire relief apparatus, which extracted large chunks of what little the gas victims received. A complex governmental form combined with an illiterate gas victim, for example, created space for an unofficial scribe who charged fifty rupees as service charges to fill out an application (Rajan 1988: 17-18). A frustrated protest followed by an arrest could mean several hundred rupees to local policemen. Multiple

stages in the loan application process, with the accompanying hassle of document procurement, form filling, and lost time, could be reduced to a relatively
bearable process by a cash payment at existing market rates. At another level,
infrastructure projects aimed at public health or slum improvement offered a
vast opportunity for a wide range of agents to make money. The rehabilitation bureaucracy around the disaster actually proved to be one of the greatest
sites of institutional innovation, as middlemen systematically identified and
occupied a variety of service niches. Indeed, the disaster created an ecology of
opportunity for lower-middle-class entrepreneurs unaffected by the gas leak,
petty bureaucrats, politicians, and, in some cases, even unscrupulous NGOs.
The problem, however, was that these economies were built largely at the
expense of the victims.

These occurrences bear an important parallel. If one contrasts rehabilitation in Bhopal with most governmental poverty alleviation programs across
India, the events following the disaster do not appear pathological but quite
normal. The governmental rehabilitation program in Bhopal, in effect, ended
up creating a poverty alleviation bureaucracy, with all its attendant problems
of inefficiency and apathy. In doing so, the rehabilitation effort inadvertently
ended up routinizing the disaster. The chronic disaster mirrored the wider and
equally reprehensible phenomenon of chronic poverty elsewhere in the country. Bhopal thus was just a microcosm, reflecting the larger macrocosmic reality of the failure of the government as an agent of poverty eradication.

THE CULTURE OF MEDICAL PRACTICE AND RESEARCH

There are some important continuities between the medical and economic
rehabilitation programs. One of these was in the politics of class, as was manifest in the day-to-day interactions between the relief administration and the
gas victims. To the doctor and hospital staff, the gas victim was an illiterate,
working-class laborer, a double negative for a class-conscious mindset.
Equally important, by being recalcitrant in refusing to respond to treatment,
the victim was being a perpetual burden.

The failure of the medical rehabilitation program, however, lay also in a
host of other factors. Among them was a particular form of scientific hubris,
one that favored certain types of evidence over others. Women's gynecological
problems, for example, were systematically denied and repeatedly attributed
as "faking," "psychological," or "due to poverty and poor hygiene" (Sathyamala 1988: 50). Again, men's problems were attributed to "compensation
neurosis" or to wider social factors, such as baseline diseases. Underlying this
language was a cultural prejudice that privileged one form of knowing over
another. Subjective testimonies did not count.

Related to this was the prevalent culture of resolving scientific controversies. The classic illustration of this was the infamous "thyiocyanate contro-versy," which arose around the question of how to interpret the results of the autopsies of hundreds of bodies in the aftermath of the gas leak. To forensic pathologists such as Professor Heeresh Chandra, the person in charge of the autopsies, there were unmistakable signs of cyanide poisoning. This diagnosis led them to a policy prescription of detoxification, which meant the adminis-tration, through series of injections, of sodium thiosulphate, a known anti-dote for cyanide. The theory argued that the cyanide radicals would in time be eliminated through urine and that the victims would slowly attain normal-ity. This theory was seemingly supported by laboratory studies (Sathyamala 1988: 41–44).

The enlarged cynogen-pool theory was, however, opposed by a powerful local figure, Professor N. P. Misra, the dean of the Gandhi Medical College. He argued that his own examinations of gas victims indicated that the gas had affected only the lungs, causing fibrosis with the resultant hypoxia, a pos-tulation that was later titled the "lung fibrosis theory." He argued further that there was no evidence in the medical literature of the phenomenon of "chronic cyanide poisoning" (Sathyamala 1988: 41–43). The cynogen-pool and fibrosis theories, therefore, began to be fiercely contested by Professors Misra and Chandra, respectively the dean of the medical college and the head of forensic pathology. At stake were not only the personal egos of these two men but also the institutionalized rivalries between the two fields they repre-sented—those of clinical medicine and pathology (Sathyamala 1988: 43). One of Misra's main arguments against the NaTs therapy was that the existing record of NaTs showed that "while 60 percent of the cases showed subjective improvement," none showed "objective improvement," as opposed to his own treatment using bronchodialators, which, he argued, showed "objective evidence of reduced airway resistance" (Sathyamala 1988: 43–44). As Medico Friends Circle and other NGO medical teams repeatedly pointed out, "there was no reason why the two theories could not go hand in hand, why there could not be systematically coordinated treatment procedures that adopted a plurality of measures with systematic record keeping that would eventually lead to closure. But the power and the egos of the individuals and the unwillingness of the ICMR to interfere, prevented this from happening" (Sathyamala 1988: 54). The inability of the ICMR to intervene effectively during the thyiocyanate controversy raises yet another issue, of a wider fail-ure of India's premier medical body. In particular, what was missing was a coordinated procedure to translate the vast amounts of medical research that was conducted and published in leading medical journals into policy guide-lines on the ground level.

Like the economic rehabilitation program, the medical response was plagued by class and gender biases that prevented effective treatment. In addition, here, too, there was a total absence of both contingency planning and the ability to mount an effective response system. Also missing was a pragmatic scientific culture that would effectively channel research energy into result-oriented ends aimed at treatment. The result was a medical rehabilitation program that could do little to prevent the transformation of the disaster from the acute to the chronic.

THE ACTIVISTS

Given the complexity of the issues involved in the disaster, civil society responses in the aftermath required enormous tact, intelligence, and, most importantly, strategic sensibilities that recognized the politics of Union Carbide as well as the limitations and opportunities open in the rehabilitation bureaucracy.

The Bhopal gas disaster spawned a wide diversity of activist initiatives (Rajan 1988: 24–36). The most visible of the activist initiatives during the first two years after the gas leak was that of the Zahreeli Gas Khand Sangharsh Morcha (Poisonous Gas-Event Struggle Front). The Morcha saw itself primarily as a political movement. Judged by the backgrounds of its members, the Morcha was extremely heterogeneous. The rank and file included many motivated gas victims, as well as dedicated volunteers from smaller towns in Madhya Pradesh state. It also included middle-class activists from cities such as Delhi, Bombay, and Calcutta, mainly student environmentalists, feminists, and public health activists.

Despite its diversity, the Morcha cohered around a common approach borne out of a revolutionary, as opposed to a reformist, mode of politics. Underlying this perspective was a basic understanding. Disasters like Bhopal, tragic as they are, had revolutionary potential. They could help shatter the faith the masses had in the institutions of the state. Hence, an organization with truly revolutionary consciousness had to use the disaster to expose the Indian state and particularly its class composition, interests, priorities, and its collusion with multinational capitalist interests. In doing so, it could build among the common people a class consciousness that would in time create the objective conditions for a revolution.

With this approach, the Morcha devised a four-pronged strategy. It would mobilize the gas victims over issues that exposed the failure of the government to provide for them. It would create alternative data to counter what it saw as governmental and company attempts at erasure. It would present "people's plans" as alternatives to the governmental programs where appropriate. Finally, it would establish a network of organizations to debate and act on the "larger issues" raised by Bhopal (Rajan 1988: 27).

For more than a year and a half the Morcha succeeded in at least three of these four aims. It mobilized the gas-affected people; used such events to "educate" the people about their class identity; kept Bhopal in the news and exposed efforts at erasure by both the company and the government; and conducted socioeconomic surveys of sections of the affected population and collaborated with the Medico Friends Circle in conducting a medical survey. In addition, the Morcha started a People's Health Clinic and collected data on the effectiveness of sodium thiosulphate, information used to file a case against the government in the Indian Supreme Court. The case resulted in the appointment of a Supreme Court Committee on alternative medical relief, with representatives from governmental agencies and the NGO community (Rajan 1988: 26–28). The Morcha also succeeded in contributing to the national and, to a degree, international debate on the wider issues raised by the disaster.

The Morcha, however, floundered in certain crucial areas. Perhaps the most important of these was its failure systematically to address the issue of rehabilitation and the wider problem of growing social and economic vulnerability. In focusing on demonstrating governmental erasure, it blinded itself to the fact that the state government did in fact have a rehabilitation program, however badly designed. Given that denial was its starting point, constructive engagement and viable alternatives were never really part of its agenda.

Perhaps the most important reason for the Morcha's failure to tackle the issue of vulnerability, however, was the extremely doctrinal and inflexible ideology that framed its activism. Missing was a sense of pragmatism, a willingness to explore the gray areas between revolution and reform. Underlying such an attitude was an inability to see social suffering as a political category unto itself, as opposed to a mere manifestation of wider structural issues, such as the class composition of the state or the rapaciousness of multinational companies. There was arguably scope for a more constructive engagement with the state, an engagement that could have been part of a pragmatic strategy that did not necessarily mean reneging on its wider understanding. For all the corruption and apathy at the lower levels of the governmental bureaucracy, many in the state administration were genuinely concerned about the failure of their programs.

Moreover, with its connections to the Indian and, in some cases, foreign intelligentsia, the Morcha had the opportunity to commission research that could have helped provide alternatives to the governmental program, creatively politicize the question of vulnerability, and thereby help it remain a potent public issue. Had the Morcha seen vulnerability as an intrinsic political problem, it might have felt compelled to act in this manner, and this in turn might have changed the landscape of the chronic disaster. A political strategy based on pressing for the implementation of such alternatives might have given the Morcha itself a new lease on life and the basis for further mobilization. As it turned out, the Morcha declined in influence and was for all practical purposes extinct within two years of its formation.

With the Morcha's decline, another grassroots movement began to emerge, one that has endured to this day. It was different from the Morcha in that it was comprised entirely of the gas-affected people. Equally important, 85 percent of its members were women. It was therefore called the Bhopal Gas Peedith Mahila Udyog Sanghatan (the Bhopal Gas-Affected Women's Trade Union—BGPMUS). The BGPMUS grew out of the shop floor and the house floor where women manufactured commodities for sale for businesses set up under STEP-UP and other schemes, not all of which were related to the official rehabilitation program.

Much of the BGPMUS's activities have concentrated on material tangibles directly targeted at mitigating the members' collective vulnerability. For example, when the state government closed down a sewing center, one of its rehabilitation projects, the BGPMUS agitated until the government reconsidered and reopened the facility in June 1987, thereby providing twenty-three hundred jobs. Again, in the aftermath of the out-of-court settlement in 1989, more than five thousand women took the train to protest outside the Supreme Court in Delhi. This agitation eventually led to the filing of a review petition by the BGPMUS, with handwritten testimonies from thousands of gas-affected women (Basu 1994a, 1994b). The BGPMUS has engaged in many similar activities over the past decade.

Unfortunately, however, the BGPMUS has, with a few notable exceptions, not been supported by the wider Indian community in attempting to find lasting ways of mitigating the chronic disaster. While there has been some logistical support, helping it file court cases and helping arrange events such as the demonstrations outside the court in Delhi, this has failed to help address the fundamental concern that has sustained all of the BGPMUS's activities—effective rehabilitation. One is left wondering how different Bhopal might be today if the strength and the tenacity of the organized women had been matched by a technical ingenuity and commitment on the part of the rest of Indian society, especially its various institutions of science and social science, to suggest how a working rehabilitation program could be practically erected.

CONCLUSION: BHOPAL AND ANTHROPOLOGY

Herein lies a final moral of this story: the failure of Indian social scientists to articulate and put in practice a vision of rehabilitation. Since this is a book on the anthropology of disasters, let us examine what anthropologists did in response to Bhopal.

It must be noted, first of all, that there were very few anthropologists present in Bhopal. Those who did write on Bhopal basically presented a critique of the modern state and modern science. One of these interventions, by Veena

Das, concludes by making a point that is particularly relevant here. Das writes that the Bhopal case "has enough residues to create . . . a new understanding of suffering," the most important of which is taking "direct responsibility" (V. Das 1995). Das's analysis is, however, directed at what she calls the "existing theodicies of the state." By this she means the languages and methods by which agencies such as the bureaucracy, organized medicine, and the legal profession produce discourses on the meaning of suffering that "legitimize the producer of the discourse rather than the victim" (Das 1995).

What Das and her colleagues (e.g., Visvanathan 1988) fail to do is to extend this analysis inward to their own discipline and vocation. Anthropologists like Das and Visvanathan were active presences on the Bhopal scene. They were not only modest witnesses, keeping Bhopal alive on university campuses, but crucial allies for activists, intervening on their behalf and traveling to Bhopal on occasion to help release them from jail. Such acts, important as they were, represented only the efforts of concerned citizens acting out of a sense of moral duty. The extent to which they drew upon anthropology as a discipline was in helping articulate a critique of statist techniques and development policy, which was by no means an unimportant thing to do. They and the discipline were, however, silent on the tangibles that mattered for the people of Bhopal. With all good intentions, all they could do was create a new theodicy of suffering, one that was empathetic to the victim's plight but which was, nevertheless, as externalizing as that of the state or indeed the activist.

What anthropology failed to do, like the scientists, doctors, lawyers, and bureaucrats it accused, was to embrace direct responsibility and address the day-to-day issues that exacerbated vulnerability and sustained the chronic disaster. Ultimately, there is nothing that anthropology could offer to a theory of recovery or rehabilitation. What is striking is that no anthropologist did fieldwork in Bhopal that attempted to make a material difference in people's lives by exploring how a meaningful rehabilitation program could be established. What is equally striking is that such a research program was not even conceived. When one juxtaposes this with the failure of the rest of the social sciences, such as the failure of the Tata Institute of Social Sciences to complete a survey, or the lack of response by other social science institutions to the state government's initial call to formulate a rehabilitation strategy (Rajan 1988), one begins to see some more reasons for the persistence of erasure and vulnerability. Like the bureaucracy and the scientific and medical communities, social scientists, including anthropologists, lacked both the capacity and the paradigms to effect an adequate response.

Part of the reason anthropology could not provide an alternative was that it operated with big and awkward categories, such as "the state," "science," and "civil society." It failed to disaggregate these entities into something that could then be reassembled with problem solving as the objective. Crucially, it persisted with an epistemological position of "the other," commenting and criticizing but refusing to get its hands dirty. Anthropologists in Bhopal could well have attempted to intervene in the bureaucracy, pointing to the lack of adequate accountability structures, class biases, gender biases, and the absence of institutionalized methods of response. They could well have suggested alternative institutional arrangements that were socially sensitive. They could also have helped break the unconstructive and uncooperative relationship between the state bureaucracy and the various voluntary activist groups attempting to assist the victims. In doing all this they could well have invoked a notion of expertise to push the bureaucracy to listen and change. This idea of expertise, based on various recent historical studies of science and society (see, e.g., Jasanoff 1995), could have been reflective and sensitive without the hubris of the omniscient, and yet very potent.

All this, however, required a commitment to problematization with the view toward problem solving, rather than one of pure description alone. Ultimately, anthropology as art failed to transform itself into anthropology as science, with a wider notion of social experimentation. While anthropologists were willing to criticize institutions such as the bureaucracy for a lack of an ethnographic imagination, their own ethnography had a very limited political imagination and was in the end insufficient to prevent the disaster from metamorphosing from the acute to the chronic.

In the decade and a half after Bhopal, however, the political landscape has changed drastically. The power of corporations is rising at the expense of citizens, as the environmental and social causes in the various trade arrangements and proposals, such as the Multilateral Agreement on Investment, testify (Barlow and Clarke 1998; Grossman and Adams 1993; Valliantos and Durbin 1998). At the same time, the capacity of nation-states to deal with disasters such as Bhopal is decreasing. Besides, social movements, while being successful on specific issues and places, largely lack an alternative global vision. In this environment, anthropology has new challenges and opportunities. Understanding corporate cultures, for example, needs a major ethnographic effort. Again, anthropologists are well positioned to help create capacity in governments and bureaucracies, especially by building into these institutions an ethnographic imagination that will eventually help make them more sensitive and accountable. To what extent the discipline is able to embrace these challenges might well decide the fate of the Bhopals to come.

NOTES

1. I gratefully acknowledge a large number of people who made this paper possible. Among them are Shiv Visvanathan, who has encouraged and supported this work

for over a decade; and a number of other people in India including Dunu Roy, Imrana Quadir, Ravi Chopra, Shekhar Singh, Ashis Nandy, Satinath Savangi, J.P.S. Uberoi, Veena Das, and my parents. More recently, I have benefited enormously from conversations with Anna Tsing, Lawrence Cohen, Paul Rabinow, Ben Crow, Michael Watts, David Goodman, Margaret FitzSimmons, Sheila Jasanoff, Ron Herring, and Barbara Harriss. I am especially indebted to Tony Oliver-Smith and Susanna Hoffman for introducing me to the field of the anthropology of disasters and for their patience and encouragement, and to Anuradha Mittal for all her support during the gestation period of this manuscript. The mistakes therein are mine alone.

2. The exact number of deaths remains a disputed figure, though most sources point to a total in excess of two thousand.

3. The term "vulnerability" is used here in the way it has been in Blaikie et al. 1994, and refers to the diminished capacity of the Bhopal victims to "cope with, resist and recover from."

4. The term "social suffering" is used here in the sense it has been used in Kleinman et al. 1997.

5. Unless otherwise specified, "Union Carbide," "Union Carbide Company," and "Carbide" in this paper refer to both the U.S. parent company and the Indian subsidiary.

6. "Setting the Record Straight: A Conversation with Edward A. Muñoz, former Managing Director, Union Carbide, India." Interviewed by Joshua Karliner, Ebb-Tides.

7. A good example of this are the efforts of Wil Lepkowski (Lepkowski 1994).

8. At the end of its battle with the GAF corporation, Union Carbide had been able to divest itself of enough assets to file a bankruptcy claim under U.S. laws. GAF, however, made U.S.$81 million even though the takeover failed. The only losers were the victims (Chouhan et al. 1994: 122).

9. See several issues of *Bhopal,* the bulletin of the Bhopal Group for Information and Action, in 1986.

BIBLIOGRAPHY

Anil A., J. Merrifield, and R. Tandon. 1985. *No Place to Run: Local Realities and Global Issues of the Bhopal Disaster.* New Market, TN: Highlander Center; New Delhi: Society for Participatory Research in Asia.

Barlow, M., and T. Clarke. 1998. *MAI: The Multilateral Agreement on Investment and the Threat to American Freedom.* Foreword by Lori Wallach and Ralph Nader. New York: Stoddart.

Basu, A. 1994a. "Bhopal Revisited: The View from Below." *Bulletin of Concerned Asian Scholars* 26, 1–2.

———. 1994b. "Interview with Jabbar Khan." *Bulletin of Concerned Asian Scholars* 26, 1–2.

Bhopal, the Newsletter of the Bhopal Group for Information and Action (BGIA), 1986–present.

Blaikie, P., T. Cannon, I. Davis, and B. Wisner. 1994. *At Risk: Natural Disasters, People's Vulnerability, and Disasters*. London: Routledge.

Burson, H. n.d. The Role of the Public Relations Professional, *http://www.bm.com/files/per/PER-R07a.html*.

Cherniack, M. 1986. *The Hawk's Nest Incident: America's Worst Industrial Disaster*. New Haven: Yale University Press.

Chouhan, T., et al. 1994. *Bhopal: The Inside Story, Carbide Workers Speak Out on the World's Worst Industrial Disaster*. New York: The Apex Press.

Cordero, J. 1993. "The Epidemiology of Disasters and Adverse Reproductive Outcomes: Lessons Learned." *Environmental Health Perspectives* 101 (S2): 131–136.

CSE. 1985. "The State of India's Environment 1984–85: The Second Citizen's Report." New Delhi: Centre for Science and Environment.

Cullinan, P., S. Acquilla, and V. Dhara. 1996. "Long Term Morbidity in Survivors of the 1984 Bhopal Gas Leak." *National Medical Journal of India* 9, 1: 5–10.

Das, S. 1985. "A Worse Aftermath." *Economic and Political Weekly*, December 14, 1985.

Das, V., 1995. *Critical Events: An Anthropological Perspective on Contemporary India*. Delhi: Oxford University Press.

Dembo, D., W. Morehouse, and L. Wykle. 1990. *Abuse of Power, Social Performance of Multinational Corporations: The Case of Union Carbide*. New York: New Horizons Press.

Dhara, R. 1992. "Health Effects of the Bhopal Gas Leak: A Review." *Epidemiologia e Prevenzione* 14, 52: 22–31.

Douglas, M. 1992. *Risk and Blame: Essays in Cultural Theory*. London: Routledge.

Ferguson, J. 1990. *The Anti-Politics Machine*. Cambridge: Cambridge University Press.

GMP. 1985a. "The Bhopal Disaster and Its Aftermath." Government of Madhya Pradesh.

———. 1985b. "Bhopal Gas Trazdi—Rahat aur Punarvas." Government of Madhya Pradesh.

Greenpeace. 1992. *The Greenpeace Book of Greenwash*. Greenpeace International. *http://www.greenpeace.org*

Grossman, R., and F. Adams. 1993. *Taking Care of Business: Citizenship and the Charter of Incorporation*. Cambridge, MA: Chapter Inc.

Hazarika, S. 1986. *Bhopal—Lessons of a Tragedy*. New Delhi: Penguin, India.

Jasanoff, S. (ed.). 1994. *Learning from Disaster: Risk Management after Bhopal*. Philadelphia: University of Pennsylvania Press.

———. 1995. *A Handbook of Science and Technology Studies*. Thousand Oaks, CA: Sage.

Kleinman, A., V. Das, and M. Lock (eds.). 1997. *Social Suffering*. California: University of California Press.

Koplan, J., H. Falk, and G. Green. 1990. "Public Health Lessons from the Bhopal Chemical Disaster." *JAMA, The Journal of the American Medical Association* 264 (21): 2795–2796.

Kumar, S. 1993. "India: The Second Bhopal Tragedy. (Eight years after the accident, not one survivor has been compensated)." *Lancet* 341 854: 1205–1206.

Kurzman, D. 1987. *A Killing Wind: Inside Union Carbide and the Bhopal Catastrophe*. New York: McGraw-Hill Company.

Lepkowski, W. 1994. "The Restructuring of Union Carbide," in S. Jasanoff (ed.), *Learning from Disaster: Risk Management after Bhopal*. Phildelphia: University of Pennsylvania Press.

Morehouse, W., and M. Subramanian. 1986. *The Bhopal Tragedy: What Really Happened and What It Means for American Workers and Communities at Risk*. New York: Council on International and Public Affairs.

Mukerjee, M. 1995. "Persistently Toxic: The Union Carbide Accident in Bhopal Continues to Harm." *Scientific American* 272, 6: 16–17.

Rajan, S. R. 1988. "Rehabilitation and Volunteerism in Bhopal." *Lokayan Bulletin* v. 6, 1/2: 3–32.

Reich, M. 1991. *Toxic Politics: Responding to Chemical Disasters*. Ithaca, NY: Cornell University Press.

Sathyamala. 1988. "The Medical Profession and the Bhopal Tragedy" *Lokayan Bulletin* 6, 1/2: 33–56.

Valliantos, M., and A. Durbin. 1998. *License to Loot: The MAI and How to Stop It*. Washington, DC: Friends of the Earth.

Visvanathan, S. 1988. "Reflections on the Transfer of Technology: Notes on the New Panopticon." *Lokayan Bulletin* 6, 1/2: 147–160.

THE PHOENIX EFFECT
IN POST-DISASTER RECOVERY:
AN ANALYSIS OF THE ECONOMIC
DEVELOPMENT ADMINISTRATION'S
CULTURE OF RESPONSE
AFTER HURRICANE ANDREW

CHRISTOPHER L. DYER
University of Rhode Island

INTRODUCTION

THE ANTHROPOLOGICAL STUDY OF DISASTERS HAS BEEN DOMINATED BY A community and individual perspective. Receiving less attention from anthropologists has been the response of institutions to disasters. Institutional response to disasters from an anthropological standpoint necessarily involves the political ecology and ethnohistory of human populations under disaster conditions and is impacted by social and economic factors which combine to create what is identified as the "culture of response" (Dyer 1996).

The culture of response emerges from underlying traditional structures that have evolved as adaptations to disaster. Torry (1978) points out that many adaptations—or maladaptations—of the culture of response can influence the recovery process. Examples include administrative inefficiency that retards recovery (Baldassaro 1975; Nugent 1973; Levine 1995), fatalistic belief systems that jeopardize life (Sims and Baumann 1972; Kates 1971), and alien technology introduced to regulate hazards that pose new sources of danger (Flannery 1972; Dyer 1996; Lees 1975; Reidinger 1974; Van Der Schalie 1974; Obeng 1977; Torry 1978). The culture of response is also tempered by political economics when power relationships dictate access to disaster recovery resources.

An institutional culture of response to disasters constitutes one level of human adaptation to these disruptive events—whether they be technological or natural in origin. Most of the work done on institutional/organizational responses to disaster events has dwelt on issues of conflict—the "we-they dichotomy" (Hoffman 1995; McFadden 1991; Oliver-Smith 1979). It is rare when disaster assistance is guided by a well-informed and culturally appropriate plan of action. Frequently, disaster assistance leads to conflict, and in some cases inappropriate assistance can hinder the ability of a population to recover from a disaster state or can even increase vulnerability to future disasters (Dyer 1996; Haque and Zaman 1993; Rajan, this volume, chapter 13). In other cases, cooperation and mutual respect replace conflict, and a good understanding by institutional agents of local cultural, social, and economic environments allows people effectively to reduce long-term losses through the integration of communities, local leaders, and community-based organizations in the recovery process (Dyer 1996).

This chapter examines the culture of response of one institution—the Economic Development Administration of the United States Department of Commerce—to the post-disaster assistance needs of Florida communities and organizations hit by Hurricane Andrew in 1992. Only one other study (Kinkaide et al. 1991) has been conducted that evaluates the impact of disaster assistance in North America several years after the event. The evaluation by Kinkaide and colleagues reported on Alberta's disaster assistance program in reestablishing individuals, farms, businesses, and communities impacted by three disasters: floods in 1986 and 1988 and a severe tornado in 1987.

Based on an assessment of the success of post-disaster recovery projects three years after the disaster event (Dyer 1996), I evaluate the EDA approach and offer lessons learned on the nature of institutional response to disaster. EDA is assessed on measures common to disaster agencies worldwide, including the general criteria of cultural appropriateness, sensitivity to the needs of the poor and underprivileged, effective communication with local leadership, and creation of social, economic, and cultural capital that exceeds what existed in the predisaster environment. I critically review EDA's protocol of post-disaster assistance and comparatively analyze the impact of funded projects three years after the disaster event. Before presenting the case study, an overview of the disaster event is appropriate.

THE DISASTER EVENT

When Hurricane Andrew struck south Florida's coastline early in the morning of August 24, 1992, it became the most costly storm in United States history. The hurricane hit with winds in excess of one hundred seventy miles per hour, killed at least forty-one people, injured many others, and caused about twenty-billion-dollars-worth of property damage. The worst physical damage inflicted by Hurricane Andrew occurred in that portion of Dade County from Kendall Avenue (beginning at S.W. 88th Street) south to Florida City. The affected zone included the communities of Perrine, Goulds, Princeton, Naranja, Cutler Ridge, Kendall, the Redlands, Richmond Heights, West Perrine, Homestead, and Florida City (Figure 1). This area contained 8,000 of the 59,000 businesses in Dade County and 120,000 jobs, providing workers with an estimated personal income of $4.5 billion.

Small business was the principal economic activity in these areas. Sixty percent of all firms/establishments employed fewer than five persons each, and 96 percent employed fewer than fifty people. The service sector—including banking, insurance, hotels, health care, business personnel, real estate, and government—accounted for nearly 63 percent of employment. Agriculture, construction, mining, and manufacturing accounted for 13 percent. The areas most damaged by the hurricane accounted for approximately 12 percent of Dade County's thirty-eight-billion-dollar personal income and 14 percent of its 878,000 jobs and 59,000 businesses (Metropolitan Dade County 1993: 9).

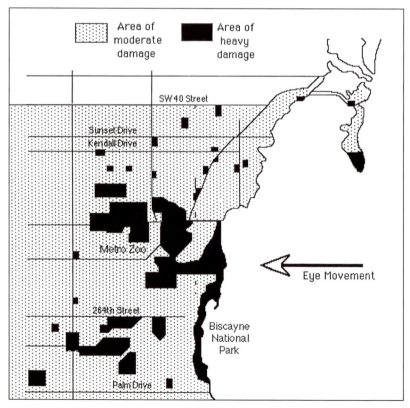

FIGURE 1. *Affected areas of Dade County, Florida.*

It is estimated that by April 1993, roughly eight months after the disaster, twenty-one thousand people were back at work in the hurricane impact area. However, 55 percent of those displaced by the disaster remained unemployed at that time. The areas south of 152 Street in Dade County and Monroe County were even slower to recover. Some 70 percent of the businesses in this area were still closed as of mid-1993. Only 16 percent of the jobs existing in this area were reclaimed by mid-1993. Those businesses that did manage to reopen struggled with the damaged infrastructure, which took months to recover.

In addition to job loss impacts, many people migrated out of the hurricane zone, which added to economic destabilization, including reduction of the local income tax base. The 1990 census recorded a population of 26,694 residents in Homestead, with the 1992 population estimated at 28,000. However, the population dropped by 40 to 50 percent after Hurricane Andrew. As of April 1993, the population had rebounded to 18,732 residents, according to the Bureau of Economic and Business Research at the University of Florida. Including seasonal visitors, the total population for April 1993 was estimated to be nearly 23,000. However, as of 1997—five years after the hurricane—the population of Homestead is estimated at three thousand less than its pre-Andrew count of 28,000 (Musilbay 1997).

Hurricane Andrew was accompanied by a devastating loss of infrastructure and organizational capacity. Over 125,000 homes were damaged or destroyed. Public buildings and private businesses were also destroyed or suffered severe damage. Power lines were severed, road signs were destroyed, and general chaos ensued until some twenty-three thousand federal troops provided relief and secured the area against widespread looting and other crimes (*Sun-Sentinel* 1992: 5 and 17; Anonymous 1993: 1–8).

One of the problems faced in south Dade prior to the hurricane was the absence of an established planning process and infrastructure between the municipalities and the county government (Beacon Council 1996). The absence of planning is most apparent in the disaster mode, where weaknesses in leadership and organizational capacity become revealed. Many of those responsible for administering city services and making decisions on the daily functioning of public facilities were overwhelmed after Hurricane Andrew, and the situation was compounded by a loss of a patterned routine and organizational capacity. Recovery efforts were hampered by the lack of partnerships and cooperative networks among the various level of government, municipalities, and private-sector decision makers.

EDA AS A DISASTER RESPONSE INSTITUTION

Providing strategic post-disaster assistance by investment of capital resources is an important role of EDA. EDA was created to stimulate growth in economically distressed areas of the United States through a strategic investment of resources under the Public Works and Economic Development Act of 1965 (PWEDA).[1] EDA is a public service agency dedicated to job creation through community assistance and infrastructure projects. EDA typically works with local-level entities—municipalities, county governments, quasi-public entities such as utilities and local development corporations, and public or private nonprofit organizations—to develop projects and offer grants for public works projects and revolving loan funds in both rural and urban areas. The agency also funds planning services and technical assistance to help communities create strategic development plans and conduct feasibility studies to overcome obstacles to economic growth.

Part of EDA's mandate is to respond to cases of, as the PWEDA legislation terms it, "a major disaster." The declaration of disaster must come from the federal executive branch as a presidential order that qualifies impacted regions and communities for federal disaster assistance from such institutions as the Federal Emergency Management Agency (FEMA), Housing and Urban Development (HUD), and EDA. Special congressional appropriations give EDA the means to furnish emergency assistance to areas struck by disasters and other economic crises, both natural and man-made. In the past several years, EDA has assisted communities throughout the United States in responding to hurricanes, earthquakes, floods, and military base closings. This chapter looks at its response to Hurricane Andrew and the impact of EDA assistance on the economy and communities of south Florida.

DISASTER, RISK, AND THE PHOENIX EFFECT

Social or economic risk after a disaster event can be increased by accelerated change in the economic and political landscape, including demographic shifts, loss of businesses, and shifts in labor skills/needs, economic priorities, and employment patterns, as well as the competing demands of various social groups (Clarke 1989; Freudenberg 1989; Perrow 1984). Counteracting post-disaster risk is partially achieved through careful planning that functions to maximize the benefits of invested recovery capital. Achieving a state of recovery that surpasses the original state and that creates new social, economic, and cultural capital beyond what existed before is here termed the "phoenix effect."

The phoenix effect is formally defined as: "a sustainable improvement in the social and economic condition of a community or organization arising from the strategic investment of capital resources after a disaster event" (Dyer 1996: 35).

To achieve this effect, the projects chosen for funding must provide long-term social and economic benefits that have the potential to rebuild and restructure the local economy in ways that, prior to the disaster, might not have happened as quickly or at all.

The phoenix effect is not an explicit goal or mandate of EDA funding, but occurs spontaneously as a socioeconomic process when project planning efficiently identifies key areas of strategic investment. EDA disaster experts select projects that in their judgment have long-term impact potential and that are good candidates for generating development funds from other public- and private-sector sources. Therefore, the initial EDA investments may act as an economic trigger to achieve results that might not have been achieved in the post-disaster climate.

The phoenix effect is hypothesized to arise from a community and institutional-level approach and is modeled on six cultural indicators of success identified in the assessment of the various funded projects. Noted as important by EDA in the project selection process, these are: 1) effective leadership, 2) effective progress, 3) job creation, 4) generating secondary resources, 5) creating partnerships, and 6) stakeholder empowerment (stakeholders are those targeted as beneficiaries of a project; empowerment includes any activity where stakeholders gain access to or control over resources for purposes of recovery from and mitigation of disaster impacts).

After Hurricane Andrew devastated parts of south Florida in August 1992, EDA devised a strategy to establish a presence in Miami and to help communities and organizations begin to recover. EDA funded thirty projects, including planning grants, revolving loan funds, infrastructure projects, building renovations and improvements, and training and technical assistance programs, for a total of over fifty million dollars. This chapter is based on an analysis conducted three years after Hurricane Andrew, of the effect of seventeen of the thirty EDA post-disaster assistance projects on the social, cultural, and economic recovery of communities, regional organizations, and community-level organizations in the impact zone.

To understand the interaction of project indicators, the EDA selection process, and impacts of selected projects on post-disaster recovery, we must first understand the operational culture of this disaster relief institution.

EDA'S OPERATIONAL "CULTURE OF RESPONSE"

EDA follows an operational culture of response that has evolved through several decades of post-disaster economic recovery activity. Beginning in the early 1960s with responses to hurricanes and floods, EDA personnel went to the field with the idea to bolster recovery but with little of a clear plan on how to do this:

> When we first started working with disasters, things were very disorganized. When Hurricane Camille hit the Gulf coast, we had a tough

time just getting down there. Roads and telephone lines were down, bridges were destroyed, and there was little left. We started work in a building with no roof. We put up a tarp, and it was a real big deal to be able to get a hot meal once in a while. We were climbing through half-destroyed buildings . . . places the locals wouldn't even go. . . . (Boyd Rose, EDA Regional Coordinator, Atlanta)

As EDA responded to various disasters, administrators refined its approach to coordinate with relief agencies such as the Federal Emergency Management Agency (FEMA) and the Red Cross. Initially, staff who took to the field found they lacked critical knowledge on economic infrastructure, engineering, marketing trends, and planning. Through time, specialists were hired who could provide on-the-spot assessment, work with local-level leadership, and provide necessary knowledge needed to evaluate recovery plans. The EDA staff supported each other on-site as they assessed the needs and reviewed the projects of the impacted area. This support system required that the staff remain on-site for the duration of time necessary to see projects through their funding approval phase. In the case of Hurricane Andrew, the site office in south Florida remained in operation for forty weeks. By staying on-site, agency personnel were able to work with local leaders and planners person to person. This contact was critical to the recovery process, for many local leaders, initially suffering from the trauma of multiple losses of place and resources, were at a loss as how to plan for recovery:

It was a shock to come in to work and find your office a disaster zone. The support structure was gone, everything was gone. No one knew how to begin making decisions—what to do first. We were in a state of shock. When the EDA folks came in, they forced us to begin planning. That got us going—gave us our sense of purpose back. (City Manager, Homestead, Florida)

EDA solicited knowledge of stakeholders in identifying the major elements of the local economy that were impacted by the hurricane. This information helped guide the selection process to insure that funded proposals best fit local recovery needs.

For the majority of assessed projects, EDA was instrumental in helping municipalities put the disaster in the context of broader economic processes. This allowed local administrators to organize their staff and resources toward the development of these economic recovery plans. To accomplish this, the relief team worked in a context framed by the social, cultural, and economic dynamics of a region. Its work was informed by on-site inspection of disaster damage, review of information on economic and infrastructure and social dynamics (taken from EDA economic district files), and an analysis of recent demographic trends (Boyd Rose, EDA Atlanta, personal communication). This included assessing the impacts of disaster events on existing community social and economic networks. Such networks extended beyond the immediate path of the Hurricane Andrew disaster. Core impact-area effects create a social and economic shock wave that ripples into the surrounding region (Dyer 1996).

With this knowledge in hand, EDA then targeted city managers, nongovernmental organization (NGO) presidents, and other likely proposal writers through invitations to a series of planning meetings. Advice was provided and recommendations made on how worthy proposals could be focused and improved. For infrastructure projects, on-site assessments were conducted. Those who conducted assessments were the same individuals who reviewed the related proposal and forwarded them to Washington for approval.

Funded projects were selected on their individual merits, not necessarily on their correspondence to a particular planning agenda. Although no bias existed in the letting of grant funds, communities with already established development organizations and effective civic leadership had an advantage. Similarly, those with less effective or little leadership, or those excluded from the political process, such as poor neighborhoods in Florida City and Homestead and Native-American tribes, had difficulty communicating their needs and recovery goals. EDA's stated goals for recovery were to 1) reestablish viable, balanced, residential communities in south Dade; 2) protect, restore, and build upon economic strengths and strategic assets; 3) expand and improve delivery of governmental relief and assistance; 4) rebuild support services; and 5) improve upon the built environment that was destroyed.

EDA selected thirty projects in four different categories with funding of $50,875,100. The four different types of projects funded included 1) planning grants, 2) public works/infrastructure grants, 3) technical assistance/business incubator grants, and 4) revolving loan funds (Table 1). These projects were selected from sixty-nine submitted proposals totaling approximately $130 million. Assessment of projects was accomplished by the utilization of the six criteria on which case studies are ranked. Guidelines for selecting disaster reconstruction projects after future disaster events were provided, and the criteria translated into assessments using the phoenix effect paradigm as a best- case-scenario model. Final selections were made by the project development team, which consisted of three field personnel and support staff in Atlanta and Washington, D.C.

ANALYSIS OF EDA'S FUNDED PROJECTS

The disaster recovery process EDA engages in is not equivalent to "normal development." The goal is to improve upon the predisaster state (Kent Lim, EDA Economic Specialist, personal communication). This is accomplished in

TABLE 1. *List of assessed EDA projects.*

Project Categories/Titles	Project Descriptions
Planning Grants	
Miami Convention and Visitors Bureau	$1 million to develop promotional materials/tourist marketing
South Florida Regional Planning Council	$200,000 for a strategic economic plan to promote international trade
Public Works/Infrastructure Grants	
Florida City	$5 million to replace and upgrade the city water treatment and distribution system
City of Homestead	$7 million for construction of water and sewer line and road improvements
City of Hialeah	$1.5 million for the rehabilitation of the old Hialeah train station into a farmers' market
Miccosukee Corporation	$1 million for public works infrastructure for commercial/residential development
Seminole Tribe	$1 million for public works infrastructure for commercial/residential development
Metro Dade County Parks and Recreation Department	$4.5 million to improve infrastructure of existing facilities and to provide additional facilities for expansion of the Metro Zoo
Metropolitan Dade County	$5 million to install water and sewer mains, sewage pumping stations, and fire hydrants along the Dixie Highway
Technical Assistance/Business Incubator Grants	
Tools for Change	$550,000 to provide technical assistance to minority businesses
Center for Health Technologies	$1 million to renovate a building for use as an incubator for health technology companies
City of Hialeah	$1 million for conversion of a manufacturing facility into a training center for computer technology transfer
Florida International University	$250,000 to fund training/technical assistance by the Small Business Development Center
Goodwill Industries	$1.5 million for building renovations and purchase of equipment to train and employ low-income/handicapped persons
Revolving Loan Funds	
Beacon Council	$2 million for a revolving loan fund to help businesses in Dade County recover
Beacon Council	$1.5 million recapitalization of existing revolving loan fund
City of Homestead	$2 million to establish a revolving loan fund to assist businesses in Homestead

part by the utilization of recovery criteria derived in a culturally appropri-ate—albeit not so described—fashion characterized by a close interface with community leaders and stakeholders in realizing feasible projects. This is rein-forced by project selection and review by the EDA staff. The assessed case studies can be ranked using the six criteria for project success. As noted, explicit, implicit, and discovered social, economic, and cultural criteria used to select and monitor projects included their capacity for 1) effective leader-ship, 2) effective progress, 3) job creation, 4) generating secondary resources, 5) creating partnerships, and 6) stakeholder empowerment. Not all criteria are appropriate to all projects. For example, job creation is not a primary goal of a planning grant. However, it is to be expected of the successful appli-cation of the resulting economic development plan.

Case studies were assessed both within and across the four categories of projects. It is important to note that the assessment of these case studies is for one point in time along a five-year continuum. Five years is the maximum allowable time for the completion (or total utilization) of earmarked EDA funds toward completion of any EDA post-disaster assistance project. Pro-jects that were unsuccessful at the time of assessment may now in fact be very successful. They also may not have improved, and if the five-year time period runs out, they may be terminated. Those that are presently successful are assumed to be economically sustainable. Table 2 ranks the projects across the six above-mentioned criteria, with 1 being the lowest ranking and 5 the high-est ranking. Values can range from a low of 0.2 (that is, all rated 1 or "poor" across all applicable categories) to a high of 1.0 (rated 5 or "outstanding" across all applicable categories). The comparative measure realized is the Development Quotient (DQ), defined as the measure of the overall develop-ment impact of a post-disaster assistance project.

An average DQ (with all criteria ranked as 3) is .60. This represents a value at which the project is "about as expected at this point." A DQ below .60 would indicate that the project development is less than expected at this point. Any score above .60 indicates a project above expectations at this point. Overall, project DQs presently range from a high of 1.0 to a low of .23. Projects with scores above .60 are suggested to have achieved the phoenix effect.

As shown in Table 2, eleven of the seventeen projects (69 percent) of the sample are exceeding expectations (above .60). For these projects alone, val-ues range from .63 to 1.0. The average score for this group is very high (.84). This indicates that most of the sixteen projects were well chosen and have accomplished much of what was planned for by EDA (e.g., created partner-ships and jobs and leveraged additional funds).

Five projects have DQs less than .60, indicating they are not meeting their expectations. Development quotients for this "below expected" category range from .23 to .53. The average DQ for this category is .42, which is well below the "expected" value of .60.

Projects that lie close to the .60 mark can be characterized as "average." These include the Dixie Highway commercial water project (.53), the Homestead Revolving Loan Fund (.52), and the Beacon Council (.60). All four of these scores are anticipated to rise as the impacts of these projects show effective progress. It must be emphasized that projects are evaluated at a single point in time and that lower-than-average scores are not necessarily a reflection of any project's future potential.

The criteria used to evaluate these projects and generate the DQ scores

TABLE 2. *Comparative development quotients for the assessed case studies.*

Project	Leader-ship	Progress	Jobs	Lever-aging	Partner-ships	Empower-ment	Total	
Development Quotients Planning Projects								
1 SFRPC	5	5	NA	3	5	5	23	.92
2 GMCVB	4	5	NA	NA	5	4	18	.90
Public Works/Infrastructure Projects								
3 Florida City Water	4	5	5	5	4	4	27	.90
4 Hialeah Farmers	4	3	3	3	3	3	19	.63
5 MetroZoo	5	4	4	5	4	4	26	.87
6 Homestead Water	4	5	4	5	5	5	28	.93
7 Dixie Highway	3	3	2	4	2	2	16	.53
8 Miccosukee	2	2	2	2	2	1	11	.36
9 Seminole	2	1	1	1	1	1	7	.23
Technical Assistance/Business Incubator Projects								
10 Goodwill	5	5	5	5	5	5	30	1.0
11 Tools for Change	5	5	5	5	5	5	30	1.0
12 HITPIC	4	3	3	5	4	3	22	.73
13 CHT	3	1	1	3	5	1	14	.47
14 FIU	4	5	NA	3	4	4	20	.80
Revolving Loan Funds								
15 Homestead RLF	2	3	2	NA	3	3	13	.52
16 Beacon Council	3	3	3	NA	4	2	18	.72

Scores can be interpreted as follows:
5 = outstanding—well above expectations at this point
4 = excellent—above expectations at this point
3 = good—about as expected at this point
2 = fair—somewhat below expected at this point
1 = poor—below expected at this point

will now be explored in the context of specific EDA projects from the anthropological perspective on disasters and reconstruction.

Effective Leadership

Lack of effective leadership is one of the most limiting factors in recovery from disaster. Poor leadership can not only delay recovery from disaster but also result in an increasing vulnerability to disaster impacts. Boyce and Hartmann (1978) record abuse of well construction aid by local leaders after flooding in Bangladesh. Actions of local leaders such as judges, magistrates, Members of Parliament, and union chairmen further marginalized the lot of victims as they took over deep tube wells supplied by the World Bank for themselves:

> Far from "trickling down" to the poorer majority, such aid actually makes them poorer. Made richer by his well, the landlord readily buys out smaller farmers when hard times befall them. (Boyce and Hartmann 1978: 240)

For the purposes of EDA, an effective leader was viewed as one who 1) articulates a vision on what project goals can be accomplished; 2) maximizes the availability of resources for the organization or community being represented; 3) maintains good communication between clients and the organization; 4) shares information on how to achieve project goals; 5) achieves the goals of a project within a time frame that maximizes the potential project benefits and allows for phoenix-effect-level impacts; 6) shares the responsibility with followers for achieving the goals of the project; and 7) is experienced in representing the organization/group due to receive EDA project funding (Dyer 1996).

The project leader for Goodwill Industries had thirteen years of experience as president of the organization when Goodwill received the EDA grant. He proved to be highly effective at maximizing the benefits of EDA building renovation funds through the use of refurbished building materials. His thrift allowed Goodwill to improve facilities beyond expectations. Effective leadership was also reflected in the job satisfaction of Goodwill employees and by the success of Goodwill in delivering quality garment products (memorial flags, fatigue pants, navy caps) to the Department of Defense (DOD) under a contract awarded after the hurricane. The leader's effective planning and organization also resulted in a thirteen-year contract with the *Miami Herald* for doing Sunday inserts. This increased both jobs and working capital for the organization.

Effective Progress

Effective progress, according to EDA, is demonstrated by projects that flexibly adapt to changing circumstances so as to move toward project objectives, even if this requires shifts in the original project timeline. Delays in project completion may be beneficial when they are due to improvements in project design or result in leveraging of secondary resources. Effective progress also means that the goals of the project are being fulfilled as planned.

EDA, in its role of providing local community infrastructure and NGO assistance after Hurricane Andrew, did not deal with the complex needs of individual home owners. Thus, its role was much more focused, and achieving effective progress tended to be less problematic. Still, lessons learned from the EDA experience have relevance in other cultural and organizational settings. In the assessment of EDA projects, a ranking system was developed that reflected the range of project success:

- Outstanding: Projects that were already completed and demonstrating benefits beyond expectations;
- Excellent: Projects that have been completed and delivered benefits as expected;
- Good: Projects in progress, or development delays were due to improvements in design or through efforts to generate additional funding;
- Fair: Projects that have just started or will start soon;
- Poor: Projects that have shown no progress and for which there is no clear schedule of when they will begin or be completed.

A project that achieved outstanding effective progress was the Homestead Commercial Water and Sewer Project. This project was completed on time, and its monies turned into significant outside funding for the construction of the Homestead Industrial Complex and Motorsports Complex. This infrastructure provides significant employment, capital, and tax benefits to the City of Homestead. Cultural capital has been created by the introduction of car racing as a recreational activity in south Dade County. Construction of both projects is complete, and hundreds of permanent jobs have been created for local residents. The Homestead Motorsports Complex inaugural race, held on the weekend of November 3–5, 1996, was attended by over sixty thousand people and was nationally televised on CBS. Commenting on the success of the project:

> The destruction of Hurricane Andrew was the catalyst for making this project come to fruition. The infrastructure provided to the sites allowed new businesses to be developed to replace those lost to the storm. This project could not have been realized without EDA assistance. (Director of Community Development and Planning, City of Homestead)

Local businesses that benefited from the event included gas stations, restaurants, local ice and paper product suppliers, and fresh produce and snack food distributors. Dade County initially committed $11 million to assist on-site improvements to the complex that have allowed it to be designed as a state-of-the-art facility.

Job Creation

Lost revenues, population, and economic opportunity are secondary impacts that can persist long after the disaster event. Job creation as a component of recovery from disasters is virtually unexplored in the sociology and anthropology of disasters. When economic losses are considered, they are done so as a measure of human failure to adjust to environmental hazards (Alexander 1993). Costs of reconstruction are the focus of economic recovery. Economic adjustment models (Russell 1970; Burby et al. 1991) have been developed which examine such things as annual costs and damages (Russell 1970), number of casualties per cost of strengthening buildings, and "cost per life saved" of strengthening buildings (Coburn et al. 1989). Yet, loss of jobs represents a major impact in any post-disaster economy. For example, the Bhopal disaster had long-term impacts on job and business recovery:

> In a context where there was little buying power because livelihoods had been debilitated by the disaster, and with little other industrial or economic activity in the city and in its immediate hinterland, the small retail units and other businesses began to collapse and close down one by one. (Rajan forthcoming: 28)

Post-disaster job creation is not a stated goal of FEMA, HUD, or any other disaster response agency. However, it is one component against which success of EDA post-disaster assistance can be measured. For EDA job creation was measured as the number of jobs predicted versus the number created. Job creation occurs when new businesses are created or old revitalized in the post-disaster recovery period. Examples of projects that are providing sustainable employment at or above predicted levels include Tools for Change, Goodwill Industries, and Florida City Commercial Water. Each of these projects created jobs above expectations.

Tools for Change, an organization providing small business loans to minorities, created or maintained jobs by providing technical assistance to one hundred forty businesses since the disaster event. In the process it generated over $16 million in additional loans. This was accomplished by careful utilization of $550,000 in EDA funds to pay the salaries of the technical assistance staff of the Tools for Change office. Technical assistance provided by the TFC team allowed clients to upgrade operations, hire new employees, or start new businesses. On average, each of the one hundred forty businesses counseled generated three jobs, for a total of at least four hundred twenty jobs. Jobs were

generated by business owners hiring new employees and by the business owners themselves being able to sustain their businesses. Most of those receiving
assistance were ethnic minorities who traditionally have a difficult time securing loans or improving existing business operations without outside assistance.

The Goodwill Industries lost over three hundred jobs when the Homestead Air Force base was destroyed and the local base store and restaurant
facility—staffed exclusively with Goodwill clients—was lost. The Goodwill
project directly generated three hundred jobs in its first two years of existence
with the Department of Defense (DOD) contract and an additional one hundred fifty jobs due to a new contract with the *Miami Herald*. It was predicted
that the project will also place twelve hundred individuals in the garment
manufacturing sector over the next eight years.

Not all job creation plans are, however, on schedule or have had the desired
impact. For example, changes in project design and administration for the
Hialeah Farmers' Market and the Industrial Teaching Factory have delayed the
job creation potential of these projects. Job creation is negatively impacted
when projects are delayed or lie dormant or when they are terminated. The
Center for Health Technologies project, which would have provided jobs in
health industries, was unsuccessful and proposed for termination.

Generating Secondary Resources

The multiplication of EDA funds into a secondary source of funding or
alternate resource (donated structures, technical assistance) is the mark of an
outstanding project. By this measure, an unsuccessful project would be one that
managed to leverage no additional resources or actually lost resource value.
Loss in value could be due to inflation accrued as the result of too- lengthy project delays or legally mandated changes in project design (e.g., post-disaster
changes in building codes). The degree of leveraging varies and can only be
compared on a project-by-project basis using the initial investment as a baseline.

Examples of highly successful leveraging of resources occurred with the
Goodwill project, the Hialeah Industrial Teaching Factory (HITPIC) project,
and the Homestead Motorsports Complex. Goodwill expanded its military
garment contract as a result of the EDA renovations, enabling project managers to attain high levels of productivity and quality control. The owner of
the *Miami Herald* was very impressed with these improvements. According to
the Goodwill president, it was this positive impression that lead to a thirteen-
year contract for newspaper inserts with the *Herald,* including one hundred
fifty new jobs and $7 million in associated renovations and equipment instal-
lation. EDA funds were also the trigger for Coulter Industries to donate a
structure to the city of Hialeah for the HITPIC, the project that established a
facility for instruction in the use of new industrial technologies. Without the
EDA funds in place, the donation would not have occurred. Also, the German

industrial firm Franhoffer would not have made an offer to the city of Hialeah to install and operate the instructional facility.

Cases where leveraging has been less than successful include the projects on the Miccosukee and Seminole reservations. For these projects, delays have produced no additional leveraging. Research into the dynamics of tribal action and past federal assistance after disaster events suggests that differences between Native-American cultural precepts and agency expectations have occasionally led to conflict over goals and expectations (Jessel 1995). While no such conflicts were reported to exist between EDA staff and tribal authorities, the overall context of relationships with the government did include conflicts with other agencies that led to delays in post-disaster assistance delivery.

Creating Partnerships

EDA views partnerships as the building blocks of post-disaster recovery. Partnerships allow for the development of economic networks that mitigate disaster recovery. Walker (cited in Dyer 1996) observes that developing cooperative networks can improve efficiency of post-disaster assistance, minimize waste of resources, and improve the quality of service delivered to disaster victims. In developing cultures, existing networks and adaptive mechanisms can allow for recovery from disaster without extensive outside assistance. In his studies of Turkana pastoralists, famine associated with drought was alleviated through support networks of in-laws and pastoral neighbors (McCabe 1990).

Partnerships can be local, regional, national, and even international. A variety of partnerships with national and international elements emerged after Hurricane Andrew. Projects such as the Goodwill Industries, the Hialeah Farmers' Market, the Hialeah HITPIC project, the South Florida Regional Planning Council, the Greater Miami Convention and Visitors Bureau, and Tools for Change all have linkages that extend beyond the local region. These are partly outcomes of the EDA planning process and are also the result of multiplier effects from the original investment of funds.

Projects that rank as average to poor on the creation of partnerships category include the Homestead revolving loan fund, the Hialeah Farmers' Market, and the Seminole Historic Village and infrastructure project. The Seminole project started late, so far realizing no partnership development. The Homestead revolving loan fund was delayed in startup because of changes in project managers. Partnerships are just now starting to develop as the initial loans are having an economic impact.

Stakeholder Empowerment

Stakeholder empowerment directly measures how effectively projects benefit community members by engaging them in project development and decision making or providing them with jobs, technical assistance, or public services. Much remains to be explored on how the social structure of communities and local organizations impact adaptation to natural disasters (White 1974; Burton et al. 1978; Kates 1971; Zaman 1994). To be effective, EDA recovery teams interact with local social organization in the decision-making process. The intent of EDA projects is to have community-level benefits (i.e., to promote the economic development of communities). This occurs most directly when community beneficiaries are involved in project planning and development. Stakeholder empowerment is indirect for those projects that provide infrastructure improvements or economic planning. Projects in progress are measured by their potential for stakeholder empowerment. Stakeholders vary for each project but are identified as those who receive direct or indirect benefits. Projects ranking high on stakeholder empowerment include Tools for Change, Goodwill, Florida City Commercial Water, and the MetroZoo.

The MetroZoo is a major recreational resource and tourist destination for south Dade whose stakeholders include zoo patrons, the Zoological Society, employees, service contractors, and suppliers. The effective use of EDA resources in zoo infrastructure repair was instrumental in its rapid reopening four months after the hurricane. Stakeholders such as the Zoological Society and the annual zoo membership actively participated in the zoo recovery process by volunteering time and resources to the zoo reconstruction process. Local residents used the zoo as a frequent recreational destination alternate to the more distant beaches of greater Miami.

Projects that remain incomplete or have been terminated rank lowest in stakeholder empowerment. In cases where projects are delayed, there is a loss of immediate stakeholder opportunity from planned jobs, public services, or technical assistance. This is the case in the Seminole Historic Village project. There is also the risk that extended delays may result in the termination of a project, giving no return to stakeholders (e.g., Center for Health Technologies). There are two negative effects here: 1) the loss of project benefits for the original stakeholder, and 2) the loss of time before funds are reallotted.

CONCLUSIONS

Disasters represent a disruption of the normal social and economic patterns of a community. Economic recovery in a disaster context differs from "normal" economic development. In many cases, particularly in developed regions, the reestablishment of the status quo can be considered an adequate or desired outcome. Initially, development resources are lost as priorities shift to deal with basic life needs. The point where outside development assistance is warranted occurs when the administrative infrastructure is sufficiently recovered for effective long-term planning to take place. Planning at this stage is a critical feature in surpassing status quo and realizing the phoenix effect.

The EDA post-disaster assistance program in the wake of Hurricane Andrew has been shown to achieve the phoenix effect for fourteen of seventeen (80 percent) assessed projects (Table 2). This was accomplished through a careful assessment of the post-disaster conditions, reliance on past experience in dealing with regional disaster assistance, and a thorough knowledge of the economic networks and political ecology of south Florida. The EDA approach fits well with what Torry calls "cultural translation." By this Torry refers specifically to enhancing communication between community and bureaucracy where victims comprise a minority ethnic or subcultural group. The EDA disaster recovery team worked through minority NGOs (Goodwill, Tools for Change) as well as among nonminority community organizations and groups (the City of Homestead), using the best available information on the socioeconomic and cultural context of the disaster regions. The idiom team members worked from arose out of their own experience in development of economic districts and from careful planning with and listening to local leaders and community representatives in the disaster aftermath. Their approach is consistent with recommendations of previous anthropological and sociological studies that stress the need to have someone on the scene who is capable of responding to local estimates of loss, assessments of needs, and reasoned projections of recovery rates for various economic sectors (Keesing 1952; Kiste 1968; Chambers 1970; Marshall 1976; Palacio 1976; Oliver-Smith 1996).

In Florida the on-site staff members became known to the organizations and communities they worked with in a manner that created social bonds and confidence more typically reserved for long-term community residents and civic leaders than outside government agents. EDA broke down the etic-emic barriers normally separating government relief agencies and disaster victims:

> The people we dealt with from EDA . . . were exemplary. They worked with us no matter what we asked of them. They know we had something special with this project in particular—that it had the potential to be a model for the rest of the nation. EDA was the trigger mechanism for the whole project. They didn't just have an idea— what they had was a vision. (City Manager–Hialieah, referring to the EDA-funded Industrial Teaching Factory Project)

EDA's "vision" was born in the early sixties in the era of the "Great Society." In this case, the Great Society philosophy translated into close and active participation in the creation and re-creation of social, cultural, and economic capital after a disaster event, in most cases achieving the phoenix effect. EDA staff working under this disaster assistance paradigm are shown here to be effective agents of post-disaster recovery. By crossing the barriers of institutional bureaucracy and reaching out to the communities, NGOs, and other organizations qualifying for assistance in the post-disaster scenario of Hurricane Andrew, EDA professionals acted much more like applied anthropologists than federal bureaucrats.

The EDA culture of response was least successful when dealing with disadvantaged populations (Homestead business incubator, Seminoles and Miccosukee infrastructure projects). Ironically, such populations are traditionally the ones of primary concern to applied anthropologists. Reasons for the failure of the EDA in these cases reveal potential inadequacies in the organizational post-disaster recovery model. As was stated, the most successful projects were often previously linked to EDA through "normal" (nondisaster) development projects. They fit the cultural "model" in being institutionally well matched to the structure and function of mainstream (core) social and cultural capital provided by EDA. For the less successful projects, cultural differences and lack of certain forms of leadership and infrastructure clearly hampered project success. In these cases, the problem represented by variant forms of local-level (community) leadership (from EDA norms) was exacerbated by the absence of project monitoring after the initial forty-week development period. Thus, critical to project success was the presence of a certain form of aggressive, individualistic leadership capable of effectively translating the goals and regulations of EDA into actions resulting in effective disaster recovery projects. Such leadership patterns were not found with the Miccosukee, who, because of diffuse leadership and management practices under their tribal form of governance, were unable to realize the benefits of their EDA project some three years after being funded. However, lack of such leadership, combined with inadequate social and economic infrastructure such as that found in the poorer neighborhoods in Homestead, possibly requires a different approach. In future disasters, EDA must find ways to work effectively with communities with diffuse leadership and management patterns in the implementation of disaster recovery projects. One approach might be characterized as "socioeconomic advocacy," where EDA assumes the focused leadership role that seems necessary under its model. If successful strategies can be developed to work with communities with disadvantaged social and economic baseline conditions, success for such marginalized cases of indigenous populations and poor minority neighborhoods would represent the ultimate phoenix effect.

Anthropology is the most holistic of the social sciences. Its perspective covers the gamut of adaptations and responses of human cultures to their biophysical, social, and built environments. The social and cultural responses of communities to the major environmental challenge represented by disaster constitute an important area for anthropological research. However, a major gap in our knowledge of disaster phenomena and response is at the institutional level of the disaster response agency. Little is known of the culture of response of contemporary disaster agencies. In fact, most U.S. government disaster response agencies resist external examination, preferring to conduct self-evaluations of disaster mitigation programs (John Feiser, EDA Economic Development Specialist, personal communication). As noted, the assessment of EDA (Dyer 1996), upon which this chapter is based was carried out only when a strong political threat to the institution from Congress was perceived by the EDA leadership (Kent Lim, EDA Economic Development Specialist, personal communication).

This study of the impact and response of the Economic Development Administration (EDA) in disaster recovery after Hurricane Andrew provides, I believe, important insights into a mostly unexplored territory of the anthropology of institutional response to disasters, particularly in their interaction with NGOs and community and regional-level organizations. It provides important lessons learned both in anthropological theory and praxis of disaster management that can be used to analyze and model institutional responses to disasters in other cultural settings.

Torry (1978) stresses the need for the construction of indices for loss and need in the appropriate direction of relief and compensation. In this study, the development of a scaled measure of project success (the development quotient) has application in cross-cultural settings where the measure of assistance impact can improve the culture of response of relief agencies. Also noteworthy are the importance of careful proactive planning for recovery, guided by an intimate knowledge of the social, cultural, and economic landscape of an impacted area, and the enlistment of local leadership in the recovery process.

NOTE

1. Public Law 89-136 USC 3121 et seq. (PWEDA).

BIBLIOGRAPHY

Alexander, David. 1993. *Natural Disasters*. New York: Chapman and Hall.

Anonymous. 1993. Untitled Editorial. *Aide* 24(1): 1–8.

Baldassaro, Larry. 1975. "Sicily's Earthquake Zone: Waiting in the Wreckage." *Nation* (September 13): 198–201.

Beacon Council. 1996. Annual Planning Report. Miami, FL.

Boyce, J., and B. Hartmann. 1978. "U.S. Aid for the Rich: View from a Bangladesh Village." *Nation* (March 4): 239–242.

Burby, R., B. Cigler, S. French, E. Kaiser, J. Kartez, D. Roenigk, D. Weist, and D. Whitington. 1991. *Sharing Environmental Risks: How to Control Governments' Losses in Natural Disasters.* Boulder, CO: Westview Press.

Burton, I., W. Kates, and G. White. 1978. *The Environment as Hazard.* New York: Oxford University Press.

Chambers, R. (ed.). 1970. *The Volta Resettlement Experience.* New York: Praeger.

Clarke, L. 1989. *Acceptable Risk: Making Decisions in a Toxic Environment.* Berkeley: University of California Press.

Coburn, A., A. Pomonis, and S. Sakai. 1989. "Assessing Strategies to Reduce Fatalities in Earthquakes," in *International Workshop on Earthquake Injury Epidemiology for Mitigation and Response,* pp. 107–132. Baltimore: Johns Hopkins University Press.

Dirks, R. 1980. "Social Responses during Severe Food Shortages and Famine." *Current Anthropology* 21, 1: 21–44.

Dyer, C. 1996. *Assessment of the Economic Development Administration's Post-Disaster Recovery Program after Hurricane Andrew.* Bethesda, MD: Aguirre, International.

Flannery, K. 1972. "The Cultural Evolution of Civilization." *Annual Review of Ecology and Systematics* 3: 399–426.

Freudenberg, W. 1989. "The Organizational Attenuation of Risk Estimates." Paper presented at the Society for Risk Analysis meeting, San Francisco.

Haque, C., and M. Zaman. 1993. "Human Responses to Riverine Hazards in Bangladesh: A Proposal for Sustainable Floodplain Development." *World Development* 21, 1: 93–107.

Hewitt, K. 1983. *Interpretations of Calamity.* Boston, MA: Allen & Unwin.

Hoffman, S. 1995. "Culture Deep and Custom Old: The Reappearance of a Traditional Culture Grammar in the Aftermath of the Oakland-Berkeley Firestorm." Paper presented at the annual meeting of the American Anthropological Association, Washington, DC.

Jessel, E. 1995. *An Evaluation of FEMA's Response to the Housing Needs of the Miccosukee after Hurricane Andrew.* Tampa: The Grey Group.

Kates, R. 1971. "Natural Hazard in Human Ecological Perspective: Hypotheses and Models." *Economic Geography* 47: 438–451.

Keesing, F. 1952. "The Papuan Orokaiva vs. Mt. Lamington: Cultural Shock and its Aftermath." *Human Organization* 11: 16–22.

Kinkaide, P., S. Bradley, and D. Kyba. 1991. *Alberta Public Safety Services: Evaluation of the Disaster Assistance Program.* Edmonton, Alberta: Emergency Preparedness Canada.

Kiste, R. 1968. *Kili Island: A Study of the Relocation of the Bikini Marshallese.* Eugene, OR: Department of Anthropology, University of Oregon.

Lees, S. 1975. "Oaxaca's Spiraling Race for Water." *Natural History* (April): 30–39.

Leighton, A. 1974. *The Governing of Men.* Princeton: Princeton University Press.

Levine, I. 1995. "A View from the Field: Operation Lifeline Sudan," in *Retrospective DHA 1995: Coordination of Humanitarian Assistance*, pp. 10–12. New York: United Nations Department of Humanitarian Affairs.

Marshall, M. 1976. "Typhoon Pamela, Uncle Sam and Political Competition in Micronesia." Paper presented at the American Anthropological Association meeting, Washington, DC.

McCabe, J. T. 1990. "Success and Failure: The Breakdown of Traditional Drought Coping Institutions among the Turkana of Kenya." *Journal of Asian and African Studies* 25, 3–4: 146–160.

McFadden, L. 1991. "Case Management versus Bureaucratic Needs: Earthquake Response in California." Paper presented at the annual meeting of the Society for Applied Anthropology, Charleston, SC.

Metropolitan Dade County. 1993. *Economic Recovery Strategies Phase One: Short Term Strategies*. Dade County, Florida: Research Division of the Metro Dade County Planning Department.

Miller, K., and C. Simile. 1992. *They Could See the Stars from Their Beds: The Plight of the Rural Poor in the Aftermath of Hurricane Hugo*. Disaster Research Center, Preliminary Paper no. 175. Newark, DE: University of Delaware.

Musilbay, A. 1997. "South Florida Still Recovering from Hurricane Andrew." *The Phoenix Republic* (August 24): 17.

Nugent, T. 1973. "After Buffalo Creek: Bureaucracy of Disasters." *Nation* (June 18): 785–788.

Obeng, L. 1977. "Should Dams Be Built? The Volta Lake Example." *Ambio* 6, 1: 46–50.

Office of the City Manager. 1996. *Metropolitan Report on Housing*. Hialeah, FL: Office of the City Manager.

Oliver-Smith, A. 1979. "Post-Disaster Consensus and Conflict in a Traditional Society: The Avalanche of Yungay, Peru." *Mass Emergencies* 4: 39–52.

———. 1982. "Here There Is Life: The Social and Cultural Dynamics of Successful Resistance to Resettlement in Post-Disaster Peru," in A. Hansen and A. Oliver-Smith (eds.), *Involuntary Migration and Resettlement*, pp. 85–103. Boulder, CO: Westview Press.

———. 1996. "Anthropological Research on Hazards and Disasters." *Annual Review of Anthropology*. Palo Alto: Annual Reviews Inc.

Ortwin, R., W. Burns, J. Kasperson, R. Kasperson, and P. Slovik. 1992. "The Social Amplification of Risk: Theoretical Foundations and Empirical Applications." *Journal of Social Issues* 48, 4: 137–160.

Palacio, J. 1976. "Post Hurricane 'Hattie' Resettlement in Belize." Unpublished research report. Department of Anthropology, University of California, Berkeley, CA.

Perrow, C. 1984. *Normal Accidents: Living with High-Risk Technologies*. New York: Basic Books.

Rajan, R. Forthcoming. "Bhopal and Beyond: An Anthropology of Relief and Rehabilitation Efforts and Prospects for a Socially Relevant Political Ecology of Disaster Management," in S. Hoffman and A. Oliver-Smith (eds.), *Culture and Catastrophe*. Sante Fe: School of American Research.

Reidinger, R. 1974. "Institutional Rationing of Canal Water in Northern India: Conflict between Traditional Patterns and Modern Needs." *Economic Development and Cultural Change* 23, 1: 79–104.

Russell, C. 1970. "Losses from Natural Hazards." *Land Economics* 46: 383–393.

Scudder, T., and E. Colson. 1982. "From Welfare to Development: A Conceptual Framework for the Analysis of Dislocated People," in A. Hansen and A. Oliver-Smith (eds.), *Involuntary Migration and Resettlement*, pp. 267–287. Boulder, CO: Westview Press.

Sims, J., and D. Baumann. 1972. "The Tornado Threat: Coping Styles of the North and South." *Science* 176: 1386–1392.

Sun-Sentinel. 1992. *Andrew! Savagery from the Sea*. Orlando: Sun-Sentinel Press.

Torry, W. I. 1978. "Bureaucracy, Community and Natural Disasters." *Human Organization* 37: 302–308.

———. 1986. "Economic Development, Drought, and Famine. Some Limitations of Dependency Explanations." *Geojournal* 12, 1: 5–18.

Van Der Schalie, H. 1974. "Aswan Dam Revisited." *Environment* 16, 9: 18–26.

White, G. 1974. "Choice of Adjustment to Floods." Research Paper no. 93. Department of Geography. Chicago: The University of Chicago.

Zaman, M. 1988. *The Socioeconomic and Political Dynamics of Adjustment to Riverbank Erosion Hazard and Population Resettlement in the Bramaputra-Jamuna Floodplain*. Ph.D. dissertation. Winnepeg: University of Manitoba.

———. 1994. "The Social and Political Context of Adjustment to Riverbank Erosion Hazard and Population Resettlement in Bangladesh." *Human Organization* 48, 3: 196–205.

VI

DISASTER AND CULTURAL CONTINUITY

DISASTER RESEARCH INEVITABLY ADDRESSES THE ISSUE OF CHANGE. DISAS-
ters disrupt physical, social, and emotional worlds. Disasters
cause loss and bereavement. Reconstruction after disaster is
fraught with difficulty and ambivalence.

Early research in disaster generally promoted the point of
view that calamities bring little social or cultural change.
Anthropology, however, with its tradition of long and on-site
field research and emphasis on social and cultural process, adds
new considerations to the question of calamity and sociocultural change. Anthropology brings to the forum issues of magnitude, how those affected are articulated into larger social
wholes, and the matter of long-run developments in such areas
as social organization, politics, ideologies, and knowledge.

Equally, anthropological investigation into disaster and
sociocultural change deals with cultural continuity, the fixed-
ness of society and culture and their resistance to change. In
some ways small groups and entire social cultural systems brace
against the alterations calamity ushers in. Yet, there are many
kinds of shifts that alter a society's composition without threatening continuity.

We consider the topic of change after a disaster as a summation to *The Angry Earth*. Every chapter in the volume in some
capacity deals with the question of social cultural change.

AFTER ATLAS SHRUGS: CULTURAL CHANGE OR PERSISTENCE AFTER A DISASTER

SUSANNA M. HOFFMAN
Independent Researcher

IN EVERY SCIENTIFIC INQUIRY THERE EXIST NAGGING QUESTIONS THAT ROUSE seemingly endless discourse. In the field of disaster studies, one such issue is whether after a catastrophe a culture and society change . . . or not.

The question is a burning and important one, which is why it has provoked continuous debate. Its import emerges from the number of contingent issues that surround it. For the leaders, dealers, and brokers of society, the changes that might occur in a society and culture after a calamity pique personal concern. Change can threaten vested interest or, on the other hand, betoken opportunity for reward. For the scientists who study the phenomenon, the question fires up long-running scholarly regards. It opens avenues to enlighten concepts about social change in general, to gain more understanding about human nature and actions, perhaps to fine-tune theory. For professionals whose aims are more practical, the answer can lead to mitigation of future disasters and devising viable, effective disaster aid.

For the victims of calamity, the matter of change or constancy impacts recovery. Implied is whether they can return to former circumstance, gain improved ones, or whether they are fated to linger in a sea of despair. The topic also encompasses a quest for satisfaction. Will the experience they endured come to naught or work to improve the horizons of those to follow? The wider inhabitants of a disaster zone suffer disquiet as well. Does the crisis mean a shift to a new social and ecological climate in which they, too, will have to make their way? Change or no change entails the intimation of adjustment and thus, for all the parties swept up in the amalgam of a disaster scenario, the question menaces and at the same time engrosses.

The concern extends to farther-reaching notice. In an era of vast globalization, the issue, in fact, looms large. Due to a number of causes—greater population, occupation of less safe habitats, more perilous technology, corporate hegemony—the frequency of events bringing tragic consequence to human communities seems to be on the upswing, and the nature of many events appears more destructive to humankind than that of former calamities. The homogenization of human habitat, governmental policies, technology, and culture, combined with the intense exploitation of natural resources, points to less elasticity among humans. The capacity of people to adapt to disasters, to contend with fluctuating or grievous circumstance, and to prevail seems in peril. Hence, numerous experts see the matter of whether human life ways alter in relation to critical phenomena encountered as indicating whether the species retains tensility or is "digging its own grave."

The debate over change in consequence to disaster runs on in part because the perspectives—more so than the parameters—of the argument vary and have been ill defined. At its barest bones, the question involves the concatenation of two sets of dichotomous variables, rather like those of a two-dimensional four-component graph, two possibilities to the top and two to the side. Beyond the initial question of whether changes occur at all, on the vertical plane lies the division of whether the changes resulting from disaster are minor or major. On the horizontal lies the polarity of whether such changes last or not. Woven together, four potentials result. Are the shifts small or large, superficial or significant? Do the seeming alterations abide for only a fleeting time or into the long run? In short, are the largely unexpected, sometimes exhilarating, sometimes discouraging, often opportunistic changes that appear to emerge as a consequence of calamity trivial or salient, temporary or permanent?

Many more elements enter beyond these bare bones, of course. Collateral to the core questions, for example, lies inquiry into what kind of changes take place and in what arena. Do the changes represent simple shifts in old patterns or utter rifts? Did the calamity initiate wholly new developments or merely accelerate processes already underway? Did the changes permeate the entire populace or subsume only a certain few? These issues, though, while ultimately important, are but shades and variations extending from the initial crucible.

So far, the points of view seem to depend somewhat on the body politic. The perspective that change does occur usually comes from the efforts of first-tier relief workers—those reconstructing the physical and human habitat—and victims in the immediate aftermath of disaster. To them, in the early days and dispositions of the event, the changes often seem major. Over time, though, they may appear lesser, rather like a pot of soup when the direction of stirring is reversed, with the same ingredients but differently settled. Still, some submit that real shuffling occurs. The view that little or no change takes place emerges from the purview of more distant analysts and agents, and often from the wider citizenry who move on with the truck of life as their fellows struggle. Whatever alterations seemingly emerge are not of great import nor pervasive. Life rolls on, reducing whatever small shifts and diversionary rubble a calamity stirs up into immemorable dust. Even victims sometimes concur. While still maintaining that they were personally transformed, in due course many assert that socially and culturally they have become living examples of an old adage: The more things change, the more they stay the same.

Differing viewpoints also arise from scientific discipline. There is among the researchers of disaster a certain segmentary opposition. In general sociologists, who have been the main discussants in the field, have held that disaster causes little social change. Indeed, until recently they considered the transformations that seemingly issue from calamity dysfunctional and argued that the predisaster situation, or "norm," should be returned to as quickly as possible. Quarentelli amended that stance and suggested that disaster be considered a catalyst for social change, not social problems (1987). The issue has been also been considered by anthropologists, the relative newcomers on the block, whose studies so far indicate a position somewhat in contradiction to prior sociological thought. Anthropology approaches the subject of human existence from a holistic and evolutionary point of view. The study looks not only at sociocultural factors, but environment, biology, adaptation, and constructed ecologies. On-site, minute, day-to-day research takes place in participation with a community. Often research is long term—very long term. It can continue over decades. Historical and archaeological records are explored (Kushner 1973; Hodder 1987). From this multifaced platform, the growing opinion of most anthropologists studying disaster is voiced by Oliver-Smith when he says: "any discussion of a disaster and its effects on a community must consider the issues of adaptation and change as well as the drama of impact" (1992: 14).

It is from this anthropological point of view that I enter the fray. I speak as an anthropologist who has personally endured disaster and encountered the shifts that transpired. I further observed those that faded or stayed through the evanescence of incident and time. I also enter as a researcher who conducted studies in a site that once underwent a truly cataclysmic catastrophe and has subsequently sustained continuous, albeit more circumscribed, rumbles. I have come to the persuasion a number of other anthropologists have reached (Torry 1978; Oliver-Smith 1992, 1996; Zaman 1989; Bode 1989; Button 1992; Paine 1992; Stephens 1995): What happens after a disaster depends to some extent on the magnitude and nature of the event, the size of the population, the complexity and background of the culture, whether one looks at small shifts or major change, and the long hand of time. From these vistas arrives the tenet that not only are there significant alterations in society and culture after Atlas shrugs, but even after Atlas merely shudders.

A BRIEF CONSIDERATION OF (A FEW) FACTORS

In this section I review a few of the factors that figure in the matter of social and culture change after catastrophe, more cataloging than analyzing them. After surveying these several "hinges" on which the issue, at least in part, swings, I present three short case studies, two main and one more narrow illustration. Of the main case studies, one outlines an extraordinarily immense calamity, the other a minor one. Without entering the debate between what constitutes society and what constitutes culture, I tackle whether calamity changes both. For the purpose of this perusal, as my introduction indicates, I follow tradition and falsely bifurcate them.

Matters of Size—Magnitude of Disaster, Population Mass, Amount of Damage

There have been occasions when truly massive social and cultural change took place as the consequence of disaster, that is, when an entire society and culture have been destroyed. The events that brought about such dire change were at times beyond mammoth. They were cataclysmic.

These instances are exceedingly rare, though perhaps they might also be rarely recorded. Quite possibly small groups of people with unique traditions have been eliminated by total or near-total destruction any number of times. Whatever devastation occurred, it was complete enough that survivors could not reconstitute their society, and as the happenings occurred before or outside written record, they have been lost to us. Within written record, most disasters chronicled, even huge ones such as Pompeii, have taken place within greater social milieus, and though the events were often momentous, with many deaths and great damage, the greater population persisted.

In conjunction with the far more common case of when a whole society is *not* destroyed, what the rare instances point out is that one element affecting the change disaster causes is size. In fact, three distinct aspects of size play a role: the enormity of the calamitous event, the relative numbers of the population impacted, and the extent of the damage wreaked. These three factors intertwine. The amount of change a disaster brings about at least in part depends on how vast the calamity is, that the population it falls upon is either significantly great or spatially contained in such a way that many or most are impacted, and/or how deep and widespread is its destruction to habitat, subsistence method, and possessions. These latter two can also be seen as levels and sorts of vulnerability amid the population.

In most disasters one or more of the three aspects is bounded, and the issue of change is thus brought into question. The disastrous event is of relatively small scale, narrowly localized, not catastrophic in extent. The impact falls upon proportionally few persons, perhaps an isolated group with a distinct cultural tradition, but more likely a small pocket or vulnerable segment of population within a larger social composite. The destruction is, one way or another, rapidly or after some time, redeemable.

In the contemporary world, because of greater prevailing social conglomerates, a disaster that once might have been large enough to destroy a culture and people now more likely affects a limited population within an entire societal whole. The question then becomes, does the loss or alteration of a small group affect the greater social and cultural evolution of the larger? There is as well another ominous qualification concerning size in today's entangled world. With far-reaching transportation, all-pervasive economics, and weakly controlled technologies, an "accident," small or large, in one place on the planet can affect, even eradicate, a people or their culture in another. Chernobyl illustrates. The effects of the nuclear meltdown have spread far beyond the local population and localized region and caused serious, possibly indelible, damage to the viability of the Sami culture of northern Norway (Stephens 1995; Paine 1992).

Some disasters are sizable enough to launch cultural change in a more curious fashion. They create legend. The notoriety of most disasters tends to disappear in short shrift, but occasional ones gain fame. What spurs the fame seems to be the illusion, more so than the reality, of scale again: specifically that the calamity destroyed a "whole" people or place. Atlantis shines in myth because the land and people are said to have completely disappeared. Pompeii echoes in tale not so much for the alterations it inspired in life ways, but because an entire city vanished. The San Francisco earthquake and Chicago fire also entered mythic vernacular as having swept away whole cities, which they did not. Legends in themselves modify life ways. They serve to remind people that untoward occurrences transpire and that peril persists. They suggest that perhaps precautions should be enacted.

Time and Change—The Diachronic Consideration

Change wrought by catastrophe also hinges on a dimension less tangible than size. It hinges on time.

As mentioned earlier, immediately after a disaster, to many—especially those experiencing the event—it appears that a host of changes occur, or will occur, in social formulations and habit. To those investigating a disaster months or years later, the opposite seems true, that little or no change eventuates. Consequently, a debate has arisen among researchers in which change viewed close to a disaster represents apples and change viewed far is oranges.

At the crux is, of course, how the two factors, time and change, have been juxtaposed and then examined, and that has been quite piecemeal.

Once the concept of vulnerability entered the exploration of disaster, a *rapprochement* concerning the two views of time and change began (see Hewitt 1983 and Blaikie et al. 1994). Investigators, anthropologists among them, began considerable assay into the long-term processes that lead to the imperilment of certain societies or segments of society. Few, on the other hand, have conducted studies of the long-term effects consequent to disaster. Such an investigation demands commitment to extended research, more the purview of anthropology than other social sciences. It requires that research take place where disaster has occurred, an infrequent occurrence, and that the research concentrate on the disaster and its effects. Rarely has any study covered the triplicate of time and change perspectives, that is, been in place to cover prior organization, the actual event, and the extended post-event eventuations. Notable exceptions are Oliver-Smith (1992), Doughty (this volume, chapter 12), and, although so far in the short term, Peacock and colleagues (1998).

Undeniably, society and culture are tenacious over time, else culture would not have arisen as a concept to explain the differing customs of a people and the continuation of those habits. Culture is carried by the people who share it, "in their heads" as Kearney points out (1984: 5), and even after a disaster their patterns, peculiarities, and understandings will reassert. Indeed, even anthropological studies have noted the return of the prior, indelible cultural stamp after a disaster (Chairetakis 1995; Doughty 1986: 35–80). What has escaped attention in the search for great shifts in society and culture is a focus on nuance. Most social and cultural change, save major revitalization, is near imperceivable, more mutability than leap (Wallace 1961). Also lacking has been a holistic perspective in correlation with time consideration. It was once thought that preindustrial societies in disaster zones lived under a "more or less continual reign of terror" from the threats around them (Sjoberg 1962: 36), that groups took little heed and made no accommodations to the hazards of their surroundings. Anthropological research has found, rather, that cultures everywhere, traditional and contemporary, take environmental dangers into account, developing mitigation and risk avoidance strategies over time that are reasonably effective (Torry 1978; McCabe 1988).

The key to a complete *rapprochement,* and a solution to the piecemeal debate, seemingly lies with the development of a multifaceted diachronic slide rule with which to view disaster. The basal rule is the long-term path of the culture through time, with marks denoting both era and incident. The slide in the center denotes the reformulation of quotients over time. The transparent movable lens above provides the examining principle that lets the researcher see into the cultural matrix as it shifts, i.e., change in traditions, ecological adaptations, political evolution. Investigators dissecting disaster need the entire slide from before to after, if possible. With such a slide rule comes the caution that the glide of reformation, despite occasional jolts, is slow and the fluctuations are usually subtle.

Deep Structure versus Surface Structure

Borrowing from the study of linguistics, the premise prevails in some realms of social science that culture and society contain two levels: surface structure and deep structure. Surface structure pertains to all the top-lying cultural minutia, particular customs and ceremonies, habits and practices. What is contained in deep structure are the invisible rules, how reality is organized and people, space, time, and other material are categorized. Surface structure, like sound bits and words, is the expression. Deep structure provides the grammar (Levi-Strauss 1963, 1966; Leach 1961; Douglas 1966; also see Bloomfield 1933; de Sausseur 1966; Chomsky 1957, 1969). As the underskeleton of culture, the deeply ingrained rules have been seen as highly constant, resistant, and slow to change. Surface structure has been viewed as mutable, more prone to transform, but in whatever guise, nonetheless organized by the principles below.

Marcel Mauss, a forerunner of this school of thought, proposed that the deep organizing principles of culture lay in the exchange systems: the trade of persons, or the kinship system; the trade of goods, or the economic system; and the trade of words, or language. He believed change took place only when one of these three fundamental systems was altered (1967). Applying this premise to disaster, change of true significance would occur only when one of the exchange systems was seriously impacted. Otherwise the shifts occurring constitute outlying fabric.

Following somewhat from Mauss, Levi-Strauss and other structuralists maintain that cultures contain deep-seated systems for ordering "reality." The underlying design pervades throughout social order and customs and is revealed on any number of levels. While overlying matter can change, the more profound organizing principles of culture are dogged. Levi-Strauss and Douglas, however, state that since the integrated whole of culture is ecologically founded, if the environment changes, all else follows (Levi-Strauss 1966: 15; Douglas 1970). Levi-Strauss finds that culture is a system of interlocking societal groups, but it is also a system of transformation (1966: 15). Structural or not, anthropology sees natural and human-made realms as interactive in ways other social scientists do not. Sahlins notes that if environments undergo change, cultures must respond anew to the changes set in motion (1964: 143). Nature and society are not two separate domains in external contact, but are intrinsically interlinked (Ingold 1992: 51). Clearly, disasters, both natural and technological, entail environmental change. Kroll-Smith and Couch specify the differing effects of the two sorts. Natural disasters rarely affect the long-term relationships between humans and their biophysical environments but alter a community's built and modified environment. Technological disasters disrupt the exchange between humans and their biophysical environment but result in comparatively little damage to built and modified environments (1991: 362).

Whether the changes that occur in society and culture after a disaster are deeply structural or more superficial bears import for whether the changes are significant or enduring. Changes in the grammar of society would constitute profound modification, alterations that would enter the fixed and ongoing warp of the people. Variation in surface structure carries more transient implication—that changes are vacillation, not mutation.

In argument that the changes that appear to erupt after disaster are surface structure, some have compared disaster to rites of passage. Van Gennep, in analyzing these transitional rituals, describes them as only seeming to bring alteration in position, rules, and other matters, while in fact the structure of society and culture remains unchanged (Van Gennep 1960: 13). Van Gennep, of course, was referring to cyclical, repetitive events, known and expected by all. Still, disaster in areas prone to chronic calamity is similarly, though not specifically, periodic. Drawing on Wallace's discussion of revitalization movements (1956), disasters are viewed by other researchers as instigators of essential change, or alterations in deep structure. The transformations calamities bring become the new structure of the society, for every catastrophe is at some level unexpected, each turbulent to its victims, and each initiates renovation.

Striding the line between deep and surface structure, the changes that occur after a calamity can also be seen in terms of Bateson's concept of ethos. Bateson defines ethos as "a culturally standardized system of organization of the instincts and emotions of the individuals" within a particular culture or group (1958: 118). The ethos of a society is obstinate but also mutable. This double edge is demonstrated by societies that, upon disaster, slide into a state of nostalgia, occasionally to the point of "mummification." The people, sometimes displaced, retain a stubborn hold on old, frequently no longer appropriate, cultural ways. Yet, in so doing, they undergo a drastic alteration of spirit (Foster 1985; Stewart 1992). Even without severe nostalgia, Bode comprehensively depicts the changes in psyche experienced by the communities of Yungay and Huaraz after the 1970 avalanche in Peru (1989).

Clearly, tradition both small and large can alter or transform after a calamity. While generally the anthropology of disaster deals only with natural and technological disasters, excluding warfare, colonization, and holocausts, a mere fifty years after the Jewish holocaust that terrible occurrence has found inclusion in Jewish religious liturgy. Forrest (1993) cites the genesis of anniversary in the aftermath of calamity. Doughty records the loss of celebration (this volume, chapter 12). Marris, meanwhile, claims that change in energy, fervor, and courage accompanies all loss (1974), and Erikson documents salient and permanent alterations in temperament and lifestyles for all the various communities he describes as having undergone what he calls "a new species of trouble" (1994).

Catastrophe as Revealer More than Changer

Cultures are in some sense like hands of cards in a game of stud poker. Some cards are up and thus "show"; some are "in the hole" and therefore hidden.

The query has been raised as to whether disasters cause change or whether they instead act to display a culture's hidden aspects. When catastrophe upends a culture's cards, are matters altered or merely disclosed (Garcia-Acosta 2000)?

It has been suggested that disasters function as the closest thing a student of society ever approaches to a natural laboratory. Calamities take a people back to their core, and in the rubble remaining, a researcher can behold the fundamental constructs that underpin the social world and, thread by thread, observe the web of the world and worldview as they are spun again. Many aspects of a society and culture are unclothed in the aftermath of a disaster. The workings of kinship, alliances, and institutions come to the fore. The varied dominions of biology, economy, and social practice appear. Groups form and divide. Authority arises and meets contestation. Precepts show their shape and relevance. The fact that calamity reveals hidden aspects of society and culture, however, often provides people the motive to alter the conditions. Looking at long historical records, Garcia-Acosta argues that as well as revelation, calamity gives birth to transformation and adjustments. After the massive Mexico City earthquake of 1985, for example, a new mindset about vulnerability suffused the Mexican population. For the first time, institutes have been formed to study the perilous mix of geological and human situations and programs enacted to mitigate the conditions (2000). Undeniably, throughout history there have been attempts to alter physical dangers that disasters exposed. Rivers have been diverted, architecture amended. The challenge has now been extended to the social factors that engender catastrophe.

Challenge, Contestation, and the Cultural Commonwealth

Cultures are always in the process of change. Diversities emanating from the vicissitudes people confront, by their very creation, filter into the cultural corpus. Responses to challenges, innovations of new objects or ideas are taken up by members of a culture and passed along. Slowly, and sometimes rapidly, the new joins the old and filters into the cultural goods held and shared by a community.

Such is the hypothesis various traditional definitions of culture and cultural change have put forth. Wallace declared that, though basically stable, culture operates in a state of moving equilibrium, ever shifting over time with accepted innovations brought about by invention, acculturation, or diffusion (1961: 143). Whether having a vitality above and beyond the persons who carry it or not, Kroeber defined culture as modifying over time in consequence to meet circumstance (1948). Kluckhohn viewed culture as a system of knowing that, while it does not modify easily, nonetheless alters (1964). Turner found that free human action, shaped by a well of experiment and innovation, engenders social and cultural change (1961), and Kearney stated that "cultures and societies exist in history, through time, and are constantly self-creating by responding to historically given conditions" (1984: 5). Some new definitions of culture are more dynamic and present culture as less unified and coherent, giving heed to the fluidity and contestation that arise within populations.

Within this view of culture as ever changing, the sorts of drastic fortuities and dramatic alterations a disaster creates are particularly the kind prone to filter into the cultural whole. Disasters set a critical stage, both bringing out and igniting arenas of contestation within society. They are great motivators of social action, and social action motivates change. People do not sink into inertia in calamitous situations. They react. New groups and leaders emerge. As disasters cause numerous difficulties, they require departure, adjustment, and answers. They throw into stark light inequalities, struggles over power, the social as well as the physical matters that imperil and increase dissatisfaction. They raise questions of a metaphysical nature. They frequently accelerate processes of change already underway.

On the other hand, in response to challenges and contestation, disasters also often promote cultural preservation and resistance to change. In particular when issues of redistribution of goods or power arise, the forces behind the status quo revive. All in all, disasters present extraordinary examples of the fluid quality of culture, the invention and reinvention of cultural goods, the areas of harmony, disjuncture, inconsistency, and coherence.

As culture from this point of view by necessity vacillates according to the alterations people must make, whether the fluctuations are short term or long, deep or surface structure, the result of any aspect of magnitude, makes little difference. Each permutation potentially distills into the prevailing cultural commonwealth. Culture can, indeed, be likened to a huge vat of dye, blended from many strands of pigment. Any alteration people make adds a drop of tint to the overall mixture. If major change happens and the shift amends the lives of many, the drop, perhaps, alters the hue significantly. If the variation that takes place is slight and taken up by only a few, the barely perceptible stain that then results nonetheless constitutes a minute shift in shade. The changes can be immediate or incremental. Either way, the new circumstance people face as a consequence of disaster and the adaptations they make, including conservation, would join the components of understanding, knowledge, and experience. Passed down to others, the newly introduced becomes part of "the way things are done."

Instances seeming to substantiate how changes from calamity filter into the whole exist. Poniatowska, in concurrence with Garcia-Acosta, points out that culture has changed in Mexico in the short time since the cataclysmic 1985 earthquake. Matters were in flux in Mexico anyway, especially in the political arena, but anger peaked with the revelations of corruption in building practices and lack of recovery aid. Consequent to the quake, far more social awareness of vulnerability entered the social structure and politics of Mexico (1995). Robinson and colleagues further describe the emergent groups that arose after the Mexican earthquake and caused the government to change policies drastically (1986).

ONE SMALL ISLAND—TWO DISASTERS

The island of Thera, where I have worked for the last thirty years, lies in the Aegean sea some seventy-two miles north of Crete. Though part of the Cyclades, Thera differs from surrounding islands, for while they are mountaintops, Thera is a volcano. As such, the island presents a case of two drastically different disasters. The one involves a colossal eruption that occurred some twenty-five hundred years ago, the other a far lesser incident, an earthquake occurring forty years ago. Both entail change, the first momentous, the second ostensibly trivial yet ultimately substantial. Each bears elements of magnitude, the factor of time, level of structure, revelation, and the acquisition of new cultural habits.

Thera is a relatively rare although not unique sort of volcano. It builds up over approximately twenty thousand years, usually in a round, almost perfect cone shape. Then, having walled itself in, it experiences a tremendous eruption in which the entire top blows away and the caldera collapses (Ninkovitch and Heezen 1965; Georgalas 1937). Thera experienced just such an explosion in around 1623 B.C.E. The volcano burst, the caldera imploded, and almost the entire land mass of the island sank back into the sea. The eruption of Thera was seven times larger than Krakatoa's, an event that on August 28, 1883, unleashed a huge tidal wave—one hundred and twenty feet high—and blast projectory, killed thirty thousand people in coastal towns on surrounding islands, suffocated crops and foliage for thousands of miles around, and left so much detritus in the air—a cloud of ash seventeen miles in altitude—it caused brilliant sunsets as far away as Chicago for over three years (Galanopoulos 1958, 1969; Doumas 1983; Mavor 1969; Pellegrino 1993).

As traces of Theran pumice stone imbedded in far-distant Mediterranean cliffs reveal, the tidal wave emanating from Thera's eruption rose seven hundred feet. Thera's explosive blast swept south and eastward with incalculable power. Every coastal town on the shores and islands of the eastern Mediterranean was most likely demolished, with only inland communities surviving. Thera itself, what was left of it, was buried under forty feet of pumice, a dry porous crust so thick it obscured all former occupation (Fouque 1869, 1879; Galanopoulis 1969; Doumas 1983; Pellegrino 1993).

There were, indeed, occupants. At the time of the eruption, the Minoan civilization dominated the eastern Mediterranean, and Thera itself held a Minoan city of approximately twenty thousand inhabitants. The Minoans were a seafaring people, traders and nautical warriors who plied many routes across the surrounding waters. They built a number of cities on the islands and mainland of what later became Greece, most of them at water's edge to provide them port. The island of Crete just south of Thera seems to have been their center, although some speculators surmise their capitol might have been tall, then-cone-shaped Thera itself. Certainly Crete held the civilization's major cities, most on the northern coast facing Thera. The largest and apparently most powerful Minoan city, Knossos, lay there. Archaeologists had always wondered why Knossos as well as other Minoan cities had fallen inward and why, shortly thereafter, the Minoan civilization abruptly ended. Discovery of Thera's cataclysm explained why (Dickinson 1994; Evans 1921; Marinatos 1939, 1948, 1950; Martin 1996; Willets 1977; Wilkie and Coulson 1985).

People did survive. A few inland settlements of the Minoan civilization, such as Phaistos, remained relatively undamaged. Those at sea, it is conjectured, might have ridden out the tidal wave. They would hardly know one passed beneath them unless they were near enough land to view themselves sailing higher. Perhaps even inhabitants of Thera survived. The citizenry seems to have heeded forewarning earthquakes and left. No bodies have been found in the ruins of the Minoan city (one was found by Fouque on the adjacent island of Therasia) and a small junk-filled room seems to indicate someone tossed in a heap of broken objects, such as might have tumbled in a tremor, and closed the door. Presumably, however, the unlucky souls of Thera merely moved to another Minoan community, not realizing how imperiled they remained (Fouque 1869, 1879; Doumas 1983).

What is clear is that those people who did survive had few of their own kind left. There was some short-lived rebirth in Minoan cities, a bit of rebuilding, some walls replaced. But largely, it appears, survivors joined with communities of Greek settlers who were infiltrating at the time. Early Greek communities suddenly experience a burst of art and pottery-making of Minoan style. Greeks apparently also took over decimated Minoan cities, for abruptly in Minoan towns, Linear A, the language that prevailed prior to the catastrophe and as yet untranslated, was replaced with Linear B, an early

Greek. The continuation of Minoan cities that seem to linger on, appears, therefore, to take place with a new and largely different population. Shortly after, the Minoan civilization disappears altogether (Bennet 1990; Chadwick 1987; Coles and Harding 1979; Dickinson 1994; Drews 1988, 1993; Sandars 1978; Ward and Joukowsky 1992; Willets 1977; Wilkie and Coulson 1985).

The destruction and disappearance of the Minoans was so complete that by the time of the blossoming of Greek civilization, no memory or record existed that anyone had lived in Greece before. The Egyptians told Solon, the first great Greek leader, on his historic visit to Egypt that he was an ignorant bumpkin who did not know his people occupied a land that had held prior inhabitants. Nothing was known of the Minoan civilization, in fact, until Sir Arthur Evans, the English archaeologist, discovered Knossos in the 1890s. It was he who named the people Minoans in honor of the myth of King Minos (Evans 1921). What they called themselves remains unknown. There are those, however, scientists and scholars among them, who believe that the tale of Thera and the Minoans lived on in the legend of Atlantis. Plato in his *Critias* and *Timaeus* chronicled the tale exactly as it was told to him by Solon's general's grandson, including the Egyptian description that an entire civilization—Plato never said continent—sunk in the course of a single day. From that seminal story, Plato, as he clearly states, went on to conjure up a hypothetical utopia. Operating without the concept of zero, Plato calculated the sunken land to be so large that it could fit only beyond the gates of Gibraltar, and thus he called the land Atlantis (Plato n.d.). However, if a zero is removed from Plato's calculations, the land size and conformation he details well fit the dimensions and placement of Crete and Thera (Galanopoulis 1958, 1960, 1969; Marinatos 1939, 1948, 1950; Mavor 1969; Doumas 1983; Pellegrino 1993).

Atlantis or not, a people that once existed, and their society and language, were erased. Another people with another culture and a completely different language replaced them. Many believe the cataclysm changed the course of Western society. Without the massive eruption and its devastating consequence, Indo-Europeans would never have gained a foothold against the commanding cultures of the Mediterranean. Thera's cataclysm allowed invading groups, the Greeks and possibly those moving into Italy (later to become the Romans), purchase and eventual domination. Both peoples later expanded. Both infused the rest of Europe with their culture and ideas (Coles and Harding 1979; Drews 1988, 1993; Mallory 1989; Ward and Joukowsky 1992). Manifestly, though, kernels of Minoan civilization filtered into Greek culture. They enter the arts and crafts. They give rise to a system of writing. What remains unknown is what other, less material customs and ideas fused into the culture and social organization of the people who became the icon of Western civilization.

When Thera erupted and collapsed more than three millennia ago, the rim of the volcano remained. Eventually people resettled the now sheer-cliffed, crescent-shaped remnant. First came Phoenicians, who were followed by early Greeks. Since that time a population of Greek-speaking people, largely horticulturalists and viticulturalists, has dwelled continuously on the island, while various overlords, Romans, Byzantines, Venetians, and Turks, have come and gone. Though its name before the cataclysm seems to have been Kallisti or Stroghili, meaning "beautiful," and "round," in later days the island became known as Thera after one of its early Greek rulers. Today it still bears this name, but is also popularly called Santorini, the Italian name for its patron saint, St. Irene (Hiller von Geartrigen 1895–1909; Naupliotou 1937).

Encircled by the cliff rim, the volcano's caldera lies sunken in the sea, but it lets its presence be known every now and then with small eruptions and jolting earthquakes. One such tremor occurred in 1956. The shaking took place in the early hours of morning, about 5:30 A.M., and though its death toll was low, only four persons, it caused tremendous physical damage. Every one of the island's twelve villages was largely destroyed, and almost the entire population, some fourteen thousand, was displaced as their homes crumbled about them. The government responded fairly rapidly and within several months began to build new homes for those whose abodes lay in ruin. As is typical in government disaster housing programs, however, the new houses were almost entirely unlike the former ones. In the first place, they sat above-ground. To conserve every inch of arable soil, from time immemorial all Thera's houses had been carved into cliffs and ravines cave-style. The island's thick pumice layer proffered a strata of natural cement in which cave homes were easily excavated, their walls merely patted down with water to solidify (Bent 1985). The new homes also stood in tidy rows, whereas former village dwellings lay curled and stacked serpentine fashion in labyrinths convoluted enough to give a modern-day Theseus a migraine. Most egregiously, the new government structures were placed in wholly new locations. Rather than clear out the rubble of the old houses—many of the old homes are *still* filled with rubble—the government appropriated nearby fields or village squares on which to erect the new buildings. In one case they constructed an entirely new village a mile or more from the old one and left the old village abandoned.

I began fieldwork in one of the villages on the island about ten years after the earthquake. I had little notion that I was working with people in the midst of disaster recovery. Ten years seemed to me a long time, and I took everything to be normal. Only the experience of my own calamity made me realize that a decade is but an eye blink in the recovery process, and the people of Thera as I first knew them were still deeply in the midst of adjustment. Now, more than forty years later, one would scarce think a disaster, or any altering circumstance, had ever happened. The row houses have been transformed into a contorted maze again. Devastated after the earthquake, the village is once more socially and economically flourishing. However, both village society and cultural heritage did change, and in trenchant ways. But only in-depth and in-place ethnographic research over a long span reveals the transformation.

To begin with, the earthquake of 1956 hugely exacerbated island depopulation, a process that had been slowly taking place since 1917. In fact, after the earthquake, the island population dropped about 40 percent. Overwhelmingly, it was the most poor who left, mule drivers and those with only a few agricultural fields. Their departure gave others with more assets the opportunity to accumulate more land holdings. As a result the economic and class structure of the village reshaped. Well-off families acquired still more, and almost all who remained in the village gathered enough land to rest secure. Only one mule driver lives in the village today.

Along with the most poor, strangely, those at the top end of the island's social ladder, their mansions in ruin, also decamped. These people, often Catholic, wealthy families, had in essence "owned" certain villages, renting out their many fields to "client" villages and villagers on half shares. They also granted employment to village sons on their shipping lines and processed island produce in their factories. Their exodus broke the back of a millennia-old patron system. Villagers found themselves suddenly on their own, freed of those they viewed somewhat as oppressors but largely as benefactors upon whose favors they depended. The departure of the wealthy also meant the disappearance of a diversified population on the island. The Catholics, present for five hundred years, yet much resented and vilified by the Greek Orthodox, were largely gone. The top level of society was open and deserted. No people of rivaling background remained.

Prior to the earthquake, the village where I worked, along with the other villages of the island, had been largely endogamous. The inhabitants married almost exclusively among one another. Village neighborhoods also strongly reflected a matrilineal and sororal principle. Women inherited houses as the main part of their dowries, and it was the custom that a mother gave her own house to her eldest daughter upon that daughter's marriage. Homes for other daughters were built next to the eldest, so that clusters of sisters lived together, and men, upon marriage, moved about the village. The spine of that tradition was broken when mothers' houses lay in ruins. Families had little choice but to purchase dowry houses scattered in various locales or build new homes on nearby fields. Recently former custom has partially returned, as families have erected second-story dowry flats atop the government-built disaster houses. But the towering additions house only one daughter. Sisters must still find other dwellings, and wealthier families, having learned the marital appeal of bestowing daughters with shiny new homes, have continued to construct new and more luxurious dowry houses ever closer to the sea. The effect has been that more and more houses are now aboveground on arable land, a practice which was viewed before as a terrible waste, and that the village's location has shifted. As a result, the social relations of the village have greatly changed. Neighborhoods no longer hold discrete and interrelated sororal clusters but mix together members of many families. Those by the sea live more isolated from others than villagers ever have.

Because of the depopulation, more marriages outside the village have taken place. Before, endogamy was so strongly in play that most villagers married back into extended family groupings as soon as parties reached the second cousin relationship allowed within the Orthodox church. Now entire strangers are entering the population, and in considerable numbers. As a product, the names of villagers are changing. Prior to the earthquake the village contained only about eight first and last names. Custom decreed that the first son be given the name of his father's father and the first daughter the name of her mother's mother. Second sons and daughters received the opposite pairing. Since families married back so rapidly into extended groupings, many young people had the same grandparents and certainly great and great-great grandparents. Accordingly, many had repetitive names. To distinguish individuals, people were more commonly known by nicknames, although, to my dismay, these, too, were inherited. Now "outsider" husbands who come to the village and their wives dowry homes bring with them different patronyms, and, since they have brought with them the more widespread Greek custom of naming both the first son and daughter in honor of the father's parents, first names have evolved as well. While this may seem nothing but a curiosity, the change has meant that the identifying marker linking individuals to families, characteristics (for most nicknames were character-based), heritages, and, therefore, to economic and political factions as well, has evaporated. It has also dissipated the strong matrilineal principle that ran parallel to the patrilineal in the village kinship system. The loss of the matri-line brings into ambivalence many concomitant issues, for example, women's place and power, their allegiance and support networks (see Hoffman 1974, 1976a, 1976b, 1997; Dubisch 1974, 1986; Hirschorn 1984; Peristiany 1965).

The island's economy has regrouped and recuperated, due greatly to the arrival of tourism. In response, many of the former residents who waved *adiou* after the earthquake have begun to return. The returnees, however, are not the same as they were before. The adults are now aged; the children are adults. Some were born in the city and for much of their lives knew the village only as their parents' place of birth and, hence, their vacation home. They have experienced city life. No longer rural, they have carried city culture to the village. They drive cars. They eat at taverns, to which they even bring their wives. They have acquired esteem for education, so valued among the larger Greek population. They send all their children, male and female, to high school and sometimes beyond. Chagrined by their example, village parents are following suit. Where no village child before was schooled beyond sixth grade, now all attend at least gymnasium, the equivalent of grades six through nine. Villagers have urbanized their habits in emulation of the more sophisticated city folk. They have given up headscarves, housecoats, and transportation by donkey. The village sense of oneness has also altered. Because of more outside marriages and increased wealth, the entire village, which used *en masse* to attended the baptisms, weddings, and ongoing funereal rites of every resident as if belonging to a single faction, no longer attends one another's occasions unless specifically invited.

The returning city folk have forgotten many of the traditions. But they are not the only ones. As kinship changed, the resident villagers let ravel the thread of custom, the patois of continuity, of habit, adage, and dirge. Sometimes it seems I'm the only one who remembers the way things were. There I am, the "foreigner," shouting out lyrics and cuing next steps in the procedure. That some of these changes result from modernization in general, from tourism and televisions, is surely true, but by no means all of them. Nor would they have brought the fluctuations with such rapidity. Disasters accelerate processes of change already underway.

Indeed, the changes that have occurred since the earthquake are quite profound. They reflect more than surface detail; they indicate alteration at deep levels where rules of marriage, naming, residence, and class category lie.

THE LEGACY OF OAKLAND—ANOTHER EXAMPLE

A third illustration arises from another disaster I know well, the Oakland firestorm. Although the Oakland fire was a major urban disaster, at the time of this writing seven years later, to the clichéd "all appearances' sake," the incident has all but evaporated from national memory. Few outside the local community remember when it occurred or even *that* it occurred. The United States is large, and a catastrophe that affects a mere six thousand persons, once the headlines fade, scarcely makes a waggle in eminence. When the subject arises, I am constantly asked a trio of queries, "It was what?" "It was when?" and "Aren't you over it yet?"

Yet, this seemingly insignificant disaster, not even big enough to garner—like Chicago, San Francisco, and Johnstown—its own myth, resulted in a fairly significant social and cultural change for the nation. I use both terms here, for while the change bore immediately social consequences, I believe it ultimately affects culture, as it alters the treatment of all disaster sufferers in the United States in future.

The Oakland firestorm was one of those rare instances when the community struck by disaster was populated by affluent and relatively powerful people. Usually it is the disenfranchised who brook the misery of disaster. One would expect that the comparative potency of the Oakland firestorm victims would aid their recovery, and, indeed, the vast majority received compensation at least for their material losses in an essentially short time, although not without struggle. Yet, as well as aiding their recovery, the affluence of the victims led them to encounter a set of national laws that unduly punished disaster victims. Oakland firestorm survivors discovered that they were required by federal statute to rebuild or repurchase homes within one year of the conflagration, although because the firestorm received national emergency status, a scant second year was granted. Should they not rebuild in time, the law required victims to pay one third capital gains tax on any compensation they received. Like most disaster victims, few Oakland firestorm survivors received settlement within the required time span, thus the law placed them in a "Catch 22" situation where they would lose a third of their compensation before receiving it. The law further required victims to pay capital gains tax on any by-then unspent compensation for personal belongings—furniture, dishware, and the like—although they had as yet no homes to furnish. As they had paid sales tax on both original and replacement purchases, the capital gain represented a third levy. In addition, the law disallowed victims from using money provided for one purpose, such as rent while displaced, for another purpose, such as construction, despite the victim's needs. Presumably, the tax laws had been enacted to discourage fraud, but in effect they punished victims. They also furthered the not-uncommon notion that victims were somehow to blame.

Oakland firestorm survivors set about rewriting the laws, calling for a four-year-from-settlement period to rehouse, no taxation on personal goods, and fluidity of monetary use. The Bush administration refused to enact the new proposals, but the Clinton administration did. Within months the new codes benefited the victims of the Mississippi flood and thereafter the victims of America's many subsequent catastrophes. As a consequence, the Oakland firestorm survivors changed social legislation, which in turn altered the government's approach to the national community. At this writing, the ultimate consequences of the Oakland firestorm are far from calculable. Still, one invaluable change has already resulted and others might well, from a calamity of rather insignificant scale.

CHANGE AND PERSISTENCE/PERSISTENCE AND CHANGE

The question was posed at the beginning of this chapter whether social and cultural change took place after a calamity or not. After reviewing some factors and several examples from an anthropologist's long-term and more subtle perspective, the answer, to my mind, is no, but also decidedly yes.

Without a doubt, cultures and societies are marked by great persistence. Even when few people survive a disaster, which is rare, for usually many do, their systems, habits, thought patterns, means of expression flow on. Culture persists in part because, in the minds of those who hold it, culture creates limitations. Culture forms boundaries on perceptions, fetters on language, walls in categories. While it is possible, it is extremely difficult for people to break through these invisible barricades to perceive in open ways or create formulations anew. Part of what drives a culture is not that new experiences do not enter, but that the lexicon in which to place new information captures it and transforms the new into the known.

But change does occur. Small matters shift. Framework alters. The Minoans, while their own society and culture disappeared, changed others. The Theran villagers, while they quickly moved on in a thick cloak of continuity, still underwent a metamorphosis. The one calamity represents an instance of enormous change, yet with traces of persistence. The other reveals overwhelming persistence, yet alterations in the very weave of life. In Oakland a catastrophe that has receded to an almost nonevent brought forth a potent policy change reflective of a political value shift. The peripheral occurrences around a calamity can, in and by themselves, bring alteration. Aider and aided interact. Awareness of the outside world enlarges. Perspectives change. Horizons expand. Interplay between community and government increases.

No social cultural juggernaut rolls so heavy or so fast as not to take on moss, and moss tilts balance ever so slightly this way or that. None rolls so directed that it does not veer when it encounters dips and hillocks. Undoubtedly the amount of change a society and culture experiences increases with the magnitude of a disaster and number of those affected. Some changes appear immediately; others through the transition of time. Some are surface matter; others impact the deep. Revelations spur corrections. What emerges from the disaster experiences ripples through, across, and down a people until widespread.

What many disaster researchers have up to now largely looked for in terms of change are large shifts in political organizations, leadership, economics, social construction, and hazard adaptations. They have also expected immediate ramifications to adhere in a lasting manner. From the anthropological point of view, the shifts are more delicate. Anthropology looks at new relationships, new amalgamations, new antagonisms. That which changes in persons alters the social and cultural corpus. Speciality, which changes drastically in calamity, alone can be an agent of social change. Social relationships take place in space, as do material practices and institutions. Disaster affects people's mapping, says Harvey (1996: 13), and it is noteworthy that disasters themselves often bear place names.

I come to the last questions brought up in the introduction. Can a cataclysmic catastrophe such as Thera's occur in our globalized world of today? Can an entire population bearing an entire culture be wiped out, or for that matter all human society and culture? As mentioned earlier, the question of whether change occurs in consequence of a disaster has gained in importance. It is no longer possible to assume that our or other social systems can adapt should disaster upon disaster unfold. The environment has been increasingly compromised. New risks to the human community have joined the old. Technology has grown increasingly volatile and toxic. Business and industrial practices maximize resource exploitation with little mind to depletion. At the same time, the social realms of all people depend more and more on global systems, adding complexity while increasing homogenization and reducing flexibility. The situation potentially increases the vulnerability of small groups, certain segments of populations, and all.

Science fiction writers and film directors have envisioned globally cataclysmic events and the drastic change of society and culture as we know it any number of times. Before we face the reality of just such a happening, we need to consider persistence of policy, change in our ways, and—the Angry Earth. How much strain can Atlas bear without breaking? How much destruction and contamination can Atlas forgive without shrugging off the totality?

BIBLIOGRAPHY

Bateson, G. 1958. *Naven*. Palo Alto: Stanford University Press.

Bennet, J. 1990. "Knossos in Context: Comparative Perspectives on the Linear B Administration of LM II-III Crete." *American Journal of Archaeology* 94: 291–309.

Bent, T. 1985. *Aegean Islands: The Cyclades, or Life Among the Insular Greeks*. London: Longsmans Green.

Blaikie, P., T. Cannon, I. Davis, and B. Wisner. 1994. *At Risk*. New York: Routledge.

Bloomfield, L. 1933. *Language*. New York: Holt.

Bode, B. 1989. *No Bells to Toll: Destruction and Creation in the Andes*. New York: Scribners.

Button, G. 1992. *Social Conflict and Emergent Groups in a Technological Disaster: The Homer Area Community and the* Exxon-Valdez *Oil Spill*. Unpublished Ph.D. dissertation. Waltham, MA: Brandeis University.

Chadwick, J. 1987. *Linear B and Related Scripts*. London.

Chairetakis, A. 1995. *The Two-Sided Mirror: A Theory of Culture and Crisis Response in Complex Societies*. Presented at the Annual Meeting of the American Anthropological Association, Washington, DC.

Chomsky, N. 1957. *Syntactic Structures*. The Hague: Mouton.

————. 1969. *Aspects of the Theory of Syntax*. Boston: MIT Press.

Coles, J., and A. Harding. 1979. *The Bronze Age in Europe*. London: Methuen.

de Saussure, F. 1966. *Course in General Linguistics*. New York: McGraw.

Dickinson, O. 1994. *The Aegean Bronze Age*. Cambridge: Cambridge University Press.

Doughty, P. 1986. "Decades of Disaster: Promise and Performance in the Callejón de Huaylas, Peru," in A. Oliver-Smith (ed.), *Natural Disasters and Cultural Responses*, pp. 35–80. Williamsberg: College of William and Mary.

Douglas, M. 1966. *Purity and Danger*. New York: Praeger.

————. 1970. *Natural Symbols*. New York: Pantheon.

Doumas, C. 1983. *Thera, Pompeii of the Ancient Aegean: Excavations at Akrotiri, 1967–79*. New York: Thames and Hudson.

Drews, R. 1988. *The Coming of the Greeks: Indo-European Conquests in the Aegean and the Near East*. Princeton: Princeton University Press.

————. 1993. *The End of the Bronze Age: Changes in Warfare and the Catastrophe ca. 1200 B.C.* Princeton: Princeton University Press.

Dubisch, J. 1974. "The Domestic Power of Women in a Greek Island Village." *Studies in European Society* 1, 1: 23–33.

————. 1986. *Gender and Power in Rural Greece*. Princeton: Princeton University Press.

Erikson, K. 1994. *A New Species of Trouble*. New York: Norton.

Evans, Sir A. 1921. *The Palace of Minos: A Comparative Account of the Successive Stages of the Early Cretan Civilization as Illustrated by the Discoveries at Knossos*. London: Macmillan.

Forrest, T. 1993. "Disaster Anniversary: A Social Reconstruction of Time." *Sociological Inquiry* 63, 4: 444–456.

Foster, H. 1985. *Recordings: Art, Spectacle, and Cultural Politics*. Port Townsend, WA: Bay Press.

Fouque, F. 1869. *Une Pompeii Antehistorique*. Revue des Doux Mondes 39.

————. 1879. *Santorin et Ses Eruptions*. Paris: Maison et Cie.

Galanopoulos, A. 1958. "Zur Bestimmung des Alters des Santorin-kaldera." *Annales Geologiques des Pays Helleniques* 9.

————. 1960. "On the Size and Geographic Site of Atlantis." *Proceedings of the Academy of Athens* 35: 401–418.

————. 1969. *Atlantis: The Truth Behind the Legend*. New York: Bobbs-Merrill.

Garcia-Acosta, V. 2000. "Historical Disaster Research," in S. Hoffman and A. Oliver-Smith (eds.), *Culture and Catastrophe*. Santa Fe: School of American Research.

Georgalas, G. 1937. "The Genesis of the Complex Volcanic Island of Thera," in M. Danezis (ed.), *Thera: Collected Writings*, pp. 10–30. Athens: Academy of Athens.

Harvey, D. 1996. *Justice, Nature and the Geography of Difference*. Cambridge, MA: Blackwell.

Hewitt, K. 1983. *Interpretations of Calamity*. Boston: Allen and Unwin.

Hiller von Geartrigen, F. 1895–1909. *Thera: Untersuchenger, Vermessungen and Aus-*

grabungen in den Jahren 1895–1898, 4 vols. Berlin.

Hirschorn, R. 1984. *Women as Property—Property as Women*. New York: St. Martin's Press.

Hodder, I. 1987. *Archaeology as Long-Term History*. Cambridge: Cambridge University Press.

Hoffman, S. 1974. *Kypseli—Women and Men Apart: A Divided Reality*. Film Distributed by Extension Media Center, University of California, Berkeley, California.

————. 1976a. "The Ethnography of the Islands: Thera," in M. Dimen and E. Friedl (eds.), *Regional Variation in Modern Greece and Cyprus: Toward a Perspective on the Ethnography of Greece*. Annals of the New York Academy of Sciences, 268, pp. 328–340. New York: New York Academy of Sciences.

————. 1976b. "Kypseli: A Marital Geography of a Greek Village," in *Lifelong Learning* 45, 58. Berkeley: University Extension, University of California.

————. 1997. "Bringing the 'Other' to the 'Self': Kypseli the Place and the Film," in S. Parman (ed.), *Europe in the Anthropological Imagination*, pp. 44–59. Englewood Cliffs, NJ: Prentice Hall.

Ingold, T. 1992. "Culture and the Perception of the Environment," in E. Croll and D. Parkin (eds.), *Bush Base: Forest Farm*, pp. 39–55. London: Routledge.

Kearney, M. 1984. *World View*. Novato, CA: Chandler and Sharp.

Kluckhohn, C. 1964. *Culture and Behavior*. Glencoe: Free Press.

Kroeber, A. 1948. *Anthropology*. New York: Harcourt, Brace.

Kroll-Smith, J. S., and S. Couch. 1991. "What Is a Disaster? An Ecological-Symbolic Approach to Resolving the Definitional Debate." *International Journal of Mass Emergencies and Disasters* 9, 3: 355–366.

Kushner, G. 1973. "Archeology as Anthropology." *Science* 183: 616–618.

Leach, E. 1961. *Rethinking Anthropology*. London: London School of Economics Monographs on Social Anthropology 22.

Levi-Strauss, C. 1963. *Structural Anthropology*. New York: Basic Books.

————. 1966. *The Savage Mind*. Chicago: University of Chicago Press.

Mallory, J. D. 1989. *In Search of the Indo-Europeans: Language, Archaeology and Myth*. London: Thames and Hudson.

Marinatos, S. 1939. "The Volcanic Destruction of Minoan Crete." *Antiquity* 13: 425–439.

————. 1948. *Le Probleme de l'Atlatide*. Athens: Societe Hellenique d'Anthropologie.

————. 1950. *About the Rumor of Atlantis*. Cretan Chronicle 4.

Marris, P. 1974. *Loss and Change*. London: Routledge.

Martin, T. 1996. *Ancient Greece: From Prehistoric to Hellenistic Times*. New Haven: Yale University Press.

Mauss, M. 1967. *The Gift*. London: Routledge.

Mavor, J. 1969. *Voyage to Atlantis*. New York: Putnam.

McCabe, T. 1988. "Drought and Recovery: Livestock Dynamics among the Ngissonyoka Turkana of Kenya." *Human Ecology* 15: 371–390.

Naupliotou, K. G. 1937. "Thera in Ancient Times," in M. A. Danezis (ed.), *Thera: Collected Writings*, pp. 61–80. Athens: Academy of Athens.

Ninkovitch, D., and B. Heezen. 1965. *Santorini Tephra*. London: Colston Papers 25.

Oliver-Smith, A. 1992. *The Martyred City: Death and Rebirth in the Andes*. Prospect Heights, IL: Waveland Press.

———. 1996. "Anthropological Research on Hazards and Disasters." *Annual Reviews in Anthropology* 25: 303–328.

Paine, R. 1992. "Chernobyl Reaches Norway: The Accident, Science, and the Threat to Cultural Knowledge." *Public Understanding of Science* 1: 261–280.

Peacock, W., B. Morrow, and H. Gladwin. 1998. *Hurricane Andrew: Ethnicity, Gender, and a New Sociology of Disaster*. London: Routledge.

Pellegrino, C. 1993. *Unearthing Atlantis, an Archaeological Odyssey*. New York: Vintage.

Peristiany, J. 1965. *Honour and Shame: The Values of Mediterranean Society*. London: Weidenfeld and Nicolson.

Plato. n.d. *Timaeus* and *Critias*. R. G. Bury, trans. Loeb Classical Library. Cambridge: Harvard University Press.

Poniatowska, E. 1995. *Nothing, Nobody: The Voices of the Mexico City Earthquake*. Philadelphia: Temple University Press.

Quarentelli, E. 1987. "What Should We Study? Questions and Suggestions for Researchers about the Concept of Disasters." *International Journal of Mass Emergencies and Disasters* 5: 7–32.

Robinson, C, J. Hernandez, R. Mata Castrejon, and H. Bernard. 1986. "It Shook Again: The Mexico City Earthquake of 1985," in A. Oliver-Smith (ed.), *Natural Disasters and Cultural Responses*. Williamsberg: College of William and Mary.

Sahlins, M. 1964. "Culture and Environment: The Study of Cultural Ecology," in S. Tax (ed.), *Horizons of Anthropology*, pp. 136–147. Chicago: Aldine Press.

Sandars, N. 1978. *The Sea Peoples: Warriors of the Ancient Mediterranean, 1250–1150. B.C.* London: Thames and Hudson.

Sjoberg, G. 1962. "Disasters and Social Change," in G. Baker and D. Chapman (eds.), *Man and Society in Disaster*. New York: Basic Books.

Stephens, S. 1995. "'Cultural Fallout' of Chernobyl Radiation in Sami Regions: Implications for Children," in S. Stephens (ed.), *Children and the Politics of Culture*, pp. 292–321. Princeton: Princeton University Press.

Stewart, K. 1992. "Nostalgia—A Polemic," in G. Marcus (ed.), *Rereading Cultural Anthropology*, pp. 552–566. Durham: Duke University Press.

Torry, W. 1978. "Natural Disasters, Social Structure and Change in Traditional Societies." *Journal of Asian and African Studies* 13: 167–183.

Turner, V. 1961. *The Ritual Process*. Chicago: Aldine.

Van Gennep, A. 1960. *The Rites of Passage*. M. Vizedom and G. Caffee, trans. London: Routledge.

Wallace, A. 1956. "Revitalization Movements." *American Anthropologist* 58: 264–281.

———. 1961. "The Psychology of Culture Change," in A. Wallace, *Culture and Personality*, pp. 120–163. New York: Random House.

Ward, W., and M. Joukowsky (eds.). 1992. *The Crisis Years: The Twelfth Century B.C.* Dubuque: University of Iowa Press.

Willets, R. 1977. *The Civilization of Ancient Crete*. Berkeley: University of California Press.

Wilkie, N., and W. Coulson (eds.). 1985. *Contributions to Aegean Archaeology*. Minneapolis: University of Minnesota Press.

Zaman, M. 1989. "The Social and Political Context of Adjustment to Riverbank Erosion Hazard and Population Resettlement in Bangladesh." *Human Organization* 48: 196–205.

INDEX